The Psychology of the Supreme Court

American Psychology-Law Society Series

Books in the Series
Trial Consulting
Amy J. Posey and Lawrence S. Wrightsman

Death by Design: Capital Punishment as a Social Psychological System
Craig Haney

Psychological Injuries: Forensic Assessment, Treatment, and Law
William J. Koch, Kevin S. Douglas, Tonia L. Nicholls,
and Melanie L. O'Neill

Emergency Department Treatment of the Psychiatric Patient:
Policy Issues and Legal Requirements
Susan Stefan

The Psychology of the Supreme Court
Lawrence S. Wrightsman

The Psychology
of the Supreme Court

Lawrence S. Wrightsman

UNIVERSITY PRESS

2006

OXFORD
UNIVERSITY PRESS

Oxford University Press, Inc., publishes works that further
Oxford University's objective of excellence
in research, scholarship, and education.

Oxford   New York
Auckland   Cape Town   Dar es Salaam   Hong Kong   Karachi
Kuala Lumpur   Madrid   Melbourne   Mexico City   Nairobi
New Delhi   Shanghai   Taipei   Toronto

With offices in
Argentina   Austria   Brazil   Chile   Czech Republic   France   Greece
Guatemala   Hungary   Italy   Japan   Poland   Portugal   Singapore
South Korea   Switzerland   Thailand   Turkey   Ukraine   Vietnam

Copyright © 2006 by Oxford University Press, Inc.

Published by Oxford University Press, Inc.
198 Madison Avenue, New York, New York 10016

www.oup.com

Oxford is a registered trademark of Oxford University Press

Library of Congress Cataloging-in-Publication Data
Wrightsman, Lawrence S.
The psychology of the Supreme Court / Lawrence S. Wrightsman.
    p. cm.
Includes index.
ISBN-13 978-0-19-530604-0
ISBN 0-19-530604-X
1. United States Supreme Court.   2. Judicial process—United
States—Psychological aspects.   3. Conduct of court proceedings—United
States—Psychological aspects.   4. Political questions and judicial
power—United States.   I. Title.
KF8748.W753 2006
347.73'262—dc22   2005025829

9 8 7 6 5 4 3 2 1

Printed in the United States of America
on acid-free paper

To the memory of Flip Kissam, whose enthusiasm

for the law smoothed my introduction to it.

Series Foreword

This book series is sponsored by the American Psychology-Law Society (APLS). APLS is an interdisciplinary organization devoted to scholarship, practice, and public service in psychology and law. Its goals include advancing the contributions of psychology to the understanding of law and legal institutions through basic and applied research; promoting the education of psychologists in matters of law and the education of legal personnel in matters of psychology; and informing the psychological and legal communities and the general public of current research, educational, and service activities in the field of psychology and law. APLS membership includes psychologists from the academic research and clinical practice communities as well as members of the legal community. Research and practice is represented in both the civil and criminal legal arenas. APLS has chosen Oxford University Press as a strategic partner because of its commitment to scholarship, quality, and the international dissemination of ideas. These strengths will help APLS reach our goal of educating the psychology and legal professions and the general public about important developments in psychology and law. The focus of the book series reflects the diversity of the field of psychology and law as we will publish books on a broad range of topics.

I am pleased to add *The Psychology of the Supreme Court* by Professor Larry Wrightsman to this series. Professor Wrightsman is a prolific and influential contributor to the field of psychology and law. In addition to his outstanding scholarly contributions, he has authored and co-authored perhaps the most widely used psychology and law textbooks, and these books have directly influenced generations of students in psychology and law. In 1999, he was recognized for his many contributions when he received the American Psychology-Law Society Award for Distinguished Contribution to Psychology and the Law. He has previously written about judicial decision making, and in this book, Wrightsman again turns his attention to this area, focusing specifically on the United States Supreme Court. This book provides a compelling and thoughtful analysis of how nine Supreme Court justices behave both individually and as a group in reaching decisions that can affect all Americans. He draws on psychological theory to examine how the values and backgrounds of each of the justices influence the decisions they make. This is a fascinating and insightful analysis, and perhaps all the more significant given the changes to the Court with the retirement of Justice Sandra Day O'Connor and the death of Justice William H. Rehnquist. Senate confirmation hearings focus on the writings and backgrounds of nominees in attempt to predict how they might vote on certain key issues. In this book, Wrightsman provides an empirically grounded approach to understanding their votes. Many Supreme Court key decisions are divided (e.g., 5 to 4 decisions), such as the juvenile death penalty or abortion rights decisions. It is therefore of paramount importance to gain an understanding of what leads justices to draw different conclusions from the same case facts, legal precedents, and other information (including amicus briefs). Professor Wrightsman's book provides a solid foundation in theory and research to explain these differences among justices, and it should be a highly regarded reference not just for psychologists but for anyone interested in the inner workings of the Supreme Court.

Ronald Roesch
Series Editor

Preface

The Supreme Court presents a challenge to understand. Its decisions and the actions of its individual justices often surprise us. As the Court's term ended in the summer of 2005, Court watchers were convinced that Chief Justice Rehnquist would resign, but instead it was Justice Sandra Day O'Connor who did so. Her surprise announcement was followed two weeks later by one by the chief justice, who adamantly stated that he would continue as long as his health permitted. But his death two months later led to another surprise—John Roberts, who had been nominated by President Bush to be an Associate Justice, was promoted to Chief Justice.

As a source of public interest, the Supreme Court generates its share of stereotypes. Upon her resignation, media accolades labeled Justice O'Connor as the "swing vote" on the Court, and while that had been largely true in the past, in the term that had just ended days before her announcement, it was Justice Breyer, not O'Connor, whose vote was the crucial fifth vote in more of the 5 to 4 decisions. In fact, in several major decisions, Justice O'Connor was on the losing side, and she wrote dissents in 11 of the 74 decided cases.

Individual justices are not just stereotyped; they are pigeonholed into conservative or liberal camps. And while these classifications reflect their votes and justifications in certain types of cases, as this book documents, the decisions and votes of each justice are more complexly determined than their simply reacting to their ideological bent. For example, in the 2004–2005 term, 24 decisions were 5 to 4; the conservative majority on the Court held together on only five. In eight of these cases, one of the conservatives formed a majority with the liberals.

Study of the Court can be approached from many perspectives. Psychology seeks to understand the Court as an organization of diverse individuals who share some goals but not others. It offers concepts and theories to describe and explain the behavior of justices. For example:

1. Chief Justice Rehnquist, in his last terms on the Court, displayed several surprising votes, for example upholding the *Miranda* ruling that required police to inform suspects of their rights and, in some cases, supporting the family and medical leave rights of individuals who sued the government. Leaders who have "paid their dues" for a number of years have earned what psychologists call *idiosyncracy credits*, the right to deviate, on occasion, from what their supporters expect of them.

2. In contrast to the predictions of experts or of a statistical model based on past votes, the Court reaches unanimous votes much more often than votes of 8 to 1. *Pressures to uniformity* exist in the Court just as they do in any other small, tightly knit organization.

3. Individuals make a difference. Every 5 to 4 vote is, of course, testimony to the difference one justice can make, but the observation is especially demonstrated when a new chief justice is on board. For example, the case of *Brown v. Board of Education* languished when it was first reviewed by the Court in 1952 when Fred Vinson was chief justice; the Court was split, and had a vote been taken, the decision could have gone either way. Justice Vinson's sudden death and the presence of Earl Warren as chief justice meant vigorous leadership that led to a unanimous endorsement of desegregation in the public schools.

The goal of this book is to describe every major aspect of the Court's functioning and explain each through the use of knowledge from the social sciences. These aspects include the nomination and confirmation of justices, the steps in the process by which the Court reviews petitions and makes its rulings, the role of law clerks, the individual qualities that make justices succeed or fail, the influence of the chief justice, and various aspects that need review and reform. The *Bush v. Gore* decision is examined in detail, in a quest to understand what led to the most important decision by the Court in recent times. Systematic efforts to predict the votes of justices and decisions of the Court are described, with statistical analyses that are new to this volume.

This book is an extension and expansion of my book *Judicial Decision Making: Is Psychology Relevant?* (published in 1999). In that book, my focus was on the impact of organized psychology, through the submission of amicus briefs, in trying to influence Supreme Court decisions. The purpose of this book is a broader one, seeking comprehension of the Court as a real-life, ever-changing organization. The psychological approach is empirical, hence the book summarizes data-oriented studies on, for example, such matters as the number of petitions submitted and acted upon, the reversal rate by the

Court, the frequency of unanimous decisions, and the number of changed votes from the conference to the final decision. But psychology also concerns itself with the impact of the personalities of the participants in the organization. Why was Earl Warren so effective as a chief justice, when Fred Vinson was not? What qualities led William Brennan, and later, Sandra Day O'Connor, to become influential?

The Supreme Court is always important in the lives of all Americans. But now it is going through a period of change, and thus it is especially important that we seek to understand why it behaves as it does.

Acknowledgments

It has been a joy to prepare this book. While the writing was mine, many others contributed to its preparation and completion. Cindy Sexton solved my computer problems. Among students at the University of Kansas, Justin LaMort assisted me greatly in finding obscure references, Mary Pitman drew my attention to websites, and Angela Rasmussen contributed to my knowledge when, on my request, she asked Justice Clarence Thomas a question during one of his visits to our campus. ("How do the justices refer to the chief justice in private? Do they call him by his first name like they do each other?" "No, they refer to him as 'The Chief.'")

Professor Ronald Roesch, editor of the American Psychology-Law Society series of books, was very prompt and encouraging, not only in obtaining reviews of the prospectus but in working with the publisher and especially in providing me with a detailed critique of the entire manuscript.

The staff at Oxford University Press has been exceedingly helpful. Joan H. Bossert, vice president/associate publisher and editorial director for science, professional, and medical books, met with me and suggested the title for the book. Mariclaire Cloutier, executive editor for Psychology, facilitated the review of the prospectus by further reviewers. Joseph Zito, associate editor for psychology, and Cristina Wojdylo, developmental editor, have provided responses to my frequent inquiries.

Needless to say, any errors in the book, despite the efforts of these folks, are mine.

Contents

The Psychology of the Supreme Court

1

The Supreme Court

The Least Understood Branch

Judges as persons, or courts as institutions, are entitled to
no greater immunity from criticism than other persons or
institutions. . . . [J]udges must be kept mindful of their limitations and of their ultimate public responsibility by a vigorous
stream of criticism expressed with candor however blunt.
—Justice Felix Frankfurter

The United States Supreme Court only occasionally penetrates the threshold of awareness of the American public. People do not typically ruminate about the Court, but periodically news about the justices, the Court, or the federal judiciary intrudes into people's consciousness. In the fall of 2004, it was the serious illness of the chief justice; in the winter of 2005 the removal of life support from Terri Schiavo, in which the Supreme Court refrained from intervening; in the summer of 2005 the resignation of Sandra Day O'Connor; and in the fall of that year, the nomination of John Roberts to replace her, then the death of Chief Justice Rehnquist, followed quickly by the substitution of Justice Roberts's seat from O'Connor's to the chief justice's. In October of 2005 President Bush nominated Samuel Alito to fill the O'Connor seat.

But despite the public's only spasmodic attention, the Supreme Court continues to exert an influence on every American. As the public gives it less consideration than the other two branches of government, it is truly the least understood branch. The purpose of this book is to apply the methods and findings of psychology and the other social sciences to further a knowledge and appreciation of the Court's processes and decisions.

As noted, sometimes the Court makes news. And on occasion it makes big news. Many admirers of the United States Supreme Court—and needless to say, most supporters of Al Gore's bid for the presidency in 2000—were disappointed when, on December 12, 2000, the Supreme Court effectively decided the outcome of that year's presidential election in favor of George W. Bush. Some observers immediately proclaimed that the Court's decision in the case of *Bush v. Gore* (2000), which reflected a narrow and ideologically predictable 5 to 4 vote, would forever tarnish the image of the Court as standing above politics. While the Court's decision still rankles many, the Court goes on with its business of deciding which appeals to decide, and then announcing its decision. No evidence exists that the impact of the Court's work has been lessened. But certainly that decision and the more recent events described earlier have caused an increased questioning of how the justices make their decisions.

The fundamental thesis of this book is that the Supreme Court is a political institution in the broadest sense, in that its members often possess long-term aspirations for what is best for the country, and their judicial opinions reflect these aspirations. That is not to say that the Court is as blatantly political as are the other two branches; membership in a political party is not inexorably linked with each of its members, and justices do not have to curry favor with the public in order to win reelection. But the justices' ideologies and values play a significant—yet complex—part in many of the Court's decisions, just as they do in the decisions by the president and by Congress. This book, in presenting a social science analysis of the Court's decision-making, documents the human qualities of the justices. A second issue, considered throughout the book and especially in the final chapter, is the difficult question: How well does the Court do its job? For example, are the best persons nominated and confirmed as justices? Is the workload too heavy (or too light), and do the justices' law clerks play too influential a role? What are the duties of the chief justice and how well have incumbents fulfilled them? Does the process by which decisions are made lead to the best decisions? Does the Court have adequate enforcement power? None of these questions can be answered without generating controversy, and certainly the resulting answers I offer will reflect some subjectivity and personal values, but sufficient information on each of these questions exists at least to provide readers with material that should help them in forming their own answers to these questions.

I. Fateful Decisions at the End of the Term

Whether by design or happenstance, the Supreme Court often manages to save its most dramatic decisions for the last. (The *Bush v. Gore* decision is the obvious exception!) In the last week of June 2005, a decision that broadened the "public use" justification in the application of eminent domain drew criticism from some liberals and from some conservatives, and the Court announced its split decisions in two cases that challenged the display of the Ten Commandments on public property. And then, only four days after the completion of the term, Justice Sandra Day O'Connor surprised almost everyone by announcing her resignation. (Court observers expected Chief Justice Rehnquist to be the one to declare his retirement.)

In the last week of its 2003–2004 term, the decisions in two important *Miranda* rights cases were announced, as well as the decisions in three appeals dealing with "enemy combatants" and detainees at the Guantanamo Bay naval base. The term before saw the closely followed gay rights and affirmative action decisions announced during the last week. (These cases are described in subsequent chapters.) In the last week of the 2001–2002 term, the Court announced two decisions that had great impact on schools and schoolchildren across America—one decision approved of a voucher program that permitted tax money to be used to pay for children to attend private schools (*Zelman v. Simmons-Harris*, 2002), and the other broadened the use of drug testing for schoolchildren participating in a variety of school-related activities beyond athletics, including marching bands, choirs, and the National Honor Society (*Board of Education of Independent School District Number 92 of Pottawatomie County v. Earls*, 2002). Each decision was met with accolades from some and severe criticism from others.

One of the fascinations in studying the Court is the quest to predict the votes of individual justices and the outcome of appeals. Of particular interest were the decisions announced in the final days of the 1999–2000 term; not only was each of these five among the most important cases considered all year, but in combination they reveal the sometimes surprising votes of individual justices. Each of these cases involved highly contentious issues, including the legality of abortion, the powers of the police, the relationship between religion and the government, and the rights of homosexual persons. Specifically, these cases led to the following decisions.

- In *Dickerson v. United States*, the Court voted to uphold the requirement that police inform suspects of their *Miranda* rights before questioning them, concluding that the provision of such rights was constitutionally based and therefore may not be overridden by an act of Congress.
- In *Stenberg v. Carhart*, the Court struck down Nebraska's ban on a type of late-term abortion, because the law was so vague that it could be interpreted to prohibit most midterm abortion methods and because it did not permit exemptions when the mother's health was at risk.
- In *Hill v. Colorado*, the Court affirmed the right of states to have an eight-foot "bubble zone" around abortion clinics; specifically, the decision upheld a Colorado law that prohibits people from counseling, distributing leaflets, or displaying signs within eight feet of others without their consent, whenever they are within one hundred feet of a health clinic where abortions are performed.
- In *Boy Scouts of America v. Dale*, the Court endorsed the right of the Boy Scouts organization to bar homosexual persons from serving as troop leaders.
- And in *Mitchell v. Helms*, the Court affirmed that the federal government may provide certain kinds of materials, such as computers, to parochial schools.

Even though all these decisions were noteworthy because of the broadly important issues they considered, as a group they did little to answer the question: What is the nature of the composition of the Supreme Court? Court-watchers had difficulty in discerning a pattern in the voting outcomes. In the five big cases at the end of the 1999–2000 term, conservatives were pleased with some decisions (in the Boy Scouts case and the one involving parochial schools) but liberals rejoiced over the decisions in the abortion cases and the thwarted threat to *Miranda* warnings. Federalism received support in some decisions but not others. The blockbuster cases that ended the more recent terms once more revealed an inconsistent ideology; in June 2003, conservatives were upset that the *Lawrence v. Texas* decision abolished the laws that criminalized sexual relations between homosexual partners, but in the affirmative action cases, both sides had reason to celebrate and also to complain, as the Court approved of the procedure used by the University of Michigan law school (in *Grutter v. Bollinger*, 2003) but rejected the procedure used in that university's undergraduate admissions (in *Gratz v. Bollinger*, 2003).

Common Wisdom about the Composition of the Court

The recent "common wisdom" has seen the Court composed of two diverse groups and one pair of less ideologically consistent voters. In the 11 years that the composition of the Court did not change (from 1994 to 2005), Chief Justice William Rehnquist, Justice Antonin Scalia, and Justice Clarence Thomas typically voted in ways that pleased political conservatives; Justices John Paul Stevens, David Souter, Ruth Bader Ginsburg, and Stephen Breyer were more likely to render votes that were congruent with politically liberal values. Justices Sandra Day O'Connor and Anthony Kennedy, while more often siding with Justices Rehnquist, Scalia, and Thomas, were frequently labeled as "swing voters," in that on certain topics (such as affirmative action, abortion, and gay rights) they sometimes voted with the more liberal group. With the appointment of John Roberts and the nomination of Samuel Alito, beginning in the 2005–2006 term, the composition was more aptly described as four conservatives, one "swing vote" who often sided with the conservatives (Justice Kennedy), and four more liberal justices (although among the latter group, Justice Breyer was becoming less consistently liberal).

While the foregoing classifications are generally consistent with voting trends, the decisions about how to vote are complexly determined. Certainly in some cases, the votes of individual justices follow their ideological bent; for example, in two cases involving police powers that were decided in the month of June 2004 (*Yarborough v. Alvarado* and *Hiibel v. Sixth Judicial District of Nevada*), the voting patterns were identical, with the five conservatives (including Justices Kennedy and O'Connor) siding with the police and the four relative liberals voting to restrict police powers. But traditional distinctions such as "liberal" versus "conservative" or profederalism versus antifederalism do not explain the votes in all cases. In some types of cases, ideology is not relevant, and in others, the votes and outcomes sometimes differed from what common wisdom would have anticipated. In the June 2002 decision on drug testing in the schools, Justice Breyer sided with the conservative majority and wrote in a concurring opinion that the drug problem in our nation's schools was so serious that mandatory drug testing was justified. Justice Breyer also voted to reject the affirmative action plan used by the University of Michigan undergraduate school in *Gratz v. Bollinger* (2003). In two of the five cases that ended the 1999–2000 term, Justice Rehnquist voted the same way as the liberal justices Stevens, Souter, Breyer, and Ginsburg. Consider especially one of these, *Dickerson v. United States*. Conventional wisdom—exemplified by those who watch the Court with intensity—predicted the outcome of this case to be a close call. In this case, Justices Stevens, Souter, Ginsburg, and Breyer seemed quite likely to vote to uphold the *Miranda* warnings as constitutional, while Justices Rehnquist, Scalia, and Thomas were expected to be opposed, given their history of lack of sympathy for defendants' rights. Again, Justices O'Connor and Kennedy were less predictable, in that they were not especially supportive of defendants' rights but on occasion had endorsed the use of *Miranda* warnings. For example, Justice O'Connor had written the majority opinion in the case of *Moran v. Burbine* (1986), in which the police had deceived a suspect's sister's attorney when he inquired if the suspect was to be questioned that evening. The suspect had been given his *Miranda* rights, had waived the right to an attorney, and later that evening did confess to the crime. But had the police erred in lying to the sister's attorney? In the majority opinion, Justice O'Connor expressed distaste for the police lying but upheld the admission of the confession into evidence and concluded that at present, the use of the *Miranda* warning offered a good balance between the needs of society and the rights of suspects.

When I say that most Court-watchers saw the outcome of the *Dickerson* case as a "close call," I mean that most expected a 5 to 4 split in the vote, with the majority most likely to uphold *Miranda*, but a 5 to 4 vote in the other direction was certainly possible. The actual vote was a surprise: 7 to 2 to uphold *Miranda*, with the majority opinion written by Chief Justice Rehnquist, who was on record as a staunch opponent of defendants' rights. Only Justices Scalia and Thomas were in the minority. (According to Professor Yale Kamisar [2000], Professor Stephen Saltzburg at the George Washington University Law Center did predict the 7 to 2 vote and the nature of Justice Rehnquist's opinion in advance. I am not aware that anyone else did.) As Professor Kamisar observed, Justice Rehnquist's opinion reads "almost as if he had reread the original *Miranda* opinion recently and discovered facts about it and its companion cases and language that he had not noticed before" (p. A-8).

How did this surprising outcome happen? Was it an indication that the conservative fabric of the Court was becoming frayed? No. If you read the majority opinion by Justice Rehnquist, you can discern two themes; one is that the erosions of the *Miranda* warnings instituted by the Court in the last 30 years have made it a more acceptable procedure; the other is his major concern about the tendency of Congress to make laws that reflect its interpretation of what the Constitution says (Greenhouse, 2000). At issue in

Dickerson was whether a law of Congress, passed in 1968, overruled the need to give a *Miranda* warning (Public Law 3501). In his decision, Justice Rehnquist seemed to be saying to Congress: "Don't tell the Supreme Court what is or is not in the Constitution; that's the Court's job, not yours." Thus the *Dickerson* decision was consistent with other decisions by the Court in the last decade that have restricted or even rejected acts of Congress that in the Court's view violated the Constitution and especially the sovereign immunity of individual states (Greenhouse, 2002a). Perhaps, at another time, when the Rehnquist-led Court was not so concerned with Congressional incursions on the judiciary's powers, *Miranda* might have been overturned (Greenhouse, 2000). But since 1995, with *United States v. Lopez*, the Court has invalidated all or part of more than 30 laws passed by Congress, mostly on federalism or separation-of-powers grounds. Thus, after reading Justice Rehnquist's decision in *Dickerson* and bearing in mind his strong support for restraining antifederalism tendencies of Congress, one is tempted to say "Why, of course, he was bound to vote this way." But most experts had not expected him to. (And it should be noted that the Supreme Court, in its most recent decisions, continues to restrict conditions in which *Miranda* warnings need to be given; it considered four cases in the 2003–2004 term and ruled against the defendant in each of them.)

Does the *Dickerson* outcome mean that the Court is a mysterious and unpredictable entity? Some observers have described the Court during the last years of the Rehnquist tenure as being "arrogant" and intolerant of other views, as well as being activist and further broadening what is a "constitutional" question and thus, by doing so, usurping responsibilities better delegated to the legislature (Ponnuru, 2000, 2004; Rosen, 2000). Others have sought a common theme in the decisions, but this was not an easy task, in that some decisions favored individuals (as in the *Dickerson* case) while others—such as the ruling favoring the Boy Scouts—did not. Chapter 10, which considers the question of the predictability of votes in detail, argues that greater understanding can come when cases are divided into different types, and that justices' ideologically based votes are more emergent in some types of cases than in others.

The Purpose of This Book

Some observers have asked: Can the Court be understood? Can we come to know why specific decisions are made? I believe that at a general level, the answer to these questions is yes. But to do so requires an understanding of how the selection of justices has become so politicized, how they painstakingly proceed in deciding cases, and how a set of nine opinionated experts with clashing opinions successfully interact with each other. For example, Chapter 2 describes the nature of the appointment and confirmation of justices, chapter 8 examines why some justices have been more effective than others, and chapter 9 examines the impact of the chief justice on the Court's functioning and decisions.

Difficulties in Understanding
Supreme Court Decision-Making

Both the executive branch and Congress have made efforts to inform the public about what they do. The president gives interviews, holds press conferences, and offers a weekly radio address. Sessions of the U.S. Senate and House of Representatives (and even some of their committee hearings) may be viewed on C-SPAN, and offices of members of Congress are open to the public. But the Court does precious little to help the public understand its processes and outcomes. Yes, it is true that as many as a million visitors have toured the majestic Supreme Court building in recent years, and if they are lucky enough to be there on the right day, visitors can watch oral arguments in the impressive courtroom. But most of the Court's important work is done behind closed portals. (In contrast to the open-door policy of the offices of members of Congress, the touring public is not permitted access to the workplaces of the justices, or even to the section of the building that houses them.) Although the Court has permitted states to televise individual trials, it has steadfastly resisted attempts to permit its own oral arguments to be televised. (At one of the annual visits by several justices to defend the Court's budget request before a Congressional committee, Justice Souter responded to a congressman's question about televising the Court's proceedings by saying it would happen only "over my dead body.") The Court has grudgingly permitted *audio* taping of its oral arguments in a very few recent, highly publicized cases (specifically *Bush v. Gore* and the challenges to the McCain-Feingold campaign financing law and to the University of Michigan's affirmative action procedure) but these were permitted to be broadcast only on a delayed basis. It is possible to obtain tapes and transcripts of the oral arguments, but it was only recently—in October 2004—that the transcripts indicated which justice was asking the question, and several of the transcripts provided in early 2005 incorrectly labeled the questioner. With the tapes, one must listen carefully with an ear trained to recognize the differences in order to know the identity of the questioner.

The judicial conferences that are held after the oral arguments, at which initial votes are taken, are so secret that not even the justices' law clerks or stenographers are present; the notes by the individual justices—some detailed, some incomplete, some mere scribbles—provide the only written record. Yes, it is also true that some of these eventually become public; Justice Blackmun's—fortunately for scholars, among the very most detailed ones—were made available by the Library of Congress in March 2004, five years after his death. It is also true that the final decisions are eventually announced publicly—the justice who has written the decision may make a short statement or read the entire opinion to the press and the public—but justices do not routinely hold press conferences that permit the media to ask them "What did you really mean?" In the words of Justice William Brennan, 'We write the opinions; we don't explain them" (O'Brien, 1997, p. xi). Only rarely do sitting justices give interviews to the press or to scholars. And sometimes when they give speeches, they reveal nothing about how they perceive their decision-making process.

The justices deny that their actions are as secret as the public assumes them to be. Lewis Powell, when he was a justice, noted that the court's oral arguments and decisions are public—"as if" (in the words of journalist Tony Mauro) "nothing else mattered" (2004b, p. 193). Justice Stevens, in a speech to the Chicago Bar Association in 2004, said: "We are the one branch of government that conscientiously tries to explain the reasons for all its important decisions" (*USA Today*, 2004, p. 14A). Yet, ironically, reporters found out about Justice Stevens's speech only after the fact. Like most of the justices, Stevens on that occasion did not release a schedule of his public appearances in advance.

But the justices are sensitive to public criticism of the Court. Beginning in 2005, several justices engaged in televised public discussions; among them was Justice Scalia, who previously had rigorously refused to permit his speeches be taped or televised. For example, in January 2005 he and Justice Breyer animatedly debated the use of international law at American University, in a session televised by C-SPAN, and in April 2005 these two justices, with Justice O'Connor, participated in a discussion at the National Archives, at which they answered questions about their decision-making, posed by Tim Russert of NBC's *Meet the Press*. Doubtless one of the reasons for this willingness to "go public" was the criticism of the federal judiciary that surfaced in early 2005.

In general, however, the justices seem to cherish their privacy; although they may choose to give speeches at judicial conferences or speak to law school classes, they value the fact that they can walk into a Washington supermarket and probably not be recognized. In January 2005, during a month-long Court recess, Justice Breyer dutifully reported for jury duty in Massachusetts, where he is a part-time resident. No one noticed him, not even the presiding judge. Only when his name was called for jury selection was his presence acknowledged. (A defense lawyer then had him excused.) The justices are not often available for the kind of appearances on morning television talk shows that frequently attract members of Congress or presidential aspirants. As Anna Quindlen wrote in a *Newsweek* column, "Ruth Bader Ginsburg has not shared her cookie recipe with the readers of *Good Housekeeping*. Anthony Kennedy has yet to appear on the cover of *People* magazine. David Souter has not gone on 'Late Night' to trade laughs with Letterman" (2000, p. 92).

The "Least Understood" Branch

Thus, while it may not be, as Alexander Hamilton predicted, "the least dangerous branch," the Supreme Court, as the pinnacle of the judicial branch, is certainly the least understood (Rehnquist, 2001). Despite the increased importance of the federal judiciary, the public seems to know very little about Supreme Court procedure and personnel. Perhaps as a result of the furor over the *Bush v. Gore* decision and the perceived increased public interest in the Court, during the 2001–2002 television season two of the major networks— CBS and ABC—chose to introduce dramatic series on the Supreme Court. But they both bombed and are now long forgotten. The one on CBS, "First Monday," featuring Joe Mantegna as a new justice and James Garner as the chief justice, was not renewed after its first season; the second, titled "The Court" with Sally Field as a justice, lasted on ABC for only a few shows.

Since the media are not privy to the judicial conferences or the period of intense negotiation after an initial draft of the majority opinion is circulated to the other justices, people assume (if they assume anything at all) that the Court hears oral arguments and then simply and straightforwardly decides. One aspect of explaining the Supreme Court, as this book intends to do, is to demonstrate that very much happens during the months-long interval between oral argument and the announcement of a decision, and to illustrate the reasons for the sometimes vast shifts between the justices' reactions during oral arguments and their eventual decisions.

Just as the public does not know about the Court's procedure, most citizens lack knowledge about the individual justices. A number of years ago, when asked to name the chief justice, only 9 percent of 1,005 randomly selected adults were able to name Chief Justice Rehnquist; 6 percent gave other names, and 85 percent did not know (Morin, 1989). Only 29 percent could give the name of even one of the justices; Justice Sandra Day O'Connor was the most frequently named, reflecting lingering aspects of her "fifteen minutes of fame" when President Reagan named her as the first woman on the Court. After this survey was done, the confirmation hearings for Justice Clarence Thomas drew nationwide attention because of Professor Anita Hill's charges, and the confrontation was nationally televised during October 1991; Chief Justice Rehnquist presided over the impeachment trial of President Bill Clinton in 1999. These events made these justices more recognizable, at least temporarily; after the *Bush v. Gore* decision, Chief Justice Rehnquist's recognition score climbed to a still low 31 percent (Mauro, 2002). Yet the public remains largely uniformed. In contrast, in the 1989 survey, 54 percent of those questioned were able to give the name of the judge on the television show *The People's Court*. Despite the supposedly naked portrayal of the justices in the bestselling book by Jon Stewart and *The Daily Show* writers, doubtless today more people can recognize "Judge Judy" than Justice Ginsburg.

The Image of the Court

Political scientist Barbara Perry, in a readable book (1999a), proposed that the prevailing image of the Supreme Court is that of "a priestly tribe"; the effect of the black robes is to give an impression of uniformity in the justices' decisions. Others, focusing on the symbolism of the robe, concentrate on its "one-size-fits-all" aspect; according to one commentator, "when a judge . . . puts on the robe, the loose-fitting nature of the garment in a very real sense hides the person's personality . . . the robe tells us that the wearer's beliefs, propensities and peculiarities are not relevant to the tasks assigned to him [or her] by society" (McLaughlin, 2000, p. A22). And for whatever reason, for many years the public has viewed the Supreme Court more favorably that it has the other two branches (Sigelman, 1979); a 1997 Gallup poll found that 71 percent of the respondents had a great deal or at least a fair amount of trust and confidence in the judicial branch, compared to 62 percent for the executive branch and 54 percent for Congress (Perry, 1999a). (By mid-2005, favorable ratings of Congress had dropped to 29 percent.)

In the film shown to visitors to the Supreme Court building, Justice Souter summarizes the source of the trust and goodwill in the judiciary:

> Most people are willing to accept the fact that the Court tries to play it straight. That acceptance has been built up by the preceding hundred justices of this Court, going back to the beginning. We are, in fact, trading on the good faith and the conscientiousness of the justices who went before us. The power of the Court is the power of trust earned—the trust of the American people.

The responses of the public to the different branches have been interpreted to conclude that the executive and legislative branches are seen as having been captured by the "evil and nasty system" of inside-the-Beltway lobbying and deal-making, while the Supreme Court is seen as part of the "constitutional system," a separate aspect of the political world (Hibbing & Theiss-Morse, 1995, pp. 87–88).

It may well be that the relative lack of awareness of the judiciary's activities contributes to the greater trust the public expresses in it. The Court contrasts itself with the two "political branches" of government; presidents, senators, and members of Congress are political in two senses: they are affiliated with political parties, and they must always bear in mind that most of them must soon face the public for reelection. Members of the federal judiciary are given their jobs for life, and so their decisions can be free of the political influences stemming from the urgency of getting reelected. But that does not mean that public opinion is irrelevant to the decisions judges make. Justices watch the television news, read their mail, and are aware of the protestors outside the Supreme Court building.

At present, the public gets most of its information about the Supreme Court from the mass media. Barbara Perry's (1999a) book examined the treatment of individual decisions by reporters from prominent newspapers and wire services; in her opinion, the media "usually get it right." Yet it needs to be recognized that those cases that lead to a split vote—especially 5 to 4 votes—are the ones more likely to be publicized than those on which the justices do not disagree. (In recent years, somewhere between 16 and 26 cases a year led to 5 to 4 votes, out of the 70 to 80 decided, thus about 20–33 percent. For the five terms ending in June 2001 through June 2005, the percentage of cases with 5 to 4 votes ranged from 21 to 33 percent.) The public would be surprised to learn that in some terms, close to half of the decisions rendered by the Court are unanimous ones (in the ten most recent terms, this percentage has ranged from a low of 36 percent to a high of 48 percent).

The Importance of Decisions

To say that the Supreme Court's decisions are often consequential ones is obvious. This importance can be demonstrated at several levels. At one level, the Supreme Court decides whether state and federal laws are consistent with the Constitution and especially with its Bill of Rights. An example was a law passed in the state of California that permitted a prosecutor to mention to the jury that if a criminal defendant failed to testify at his or her trial, it "surely proved" the defendant's guilt. In the trial of Admiral Dewey Adamson ("Admiral Dewey" were his given names), the defendant in a murder trial—on the advice of his attorney—did not take the stand because he possessed a criminal record. The prosecutor pointed out to the jury that he chose not to testify, and claimed that if Adamson had been innocent, it would have taken 50 horses to keep him off the stand (Urofsky, 1991). Not surprisingly, Adamson was convicted; his attorney appealed and challenged the California law as a violation of the Fourteenth Amendment's guarantee of due process. When the Court first considered this specific question (in *Adamson v. California*, in 1947), it upheld Adamson's conviction because it concluded that the prosecutor's comments had not created an unfair trial. But almost 20 years later, in the case of *Griffin v. California* (1965), the Court overturned its *Adamson* decision and ruled unconstitutional the California law allowing prosecutors to comment on defendants' failure to testify. The Court noted that, of course, jurors may draw inferences about guilt if the defendant chooses not to take the stand, but "when the court solemnizes the silence of the accused into evidence against him [it] is quite another [matter]" (p. 614).

At another level, one of the tasks of the Supreme Court is to resolve inconsistencies in decisions made by different lower federal courts, especially the 13 federal circuit courts of appeals. For example, early in 2002, the District of Columbia Circuit Court of Appeals ruled that an employee of the U.S. Commerce Department may seek damages from two supervisors who allegedly read her personal files that she had been assured would be kept confidential (*Stewart v. Evans*, 2002). But that ruling was inconsistent with one by the Ninth U.S. Circuit Court of Appeals, which held in 1991 that federal employees could not initiate such actions because Congress had intended the Civil Service Reform Act to be the sole remedy for federal employment disputes. This is the type of conflict that receives priority when the Supreme Court decides which cases to consider.

Another purpose for the Supreme Court is to rule on the constitutionality of actions by other branches of the federal government. (For example, the *Dickerson* case described earlier dealt with the legitimacy of an act of Congress that in effect abolished the requirement to read suspects their *Miranda* rights.)

In response to the terrorist attack of September 11, 2001, Attorney General John Ashcroft initiated a number of actions, including the detention of more than a thousand persons, the proposal to use military tribunals to try alleged war criminals, and the establishment of a new system for monitoring certain types of attorney–client conversations. Each of these has been challenged, and the Supreme Court during the 2003–2004 term began to consider the constitutionality of some of these actions of the executive branch.

Frequently we hear of people who, feeling wronged, swear to take their case "all the way to the Supreme Court." The Court's function, however, is not necessarily to right all wrongs. It must be selective in what cases it chooses to hear, and priority is given to the types of cases that fit the categories described here. In following what some would say are its narrow goals, the Supreme Court can sometimes be out of touch with the needs of the country. Not only may it ignore some vital issues, but its rulings may obstruct national progress. In the 1930s, as the United States plunged deeper into the Great Depression, President Roosevelt convinced the Congress to pass a number of innovations responding to the rapidly developing economic disaster. The Supreme Court, during President Roosevelt's first term, struck down many of these acts as unconstitutional, even though public opinion strongly supported the president's actions. Thus, temporarily at least, the Court served as an obstacle to solving a national crisis.

Supreme Court Decisions Can Affect the Lives of Many Individuals

At the individual level, decisions by the Court literally carry life-or-death implications. We are all aware that the Supreme Court has ruled that the death penalty is constitutional. Until recently, those convicted of murders committed when they were as young as 16 could be executed. (In the 2004–2005 term, the Court, again in a 5 to 4 decision, in *Roper v. Simmons*, overturned its previous endorsement of the death penalty for juveniles.)

In the last decade, the Court has rejected several opportunities to discard its 1973 decision of *Roe v. Wade* and rule that the right to an abortion is not implied in the privacy guarantees of the Constitution. Were it to do so, the lives of millions of U.S. citizens might be affected, as it would be up to each state's legislature to determine the legality of abortion in that state. In another example of widespread impact, an untold number of parents were dismayed when the Court, in 1996 (in *American Civil Liberties Union v. Reno*) struck down an act of Congress that had imposed large fines and prison terms upon persons who transmitted pornography on the internet so that it might be seen by children. And, as noted earlier in the chapter, several decisions by the Court have established the legality of random drug tests for students participating in athletics and other school-sponsored activities. Justice Scalia's opinion in one of these cases (*Vernonia School District v. Acton*, 1995) reflected a belief that children do not possess the same rights as adults.

Even Presidents of the United States
Go before the Supreme Court

Decisions by the Supreme Court can affect not only the lives of ordinary citizens but also that of the president. Interestingly, when, in the last half-century, presidents have had their decisions or choices reviewed by the Court, they have generally come out the loser. When President Truman issued an executive order seizing private steel mills in 1952, so as to prevent an impending strike that would harm the United States' efforts in the Korean War, the Supreme Court ruled the action improper because Congress had not provided authorization (*Youngstown Sheet and Tube Co. et al. v. Sawyer*, 1952). When President Nixon refused to respond to a request from the Watergate special prosecutor, Leon Jaworski, for White House tapes, the Supreme Court—in a unanimous decision—ruled that presidential immunity and executive privilege were not unconditional (*United States v. Nixon*, 1974). The president was ordered to relinquish the tapes, and they were found to contain statements linking him to a White House conspiracy to obstruct justice. Within only three weeks of the announcement of the Court's decision (which came on July 24, 1974), Nixon resigned the presidency. President George W. Bush found, in June 2004, that his administration's decision to detain foreign-born terrorist suspects without review was rejected by the Court, in a 6 to 3 decision (*Rasul v. Bush*, 2004).

President Clinton versus Paula Jones

President Clinton went before the Supreme Court twice and, in effect, lost both times. In *Clinton v. City of New York* (1998), the Court rejected an act of Congress that had given the president the opportunity to carry out line-item vetoes. The other decision (in *Clinton v. Jones*, in 1997) was much more important for President Clinton and, it developed, for the nation. When, in May 1994, Paula Jones filed a complaint against Clinton for sexual harassment (alleged to have occurred on May 8, 1991, at the Excelsior Hotel in Little Rock, while he was governor of Arkansas), he sought to delay any legal actions, including a possible civil trial, until after his term as president had ended. On May 27, 1997, the Court announced its unanimous decision; it was that the court proceedings should go forward, that no constitutionally based presidential immunity existed that required delaying such actions until Clinton had left office in January 2001. "Like every other citizen," the Court opinion said, "respondent [Paula Jones] has a right to an orderly disposition of her claims" (*Clinton v. Jones*, 1997, p. 1652).

At the time of its announcement, the decision was instantly a popular one with much of the public and most of the media; political journalists were in agreement that not even the president of the United States is "above the law." Some of their comments reflected an observation that Justice Scalia made during the oral arguments: "But we see presidents riding horseback, chopping firewood, fishing for stick fish, playing golf" (Bugliosi, 1998, p. 98). Thus, the reasoning went, if President Clinton had time to play golf, he had time to consult with his lawyers about preparation for a trial or a settlement. A public opinion poll found that 68 percent of the respondents felt that the president should go to trial as soon as feasible, while only 23 percent supported a delay (Bugliosi, 1998). Little did most of us foresee the implications of this decision. Paula Jones's lawyers persisted in seeking information about potentially relevant behavior by Mr. Clinton; on December 5, 1997, they submitted to the presiding judge a list of persons whom they wanted to depose, and Monica Lewinsky's name was on the list. Meanwhile, Kenneth Starr, the independent counsel investigating President Clinton's land holdings in the Whitewater real estate development matter, learned in January 1998 of President Clinton's affair with Ms. Lewinsky. The president's deposition given to Paula Jones's lawyers on January 17, 1998, contained statements that were, at best, evasive, and potentially perjurious. Those statements, and his statements to a grand jury in August 1998, led the House of Representatives to approve two articles of impeachment in December 1998, and during the first two months of 1999, President Clinton was put on trial before the Senate, with Chief Justice Rehnquist presiding. On February 12, 1999, the president was acquitted.

The United States survived this agonizing process, although the exposure of the actions of a sitting president seems to have immeasurably damaged the public's confidence in its leaders. Doubtless some Americans have rethought the wisdom of failing to delay a civil action against a president involving charges of a personal nature that allegedly occurred before he became president. Two observers have been especially critical of the Supreme Court for its decision in *Clinton v. Jones*. A book by trial attorney Vincent Bugliosi (1998) offered pungent criticism of President Clinton's attorneys for construing the matter as a separation-of-powers case; instead, Bugliosi argued, the central issue was public interest versus private interests, specifically, "whether or not the American public's interest in the effective function of the office of the president outweighed the private interest of Paula Jones in having the lawsuit go forward without delay" (p. 45). Bugliosi denied that the issue was whether the president was "above the law"; there was no question that Ms. Jones had the right to bring the charges. "The issue was not *whether* Paula Jones should have her day in court, but *when*" (p. 36, italics in original).

But Bugliosi was equally critical of the Court, saying that its ruling was "less profound than what we could expect of even a layperson of below-average intelligence" (1998, p. 1). Specifically, he claimed that however the appellate attorneys construed and argued the case, the Supreme Court should have seen that the central issue was the salience of the need for effective functioning by the office of the presidency. He argued that the Court should have asked—and answered—the question "What conceivable argument could possibly be made for the proposition that Jones' right to proceed to trial now with her private lawsuit is more important than the public's right to have its president undiverted and undistracted in the performance of his duties running the country?" (p. 48) Trial courts do that for people they have never heard of, and they are particularly sensitive to the defendant's schedule if he or she is a prominent person. Bugliosi demanded: "Show me a judge in Chicago, for instance, who would not postpone a civil lawsuit against Michael Jordan [then the star player for the Chicago Bulls] until the end of the entire season, if for no other reason than to avoid a lynching by the people of Chicago. In short, the Court gave the President of the United States *nothing at all*" (p. 44, italics in original). And it did so without a solitary vote of dissent!

Furthermore, Bugliosi concluded that previous appellate decisions could have been brought to bear on the decision. For example, federal appeals courts have had to decide on timeliness with respect to civil suits against military personnel. The Soldier's and Sailor's Civil Relief Act of 1940 permitted the suspension of the "enforcement of civil liabilities . . . of persons in the military service of the United States in order to enable such persons to devote their entire energy to the defense needs of the nation" (Bugliosi, 1998, p. 49), and appellate courts have upheld this law, even in peacetime suits. It is true that Congress did not expressly include the president of the United States in this 1940 legislation. The majority opinion in *Clinton v. Jones*, written by Justice John Paul Stevens, even suggested that "If Congress deems it appropriate to afford the President . . . protection, it may respond with appropriate legislation" (1997, p. 1652). But could not the previous case have been applied?

The Court's opinion in *Clinton v. Jones* also reflected some assumptions that, in hindsight, seem ill advised. These include the following.

> "If properly managed by the District Court, it appears to us highly
> unlikely to occupy any substantial amount of [the President's]
> time" (1997, p. 1648).
> "If a trial is held, there would be no need for the President to attend in
> person, though he might elect to do so" (1997, p. 1643).

Furthermore, during the oral arguments, Justice David Souter told President Clinton's attorney, Robert Bennett, that pretrial discovery "does not personally involve the President. . . . I mean, the President isn't going to attend those depositions, you are" (Bugliosi, 1998, p. 97). In actuality, defendants do sometimes attend depositions of all critical witnesses.

The other detailed criticism of the Court's decision in *Clinton v. Jones* came from a source who drew immediate attention. Judge Richard Posner has served as the chief judge of the U.S. Court of Appeals for the Seventh Circuit and is a widely quoted author of more than 30 books and numerous articles. He has, for a long time, been interested in the relationship of sexual behavior to determinants of morality and legality. His book on this case, *An Affair of State* (1999), was highly critical of his fellow judges, and he minced no words in his evaluation of the Supreme Court's decision in *Clinton v. Jones*. Here is one example of what he wrote:

Part I of the main opinion begins, absurdly to the layperson, with
the statement that "Petitioner, William Jefferson Clinton, was
elected to the presidency in 1992, and re-elected in 1996." Anyone
who doesn't know these things has no business reading the
opinion. The danger, when a judge pads an opinion with sentence
after sentence that does no work, that merely labors the obvious, is
that he will run out of steam before he gets to the hard part of
writing an opinion, which is analyzing the issues. After telling us
who Clinton is, the opinion summarizes the allegations of Jones'
complaint, and this is unnecessary too because nothing in the
Court's reasoning turns on the nature of Jones' complaint; it
might as well have been a personal injury complaint arising from a
traffic accident. (pp. 225–226)

Judge Posner went on to write:

After skirmishing inconclusively with the as-usual inconclusive
historical materials, the Court takes up the question whether the
immunity sought by the President might be justified by the public
interest in his being able to "devote his undivided time and
attention to his public duties" (p. 1646). The Court naively grants
the premise of the argument, quoting Lyndon Johnson's self-
serving declaration that he didn't get enough sleep as president
and so buying into the erroneous idea that the more important the
job, the longer the hours. (1999, p. 226)

Judge Posner noted that in neither Justice Stevens's majority opinion nor
Justice Breyer's concurrence is any consideration given to the fact that Paula
Jones's suit was about sex, and he proposed that

it should have been apparent to them that depositions and a trial
in a case in which the President was alleged to have solicited a
woman for oral sex were likely to bring details of the President's
sex life into public view . . . [a]nd it should have been apparent to
the justices that public exposure of the details of the President's
sex life could undermine the President's authority and effectiveness. (1999, p. 227)

But that was not all there was to Judge Posner's critique; he even expressed
doubt that the justices have the skill to handle the challenges of this unusual
appeal. After an aside in which he observed that "the Supreme Court has not
shown a deft hand in dealing with cases involving sex" (1999, p. 227, n. 19),
he wrote:

It would, though, have required great skill to write an opinion that
gave the President immunity from being sued over sex without
making plaintiffs in sexual harassment suits seem like second-class

citizens. Either justices lack that skill or they just did not understand the mischievous potential of the case. (p. 227)

Judge Posner suggested an alternative to the decision: "At the very least, the Court could have instructed the district judge to manage the litigation in a manner designed to minimize embarrassment to the President" (1999, p. 228).

In a book such as this one, whose purpose is to understand the basis for Supreme Court decisions, Judge Posner's suggestion to the justices is fascinating; in a sense, he has asked them to be *more* political; "[n]one of the justices has substantial political experience. Most of them are professional judges . . . and there is nothing in the training or experience of a judge calculated to impart political savvy" (1999, p. 228). He urged them to go beyond legal reasoning: "[t]he justices should have known that they could not base their decision . . . in *Jones* on political insight (let alone on conventional materials for judicial decision-making—previous decisions, and historical materials, none of which spoke to the case at hand) because they didn't have any" (pp. 228–229).

The sensible approach, he argued, would have been to decide as little as possible.

> In *Jones*, the path of prudence would have been to grant the
> President immunity against having during his term in office to
> defend against (or, at the very least, having to submit to being
> deposed in) a sex case, while leaving open the possibility that
> immunity might not extend to types of cases less likely to humili-
> ate and confound the President. (p. 229)

The respected political columnist David Broder agreed with Judge Posner, concluding that "the Court is often tone deaf when it comes to political issues" (1998, p. 6B).

Despite this onslaught of criticism, Justice Stevens, who wrote the majority opinion, has stuck by his guns. In one of those rare occasions in which justices comment on their own decisions, Justice Stevens said to a group of judges in Milwaukee on May 24, 1999, that he had received mail calling his ruling "one of the dumbest opinions ever written" but that "I don't think any one of the Court would change a word in the opinion if they had to do it over again" (Mauro, 1999a, p. 4A). He also revealed that "the only thing that was ever seriously considered was postponing the trial, not the depositions."

What Determines the Decision?

The controversy over the decision in *Clinton v. Jones* reaffirms the urgency of understanding how decisions are made. The focus of this book, especially in chapters 5 and 6, is on the decision-making process. The traditional explanation, called by scholars the *legal model*, proposes that judges consider what past decisions are relevant to the issue at hand, extract the direction of their conclusions, and use legal reasoning to form their judgments. Many of those political scientists who study judicial behavior challenge this assumption. In the *attitudinal model* they advocate instead, judges' attitudes and values play a predominant role in their initial reaction to the case; furthermore, other considerations besides the issue at hand may influence judges' final votes. The attitudinal model has been, in the last 20 years, the prevailing view among scholars, but it has been reevaluated recently by some political scientists, some of whom emphasize the powerful effects of the *institution* of the Court on decisions made. Other social scientists who move away from a narrow attitudinal model suggest that *rational choice* underlies decisions. And then social psychologists have offered a *social cognition* model, which seeks to incorporate aspects of several earlier models.

Challenges to the Legal Model

If all justices followed the legal model absolutely, it could be argued that uniformity of opinion would result. There would be no split votes. Yet, as noted earlier, up to two-thirds of all cases lead to a split vote, with around one-fourth of the cases resulting in a 5 to 4 vote. Justices may view the same previous cases in a different light, or choose to emphasize different previous cases in making their decision about the current one.

Sometimes differences can be traced to different interpretations of the meaning of the same phrase, or even one word. For example, in April 2005 the Court decided the case of *Small v. United States*. Gary Small had previously been convicted of a crime while in Japan. Upon returning to the United States, he purchased a gun, and in so doing, said that he had not been previously "convicted in any court." He was arrested for violating the law that prohibited convicted felons from owning firearms. But does "convicted in any court" mean in the United States or worldwide? By a vote of 5 to 3 (Rehnquist was absent) the Court ruled that the law meant "any" in the U.S. only. Thus even if one accepts the legal model as a legitimate explanation of decision-making, variability can still exist between justices.

A Case with Nine Different Opinions

The ultimate in variance is a case leading to each justice adopting a different position, but on rare occasions this happens. In the case of *Furman v. Georgia* (1972), which dealt with the question of whether the imposition of the death penalty violated rights in the Eighth and Fourteenth Amendments, nine justices wrote *nine* different opinions. Five justices agreed that imposing the death penalty upon William Furman, a black man who murdered a white man, violated the provision against cruel and unusual punishments, and so (for four years) executions in all states were suspended. But the five in the majority—

all of whom had served with Chief Justice Earl Warren—could not agree on the proper rationale for this decision. Justice William O. Douglas concluded that the death penalty was applied against minority-race members and the poor in a discriminatory fashion that violated the equal protection clause. Justice William Brennan concluded that the death penalty served no penological purpose, compared to imprisonment, and furthermore, was inconsistent with the rights of human dignity implied in the Eighth Amendment. Justice Potter Stewart argued that the death penalty was cruel and unusual punishment because it was imposed in—to use his words—a "wanton" and "freakish" manner. Justice Byron White was in the majority because the infrequent use of the death penalty meant it violated the provision against cruel and unusual punishments. And the last of the majority, Justice Thurgood Marshall, concluded that it was cruel and unusual for three reasons: it served no valid legislative purpose, it was morally indefensible because it inflicted physical pain, and it was excessive and arbitrary, hence discriminatory. These justifications overlap, but what is noteworthy is that each of the five justices in the majority needed to write a separate opinion. Likewise, each of the four justices in the minority (Harry Blackmun, Warren Burger, Lewis Powell, and William Rehnquist, all appointed by President Nixon) also prepared separate dissents.

Votes That Are Consistent with Ideological Alignments

One argument for the impact of attitudes and values on votes of the justices is the emergence of consistent voting alignments within the Court. During Justice Thomas's first term on the Court, much was made of the fact that he voted the same way as Justice Scalia in all but one of 80 cases (and the one deviation was a minor tax case). More recently, in the 2001–2002 term, these two justices disagreed in only one of the 20 most publicized cases. In a recent term, Justices Rehnquist and O'Connor voted the same way in 93 percent of the cases, Justices Scalia and Thomas in 90 percent of the cases (96 percent of the criminal cases), and Justices Ginsburg and Souter in 91 percent of the cases (and 100 percent of the criminal cases). Certain groups of justices "think alike," and the tendency occurs both in the conservative bloc and in the relatively liberal bloc. But, as I illustrate in chapter 10, this effect is present in certain types of case more than others.

I will argue in chapter 10 that this ideological-clustering effect occurs more often in cases involving defendants' and prisoners' rights, cases in which an individual brings suit against a large organization, and cases involving rights and restrictions on minorities. An example of a case in which the vote pattern followed directly from ideological differences was the decision in *Department of Commerce v. United States House of Representatives* in 1999. While the title sounded innocuous enough, the issue at hand was a politically volatile one. In this case, the majority decided that the census in the year 2000 would use the traditional head count method rather than a statistical sampling procedure that permitted adjustments for missing respondents. (It was estimated that in the previous census, in 1990, some four million people, or 1.6 percent of the population, were not included.) Those "missing" are disproportionately urban, poor, and members of racial and ethnic minorities—groups that tended to vote Democratic—and the Clinton administration had argued for their inclusion (Greenhouse, 1999). Justice O'Connor wrote the majority opinion and was joined by the other conservative members of the Court (Justices Rehnquist, Thomas, Scalia, and Kennedy). In dissent were the four relatively liberal justices, including the two appointed by President Clinton. As Kenneth Prewitt, director of the United States Bureau of the Census, observed:

> Technical decisions (for example, how many forms to mail) normally made by career professionals are today routinely reviewed by an oversight apparatus intent on influencing how the census will be conducted. Regrettably, the division of views falls along partisan lines. Even the Supreme Court divided along conservative and liberal lines in its recent decision. Science by partisan vote is a risky enterprise. (Prewitt, 1999, p. 7)

But not all votes fall along ideological lines, as was illustrated in the *Dickerson* case earlier and as will be amplified in chapter 10. Liberals and conservatives can agree, and often do; in fact, it is noteworthy that in the 2002–2003 term, the pair that disagreed with each other most often, Justices Thomas and Breyer, still concurred on 50 percent of the outcomes.

Not only do some types of cases fail to provoke an ideological focus but justices can and do vote in ways that are inconsistent with their ideologies, attitudes, and values. For example, in 1989, in the case of *Texas v. Johnson*, the Supreme Court had to deal with the constitutionality of a law that had convicted Gregory Johnson of burning a United States flag during a protest outside the 1984 Republican national convention in Dallas. The majority of the Court, following First Amendment considerations, ruled that laws like this one against flag-burning were unconstitutional, because even desecration of a flag was a form of symbolic speech. Justices Scalia and Kennedy were members of the majority despite their deeply held reverence for traditional values. In his concurrence to the majority opinion, Justice Kennedy acknowledged his feelings but wrote: "The hard fact is that sometimes we must make decisions we do not like. We make them because they are right, right in the sense that the law and the Constitution, as we see them, compel the result" (*Texas v. Johnson*, 1989, pp. 420–421).

Another Way of Looking at Decisions: Judges Are Human Decision-Makers

Judges are human—that statement is obvious. Numerous observers have specified what qualities an ideal justice should possess; Henry Abraham (1992) identified six: absolute personal and professional integrity, a lucid intellect, professional expertise and competence, appropriate professional educational background or training, the capacity to communicate clearly (especially in writing), and judicial temperament. The 110 justices over the history of the Court have met these criteria to varying degrees, as will be illustrated in several subsequent chapters.

But what does it mean to be human? It means to have biases but sometimes to be able to overcome those biases. It also means to make mistakes, on occasion. One of the last books that the eminent scholar Bernard Schwartz prepared on the Supreme Court was *A Book of Legal Lists* (1997), which included his opinion of the 10 worst decisions in history. Some were to be expected: *Dred Scott v. Sandford* (1857), *Plessy v. Ferguson* (1896), and *Korematsu v. United States* (1944). Some of his choices reflected Schwartz's own biases, but no one would disagree with the conclusion that some Supreme Court decisions have been mistakes. Even the justices tacitly acknowledge that, when they later reverse some of their own decisions.

To be human also means to be concerned with one's own self-interests but also concerned with the reactions of others to one's choices, and even, at times, concerned with the attainment of higher goals. I believe that both the legal model and the attitudinal model fail to represent fully the human aspect of the judging process, each being deficient by emphasizing opposite qualities. The legal model bleaches the decision-making process of its colorful human ingredients; it can be portrayed as an ultralogical, if not mechanical, analysis of applications of relevant statues and decisions. The attitudinal model, taken to its extreme, fails to recognize the constraints upon the judge as a professional person. An adequate description of judicial decision-making needs somehow to recognize the contribution from these two models but also to present a richer conception than that represented by just one or the other. Subsequent chapters, especially chapters 5 and 6, present a theory of judicial decision-making that reflects each of these models.

Examples of Judicial Opinions Reflecting Human Qualities

Several examples are offered here to support the claim that justices are *human* decision-makers. Some are majority opinions, some dissents. And of course in each of the following examples, not all the judges reflected the same human values.

DeShaney v. Winnebago County (1989)

In the summer of 2002 publicity about a five-year-old girl from Miami led to the revelation that her disappearance had gone undetected for 15 months by Florida social services caseworkers who were supposed to be monitoring her welfare. This led to further disturbing disclosures about failures, in other states, of agencies given responsibility for the protection of children. The magnitude and breadth of these cases led some to seek a way to punish government agencies and professional employees who failed to provide the expected standard of vigilance and care. Unfortunately for those who were advocates of children's protection, the Supreme Court had, 13 years earlier, limited their avenues for sanction in a case with equally serious consequences for a child named Joshua DeShaney.

The parents of Joshua DeShaney had divorced within a year after he was born (in 1979), and the father, Randy DeShaney, was granted custody. For more that two years, young Joshua was beaten by his father. Social workers in the Wisconsin county in which Joshua and his father lived became aware of the more-than-questionable circumstances of the family's interactions in January 1982. Joshua was brought to the hospital for treatment by Randy's girlfriend; he was covered with bruises and abrasions. His father denied that the injuries were a result of his abuse. Two months later, the hospital once more treated Joshua for suspicious injuries, but no evidence of abuse was found. Several times when county social workers tried to see Joshua at home, his father denied them access. By the age of four, Joshua had been beaten so repeatedly and severely that he had suffered extensive brain damage and had to be permanently institutionalized. His father was convicted of child abuse (and served less than two years in prison). But that was not punishment enough to satisfy Joshua's mother (who lived in Wyoming and had not had the opportunity to observe the day-to-day developments). She brought a civil suit against the Department of Social Services of Winnebago County, Wisconsin, claiming that the social workers had failed to intervene when they had reason to suspect the boy was in danger. Did this failure to act violate Joshua's Fourteenth Amendment right not to be deprived of life or liberty without due process of law? Specifically, did Joshua's mother have a right to sue the state?

Consider what was before the Supreme Court; any person would feel sympathy for an innocent child who had suffered as Joshua had. But should the Court allow the state to be sued when the actual cause of suffering was a series of acts by another individual? What are the duties and responsibilities of state officials when abuse is suspected? Clearly, precedent has made clear that positive abuses of power by state officials are violations of due process. But what about a failure to act?

Two justices sympathized with Joshua but expressed their position on the legal issues in different ways. Justice Brennan applied a logical argument to support his conclusion that the state should be accountable: "inaction can be every bit as abusive of power as action . . . oppression can result when a state undertakes a vital duty and then ignores it" (*DeShaney v. Winnebago County*, 1989, p. 1012). Justice Blackmun expressed his opinion in even more human terms:

> Poor Joshua! Victim of repeated attacks by an irresponsible, bullying, cowardly, and intemperate father, and abandoned by respondents who placed him in a dangerous predicament and who

knew or learned what was going on, and yet did essentially nothing
except . . . "dutifully recorded these incidents in [their] files."
(*DeShaney v. Winnebago County*, 1989, pp. 1012)

But the human feelings of Justices Brennan and Blackmun *did not prevail.* In contrast, the majority opinion of the Court, written by Chief Justice
Rehnquist, concluded that Joshua's mother did not have the right to sue the
state; instead, the purpose of the due process clause of the Fourteenth Amendment "was to protect the people from the states, not to insure that the state
protected them from each other" (*DeShaney v. Winnebago County*, 1989,
p. 1003). The state had not placed Joshua in a position of danger; Joshua was
in his father's custody, not the state's. Yes, continued the majority opinion,
states could—if they chose to—enact laws that placed the liability on such
officials under similar circumstances, "but they should not have it thrust upon
them by this Court's expansion of the Due Process clause" (*DeShaney v.
Winnebago County*, 1989, p. 1004). (Justice Rehnquist's opinion was joined
by Justices White, Stevens, O'Connor, Scalia, and Kennedy.)

The majority opinion was not devoid of human feeling; it reflected awareness of the human temptation to be responsive to Joshua's mother's goal of
achieving accountability. "Judges and lawyers, like other humans," it wrote,

are moved by natural sympathy in a case like this to find a way for
Joshua and his mother to receive adequate compensation for the
grievous harm inflicted upon them. But before yielding to that
impulse, it is well to remember once again that the harm was
inflicted not by the state of Wisconsin, but by Joshua's father.
(*DeShaney v. Winnebago County*, 1989, p. 1007)

Thus an unyielding and seemingly logical application of settled rules
comes in contact with the human tendency toward mercy, "viewed as making exceptions to those rules for cases where they produce heartless results"
(Strauss, 1990, p. 86). But as Justice Brennan's dissent noted, it is more than
sympathy that could drive a decision favoring the right to sue a state; a logical
analysis could also be offered to support this view. By establishing departments
of social services, states have, in effect, removed private sources of aid. When
people see a child being mistreated, they report it to the state and assume the
problem will be rectified. The Wisconsin Child Protection Act provides for
various governmental institutions, employing social workers, to protect such
children. Thus when the state fails to respond, the individual is worse off,
because there is no private "safety net."

Furthermore, a claim that the state "failed to act" does not accurately describe the situation. Justice Brennan wrote: "It simply belies reality, therefore,
to contend that the state 'stood by and did nothing' with respect to Joshua.
Through its child-protection program, the state actively intervened in Joshua's
life and, by virtue of the intervention, acquired even more certain knowledge
that Joshua was in grave danger" (*DeShaney v. Winnebago County*, 1989, p. 1011).

Income Tax Cases

Nobody likes to pay their income taxes. In 1894, Congress imposed an income tax of 2 percent on incomes above $4,000, but the majority of the Supreme Court ruled that the tax was unconstitutional, on the grounds that it punished the citizens of those states that had a higher wealth per capita. Interestingly, the five justices who voted that the tax was unconstitutional all came from states that had, according to the census of 1890, wealth per capita that was above average. The four justices who found the tax constitutional all came from states with lower per capita income (King, 1950, p. 214).

But when a new federal income tax was instituted in 1918, some federal judges went further. They refused to pay it, for an unusual—and in their opinion, incontrovertible—reason; because article 3, section 1, of the Constitution, orders that federal judges' salaries "not be diminished during their continuance in office." In 1920, the Supreme Court justices agreed to hear an appeal on this question, and their decision not only affected the take-home income of the judges who appealed, but also their own. How would the justices decide? And why?

In the case of *Evans v. Gore* (1920), the petitioner was a federal district judge for the Western District of Kentucky, who claimed that the federal income tax diminished his compensation and thus was unconstitutional. (Another article of the Constitution, article 2, contains a similar restriction against reducing the president's salary.) Justice Willis Van Devanter wrote the opinion for the Court, and acknowledged "regret that its solution falls on us" (p. 247). He also added, gratuitously, that each member of the Supreme Court "has been paying the tax in respect of his salary voluntarily and in regular course" (p. 247). Justice Van Devanter's opinion quoted extensively from the writings of Alexander Hamilton, Chief Justice John Marshall, and President Wilson, among others, especially on the need for an independent judiciary. He concluded:

> These considerations make it very plain . . . that the primary purpose of the prohibition against diminution was not to benefit the judges, but like the claim in respect to tenure, to attract good and competent men [*sic*] to the bench and promote that independence of action and judgment. (*Evans v. Gore*, 1920, p. 253)

Judge Van Devanter expressed sympathy for the judge who appealed:

> Here the plaintiff was paid the full compensation, but was subjected to an involuntary obligation to pay back a part, and the obligation was promptly enforced. Of what avail to him was the part which was paid with one hand and taken back with the other? Was he not placed in practically the same situation as if it had been withheld in the first instance? (p. 254)

Precedent supported the conclusion that with regard to earlier income tax legislation, federal judges and the president had been exempted. Chief

Justice Roger Taney, in 1862, objected to an income tax of 3 percent on all civil officers of the United States, and in 1869 the attorney general of the United States rendered an opinion that the tax should be considered invalid with respect to federal judges and the president. Amounts that previously had been collected were refunded.

So the decision in *Evans v. Gore* was that federal judges were exempt from the tax. But two justices, Louis Brandeis and Oliver Wendell Holmes, Jr., dissented; the latter wrote:

> To require a man to pay the taxes that all other men have to pay cannot possibly be made an instrument to attack his independence as a judge. I see nothing in the purpose of this clause of the Constitution to indicate that the judges were to be made a privileged class, free from bearing their share of the cost of the institutions upon which their well-being if not their life depends. (*Evans v. Gore*, 1920, p. 265)

The majority decision in the 1920 case was affirmed in *Miles v. Graham* in 1925, with Justice James McReynolds, for the majority, writing that "there is no power to tax a judge of a court of the United States on account of the salary prescribed for him by law" (p. 509). Only Justice Brandeis dissented.

It was not until 1939 that the justices allowed themselves to be taxed. Joseph W. Woodrough was appointed United States circuit judge in 1933. He claimed his judge's salary of $12,500 to be constitutionally immune from taxation, and he paid the tax only under protest. In a surprisingly brief, six-page opinion for the majority of the Court, Justice Felix Frankfurter reversed the previous decisions and concluded that federal judges were required to pay the tax; "[t]o subject them to a general tax is merely to recognize that judges are also citizens, and that their particular function in government does not generate an immunity from sharing with their fellow citizens the material burden of the government whose Constitution and laws they are charged with administering" (*O'Malley v. Woodrough*, 1939, p. 282).

The Supreme Court continues to obsess about the tax status and pay of federal judges. In May 2001 the Court ruled that Congress's extension of the Medicare tax to federal judges in 1982 was constitutional but that the imposition of the Social Security tax in 1984 was not (*United States v. Hatter*, 2001). Justice Breyer wrote the majority opinion, saying that the Medicare tax was a general tax that applied to all taxpayers and "there is no good reason why a judge should not share the tax burdens borne by all citizens" but the Social Security tax that, in theory, was newly applied to all federal employees, in reality exempted nearly all of them except judges, and so was discriminatory and hence invalid (Greenhouse, 2001b).

More recently, several justices, including William Rehnquist while he was chief justice, have tried to publicize the position that the income of federal justices has fallen in reality because increases have not kept up with inflation and with the massive increases in salaries and shared profits by attorneys in private law firms. Even the justices' own law clerks outstrip them in income within a year or two of leaving their clerkship (Greenhouse, 2002b). Currently, the salaries of Supreme Court justices remain around the $200,000 level ($203,000 for associate justices and $212,100 for the chief justice), and they have relinquished their right to earn outside income, except for a small amount permitted for summer teaching. (In 2004, for example, Justices Kennedy, Thomas, and Scalia received between $4,000 and $8,500 for teaching summer law school classes [Mauro, 2005d].)

Conclusions

Humans are complex. Did the judges who objected to being taxed do so as a matter of principle or precedent, or was it a reflection of the justices' self-interest, rationalized by a referral to higher principles? It is difficult to know the cause—or, more likely, causes—of an individual decision. But when we examine the votes in a number of cases, and when we read what the justices have written in their majority opinions, concurrences, and dissents (*especially* their dissents!), certain themes emerge that lead to somewhat greater understanding and predictability. But first, in order to understand judicial decision-making, we need to consider the background of justices and the process by which they are selected for the Court. This is the topic of chapter 2.

2

The Selective Nature
of Supreme Court Justices

We seem unwilling to consider the many ways in which we damage judicial independence when presidential candidates promise to pack the Court if elected, and their opponents can offer nothing better than solemn undertakings to pack the Court the other way.—Stephen L. Carter, *The Confirmation Mess* (1994)

One would think that presidents, when faced with the opportunity to nominate someone to the Supreme Court, would think long and hard about possibilities and then select someone who fits the criteria of an "ideal justice." But that is not always the case.

- President Harry Truman was known for allocating favors to his friends and "cronies"; every one of his four appointments to the Supreme Court was someone he knew well and liked. In his memoirs about his years on the Court, Justice William O. Douglas (1980) recounted the following.

    [I]n the early fall of 1949 Wiley Rutledge died, leaving a vacancy on the Supreme Court. Tom Clark went to [President] Truman and recommended that he name [Secretary of the Army Robert] Patterson to the vacancy. Truman agreed to send Bob's name up the following Monday. Meanwhile Shay [Sherman] Minton, previously named to the Court of Appeals for the Seventh Circuit, flew to Washington and walked into the White House to see the President.

    "What can I do for you, Shay?"

    "Harry, I want you to put me on the Supreme Court to fill that new vacancy."

    "Shay, I'll do just that," Truman replied. (Douglas, 1980, p. 247)

    And he did.

- When President George H. W. Bush announced Clarence Thomas as his nominee to replace Justice Thurgood Marshall, he went out of his way to describe Thomas as "the best person for the position," adding "the fact that he is Black and a minority has nothing to do with this."

- Although it is difficult to be certain, it appears that when President Nixon, in 1971, faced the task of appointing an associate justice, William Rehnquist was his *eighth* choice; in Oval Office conversations he had earlier referred to Rehnquist (who was on the White House staff) as "Renchburg." He also ridiculed Rehnquist's style, once asking who was "the guy dressed like a clown," referring to Rehnquist's mutton-chop sideburns, Hush Puppies, pink shirt, and psychedelic tie (Dean, 2001, p. 86; Woodward & Armstrong, 1979, p. 189).
- Informed knowledge has it that the main reason that President Woodrow Wilson appointed James McReynolds to the Court was that, as Wilson's attorney general, McReynolds had been obstinate, opinionated, and unable to work with the president and the rest of the Cabinet (Blaustein & Mersky, 1978).

These examples reflect that fact that even though the nomination of justices to the Court is one of the supremely important activities of a president, sometimes the choice is made with little thought or for less than ideal reasons. And, of course, no candidate is guaranteed to pass the (recently) rigorous and often highly political assessment by the United States Senate. This chapter examines the nomination and confirmation processes from the perspective of their effectiveness as ways of bringing the best candidates to the Court.

The Justices—Not Representative

A total of 110 men and women have been Supreme Court justices over the more than two hundred years of the American republic. This figure might imply that they have some special qualities that have singled them out. This chapter will argue that they are certainly not representative of the entire population, or even of that subset of the population from which they are chosen. Ironically, the most salient quality that all the present justices share—training in the law—is *not* a requirement for appointment to the Court. And going beyond this quality, we find that many of the justices do share common backgrounds and experiences. Is this good?

Background of Justices

An investigation of the first 100 Supreme Court justices found that only 12 came from "essentially humble origins" (Schmidhauser, 1979, p. 49). Among justices chosen in the last half of the twentieth century, only the following four were members of families with working-class backgrounds.

- Earl Warren, whose father worked on the railroad
- Thurgood Marshall, son of a Pullman steward
- Warren Burger, whose father was a railroad car inspector and traveling salesperson
- Clarence Thomas, whose father abandoned the family

Similarities

The vast majority of justices have come from comfortable circumstances, and "were chosen overwhelmingly from the socially prestigious and politically influential gentry class in the late eighteenth and early nineteenth century, or the professional upper middle class thereafter" (p. 49). More than half had fathers who held professional or business positions; 27 of the first 100 justices had judges in their families, and 12 of these had judges as fathers (Bader & Mersky, 2004; Blaustein & Mersky, 1978). The backgrounds of the justices contrast, interestingly, with those of the presidents; of the last 12 presidents, Nixon, Truman, Reagan, and Clinton came from modest backgrounds, and only Roosevelt, Kennedy, and the Bushes from "socially prestigious" families.

The wealth of their ancestors is also manifested in the financial status of the recent and current justices. According to financial disclosure reports, at least five are millionaires. Justice Ginsburg reported a net worth between $7 million and $33 million; Justice Breyer between $4 million and $15 million. Perhaps it is not surprising, or even a matter of concern, that as a group they are richer than all but a small percentage of Americans. It is even understandable in some instances—for example, three recent or current justices (Roberts, Ginsburg, and O'Connor) have spouses who are partners in highly successful law firms. Another, Breyer, has inherited money. But representative they are not.

Differences

Religious diversity is a part of American life and is increasingly a part of the makeup of the Court. Of the first 100 justices, 89 were Protestants, six were Roman Catholics, and five were Jews (Blaustein & Mersky, 1978). There was a "Jewish seat" on the Court from the appointment of Louis Brandeis in 1916 until the resignation of Abe Fortas in 1969 (Ginsburg, 2003), and when President Nixon was considering Justice Fortas's replacement, he asked his attorney general "Is Rehnquist Jewish?" (Dean, 2001, p. 86). "He looks Jewish," Nixon said.

In contrast to earlier times, the Court beginning the 2005–2006 term was quite religiously diverse, with two Jews (Justices Ginsburg and Breyer), four Roman Catholics (Justices Scalia, Thomas, Kennedy, and Roberts), and only three Protestants. Diversity with regard to gender, ethnic group, and race has also become increasingly important. President Reagan, in a campaign pledge, promised to appoint the first woman to the Court, and did so. When the first

African American on the Court retired, President George H. W. Bush felt pressure to replace him with another black justice, and he did. As speculation about vacancies surfaced in the early part of George W. Bush's second term, Hispanic Americans—especially Alberto Gonzales—received consideration, although President Bush eventually chose two Anglo American males and an Anglo American woman to fill the vacancies.

Diversity in geographic region does not appear to be salient, as it was 150 years ago, and 19 of the 50 states have never had one of their natives named to the Court. President Nixon was the most recent president who sought specific regional representation; he failed in his bid to appoint two southerners to the Court and temporarily abandoned his quest. Later, Lewis Powell, of Virginia, reluctantly agreed with Nixon's entreaty to be nominated. One reason for the lack of recent emphasis on geography is that people move; William Rehnquist grew up in Wisconsin, went to law school in California, practiced law in Arizona, and was working for the federal government in Washington, D.C., at the time that he was appointed to the Court. Clarence Thomas is a native southerner on the Court, but he went to school in New England and worked as an attorney in Missouri before he moved to Washington, D.C. Among current or recent justices, only David Souter, Anthony Kennedy, and Sandra Day O'Connor remained geographically close to their roots before they were appointed to the Court.

Judicial Experience

Other factors than geography have become more salient over time in the selection process. Today's Court is different from the past ones in that, during the period between 1994 and 2005, eight of the nine justices had prior experience as a judge, mostly at the federal circuit court level or as a state appellate court justice. The only one without such experience, William Rehnquist, then the chief justice, had been on the bench for more than 30 years. Thus, each had a long experience and a professional identity as a judge. In contrast, when Earl Warren was named chief justice in 1953, only Justices Minton and Black had prior experience on the bench, and Black's was only 18 months, as a part-time police court judge in Birmingham, Alabama, early in his career. In fact, President Eisenhower—after he appointed Earl Warren—required that all his subsequent nominees would have prior judicial experience, and this "rule" was followed by most of the more recent presidents. Four of President Nixon's six nominees had served on the bench; the one whom President Ford nominated did; and all five of Reagan's and both of George H. W. Bush's and the first and third of G. W. Bush's were already judges.

Judges as Political Beings

The common characteristic in the current justices that is perhaps overlooked is that they are all political in their orientation. "Political" needs to be clarified here; most have not run for political office, but each has been significantly involved in political activities or held previous positions in the government that were political party–based appointments. Typically, those lawyers nominated by their states' senators to be federal judges have been visible because of their willingness to work for a political party. Among current or recent justices, Rehnquist, O'Connor, Souter, Scalia, Thomas, Alito, and Roberts all had either worked for the Republican Party or had held positions in a Republican-led state or federal government. Justice Breyer had been counsel for the majority (Democratic Party) of a congressional committee. Justice Kennedy had been a lawyer and lobbyist in Sacramento before being appointed as a federal judge. One has to go back to the appointments of Justices Blackmun and Powell in the early 1970s to find justices who were not partisan in the sense of having been actively involved in a political party.

The Nomination Process

The process of choosing a justice can be described by the following five steps (Goldman, 1991).

1. The administration selects an individual to be recommended to the president to fill the vacancy.
2. The president formally nominates the individual, and the White House sends the nomination to the U.S. Senate.
3. The Senate Judiciary Committee considers the nomination and votes whether to approve and send the nomination to the full Senate.
4. By a simple majority vote, the Senate decides whether or not to confirm the nominee. During the twentieth century, the Senate confirmed 89 percent of the president's nominees; Clarence Thomas was confirmed by the narrowest of margins, 52 to 48.
5. The president signs the commission, which is delivered to the individual, who then takes the oath of office.

When a vacancy on the Court surfaces, what is the process by which a president chooses a replacement? The Constitution gives little guidance; it simply says that the president "shall nominate, and by and with the advice and consent of the Senate, shall appoint Judges to the Supreme Court" (article 2, section 2). As noted earlier, the "consent" of the Senate has been operationalized as a simple majority vote.

Presidents have differed in the way they have responded to the opportunity to name a justice. Vacancies sometimes occur suddenly, but sometimes the president has advanced warning. Six months prior to his actual resignation, Justice Blackmun told President Clinton that he was planning to resign soon. Regardless of advanced notice, the president may want to be prepared with a list of possible nominees. President Carter used judicial selection commissions to generate names for appellate court nominations, but Carter is the only recent president who completed his term in office without the opportunity to name a Supreme Court justice. In contrast, President Reagan dropped the commission and created an Office of Legal Policy in the Justice Department. After it was announced in October, 2004, that Chief Justice Rehnquist had thyroid cancer, the White House developed a list of possible replacements, even as he remained on the Court.

More important, presidents have differed in how personally involved they became in the selection process; the behavior of Presidents Roosevelt, Truman, and Johnson reflected great involvement; in contrast, Presidents Reagan, George H. W. Bush, Clinton, and George W. Bush used a more traditional referral process.

Are There Constraints on the President?

On first thought, the president's task in selecting justices seems to be an attractive and straightforward one. During his presidential debates during both the 2000 and 2004 election campaigns, George W. Bush said that he would appoint justices like Clarence Thomas and Antonin Scalia to the Court, and that commitment clearly communicated very specifically the orientation he sought. Ronald Reagan, during his campaign, also promised to appoint judges who reflected "judicial restraint," a term that one set of authors said translated into "agree with me on social and political issues" (Murphy, Pritchett, & Epstein, 2002, p. 141). But various constraints operate on the president; these are eloquently expressed by Yalof:

> Consider the political tightrope modern presidents must walk as they attempt to choose nominees in this highly charged political atmosphere. Organized interests on all sides of the political spectrum may try to influence their choice of a candidate at the outset. Senators, attuned to these changes in the political environment, may assume more aggressive postures against a rumored nominee even before the President has formally designated him or her for a Supreme Court seat. Increased media attention may scare some potential nominees away, further constraining presidential discretion. (1999, p. 168)

Individual Differences

Presidents respond to these constraints in different ways. Political scientist Sheldon Goldman (1997) has distinguished among three types of goals the president may have in selecting federal judges; these goals can apply to the selection of Supreme Court justices, too:

1. Personal goals, including the desire to assist a personal friend or associate with a nomination, as reflected in President Truman's nomination of Sherman Minton described earlier.

2. Public policy goals, including the furthering of values supported by the president, as reflected by President Johnson's nomination of Thurgood Marshall as the first African American to sit on the Court.
3. Partisan goals, in hopes of preserving or increasing political support for himself and his party, as reflected by President Nixon's failed efforts to nominate several southerners to the Court, before the successful confirmation of Lewis Powell. According to a book by John Dean (2001), who was President Nixon's legal counsel, Nixon considered naming the first woman to the Court, despite his gender bias. "I don't think a woman should be in any government job whatever," he told Attorney General John Mitchell, "mainly because they are erratic . . . and emotional. . . . I lean to a woman only because, frankly, I think at this time [prior to the 1972 reelection] we got to pick up every half a percentage point we can" (p. 113). And Nixon did decide to nominate California Judge Mildred Lillie, but the American Bar Association (ABA) rated her as "not qualified," and she was dropped. Later, both Presidents Carter and Clinton sought to satisfy core constituents of the Democratic Party by increasing the percentage of appointees who were African American, Hispanic American, or female (Murphy, Pritchett, & Epstein, 2002).

These differences are reflected in the different ways that presidents determine their nominees. The contrasts among Presidents Truman, Eisenhower, and Johnson are illuminating.

Harry Truman

Harry Truman had the opportunity to appoint four justices to the Supreme Court, including a chief justice. Yalof proposed that Truman

> was determined to nominate justices who came directly from his own tight-knit political circle. Truman wanted to feel a sense of "personal comfort" with each of his nominees, in part because he believed that those who knew him well would be more understanding about such forays outside the traditionally enumerated powers of his office. (1999, p. 20)

The first of his appointments was a Republican, Harold Burton, but Burton had been a close colleague when Truman was in the Senate. When he was given the opportunity to name a chief justice, he chose Fred Vinson, at that time the secretary of the treasury in Truman's cabinet and Truman's "favorite poker companion" (Clifford, 1991, p. 70). His third and fourth nominees, Tom Clark and Sherman Minton, reflected Truman's domination of the selection process; "he made no pretense at all of consulting others" (Yalof, 1999, p. 37). Experienced Court observers do not include any of President Truman's appointments on lists of the most distinguished justices of the twentieth century.

Dwight D. Eisenhower

The conventional wisdom about Dwight D. Eisenhower, while he was president, was that he was quite uninvolved, disengaged, and more concerned about his golf game than the welfare of the country. But the revisionist view, spurred by Fred Greenstein's (1982) book, has portrayed Eisenhower as skillful and politically sophisticated in his actions. His choice of a justice to fill the vacancy resulting from Sherman Minton's resignation reflected the political nature of his thinking. Eisenhower had several criteria in mind; for example, early in 1955, well before there was a vacancy, he expressed the wish to his associates that the next vacancy be given to a Roman Catholic. Recognizing that the Catholic vote would be important in his 1956 reelection campaign, he asked his attorney general, Herbert Brownell for "the name of some fine prominent Catholic to nominate to the bench" (Yalof, 1999, p. 55), even before another vacancy surfaced. Later, as the election heated up, Eisenhower wanted to communicate to the public that he had really meant his pledge to be more nonpartisan than Democratic presidents had in appointing judges. His first two appointments to the Court (Warren and Harlan) had been Republicans, as well as all but a handful of his appointments to the lower federal courts. So he told Brownell to be on the lookout for a well-qualified Democrat to appoint. And, as mentioned earlier, Eisenhower had already instituted his policy of appointing justices who had some previous judicial experience; his second appointment, John Marshall Harlan II, had served briefly on the U.S. Court of Appeals.

So, on September 7, 1956—two months before Election Day—Justice Minton informed President Eisenhower that he wished to resign; the President reminded Brownell of the three criteria. David Yalof, who interviewed Brownell much later, described the process as follows.

> Brownell met with his deputy, William Rogers, to pass on the President's marching orders: canvass the field for a candidate who was a Catholic, a Democrat, and who possessed substantial experience as a judge. The attorney general also knew Eisenhower wanted to appoint a justice below the age of sixty-two, preferably with some background in the state courts. "This was a tall order," Brownell later remembered, "as there weren't that many judges out there that would fit all of Eisenhower's instructions." (1999, p. 58)

This was a time before the ease of computer searches, and Attorney General Brownell probably wasn't aware of just how few persons there were who did fit the criteria. Yalof did a systematic search almost 50 years later and concluded that at most, only three people in the country fit all of the criteria, including the age limit, and two of those were flawed. Although Eisenhower and Brownell did not realize it, the only one who fully possessed all their qualifications was the person they chose, William J. Brennan, a 50-year-old justice of the New Jersey Supreme Court.

Given his delight in finding someone who met the president's stringent criteria, Brownell perhaps did not explore in enough detail whether Brennan's judicial philosophy was consistent with the president's hopes to appoint a moderate-to-conservative Democrat. Yalof noted that Brennan had impressed Brownell and Rogers only four months earlier when he spoke at the attorney general's conference in Washington, D.C. But there is some question whether the speech Brennan gave was his own or one that Arthur Vanderbilt, the chief justice of the New Jersey Supreme Court and his boss, had asked Brennan to give in his stead. At any rate, Brennan was nominated and confirmed, and went on to become a thorn in the side of conservatives and a skillful justice who was the core of the liberal thrust of the Supreme Court from the late 1950s to the late 1960s.

Lyndon Johnson

President Johnson was known for his ability to persuade others to do as he wished them to do. But he, more than any other president, went further in successfully creating vacancies so that he could appoint his personal choices to the Court. (Franklin Roosevelt tried to, as will be described later in this chapter, but failed.) As noted, one of Johnson's long-term goals, after he suddenly became president in 1963, was to appoint the first African American person to the Supreme Court. But he had other goals for his first appointment; later in this chapter, we describe how he got the reluctant Abe Fortas onto the Court as his initial nominee.

In early 1967, Johnson began to implement his plan to create a vacancy. After his attorney general, Nicholas Katzenbach, moved to another position in the government, Johnson nominated Ramsey Clark as his replacement. While Clark had been an assistant attorney general and was a likely nominee, central to Johnson's choice was the fact that Ramsey Clark's father, Tom Clark—a Truman appointee—was then a justice. Would not this force the father to resign because of a "conflict of interest"? Yalof has eloquently described the next developments:

> The President raised the possibility directly to Ramsey Clark
> during a telephone conversation on January 25, 1967. "You think
> you could be attorney general with your daddy on the Court?"
> Johnson asked. "Well, I think that other people ought to judge
> that," Clark replied, "but I know as far as I'm concerned that
> would not affect my judgment. I don't think it would affect
> Daddy's judgment." Ramsey Clark believed that—even at the age
> of 67—his father was still performing at the peak of his abilities.
> Under no condition did he want him to resign. Ramsey Clark
> appealed to the president's political instincts: "In the police
> community and some other conservative areas Dad ranks awfully
> high. For you to replace him with a liberal would hurt you." Yet as

was often the case, the President would not budge. Johnson replied: "If my judgment is that you become attorney general, he [Tom Clark] would have to leave the Court, for no other reason than the public appearance of an old man sitting on his boy's case. Every taxi driver in the country, he'd tell me that the old man couldn't judge fairly what his old boy is sending up. (1999, p. 88)

And that is what happened. Justice Tom Clark immediately announced that he would resign at the end of the current term, and thus Johnson was able to nominate Thurgood Marshall as the first black justice on the Supreme Court.

How Important Is Personal Compatibility?

With respect to the need to be personally compatible as a criterion for selection, presidents differ, and their needs seem to be consistent with their personality. Bill Clinton, who loved to talk to people and was uncomfortable when he was not with other people, interviewed two finalists for his first appointment and chose the one with whom he felt congenial. In contrast, Ronald Reagan—known as superficially affable but lacking in close friends—was "at no time . . . tempted to choose nominees whom he knew personally" (Yalof, 1999, p. 134). Furthermore, he never vetoed the judgments of his staff in screening prospective candidates. Other than having nominees satisfy the conservative-ideology criteria, he kept hands off, with the exception of expressing his wish to name the first woman to the Supreme Court.

For some presidents, as seen earlier with Truman, compatibility was essential. For some of these, at least in the personal interview, there had to be some spark. When President Clinton faced his first vacancy on the Court with the resignation of Byron White, he was urged by some of his aides to nominate Stephen Breyer. So Breyer was invited to join the president for lunch at the White House. The meeting did not go well; Clinton told his assistants that he felt "Breyer was selling himself too hard, that his interests were too narrow, that he didn't have a big heart" (Drew, 1994, p. 215). He chose Ruth Bader Ginsburg instead, although Judge Breyer did become Clinton's second nominee a year later, when Harry Blackmun retired. (President Clinton's autobiography, published with great fanfare in mid-2004, is almost 1,000 pages long, but he devotes only two unrevealing pages to his nominations to the Supreme Court.)

Do Current Justices Play a Role?

The separation of the three branches of government is fundamental. The executive branch nominates judges, the legislative branch (specifically the Senate) confirms or rejects, and the judicial branch has no part in the process. But in actuality, certain justices and certain presidents have had close, informal relationships. Before he became a justice, Felix Frankfurter was one of Franklin Roosevelt's closest advisors, and he continued to be so after Roosevelt named him to the Court. Justice Frankfurter convinced President Roosevelt to appoint Harlan Fiske Stone as chief justice; as a representative of the Court, he argued, Stone would foster national unity (Urofsky, 1991). Be that as it may, Stone certainly did not foster unity within the Court, as chapter 9 illustrates.

While on the bench, Abe Fortas would call up President Johnson to relay advice. Chief Justice Burger had "back-channel" communications with President Nixon. Do these contacts extend to the task of selecting new justices? On some occasions, yes.

In 1921, President Harding appointed William Howard Taft, a former president, as chief justice of the United States. He also had the opportunity to appoint three associate justices (Beauregard, 2001). Taft and Harding had been friends for a long time, and Taft, as chief justice, began to take an active role in the identification of candidates for federal judgeships. In fact, he made every effort to appoint justices who shared his views (Murphy, 1965). President Harding did not object. In 1922, a vacancy developed, and Taft coordinated an informal screening of candidates; his final choice was Pierce Butler. On October 30, 1922, Chief Justice Taft wrote to President Harding:

> In your consideration of candidates for the Supreme Bench, I think I spoke to you of Pierce Butler of Minnesota. I have known him for a number of years very well indeed. . . . He is a Democrat of the Cleveland type, but really one I think would make a great justice of our Court, such a man of rugged character and force as Justice Miller was. (Danelski, 1964, p. 54)

The next day President Harding acknowledged the letter, and soon thereafter Pierce Butler was nominated and confirmed.

Do Persons Seek It Out?

Can candidates—at least, those who consider themselves eligible for a justiceship—do anything to make themselves more likely to be chosen? Or is it a surprise to most nominees when they are contacted by the White House? Harry Blackmun, in an interview made shortly after he retired from the Court, said that back in 1970 he had the idea that he might get nominated because President Nixon had said that he wanted justices with judicial experience and Blackmun was one of the few Republican-nominated circuit court judges at that time. As the likelihood of a vacancy increases, both the media and the White House generate lists of potential nominees, and to some extent, persons can lobby to get on these lists.

Examples: Warren Burger and Ruth Bader Ginsburg

Warren Burger began campaigning to be named to the Court as it became apparent that Chief Justice Warren would soon be retiring. He capitalized on his longtime friendship with Herbert Brownell, who was assisting Nixon, as a new president, in staffing. At the time, Burger was the chief judge for the U.S. Court of Appeals for the D.C. circuit—considered the most important of all the 13 circuit courts—so he certainly would have been on a new administration's list. But even before Nixon took office, Burger wrote Brownell:

> I know you have many loyalties and demands on you and I shall never embarrass you with any request of mine. But the Midwest (from Ohio to the Rockies is hell of a lot of the USA!) is not represented on the "topside" & ought to be. Before RN gets firmly fixed I hope that thought will be put to him. I have never known him well and probably suffer some guilt by association. But last year he wrote me spontaneously on my Ripon College criminal justice speech . . . hence he is not unfriendly. (Yalof, 1999, p. 102)

When President Clinton had an opportunity to make his first appointment to the Court, the husband of Ruth Bader Ginsburg, Martin Ginsburg (a prominent Washington, D.C., tax attorney) "orchestrated her nomination behind the scenes" (Perry, 1999a, p. 84). It is claimed that Judge Ginsburg altered one of her speeches to make her viewpoint sound more consistent with the Clinton administration's perspective.

Or Is It Thrust upon Them?

In contrast, several justices in the last 50 years have been less than eager to serve. Lewis Powell was 65 years old and had recently completed a term as president of the ABA when asked by President Nixon to accept an appointment. Powell was content to continue as an attorney in Richmond, Virginia, and on several occasions declined the nomination. But President Nixon was persistent; he had promised to appoint a southerner to the Court, and, as noted earlier, two of his earlier nominees had been rejected. So Powell reluctantly acquiesced. Similarly, David Souter, an intensely private person, was so appalled by the media scrutiny he received after he was nominated by President George H. W. Bush that he considered withdrawing his name before the confirmation hearings (Rudman, 1996).

The response from Abe Fortas reflected even greater reluctance. Fortas, who in the early 1960s was a prominent Washington, D.C., lawyer, was one of President Johnson's closest friends and confidants, and Johnson wanted him on the Court. Even before Johnson was vice-president and president, Fortas had drafted speeches for him and advised him on a variety of matters. But the problem facing Johnson was there was no vacancy. He singled out Justice Arthur Goldberg as a possibility. Goldberg, a Kennedy appointee and the newest justice on the Court, was happy there, but Johnson "insisted that it was in Goldberg's and the nation's best interests that he leave the Court immediately" (Yalof, 1999, p. 82). He persuaded Justice Goldberg to take the position of U.S. Ambassador to the United Nations, so that a vacancy existed for Fortas. But Fortas did not want to take the severe pay cut that would be a part of being a justice; in fact, his wife, also a prominent attorney, was adamant about it.

Fortas was, at that time, one of the founding partners of arguably the most powerful Washington, D.C. law firm, Arnold, Fortas, & Porter (later Arnold & Porter), and he was committed to the continued growth and development of his firm. He was unresponsive to Johnson's continued and persistent entreaties. He declined the president's offer at least twice even before Goldberg's resignation was made public (Yalof, 1999). After the resignation, Johnson asked Attorney General Katzenbach to generate a list of possible nominees for the vacancy. Yalof interviewed Katzenbach, much later, for his book, and reported:

> Katzenbach recalled telling the president: "Why bother with a list? The person you really want to appoint to the Court, the one who is closest to you, and who is eminently qualified to be on the Court, is Abe Fortas." But Johnson urged Katzenbach to investigate "all possible options." Katzenbach left the meeting convinced that Fortas was the presumptive nominee. Still, on July 23, 1965, he dutifully submitted a six-page memorandum to the President describing various other candidates worthy of consideration. Katzenbach addressed a number of factors to be considered in choosing a successor to Goldberg, including: the Court's partisan balance (at the time there were five Democrats and three Republicans on the Court); geography (the candidate "should come from the middle, mountain states, border states or New England"); religion ("I think it undesirable for there to be no Jew on the Court for too long"); and age ("Ideally, the appointee should be between 50 and 60 years of age"). He also touched on issues of "judicial philosophy" ("The appointee should reflect you . . . an open-minded, judicious liberal") and background ("[You are] free to choose from the federal and state judiciary, private practice, or the academic world"). Fortas fit most of the criteria quite comfortably; he was a native son of Memphis, a Jew, and 55 years old. Before proceeding to other candidates, Katzenbach declared that "from a completely objective viewpoint Abe Fortas has every qualification for the Court. If you did not know him he would be my first recommendation—and still is." (pp. 83–84)

President Johnson persisted in his quest. As Yalof described it,

> [a]s Katzenbach suspected, Johnson had no intention of considering his lengthy memorandum. Instead, the President planned to use every means at his disposal to persuade Fortas to accept the nomination. As Goldberg summed up the situation to his increasingly

anxious group of clerks: "The President says he's going to appoint Abe and Abe says no. The President won't even consider other names. He's going to wear him down. He'll wait until the end of time." The President sought help in this effort from Fortas's original mentor at Yale and in Washington, D.C., Justice William O. Douglas. But Douglas also had little luck persuading Fortas. Issuing yet another "firm refusal," Fortas told Douglas that his "personal affairs would not permit him to leave private law practice at that time." Just as Johnson remained steadfast in his choice, Fortas's refusal seemed equally inflexible.

Finally Johnson literally "ambushed" Fortas with the nomination on July 28 [1965]. That same day the President was scheduled to announce plans to escalate dramatically the war effort in Asia. On the way to the press conference, Johnson stated his case simply to Fortas: "I'm going to send your name to the Supreme Court, and I'm sending fifty thousand boys to Vietnam, and I'm not going to hear any arguments on either of them." Under the gun, even Fortas was unable to resist the President's powerful appeal. (Yalof, 1999, p. 85)

The Confirmation Process

Presidents can have an effect on the composition of the federal judiciary long past their term in office. For example, in mid-2005, seven judges on the Seventh Circuit Court of Appeals had been appointees of President Reagan 20 years before. But the Senate can create a hurdle in the appointment process; most presidential nominees get confirmed by the Senate, but not all do. In the last 30 years, five nominees to the Supreme Court have either been rejected by the Senate or have withdrawn their names as it has become clear they would not be confirmed. In October 2005, Harriet Miers withdrew her name.

Confirmation Required for All Federal Judges

It is the responsibility of the U.S. Senate to "advise and consent" with respect to the appointment of all federal judges, not just justices of the Supreme Court. At present there are 868 federal judgeships (federal district judges plus the appellate judges on the 13 circuit courts of appeals and the justices on the Supreme Court). At any given time, vacancies exist, predominantly at the district court level and often at the circuit court level. Prior to 2005, the last Supreme Court vacancy was in 1994, and the period from 1994 to 2005 without a vacancy was one of the longest in the Court's history.

When a vacancy at the district court level occurs, the president has traditionally solicited recommendations from the two senators from that state; the president then nominates a replacement. Typically, the president nominates members of his own party, even if he pledges bipartisanship. President Eisenhower promised a 50–50 appointment rate but ended up selecting 186 Republicans and 15 Democrats to the federal bench (Chase, 1972). Similarly, more than 92 percent of Reagan appointees were Republicans, and 90 percent of those appointed by Presidents Carter and Clinton were Democrats (Goldman & Slotnik, 2002). For bipartisan appointments, the high-water mark—the term is relative—was apparently achieved by President Herbert Hoover, with 13 percent of his federal judgeship appointments coming from the other party (Roche & Levy, 1964).

Traditionally, most nominees have been expeditiously reviewed by the Senate's Judiciary Committee and accepted by the Senate, without much publicity. However, in the last two presidential administrations the process has slowed down, partially because in President Clinton's second term and in a portion of President George W. Bush's first two years, the majority of the senators were members of the other party than the president's. Two consecutive nominees of President Bush for the Fifth Circuit Court of Appeals were rejected by the Judiciary Committee in 2002, while the Democrats held a majority in the Senate. In March of that year, a federal district judge from Mississippi, Charles W. Pickering, was rejected, with the Democrats on the committee claiming that his record on racial issues and in abortion cases reflected a bias. (Capitalizing on a brief adjournment by the Senate in the middle of its term, President Bush later gave Judge Pickering a recess appointment early in 2004, meaning he could serve for a year without Senate approval; the president later did the same thing for William H. Pryor, Jr., for the Eleventh Circuit.)

The Judiciary Committee later rejected another nominee for the Fifth Circuit, Patricia R. Owen. Judge Owen had received a unanimous rating of "well-qualified" by a committee of the ABA. (Since 1947, the ABA has operated a Committee on the Federal Judiciary, which rates candidates as "extremely well-qualified," "well-qualified," "qualified," or "not qualified.") All 10 of the committee's Democrats voted to reject Judge Owen, who was a member of the Texas Supreme Court, claiming that she "had gone out of her way to favor corporations over individuals and had improperly tried to insert her own anti-abortion views into court rulings" (Lewis, 2002, p. A1). They even quoted the words of Alberto R. Gonzales, at that time President Bush's counsel, who had served with Justice Owen on the Texas Supreme Court; he had written in a June 2000 ruling that her dissenting opinion in a parental notification case was "an unconscionable act of judicial activism" (quoted by Lewis, 2002, p. A1). President Bush resubmitted her name four years later, as the Senate contained a greater number of Republicans (55 votes) as his second term began. After the threat of a filibuster, Democrats achieved a compromise that permitted the Republican majority, in May 2005, to confirm her nomination (by a vote of 55 to 43), as well as four other circuit court nominees. As his second term progressed through 2005, more than 25 percent of the sitting federal judges were President Bush's appointees.

History of the Confirmation Process for Justices

Once nominated, candidates for Supreme Court justiceships make "courtesy calls" to the offices of senators on the Judiciary Committee if the senators are willing. It is now expected that Supreme Court nominees appear before the Judiciary Committee of the Senate to be questioned, but it was not always the case. The first to appear was Harlan Fiske Stone, in 1925, and he did so at his own request, after the committee had met once and had heard fierce opposition to his appointment from Senator Burton K. Wheeler of Montana. (While attorney general, Stone had conducted an investigation of Senator Wheeler.) The Coolidge administration hastily arranged for the Judiciary Committee to reconvene, so that Stone would have an opportunity to defend himself. As Carter (1994) observed, he did so with admirable skill, and was confirmed by a vote of 71 to 6.

Over the next 30 years, nominees sometimes testified and sometimes didn't. William O. Douglas, though seen by some as an extremist, was not asked to testify. Felix Frankfurter, when asked to, at first declined, citing a concern about missing classes he was supposed to teach at Harvard, as well as his goals for an independent judiciary. But when led to believe that he wouldn't be confirmed if he didn't, he reluctantly appeared before the committee, and was confirmed unanimously. Sherman Minton, after he was nominated in 1949, refused to testify, citing the impropriety of asking a federal judge to do so. The Judiciary Committee accepted his response and reported his nomination favorably to the entire Senate.

According to Stephen Carter's useful review, routine appearances before the committee were established as a result of the *Brown v. Board of Education* decision in 1954. Southern prosegregation senators who dominated the committee were outraged by what they saw as judicial usurpation of states' rights, and insisted that future nominees appear before the committee. The very next nominee, John Marshall Harlan II, in 1955, agreed to appear, and the "tradition" was established.

But for a while, the content of the questions was narrow. Carter wrote:

> For the next twelve years, every nominee appeared and every nominee was grilled about the segregation decisions. As the era of the Warren Court continued, the questioning broadened, and potential justices found themselves asked about their views on everything from communism to defendants' rights to prayer in the public schools. For example, William Brennan, nominated in 1957 by President Eisenhower, faced a series of politically clever if legally naive questions from Senator James O. Eastland, chair of the Judiciary Committee, about the legitimacy of the Court's methodology in *Brown*. (Typical: "Do you think the Constitution of the United States could have one meaning this week and another meaning next week?") He was also roughed up by Senator Joseph McCarthy, whose star was by then failing but who still

knew how to smear a witness. (Typical: "I have maintained . . .
that you have adopted the gobbledygook that communism is
merely a political party, is not a conspiracy. . . . Do you consider
communism merely as a political party?") Picking his way through
these mine fields, the usually forthright Brennan understandably
refused to answer directly, and in the end, the committee dropped
these lines of questioning. (1994, p. 67)

How the Process Has Changed over the Years

John Maltese's (1995) review of the confirmation process illustrates why the
process has changed since the first appointments in 1789. In the 1850s, two-
thirds of the Court's cases dealt with salient issues of contracts, commercial
law, trusts, admiralty, and property (Schwartz, 2004). In the last half of the
nineteenth century, social and technological changes led to the rise of organized labor and other interest groups that began to make their wishes known
to the Senate, if not to the president. The popular election of senators, as a
result of a constitutional amendment in 1913, removed a kind of complacency
resulting from senators' awareness that they only had to persuade their fel-
lows in their state's legislature to reelect them to office. And it was not until
the 1920s that floor debates over nominees began to be done in public; previously the Senate had met in executive session to consider Supreme Court
appointments.

The Brandeis Nomination and Confirmation

President Woodrow Wilson's first appointee to the Court, James C. McReynolds,
did not fulfill Wilson's goal of appointing justices who would support governmental regulation of business. So for his second appointment, Wilson turned
to Louis D. Brandeis, "a progressive crusader, a trust-busting reformer who
actively supported trade unionism" (Maltese, 1995, p. 49). By 1916, at the time
of his appointment, Brandeis—a Boston attorney—was recognized nationally
as a leading force in the reform movement and a champion of labor. As Todd's
biography notes, Brandeis "represented to men of property [a] kind of men-
ace. . . . [He was] dedicated . . . to breaking down the traditional American way
of life under which the freedom to accumulate was sacred in the eyes of those
who worshipped property" (1964, p. 64). The powerful, propertied class looked
upon Brandeis as a radical revolutionary. One of them said:

> If a man like Brandeis, with his wild ideas of a shorter day [for
> workers] and higher pay to go with it, his advocacy of the income
> tax [which was seen as punishing the rich], his schemes to break
> business into ruinously competitive units, his tight-control plans for
> public utilities—if such a man should come to a position of real
> power, then America would never be the same again. (pp. 64–65)

Urofsky's biography of Brandeis observed that what especially upset the Boston establishment was "that Brandeis, a graduate of Harvard Law School and a man who had given every indication of becoming a fine—and trusted—corporate lawyer, had broken away to become a reformer, and the targets of his reforms had frequently been Boston's own social and economic elite" (1981, p. 112). Even A. Lawrence Lowell, the president of Harvard University, actively attempted to have the Senate reject his nomination.

It is difficult to think of a crusading lawyer in contemporary life who resembles Brandeis's challenges to the establishment—perhaps Ralph Nader, when he was leading "Nader's Raiders" in lawsuit after lawsuit against large manufacturers in the 1960s and 1970s, would come closest. Like Nader, Brandeis had semiascetic qualities. He and his wife had decided how much income was necessary to maintain a modest lifestyle; anything he earned after that was invested or paid back to his law partners to compensate them for the cases that he did not take or accepted on a *pro bono* basis. And, like Nader (until Nader's runs for the presidency in 2000 and 2004), Brandeis did not seek public office; until he was nominated for the Supreme Court, he operated out of his law firm in Boston, assisting in suits to protect utilities customers from high prices, to prevent monopolies by the railroads, to ensure that the number of working hours was regulated, and to further similar activities that always had as their goal to better the working conditions of the average citizen.

Wilson's nomination of Brandeis stunned the Senate; critical senators claimed that Brandeis lacked "the judicial temperament." Anti-Semitism also played a role, as Brandeis was the first Jew ever appointed to the Supreme Court. But even if 1916, it was not acceptable, in the eyes of some at least, for a public figure like a senator to express such prejudices, and some senators were caught in a bind. However, in the eyes of most observers and biographers, the main concern was Brandeis's ideology (Maltese, 1995).

The confirmation hearings for Brandeis were a landmark for two reasons: (1) they represented the first time that the Senate Judiciary Committee held its hearings in public, and (2) they were the first after the ratification of the Seventeenth Amendment to the Constitution, providing for the popular election of senators rather than their selection by state legislatures. Thus, senators were aware that unpopular votes could cause the public at large to reject them for reelection; they had a new constituency, and for a large part of the electorate, Brandeis was a hero (Maltese, 1995). Thus a significant number of senators who were privately opposed to Brandeis refused to do so publicly, and he was confirmed by the Senate by a vote of 47 to 22.

In a survey of experts on the Supreme Court who were asked to rate the first 96 justices on the Supreme Court, 12 were classified as "great"; not only was Justice Brandeis one of those 12, but he was second, behind Chief Justice John Marshall, in the number of scholars (62 of 65) who rated him as "great" (Blaustein & Mersky, 1978).

Recent Adversarial Nature

Both liberal and conservative observers agree that the confirmation process has become more adversarial and contentious in the last two decades. Just as President George W. Bush in 2003 complained about the rejection of his candidates for federal judgeships, President Clinton found opposition from the predominantly Republican Senate in his second term. One observer recently wrote:

> The judicial confirmation process has reached a new low. There have been occasional confirmation battles over U.S. Supreme Court nominees in the past, but such battles have become less principled in recent decades. Over the last 20 or so years, the Senate also has slowed down the confirmation process toward the end of a presidential term if the President and the Senate majority are from different parties. (Gaziano, 2002, p. A24)

Why is this the case? Some blame it on what they see as the increased power of the courts in the last half-century (Gaziano, 2002). Others focus on the split nature of the current Supreme Court and the frequency of ideologically driven 5-to-4 votes. Still others note how the issue of the Court's composition has been catapulted into presidential election campaigns. During the 2004 election campaign, George Bush—who did not have an opportunity to nominate a justice during his first term—reaffirmed his description of Justices Scalia and Thomas as models for any appointments he would make, and John Kerry said he would seek justices who did not let their ideologies influence their decisions.

But we can extend the period of contentious confirmation hearings back to the 1960s. In the last 40 years, the confirmation hearings for three nominees have achieved this new level of rancor: Thurgood Marshall, Robert Bork, and Clarence Thomas. The hearings for Judge Bork were the first that drew extensive television coverage, and many of us still remember watching in fascination the confrontation between Clarence Thomas and Anita Hill in October 1991.

But President Johnson's desire to place the first African American justice on the Court challenged a Senate that, in 1967, still manifested overt racial prejudice. The book-length review of the confirmation process by law professor Stephen Carter concluded that "Thurgood Marshall was subjected to a degree of racist smear [sic] that the confirmation process had not seen before and has not seen since" (1994, p. 5). He suggested that conservatives who believe that Robert Bork or Clarence Thomas "encountered unprecedented animosity" should study the news accounts and transcripts of the "openly racist" campaign against Marshall.

He amplified:

> Many of the questions, on the surface, were directed at showing Marshall to be outside the mainstream, albeit in rather diabolical

ways. Senator Eastland [who still chaired the Judiciary Committee 12 years after Justice Brennan's hearing] observed that one of Marshall's judicial opinions had cited in support of a particular historical proposition a book by Herbert Aptheker and wanted to know whether Marshall had known at the time that Aptheker "had been for many years an avowed Communist and was the leading Communist theoretician in the United States." Marshall said he had not known. Later, on the Senate floor, Eastland strongly implied that he did not believe Marshall's denial, adding a challenge to Marshall's veracity to this slur on his loyalty. Other questions were more obviously hostile. Senator Thurmond demanded that Marshall call immediately to mind such minutiae as the views of Senator Bingham on whether the Congress could enforce the privileges and immunities clause of Article IV, and the names of the members of the congressional committee that reported out the Fourteenth Amendment. (Carter, 1994, p. 76)

While these examples may not appear to some to be as "openly" racist as Carter claims, they are reflections of the negative stereotypes held by whites who are prejudiced against blacks—that they are leftists attracted to extreme causes, that they lie, and that they are ignorant or at least uninformed.

What Is the Net Result?

If you were to ask scholars what criteria a president should consider when nominating a justice, they would suggest—as did Abraham in chapter 1—scholarship, analytical powers, writing ability, general knowledge, willingness to work hard and take responsibility, courage, and character. But some presidents have disregarded these considerations, as we have seen, and have based their choices on less relevant criteria. Some results have been better than others; an analysis of the first 96 justices, which sought to distinguish between the favorable and unfavorable appointments, concluded as follows.

Our analysis has not uncovered any one trait which clearly distinguishes the capable from the incapable. Nevertheless, several patterns tend to emerge. On one hand, if we were to develop a profile of an individual with a strong likelihood of becoming an excellent jurist, he [sic] would be a person raised in a northeastern urban area as a member of a business-oriented family. His ethnic roots could be traced back to the European continent and he would be Jewish. He would have received his education from high-quality institutions and would have experience in the academic community as a legal scholar. He would have been appointed to the Court at a relatively early age, without prior judicial experience, and serve in that institution for more than twenty-five years.

On the other hand, if we were to describe the background of a typical Supreme Court "failure," he would be a man from the midwestern United States, raised in a small town and from family engaged in farming. His ethnic origins would be Scottish or Irish and he would be affiliated with a "low church" Protestant denomination. He would have attended mediocre educational institutions and his career would have been closely tied to partisan political activities. His appointment to the Court would have occurred during his mid-fifties and he would serve less than five years. These, of course, are general profiles. There are exceptions to every broad generalization, as attested to by the fact that McReynolds served more than a quarter-century and Cardozo but six years. Yet McReynolds is universally rated a "failure" and Cardozo a "great." (Blaustein & Mersky, 1978, pp. 69–70)

If these differences can be "postdicted" (i.e., predicted after the fact), can future effectiveness be predicted? Blaustein and Mersky, in a book completed shortly after Warren Burger was appointed Chief Justice, wrote:

Among the most recent five, Chief Justice Burger appears to have the most strikes against him. While his age at appointment (62) and ethnic background (Swiss/German) are similar to those justices who have served well in the past, his family origins (rural, farming), region (Midwestern), religion (Protestant), education (University of Minnesota and St. Paul College of Law), and judicial experience (thirteen years) are factors, which, over the history of the Court, have been associated with less than distinguished levels of performance. (1978, p. 71)

In Comiskey's (2004) survey of scholars, Chief Justice Burger received a mean rating of 1.84, closer to "fair" than to "poor" and significantly below the average of all judges of 2.46.

Are the President's Goals Confirmed?

Presidents seek to appoint federal judges who reflect their goals and priorities. How well do they succeed?

Certain presidents have been explicit about the values and outcomes they wanted—or wanted to avoid. More than one president has been angered by some of the decisions of his appointees. Theodore Roosevelt appointed the distinguished law professor and judge Oliver Wendell Holmes, Jr., to the Supreme Court and expected Holmes's decisions to reflect his philosophy. But when Justice Holmes chose to disagree in an important antitrust case, President Roosevelt claimed "I can carve a better judge out of a banana" (Auchincloss, 2001, p. 53). President Truman, reacting to his own appointees' votes against him in the *Youngstown Steel* case described in chapter 1, observed: "Whenever you put a man on the Supreme Court he ceases to be your friend" (Roche & Levy, 1964, p. 7).

President Nixon abhorred what he called the "liberal jurisprudence" of the Court while Earl Warren presided over it, and President Reagan sought justices who passed an ideological litmus test on certain issues central to his policy goals. While campaigning, Reagan had charged Democrats with "placing a bunch of sociology majors on the bench" (H. Schwartz, 1988, p. 119). Both President Nixon and President Reagan named only those judges whom they believed shared their "strict constructionist" judicial philosophy and conservative position on deregulating business, and who agreed with them on various social policies, such as affirmative action and abortion (O'Brien, 1993). In President Reagan's case, his expectations for Justices Rehnquist and Scalia were confirmed, but less so for Justice O'Connor. President Nixon must have been dismayed to see Justice Blackmun become more liberal as he served more years on the bench.

Certainly the most widely cited example of a presidential appointee whose values and decisions did *not* conform to the wishes of the president who appointed him was Earl Warren as chief justice, appointed by President Eisenhower. Warren had no previous experience as a judge but was a highly regarded governor of California. The president was "convinced that the prestige of the Supreme Court had suffered severely . . . and that the only way it could be restored was by the appointment to it of men of national reputation, of integrity, competence in the law, and statesmanship" (O'Brien, 2000, p. 65). Warren had national stature, unimpeachable integrity, middle-of-the-road views, and a "splendid record during his years of active law work" as attorney general of the state of California (p. 65). After his appointment, however, Warren led the Court in a number of decisions that went against Eisenhower's values. As frequently observed, much has been made of Eisenhower's reaction to the *Brown v. Board of Education* (1954) decision; it caused Eisenhower (after he had left office) to call his appointment of Warren "the biggest damn-fooled mistake" he had ever made (p. 69).

Presidential Appointments to the Federal Courts

To determine systematically if a president's goals and values are fulfilled in his judicial appointments, we can consider the appointments at all levels, not just the Supreme Court. For example, political scientists C. K. Rowland and Robert A. Carp (1996) studied federal trial judges' decisions between 1933 and 1988 and found that 48 percent of the decisions rendered by appointees of Democratic presidents were in the liberal direction, compared with only 39 percent of the decisions made by judges who had been appointed by presidents from the Republican Party. The effect was even greater in cases involving civil rights and civil liberties.

For some presidents, the effects were quite pronounced. For example, a comparison of Carter appointees with Reagan appointees shows the following: on race discrimination cases, 78 percent of the decisions of Carter appointees were liberal, as compared with only 18 percent by Reagan appointees; for right-to-privacy cases, the difference was 78 percent to 45 percent; for women's rights issues, 56 percent to 36 percent.

In contrast to the two aforementioned presidents, President Clinton's appointees to the federal bench generally tended to be moderate and non-ideological (Berkman & MacLachlan, 1996). For example, in cases involving civil rights and civil liberties, federal district judges named by President Clinton made liberal rulings 39 percent of the time (for cases through 1996); this was the same percentage as judges named by President Ford, a Republican (Stidham, Carp, & Songer, 2002). The most obvious difference in Clinton's nominees from the appointees of previous presidents was an increased number of women and minority group members. With regard to diversity of appointments, those judges appointed by President George W. Bush during his first term were not as diverse as Clinton's but more so than those by other recent Republican presidents (Goldman, Slotnick, Gryski, & Schiavoni, 2005). At the same time, they reflected his conservative agenda (Solberg, 2005).

The Most Extreme Example of a President Intervening: Roosevelt's Court-Packing Plan

When Franklin Roosevelt assumed the presidency in March 1933, his primary task was to deal with the nationwide economic depression. With public opinion strongly behind him, he persuaded Congress to pass a number of acts that created new government agencies and other mechanisms designed to resuscitate the economy. But the Supreme Court, following its laissez-faire philosophy and its tradition of limiting the power of the federal government, struck down the laws as unconstitutional.

The issue of the regulation of child labor can serve as an example. The shift from agricultural work to factory work around the beginning of the twentieth century meant that many children were forced to work long hours in unhealthy conditions, without the nearby supervision of their parents, as they had when working on a family farm. Abuses became commonplace. Attempts to deal with this problem, initiated before the depression intensified and before Roosevelt became president, began with a series of laws passed by state legislatures; by 1910, most states had restrictions on the employment of children, although many of these statutes were narrowly drawn and riddled with loopholes. Progress over the next few decades became erratic. In 1916, the federal government took over; Congress passed the Keating-Owen Child Labor Act, which banned certain types of working conditions for children. Homer Dagenhart, the father of two sons employed in a cotton mill—one younger than age 14—filed suit, asking the North Carolina district court to enjoin enforcement of the act. Two years later, in the *Hammer v. Dagenhart* (1918) decision, the Supreme Court, by a narrow 5 to 4 vote that overrode Justice Oliver Wendell Holmes's passionate dissent, nullified this act, concluding that

Congress had exceeded its authority to regulate interstate commerce (Ball, 1978). The next year Congress passed—almost unanimously—a law that put an excise tax on any goods manufactured with child labor; three years later, the Supreme Court found it an unconstitutional intrusion on states' affairs (in *Bailey v. Drexel Furniture Co.*, 1922). Another approach by Congress—in 1924—was a proposed constitutional amendment to establish protections for child labor, but despite widespread popular approval, only 20 of the required 36 states approved the proposal.

As the Great Depression intensified, Congress saw the need to protect adult workers from being replaced by children and again adopted restrictions on children's work as a part of the Roosevelt-initiated National Industrial Recovery Act. But once more the Supreme Court interceded; in a highly unpopular decision, *Schechter Poultry Corporation v. United States* (1935), the Court ruled unanimously that Congress had unconstitutionally delegated its legislative powers to the president, as well as exceeding its powers to regulate commerce. (The *Schechter* appeal has been called the "sick chicken" case because the Schechter Corporation was alleged not only to have violated wage and hour provisions of the code but also to have been successfully shipping diseased poultry to unsuspecting buyers because no effective inspection occurred *within* the state.) Congress, at Roosevelt's urging, had passed a law creating the National Recovery Administration (NRA), which was granted the power to regulate wages and working hours. The Court ruled that the Brooklyn-based kosher poultry business run by the Schechter brothers was exclusively intrastate in character; thus their violation of the NRA regulations could not by punished by the federal government (Kennedy, 1995). Even their sale of diseased poultry was beyond the federal government's reach; the Court decreed that the federal government regulated *interstate* commerce only.

In fact, on a single day, May 27, 1935, which came to be labeled Black Monday, the Supreme Court announced three unanimous decisions (one was *Schechter*; another threw out an act that had provided mortgage relief to farmers) that eviscerated crucial aspects of the President's New Deal. "We have been relegated to a horse-and-buggy definition of interstate commerce," Roosevelt complained the next day (Kennedy, 1995, p. 88).

As Roosevelt's first term wound down in late 1936, it was clear that the conservative-dominated Supreme Court was not going to permit the president to implement legislation aimed at the relief of economic hard times; nonetheless, Roosevelt did not make the Court's obstructionism much of an issue in his reelection campaign. But after his overwhelming victory in November 1936, he made a bold move, proposing a court reform bill under the guise of improving judicial efficiency. His proposal—made only two weeks after his second-term inauguration—was that the president would appoint one new justice for every justice over the age of 70 (up to a limit of six) who chose not to resign. The language of his message to Congress reflected his exasperation with the Court's restrictions on federal regulatory power: "Aged or infirm justices are inclined to avoid an examination of complicated and changed conditions. . . . older men, assuming the scene is the same as it was in the past, cease to explore or inquire into the present or the future" (Kennedy, 1995, p. 88). (Ironically, the New Deal's most consistent and influential ally on the Court was Louis Brandeis, who was then 80 years old.) Six justices were beyond the age of 70, so Roosevelt's proposal, if passed, would have radically altered the Court's composition, increasing the number of justices from 9 to 15. But what came to be called the "court-packing" proposal was in itself widely disliked; the public, the press, and Congress all rejected it (Caldeira, 1987). As Segal and Spaeth put it, "[t]hough many of the Court's decisions were unpopular, the notion of judicial independence was not" (1993, p. 96).

Although the legislation requested by the president was never adopted, he got what he wanted (Leuchtenburg, 1995). For it wasn't only the president who was being criticized; the Court was feeling pressure from the public for impeding the president's program of reform. For whatever reason, in subsequent cases, Justice Owen Roberts shifted his vote to endorse federal legislation—what became known as the "switch in time that saved nine." In a decision announced in March 1937, only a month after Roosevelt announced his plan, the Court—with Roberts as the deciding vote—overturned a 40-year-old doctrine that had guaranteed the freedom of a contract (*West Coast Hotel Co. v. Parrish*, 1937). Two weeks later, the Court upheld the National Labor Relations Act, which granted the right of labor to bargain collectively and provided government intervention to prevent unfair labor practices (*National Labor Relations Board v. Jones and Laughlin Steel Corporation*, 1937). Then, within the next month, the Supreme Court concluded that it was constitutional for Congress to establish a tax that would generate income to fund the payment of social security benefits.

With respect to the regulation of child labor, the "Nine Old Men" of the Court also did an about-face. Congress in 1938 passed the Fair Labor Standards Act, which included child-labor protections among the multitude of wage and hour provisions. For example, the law prohibited manufacturers, producers, and dealers from shipping goods that were the product of "oppressive" child labor. The Supreme Court, in *United States v. F. W. Darby Lumber Co.* (1941), unanimously and expressly overruled *Hammer v. Dagenhart* and concluded that the Fair Labor Standards Act was a valid exercise of Congress's authority to regulate commerce.

In May 1937 one of the conservative justices, 78-year-old Willis Van Devanter, resigned; this permitted President Roosevelt, five years into his administration, to make his very first appointment to the Court and shift its balance. (By the time of President Roosevelt's death in April 1945, eight of the nine justices then on the bench were his appointees.) Roosevelt lost the battle to expand the Court, but he won the war (Pritchett, 1948; Segal & Spaeth, 1993).

Do Presidents Do a Good Job of Identifying Nominees?

How good a job do presidents do here? It is impossible to give a short answer, because of the inconsistencies. Some presidents do a better job than others, but the quality of appointments by a given president may differ widely. Woodrow Wilson's first appointee, James McReynolds, is, according to a survey of 65 eminent scholars, one of the eight "failures." But his second, Louis Brandeis, was one of the 12 "greatest" (Blaustein & Mersky, 1978). Likewise, one of Eisenhower's appointees, Earl Warren, is among the 12 "greats"; a second, William Brennan, is considered one of the most effective justices of the last half-century; and a third, John Marshall Harlan II, is rated a "near great," but the other Eisenhower appointee, Charles Whittaker, is arguably the greatest failure of any of the first 110 justices.

However, a few presidents stand out—in one extreme or another. Three of Truman's four appointments are among the eight "failures"—Burton, Vinson, and Minton. The fourth, Tom Clark, was among the 55 rated "average." In contrast, three of Franklin Roosevelt's nine appointees were rated "great" (these were Black and Frankfurter, plus Stone, who was already an associate justice but was named chief justice by Roosevelt). Furthermore, three of the fifteen "near greats" were Roosevelt's (Douglas, Jackson, and Rutledge); two were average (Reed and Murphy); and only one was a "failure." The latter, James F. Byrnes, did not enjoy the judicial life and resigned after only 16 months to accept a position in the White House and later to reenter politics. In the scholars' classification of the first one hundred justices, there had not been a "great" justice since Earl Warren, but this survey is now more than 25 years old. But a recent survey finds the same outcome; Comiskey (2004) surveyed 128 law professors and political scientists and asked them to rate the 52 justices appointed during the twentieth century. Of the 11 rated as "excellent," three—Chief Justice Warren and Justices Brennan and Harlan—were appointed by President Eisenhower. No justice appointed more recently was rated as excellent.

How Should the Process Be Changed?

If the process needs improvement, two suggestions seem paramount. First is the obvious. Presidents should submit the best qualified nominees to the Senate for review. Back when President Nixon had failed in his attempt to get one judge accepted and he had submitted a second, soon-to-be rejected nominee, Senator Roman Hruska of Nebraska, Nixon's legislative floor leader, went down in history with his statement about the nominee, G. Harrold Carswell of Florida: "Even if he is mediocre, there are a lot of mediocre judges and people and lawyers. They are entitled to a little representation, aren't they, and a little chance? We can't have all Brandeises, Cardozos, and Frankfurters, and stuff like that there" (Abraham, 1992, pp. 16–17). But we should aspire to such eminent nominees. How can it be done?

David Yalof's (1999) book had as its specific purpose the examination of the process of nomination of Supreme Court justices; he presented 28 case studies of nominations from the Truman administration through the Reagan administration (plus an epilogue on appointees by George H. W. Bush and Clinton). His conclusion: "modern presidents have *too much* information about prospective candidates at their disposal" (p. 187, italics in original). They have available sophisticated technological resources so they can access previous opinions—either judicial or any other public form, such as speeches, articles, and books—and they have larger executive branch staffs than did presidents 50 years ago. But shouldn't this be an advantage?

With regard to the confirmation process, Stephen Carter, in his 1994 book *The Confirmation Mess,* reviewed several recently-floated proposals he considered to be ineffective, and then suggested a provocative change: require a confirmation to meet a two-thirds standard rather than the simple majority of the senators. This, he proposed, would lead to the nomination of moderate candidates, as they would be the only ones who would satisfy a divided Senate. But in the present adversarial atmosphere, how many nominees could receive a two-thirds vote? The concluding chapter of this book considers this and other reforms to the nomination/confirmation process.

3

Steps in the Decision-Making Process

I made three arguments in every case. First came the one I
planned—as I thought, logical, coherent, complete. Second was
the one actually presented—interrupted, incoherent, disjointed,
disappointing. The third was the utterly devastating argument
that I thought of after going to bed that night.—Justice Robert
Jackson, on his experiences arguing before the Court as solicitor
general, in "Advocacy before the Supreme Court" (1951)

Decision-Making—An Individual
or a Group Process?

Those claiming to have been wronged by the legal system—whether they believe they have been falsely convicted of a crime or they feel that their legitimate grounds for a successful lawsuit have been rebuffed—often threaten to
take their grievances "all the way to the Supreme Court." But few find the Court
to be responsive. When a petition does get submitted to the Supreme Court
for resolution, a series of steps is initiated. This process contains a number of
decision points, and judicial decision-making occurs at every one of these
points (Menez, 1984). Each decision requires a choice, and the justices' choices
reflect human characteristics as well as legal ones.

The time between the submission of a petition for review by the Supreme
Court and the announcement of the Court's action on this petition is always
measured at least in weeks, usually in months (for the few petitions accepted
for review), and sometimes in years. The time lag is quite variable. The vast
majority of petitions are dispensed with rather quickly. A significant number
get past the first hurdle for review, but of those, fewer than one hundred a
year (of the eight thousand submitted annually) are accepted for a full review
and decision by the Court. Even among those that are granted full review, the
timetable varies; those that are accepted in September may have their oral
arguments in January, while those accepted in April may have a seven-month
delay in hearing oral arguments. For a given term, the docket is usually filled
by mid-January; for the 2004–2005 term, by January 14, 2005, the Court had

already agreed to decide 75 cases, about its usual number of decisions in recent terms. Thus a petition that is accepted for review in February will not have its oral arguments until the beginning of the next term, that is, the next October at the earliest.

The length of time between the oral arguments and final disposition of the petition also varies; other than expedited cases like *Bush v. Gore*, perhaps the modern record for a short turnaround time goes to two cases, titled *Reed v. Reed* (1971) and *Harris v. Forklift Systems Inc.* (1993)—only 27 days from the oral arguments to the announcement. But these cases were extraordinary in other, contributing ways: the vote on each case was 9 to 0, and each opinion was only six pages long. At the other extreme, some cases— the most famous ones being *Brown v. Board of Education* (1954) and *Roe v. Wade* (1973)—were not resolved until they were carried over to the next term.

For the few chosen, the steps in the decision process, while quite clearly specified, are only partly visible to the public. The purpose of this chapter is to describe what is known about each step in the process. Even some decisions during the "secret" aspect of the process—such as the decision conference—have eventually become better understood because several justices, mostly recently Justice Blackmun, have made available to libraries their extensive files (including memoranda, correspondence with other justices, and tabulations of votes).

During several steps in the process, the justices of the Supreme Court operate much like nine individual, autonomous law firms, with their law clerks serving somewhat like associates in the firm, responsive to the needs of the sole partner. For example, after the chief justice has culled possible candidates from the mass of submissions, each justice is expected to review the cases prior to a meeting whose purpose is to decide whether to take on each case. Later in the process, after this decision to grant certiorari (that is, to review the case) and after the oral arguments and case conference, each justice again operates individually to prepare a decision draft, a concurring opinion, or a dissenting opinion.

But at other points during the process, the outcome reflects a group interaction. While decisions are based on the votes of individual justices, these votes certainly have the potential to be influenced, even determined, by the comments of other justices or perceptions of them. The authors of an influential book on Supreme Court decision-making (Maltzman, Spriggs, & Wahlbeck, 2000) subtitled their book "The Collegial Game," and much of the process is just that; not only may individual votes reflect how other justices are voting but also opinion drafts may be altered out of consideration of the views of other justices. As Maltzman, Spriggs, and Wahlbeck put it, "[a]lthough each justice pursues his or her own goals, each is also required to work within a collegial setting, with no single view of policy determining the final shape of the law" (2000, p. xi).

Case Selection

How much control do Supreme Court justices have over their agenda? Some would say that the justices are in a very powerful, self-determining position; for example, a former law clerk to two justices, Stephen McAllister, wrote: "The Supreme Court has almost complete control over its docket. Through the mechanism of granting or denying *writs of certiorari*, the Supreme Court can decline or agree to review cases for any reason, or no reason at all" (1995, p. 26). But Justice O'Connor has said that the process is a reactive one, proposing that justices cannot initiate but merely respond. The latter position would imply that even if a justice had a specific policy goal—say, to eliminate gender discrimination or to return those powers to the individual states that have been "usurped" by Congress—he or she would be unable to do anything unless the right case came along. But this viewpoint ignores the possibility that among the massive number of petitions submitted each year, one might fit the justice's criterion. Justices with policy goals can instruct their law clerks to be on the lookout for cases that fit.

While certainly law-related constraints operate to influence which few petitions are chosen for review, justices and their law clerks are human, with their own idiosyncratic preferences. McAllister makes a telling comment about this aspect of case selection:

> Supreme Court law clerks are unlikely to have had much exposure to or to be particularly interested in state law or commercial law issues. Both the law clerks and the justices demonstrate remarkably little interest in commercial cases, even when they involve vast sums of money or are of considerable practical importance to an entire industry or industries. Instead, they appear far more interested in the "sexier" constitutional issues involving individual rights, in particular such areas as religion, speech, and due process, or in unusual issues involving obscure provisions in the Constitution or arcane federal statutes. Thus corporate entities and business interests generally may have a more difficult time persuading the Supreme Court to grant *cert.* (1995, p. 27)

As noted, each year approximately eight thousand petitions for certiorari are submitted to the Supreme Court—that means a relentless 150 or more arrive *each week*. Based on his interviews with justices and their law clerks, H. W. Perry, Jr. (1991) concluded that the first step in the culling process was to dispose of those appeals that were seen as frivolous; these decisions are made almost always on the law clerks' recommendations. Chief Justice Rehnquist was quoted as saying "a lot of filings are junk" (O'Brien, 2000, p. 237) and estimated that between one thousand and two thousand petitions each year were "patently without merit" (Rehnquist, 1987a, p. 264), and similarly, while he was on the bench Justice Brennan concluded that 70 percent of the docketed cases did not merit discussion (Stern & Gressman, 1978).

In a typical term, about two-thirds of the petitions are *in forma pauperis* appeals (called colloquially "i.f.p." cases). In most of these, a convicted prisoner is challenging his or her conviction or sentence. During the 1970s, one such "jailhouse lawyer" filed seven hundred appeals in state and federal cases (O'Brien, 2000). Since these petitioners are indigent, the Court waives the filing and other fees for them. These cases can be distinguished from the paid cases by their docket number; paid cases begin with 1; i.f.p. cases with 5000. In the 2003–2004 term, one of the i.f.p. cases granted certiorari (*Tennard v. Dretke*) had the number 02–10038, thus indicating that more than five thousand i.f.p. petitions had been submitted.

In forma pauperis cases are less likely to be chosen by the Court for review than are paid cases; in a typical year only ½ of 1 percent (approximately 15) of them were granted certiorari, while for paid cases that rate was 3.7 percent (Stewart, 1994). But the Court does not automatically disregard them; in the 2003–2004 term, 9 of the 73 decided cases resulted from i.f.p. petitions. Perhaps the most notable i.f.p. petition ever to be accepted for review was the case of Clarence Gideon (*Gideon v. Wainwright*, 1963), who literally submitted a handwritten (in pencil) petition that led to the landmark decision that indigent defendants had a right to a court-appointed counsel (Lewis, 1964).

After winnowing out the numerous "frivolous" cases, the justices may ask if the appeal stems from a doctrinal conflict existing between the decisions in different circuit courts (Caldeira & Wright, 1988; Ulmer, 1984). A high priority of the Supreme Court should be to resolve these circuit disagreements. Ulmer has provided examples of just how much in conflict several circuit court decisions can be. At one time or another, different courts of appeals have held that:

> (1) under federal law, a bank robber who perpetrates a kidnapping while robbing a national bank commits one offense or commits two offenses; (2) under the Internal Revenue Code, the legal expenses of a corporate liquidation are deductible as an ordinary business expense or are not deductible; and (3) conviction for making a threat against the president of the United States requires proof that the defendant intended to carry out the threat or does not require such proof. (1984, p. 902)

Given the foregoing considerations, what qualities of an appeal cause a justice to vote to grant certiorari? Political scientists have utilized what is called *cue theory* to describe the process; certain petitions stand out by possessing qualities that make them worthy of further scrutiny (Ulmer, Hintze, & Kirklosky, 1972). Initially, researchers concluded, on the basis of analyses of dockets in the 1960s and 1970s, that salient cues included the reputation of the attorneys filing the petitions, the reputation of the lower court judge or circuit of origin, the type of conflict involved, and the participation of the federal government (Tanenhaus, Schick, Muraskin, & Rosen, 1978). Later research found that other characteristics had come to serve as cues (Caldeira & Wright, 1988; O'Brien, 2000). For example, certain circuits are seen as ideologically distinct; currently, the Ninth Circuit is seen as the most liberal and the Fourth Circuit as the most conservative. Research generated by cue theory has concluded that when the Supreme Court is predominantly conservative, as it is now, it is more likely to review liberal decisions by circuit courts, but when the Court was more liberal, it more often granted certiorari to conservative circuit court decisions (Carp, 2003).

And, of course, petitions that raise the possibility that an executive-branch or legislative action has violated the Constitution ordinarily should receive the greatest of attention. But the selective nature of cases chosen for review cannot be overlooked. Here, discretion is complete. Cases that seem to bear on constitutional issues may be ignored; direct conflicts between circuit court decisions do not necessarily mean they will be resolved. For example, early in 2005 the Court denied certiorari to an appeal of a lower court ruling that had said that South Carolina's license plates bearing the slogan "Choose life" violated the Fourth Amendment. But the ruling that the Court let stand was in direct conflict with the ruling of another circuit court that essentially permitted such license plates in Louisiana and Mississippi (Associated Press, 2005). According to Ulmer (1984), a review by Feeney (1975) identified many circuit court conflicts in one year that were denied review by the Court. In the words of a former solicitor general of the United States, Erwin Griswold, "[n]o one knows for sure why the Supreme Court lets in litigants. . . . Review is now a matter of grace; it's like the royal prerogative in England" (Ulmer, 1984, pp. 902–903).

The Court Is Not a "Court of Last Resort"

Many members of the public assume that the Supreme Court functions as a "court of last resort." While that is true in specific death-penalty appeals, it does not apply to the vast majority of petitions submitted for review. Fred Vinson, when he was chief justice, wrote:

> The Supreme Court is not, and never has been, primarily concerned with the correction of errors in lower court decisions. . . . The function of the Supreme Court is, therefore, to resolve conflicts of opinion in federal questions that have arisen among lower courts, to pass upon questions of wide import under the Constitution, laws, and treaties of the United States, and to exercise supervisory power over lower federal courts. (1961, p. 55)

The "Discuss" List

Prior to each conference to discuss petitions, the chief justice circulates a list of those petitions that, in the chief's opinion, are worthy of consideration for review. Other justices can move a particular petition from the "dead" list to this "discuss" list merely by notifying the chief justice prior to the conference (Caldeira & Wright, 1990b). The vast majority of certiorari petitions do not make the "discuss" list; thus, they are automatically denied without even a formal vote. Even if a petition gets on the "discuss" list, that does not ensure that the Court will grant certiorari; in fact, it has been estimated that as few as 30 percent of the petitions placed on the "discuss" list are granted even cursory review (McAllister, 1995), and in recent years this percentage has dropped. Despite the nominal purpose of this meeting, some petitions on the "discuss" list do not even get discussed at the conference.

The Frequency of Granting Certiorari

The decision to hear a case means that the petitioner's or appellant's petition has been accepted for review, which leads to the submission of written briefs and the presentation of oral arguments. (Rarely, the Court will issue an opinion on an accepted case without hearing oral arguments.) In the 1980s and early 1990s, the Supreme Court was accepting 150 or more cases per year; the high points were the 1982 and 1983 terms, with 174 cases each term disposed of by a signed opinion. But in the last decade, the number has dropped sharply. In the Court's 1993 term, 7,786 petitions were on its docket; of these, the Court agreed to act on only 84. Since then, the Court has decided an average of fewer than 80 cases annually—74 in the term ending in June 2005—even though the number of submissions has remained about the same.

Many reasons have been offered for the dramatic decrease in granting certiorari. Some have even speculated that the justices have gotten lazy. I will consider the workload issue later, in chapters 4 and 11, but perhaps a more amenable reason is that, at present, the Court is composed almost entirely of persons with many years of experience as appellate judges (even before their appointment to the Supreme Court) and they are in more general agreement than in the past as to what constitutes an "appealable" or "certworthy" case. Numerous accounts describe the constituency of the Court as more congenial than in the past, despite the justices' ideological differences, and perhaps that is manifested in a stronger agreement about just which cases qualify as meeting the demanding standards for the Court's review.

The Presumption to Reject

In deciding to grant certiorari, it is not guaranteed that every justice has examined every petition on the "discuss" list. The law clerks have prepared detailed memoranda on each petition and these serve as the basis for the justices deciding to consider a given petition in more detail. These memoranda have five parts: a brief summary, that includes the statement of the issue; a description of the facts and the lower courts' proceedings; the arguments of the petitioner for granting certiorari (and of the respondent against granting certiorari, if an opposition has been filed); a discussion and analysis of the issues and arguments; and a recommended disposition (McAllister, 1995). But this memorandum is not necessarily prepared by the justice's own law clerk; all the justices, except Justice Stevens, participate in the "certiorari pool system," in which petitions are sent to all the chambers but the law clerks divide the responsibility of writing the memos. Thus only one law clerk has the initial responsibility for advising eight of the justices how to dispose of the petition. However, justices often ask their own law clerks to update those petitions that make the chief justice's "discuss" list.

It is important to realize that there is a heavy presumption on the part of the justices and their law clerks that most petitions will be *denied*. Thus:

> The pool memo writers generally scrutinize the petitions carefully and will be especially careful in examining any petition that appears potentially certworthy. Law clerks do not like to be embarrassed by recommending a grant of certiorari only to have their peers and all or most of the justices disagree with them and deny the petition. Similarly, justices and law clerks do not like to see certiorari granted in a case to discover much later that the case does not cleanly raise, or that the Court for some reason, cannot reach, the certworthy issue. A "bad" grant is an embarrassment. A "bad" denial goes unnoticed and the Court may address the issue another day in another case. Thus, the petitioner bears a heavy burden in overcoming the law clerks' and justices' initial skepticism that a case will merit plenary review. (McAllister, 1995, p. 30)

Petitioners may claim that their case is the "first in American history to raise this issue," or "the only one of its kind," or they may brazenly assert a conflict that does not really exist. Ulmer (1984), after analyzing certiorari petitions over a number of terms from 1947 to 1976, found that attorneys puffed or padded their claims of conflict with precedents about half the time, although in more recent years the percentage declined. As McAllister has noted, "law clerks delight in identifying false claims of 'conflict' and once they do so, the petitioner has damaged its credibility with the Court and everyone at the Court is likely to lose interest in the petition" (1995, p. 34).

The Rule of Four

For the Supreme Court to grant certiorari, at least four justices (regardless of how many actually vote) must agree that the case is of sufficient importance to warrant the Court's attention and review. This "rule of four" is of uncertain origin, but since at least 1924 it has been a matter of public record (Epstein & Knight, 1998). However, it remains controversial. Scholars have noted that "four is the perfect number, striking a sensitive balance between principle and pragmatism" (Urofsky, 1997, p. 97). If five votes were required, it would—as Urofsky observed—tend to prejudge the case. If only a couple of votes were needed, the docket would become overburdened with less-than-significant issues. But sometimes when three justices want to take a case, a wavering justice will go along—"join three"—to grant certiorari. (This occurred in the case of *DeShaney v. Winnebago* case described in chapter 1.) An analysis of docket books (O'Brien, 2000) found that as many as 23–30 percent of those cases that are granted certiorari receive four, *and only four*, votes, leading to the question: What does it mean to grant certiorari?

As noted, the predisposition is to deny certiorari. In recent years, the Court has rarely indicated why it has decided not to review a petition, but when a petition that raises an important issue is denied, speculation about the reasons is inevitable. For example, the Court's denial of certiorari in the case of *Hopwood v. State of Texas* in 1996 garnered extensive publicity because the appeal dealt with affirmative action policies in college admissions. The prestigious law school at the University of Texas had set lower test-score admissions criteria for African American and Hispanic American applicants than for white applicants and had established a separate review board for the minority applicants.

Why did the Supreme Court shy away from such an important issue? On an ideological level, we may speculate that five of the justices agreed with the thrust of the Fifth Circuit's ruling that the procedure of separate standards for minority applicants was illegal. Possibly four of the justices disagreed with the Fifth Circuit's decision (the most likely would be Justices Breyer, Ginsburg, Stevens, and Souter). But *not all of these four* (or any four) were willing to grant certiorari. Perhaps predominant was the fact that the issue was not viable since the program was no longer in operation; that was Justice Ginsburg and Justice Souter's announced reason (Kloppenberg, 2001). Perhaps the Court did not want to take on a complex and controversial affirmative action case—but the Court has since done so, and heard oral arguments during the 2002–2003 term for two cases dealing with the University of Michigan affirmative action procedure.

Commenting on the denial of certiorari in the *Hopwood* appeal, one civil rights scholar, Neal Devins of the College of William and Mary law school, suggested at that time:

> With respect to affirmative action in general, my guess is the Court hasn't quite figured out what its position is. I suspect it would just as soon let the lower courts play around with affirmative action to see if some consensus is achieved, or at least it has a better sense of its own feeling. (Coyle, 1996, p. A10)

The fact that the Court avoided such a case in 1996 but in 2002 agreed to review a similar pair of cases may support this claim that it seeks input from several circuit courts before responding.

It is even possible that with regard to the certiorari decision on the *Hopwood* appeal, the relatively liberal justices did not push to grant review because they feared that the likely decision could rule out affirmative action programs in colleges and universities throughout the whole country. Such a possibility reminds us that justices are human, that they count votes, and they may decide to cut their losses rather than forcing an issue. Perry (1991) labeled this process *defensive denial,* and Epstein and Knight (1998) have offered it as an example of strategic voting behavior, a phenomenon I will describe extensively in chapter 6.

The Meaning of Denying Certiorari

What does it mean when the Supreme Court denies certiorari for a given petition? Even the Court's justices have differed in responding to this question. Justice Robert Jackson felt that it meant that the lower court's decision should stand, but Justice Felix Frankfurter did not believe that it meant approval of the lower court's decision at all, but only that the majority of the justices did not think that the matter should be further adjudicated (Menez, 1984). Justice Stevens, in a rare public comment when certiorari was denied, wrote that "the denial of a petition of *certiorari* is not a ruling on the merits. Sometimes such an order reflects nothing more than a conclusion that a particular case may not constitute an appropriate forum in which to decide a significant issue" (Kloppenberg, 2001, p. 165). While he was chief justice, William Rehnquist was explicit that no conclusions about the merit of a prior decision should be drawn from the Court's refusal to hear an appeal. But for those thousands of prisoners who have claimed that their convictions or sentences were unjust, the practical effect of denying certiorari is, of course, no change in their status, hence a defeat.

Certiorari Votes and Votes at the Case Conference: Do the First Predict the Second?

The vote by an individual justice that certiorari should be granted can occur for a number of reasons: that the case fits the criteria for the kinds of cases the Supreme Court should be deciding, that the lower court's decision was wrong, or that reviewing the case would facilitate the achieving of the justice's policy goals. If a petition does obtain the four votes necessary to hear the case, the next question is whether an individual justice's vote on the certiorari decision is indicative of his or her vote at the conference. This question is impossible to answer, for only rarely have the votes whether to grant certiorari been announced or "leaked" to the public. (And, of course, votes at the decision conference are supposed to be secret also, but some of these records have been made available, much later, to scholars.) We do know, however, that in at least one important case, *Tinker v. Des Moines Independent Community School District* (1969), the justice who eventually wrote the majority opinion in favor of the petitioner (Abe Fortas) initially voted to deny certiorari to the same petitioner (Johnson, 1997). Much can happen, and does happen, between the initial decision and the final ruling. The decision to grant certiorari is an important one that needs thorough examination, but much less has been written about it than about votes at the judicial decision conference and changes in votes during the opinion writing. (The exception is the book-length treatment of the certiorari process by H. W. Perry, Jr. [1991], who interviewed five justices and numerous clerks and reported a variety of anonymous comments by them regarding the process.) Chapter 6 examines the various theories about why justices vote the way that they do at the conference to discuss petitions and at the case conference; in the last decades, political scientists have been proposing that some judges select those cases for review that achieve their policy goals (Baum, 1997; Epstein & Wright, 1998).

The Interval between Granting Certiorari and the Oral Arguments

If the Court grants certiorari, the two parties—the petitioner and the respondent, also called the appellant and the appellee—ordinarily have 90 days to submit written briefs. Note that these briefs have a different thrust; earlier the petitioner needed to show why his or her appeal warranted review by the highest court; now, instead, the emphasis is on why the Court should make a specific decision overturning the lower court's rulings. Some of the arguments may be the same, but petitioners and their appellate attorneys err if they assume the two types of briefs have the same specific goal. Likewise, those respondents who had opposition briefs at the certiorari stage need to rethink their approach, as it proved unsuccessful earlier.

Amicus Briefs

The briefs by the petitioner and the respondent, which are limited to 50 pages, are made available to the public. Other parties, interested in the outcome, may also be permitted to submit briefs, called amicus curiae ("friend of the court") briefs (which may not exceed 30 pages in length). Historically, amicus briefs were offered by bystanders or others who had no vested interest in the outcome, but had knowledge relevant to the evidence or a point of law in the case. The inclusion of such briefs has been traced back to an appearance by Henry Clay before the Supreme Court in 1821 (Krislov, 1963), although more than a century would pass before anything about amicus briefs was incorporated into the Supreme Court's rules of procedure (Menez, 1984).

The assumption of an impartial observer reflected in the term amicus curiae is now often a misnomer, as many of the organizations submitting such briefs are aligned with one party in the dispute. They have thus been classified as *advocacy briefs*, taking a position on some public policy or issue (Roesch, Golding, Hans, & Reppucci, 1991), in contrast with a second type, called *science-translation briefs*, that seek to inform the Court objectively about the state of knowledge on a topic. Professional organizations and interest groups have not been reluctant to submit amicus briefs to the courts. In the 2003 University of Michigan affirmative action cases, more than one hundred amicus briefs were filed, a record. One reason for organizations to submit briefs is as a response to pressure from their members to try to influence public policy; an organization lacking very much in financial resources or legal staff may find an amicus brief a much less expensive way of participating in a case than initiating a court action on its own (Wasby, 1992).

But not just anyone can submit an amicus brief. For Supreme Court cases, an organization wishing to submit a brief must either obtain permission from each party or petition the Supreme Court for permission (Tremper, 1987). The most frequent participants are interest group organizations, business groups and corporations, and individual states' agencies (Caldeira & Wright, 1990a); amicus briefs by individuals are rare. Briefs may be submitted prior to the decision whether to grant certiorari—perhaps to alert the Court of the petition's importance—as well as after the case has been accepted for review. In fact, at the point when the justices are deciding whether to grant certiorari, the submission of a large number of amicus briefs apparently increases the likelihood that certiorari will be granted (Caldeira & Wright, 1988, 1994), but if amicus briefs are submitted arguing that the case should not be heard, the result is also to improve the chances that it will be! Baum (1997) saw the latter result as reflecting the Court's concern with achieving legal accuracy and clarity.

Do amicus briefs get cited, or are they ignored? Certainly some get noticed, for the Court cites amicus briefs in 15–20 percent of its decisions (Kearney & Merrill, 2000; O'Connor & Epstein, 1983). And they get read by someone, but probably in those rare cases that generate 40, 50, or more amicus briefs, the law clerks are given the task of doing an initial pruning of their contents, because some briefs, despite the admonitions, make no arguments beyond those prepared by the parties in the case. (Justices refer to these as "me, too" briefs.) At a panel discussion in the spring of 2005, Justices O'Connor and Ginsburg admitted that they don't read all the briefs. Justice Ginsburg said that she has her law clerks sort these briefs into three piles: "must-read briefs; those she could skim or read selected pages from, and the 'skip' pile that she does not need to read at all" (Mauro, 2005b, p. 12). The first pile is "very thin," she admitted.

But the fact that amicus briefs sometimes get cited is not proof that they are influential; "the citations may reflect nothing more than the inability of a law clerk to find a better source than a brief to support a proposition or, worse, his or her unwillingness to find a better source" (Phillips, 2004, p. 118).

So do individual amicus briefs have their desired effect? A few do; most do not. Carter Phillips (2004), who has prepared a number of amicus briefs, has suggested three types that are more likely to achieve their goals:

1. *Those that reflect considerable expertise on nonlegal information that may broaden the court's knowledge and influence the court's decisions:* these are called "Brandeis briefs," because the first submitted to the Court

was prepared by Louis Brandeis (a decade before he was a justice). The case of *Muller v. Oregon* (1908) dealt with the allowable length of working hours for women laundry workers. Brandeis prepared a 113-page brief that presented social science expertise on the effects of working conditions on female workers. The Court cited the brief favorably in its decision, albeit acknowledging that the authorities were not legal sources.

2. *Those that can alert the Court to potential unintended consequences of a decision by the Court:* Phillips called these "Whatever you do, just don't hurt me" briefs (2004, p. 123). Here a third party wants to ensure that any decision in a particular case does not adversely affect its interests.

3. *Those that show a potentially profound effect of the decision for a wide array of groups and individuals*

The impact of this type of brief is illustrated by Justice O'Connor's decision in the affirmative action case of the University of Michigan's law school, *Grutter v. Bollinger* (2003); she wrote: "the Law School's claim of a compelling interest is further bolstered by its *amici*" (p. 2340). She cited several such briefs, including one from several professional organizations arguing that ethnic diversity "promotes learning outcomes" and one by leading military officers who argued that diversity was crucial to "the military's ability to fulfill its mission to provide national security" (p. 2340).

The Role of the Office of Solicitor General

Previously I noted that the vast majority of petitions are denied certiorari; while the presence of amicus briefs may increase the likelihood of acceptance, the rate is still low. But when the Office of the Solicitor General submits an amicus brief requesting the Supreme Court to grant certiorari, the petition is much more likely to gain approval for review (Caldeira & Wright, 1988). For example, in the 1995 term, certiorari was granted a whopping 78 percent of the time when the government requested it (Baum, 1997). Likewise, when a case is decided by the Court, litigants whose side has been joined by the solicitor general's office are much more likely to win (George & Epstein, 1992; Segal & Reedy, 1988). As noted by Baum (1997), scholars have offered a variety of explanations for the solicitor general's rate of success:

- The expertise of the solicitor general's office in litigation (Provine, 1980)
- The office's perceived expertise, which gives greater weight to its viewpoints (Scigliano, 1971)
- The justices' gratitude to the executive branch for its self-restraint in petitioning for certiorari (Scigliano, 1971)
- The Court's dependence on the executive branch to give implementation and legitimacy to its decisions (Puro, 1981; Salokar, 1992)

- An unusually strong set of petitions because of the solicitor general's careful screening of cases (O'Connor, 1983)
- Overlap in perspective between the current president's appointments to the Court and the solicitor general's office (Scigliano, 1971)

According to Baum's review, the most systematic research on possible reasons is that of McGuire (1996), who analyzed decisions during the 1977–1982 terms. McGuire concluded that "the expertise of lawyers in the Solicitor General's Office based on their experience before the Court accounted for at least the preponderance of their high rate of success" (Baum, 1997, p. 33).

Oral Arguments and the Court's Schedule

The Supreme Court operates on an annual term basis, always beginning on the first Monday in October. For example, a petition filed between October 4, 2004, and October 3, 2005, was given a docket number indicating that it was filed during the October Term 2004 (or "O.T. 2004"). The end of the term, or at least the end of work for the justices, is harder to specify; the Court traditionally remains in session until it has issued opinions in all cases that were reviewed during that term (McAllister, 1995). (The final oral arguments for the term occur in mid- to late April; the last for the O.T. 2004 term were on April 25, 2005.) Typically the final announcement of opinions occurs in late June or early July. One of the less publicized—and doubtless less popular—functions of the chief justice is to try to facilitate resolution of those cases that still, in May and June, lack closure. The chief justice, if not the other justices, is mindful of travel arrangements and commitments during the summer, and so each decision is either pushed through or, in rare instances, held over until the next term.

During the summer recess, the justices may travel, and teach law courses either in the United States or abroad. Case conferences are ordinarily not held, except for emergencies. The justices do reconvene during the last week of September to take initial action on those petitions and other matters that have accumulated over the summer.

The Structure of Oral Arguments

The Court hears oral arguments during seven two-week periods between early October and late April. Ordinarily, in those weeks when the Court is hearing oral arguments, two are scheduled for each Monday, Tuesday, and Wednesday. In the nineteenth century, when fewer appeals sought resolution by the Court, virtually unlimited time was allowed for each oral argument (O'Brien, 2000); in the important case of *Gibbons v. Ogden* in 1824, the Court heard oral arguments for 20 hours over a five-day period. But in those days, briefs were rarely submitted by friends of the Court or even by the litigants (Johnson,

2004). As these increased, gradually the time allotted for each case became more and more restricted, and since 1970 each side is permitted only 30 minutes to present its case. Only rarely is additional time given (Rehnquist, 2001).

The Behavior of Attorneys at Oral Arguments

Attorneys are encouraged not to just repeat what is in their written briefs; it is assumed that the justices have read those. Supreme Court Rule 44 says: "Oral argument should undertake to emphasize and clarify the written argument appearing in the briefs theretofore filed. The Court looks with disfavor on any oral argument that is read from a prepared text" (Stern & Gressman, 1962, p. 564).

Stephen McAllister's advice to lawyers amplifies these points:

> An attorney scheduled to present oral argument to the Supreme Court of the United States should prepare the case thoroughly, prepare some more and then prepare again. Nine experienced judges with the assistance of their energetic and enthusiastic law clerks will have scrutinized virtually every aspect of the case by the time the Court hears oral argument. Lack of preparation on counsel's part will quickly become apparent in oral argument and may affirmatively hurt the chances of ultimate success. . . . Pre-argument preparation also should include researching the positions of the individual justices in the area of federal law at issue. . . .
>
> In presenting oral argument, the attorney should identify one or two primary objectives and structure the presentation to emphasize those points. Oral argument is not the time to offer a long and complicated analysis of the case. A good oral argument demonstrates the fairness of the litigant's position and gives the Court the impression that, if the litigant prevails, the United States will be a better place or, perhaps, the Court will be enforcing the intent of the Framers of the Constitution or of Congress that enacted the particular statute at issue.
>
> The attorney presenting oral argument should become so conversant with the case, its facts and the arguments in support of or contrary to the client's position that a prepared text or notes are unnecessary. The goal is to have a conversation with the justices, or at least with those that demonstrate an active interest in the lawyer's arguments. Nothing will be less effective than a prepared speech delivered as oral argument. (1995, pp. 39–40)

Despite the importance of the situation, the magnificent courtroom, and the visibility of the justices, not all attorneys present a style that is congenial with the expectations of the justices. It is an intimidating experience for the novice. The justices are "less than 10 feet away, and their near-semicircular bench is low to the ground so they are looking you right in the eye" (Cullinan,

2004, p. 30). Increasingly, many of the attorneys who argue cases before the highest court are "repeat players" and among the legal elite who specialize in appellate advocacy (McGuire, 1993). But occasionally a relatively new associate at a law firm gets the opportunity. That was the case when William Colby, an associate in a Kansas City, Missouri, law firm argued the appeal of Nancy Cruzan before the Supreme Court in 1989. Nancy Cruzan had been injured in an automobile accident and had been in a persistent vegetative state for six years; her parents wanted permission for her to be allowed to die (Colby, 2002). William Colby had represented her through a long series of trials and appeals, and when the Supreme Court took the case, he rejected advice to turn the case over to an experienced appellate attorney; "I was young and headstrong enough to think I could do the argument," he reported (Mauro, 2003d, p. 7). Colby lost the appeal 5 to 4, but the Court's opinion did permit a right to die if new evidence surfaced about the person's earlier intent, and a new trial a year later permitted Nancy Cruzan to die with dignity.

Even rarer is for a petitioner or respondent to represent himself or herself, *pro se*, but it happened during the 2003–2004 term, in the case of *Elk Grove Unified School District v. Newdow*. Michael Newdow, a lawyer, unsuccessfully argued that the "under God" portion of the Pledge of Allegiance violated the First Amendment.

It would be fun to be a fly on the wall at the justices' lunches right after the oral arguments, to note how often they mention inept attorneys at oral arguments. The papers of Justice Blackmun, released in March 2004, indicated that he routinely recorded succinct evaluations of the attorneys appearing before the Court, including even mentions of their appearance, such as "looks tired" or "dark mustache"; he even graded their performance on occasion (Mauro, 2004c, p. 81). When Ruth Bader Ginsburg argued before the Court for the first time, long before she was named a justice, Blackmun gave her a "C plus," noting that she was "very precise" and that she read her statement (p. 81), and he described her brief in another case as "a very lengthy brief filled with emotion" (Greenhouse, 2004a, p. A17).

Chief Justice Rehnquist, on the basis of 30 years of observing lawyers appearing before the high court, classified attorneys and their oral arguments into four categories:

- The lector, who reads his or her argument. "Questions from the judges, instead of being used as an opportunity to advance one's own arguments by response, are looked upon as an interruption in the advocate's delivery of his 'speech,' and the lawyer after answering the question returns to the printed page at exactly where he left off" (2001, p. 245).
- The debating champion, who is "so full of his subject, and so desirous of demonstrating this to others, that he doesn't listen carefully to questions" (p. 246). His or her responses to questions reflect stock answers, usually not helpful to the justice who has asked the question.

- The advocate called by Justice Rehnquist simply "Casey Jones," because "he is like an engineer on a nonstop train—he will not stop to pick up passengers along the way" (p. 247). "He speaks very rapidly, without realizing that when he is arguing before a bench of nine people, each of them will require a little time to assimilate what he is saying" (p. 247).
- The spellbinder (less frequent than 50 years ago), the opposite of "Casey Jones" in that the advocate has a good voice and a "presence" that permit him or her to converse with the justices, but this type lets his or her "natural assets be a substitute for any careful analysis of the legal issues" (p. 247).

Even more egregious are the specific errors that occur during oral arguments.

> Imagine, for example, Justice Blackmun's surprise when, one day, a couple of terms after Justice Brennan retired, an attorney responded to Justice Blackmun's question by referring to him as 'Justice Brennan.' Although Justice Blackmun kindly let the mistake pass without comment, not a single justice on the bench that day failed to note the attorney's error. (McAllister, 1995, p. 41)

And more recently, while Walter Dellinger was solicitor general in the Clinton administration, he—incredibly—referred to Justice Ginsburg as "Justice O'Connor" on more than one occasion.

The Justices' Questioning

In presenting oral arguments, the petitioner's attorney always goes first. It is likely that the presentation, whichever side is making it, will be interrupted by questions from individual justices. Johnson's (2004) survey of 75 oral arguments found an average of 88 questions per case, and as many as 150 interruptions have been recorded during a single case's oral argument. For an attorney—for anyone—the experience can be disconcerting; the questions are often penetrating, and the justices' observations are sometimes intemperate. The judges can even get into arguments among themselves, while the attorney stands there helplessly, watching the 30 minutes evaporate. In a 1982 death-penalty appeal, Justices Rehnquist and Marshall clashed; after Rehnquist pushed the point that execution of a prisoner would be cheaper for the court system than a long imprisonment, Justice Marshall sarcastically interjected "Well, it would be cheaper just to shoot him when you arrested him, wouldn't it?" (Barbash, 1983). Discussions between justices can even stray far from the subject at hand; Justices Rehnquist and Stevens once disagreed about the position played by Hall of Fame baseball player Kiki Cuyler (Mann, 1983).

What are we to make of the justices' questions and comments during the oral arguments? First, justices differ in their behavior during oral arguments— how attentive they appear to be, how many questions they ask, and the style of their questions and comments. Justice Scalia is well known among Court-watchers for the persistence and zeal of his verbal jousts; he even concedes that he can become overbearing, saying, "It is the academic in me. I fight against it. The devil makes me do it" (O'Brien, 2000, p. 261). Early in her time on the Court, Justice Ginsburg developed a reputation for frequent inter-ruptions—even of other justices—and numerous questions (Cooper, 1995; O'Brien, 2000). Justice O'Connor could be counted on for asking a first ques-tion that might set a framework for future ones. Justice Breyer's questions remind some observers that he was formerly a law professor. At the other extreme is Justice Thomas, who may not raise a single question or comment during oral arguments throughout a whole term; he has explained that he doesn't interrupt because he has been in the attorney's position and wants to hear what the attorney has to say. But in one memorable session, Justice Thomas, by his comment, had an enormous impact on the oral argument. The case was *Virginia v. Black* (2003), dealing with the legality of cross burn-ing by the Ku Klux Klan. Justice Thomas interrupted the petitioner and with great emotion described the impact of the KKK in a reign of terror that in-cluded lynchings of blacks; he further labeled the cross as a symbol of that reign of terror.

Rod Smolla, the advocate for the respondent, described the reaction in the courtroom:

> In all my life as an advocate and observer of legal proceedings, I have never seen the mood in a courtroom change so suddenly and dramatically. The impact of Justice Thomas's remarks was pal-pable and physical. Justice Breyer, who sat next to Thomas on the bench, drew closer to him, putting an arm on his back in a gesture of collegial respect and good will. Justice Scalia, who sat on the opposite side of Thomas but nearly facing him (because of the curvature of the bench), seemed to viscerally connect with his fellow justice, nodding in agreement as he spoke. (2004, p. 164)

To some extent, these differences are related to the salience of the par-ticular issue for that justice, but are they also a function of the personality or style of the justice, reflecting the presence of exuberance or reticence, for ex-ample? Or perhaps they reflect some deep-set substantive characteristics such as open-mindedness and need for cognition.

Can Justices' Votes Be Predicted from Their Questions?

Can we draw conclusions about the future vote of a justice from his or her questions during oral arguments? Frequently, newspaper reports of the oral arguments for a specific case will describe a justice's questions and comments as reflecting "skepticism" or "doubt" about the claims of one side, but are such reactions manifested in the judge's eventual vote? Stephen Wasby and his colleagues concluded that "oral argument at times—but certainly not always—has been directly relevant to the Court's disposition of a case—and at times determinative of the outcome" (Wasby, Peterson, Schubert, & Schubert, 1992, p. 30).

Sarah Shullman (2004) observed seven oral arguments before the Supreme Court, tallied the number of questions each justice asked the petitioner's attorney and the respondent's attorney, and categorized the questions as helpful or hostile. She then awaited the announcement of the decision and the votes for each side. More questions were asked of the attorney for the losing side than the winning side, and the content of the questions asked the eventual losing attorney were more hostile than helpful. John Roberts (2005), a frequent advocate before the Court before he was appointed to the D.C. Circuit Court and then as Chief Justice of the United States, took 14 arguments from the 1980 term and 14 from the 2003 term and found a result generally consistent with Shullman's findings: more questions were asked of the eventual losing party than of the winning party in 24 of 28 cases, or an 86 percent accuracy rate. As Roberts dryly observed in his article, "the secret to successful advocacy is simply to get the Court to ask your opponent more questions" (p. 75). (Given Justice Roberts's appointment to the Supreme Court, one wonders if he is influenced by his findings when he chooses questions to ask.)

These studies are based on limited samples, and the cliché that "further research is needed" is appropriate here. But two tentative conclusions may be advanced: first, despite the uncertainty of advocates, outcomes may be foretold in many cases (Mauro, 2005c). Second, the common wisdom that justices' questions are often those of devil's advocates, that is, posing questions to both sides to elicit their weakest arguments, seems colored by the justices' own preferences and predilections. Chapter 10 describes systematic efforts to predict case outcomes, comparing the predictions of experts and a statistical formula. The "success rate" of 86 percent found by Roberts should be borne in mind when reading the results of these approaches to prediction.

The justices' motivations behind their questions are diverse and difficult to discern. A question may reflect hostility more than it reflects a genuine desire to know the answer; another justice may use questions to clarify his or her thoughts on the issue. In addition, questions may reveal that a justice has misunderstood an important aspect of the case, or has read a precedent differently from the way one of the attorneys thinks it should be read (Rehnquist, 1987a). While Johnson (2004) has provided a classification system for the content of questions asked, we need a system that reflects motivations of the questioner. Aaron Hull (1997) has suggested that justices' questions during oral arguments can be grouped into three categories:

- *Affirming questions* are those asked to aid an attorney is answering a question, or to provide a new direction of thought. They are "generally signaled by a calm voice tone of the justice, and an enthusiastic affirmative response by the attorney" (p. 28).

- *Inquisitive questions* regarding case facts alone, as in case-framing at the beginning of the oral argument; for example, "Mr. Smith, isn't this case about . . . ?"
- *Challenges*, or abrupt interruptions of attorneys in a harsh tone of voice, the net result of which is often to corner the attorneys into saying things that are potentially damaging to their case.

But it should be recognized that some questions, while directed at an attorney, are really intended to be heard by another justice, perhaps to try to persuade that justice (Wasby, D'Amato, & Metrailer, 1976). Justice William O. Douglas wrote, for example, "I soon learned that . . . questioning from the bench was . . . a form of lobbying for votes" (Cooper, 1995, p. 72). But perhaps they function, as in the aforementioned exchange between Justices Marshall and Rehnquist, as simply a barb thrown at an adversary. Despite the claims of collegiality, conflicts between justices may be observed during the oral argument sessions. Cooper described these as follows: "Apart from tactical uses, some justices have used oral argument to act out publicly some of the usually unseen conflicts within the Court. Far from planned tactical skirmishes, these public spats may sometimes simply be matters of the moment. Others are part of an ongoing pattern" (1995, p. 72).

During his long tenure on the Court (described in detail in chapter 8), Justice Felix Frankfurter often drew the wrath of his colleagues, especially because of his know-it-all professorial manner on the bench. Justice Douglas enjoyed needling him, and even Chief Justice Warren once lost his temper. During one oral argument, while Chief Justice Warren was questioning the lawyer, Justice Frankfurter interrupted Warren and reworded his question, causing Warren angrily to shout, "Let him answer my question. He is confused enough as it is" (p. 73).

The Impact of Oral Arguments

Systematic study of the impact of oral arguments on attitude formation and change is limited. In their review, Segal and Spaeth concluded that the extent to which oral arguments affect the justices' votes was "problematic" (1993, p. 208). Most scholars of the Court "still adhere to the view that the oral arguments are little more than window dressing and have no effect on how justices make decisions" (Johnson, 2004, p. 3). Chief Justice Warren, similarly, found oral arguments "not highly persuasive" (O'Brien, 2000, p. 260). After all, the justices have previously read the extensive briefs and reviewed the relevant court decisions. Most have probably discussed the case with their law clerks. Furthermore, some don't consider the oral arguments that informative. As he listened, Justice Douglas engaged in multitasking—he answered his mail or drafted sections of his many books. Justice Oliver Wendell Holmes, Jr., considered oral arguments so unimportant that he often took catnaps while on the bench (O'Brien, 1997).

Given these observations, why continue the procedure? A recent book by Timothy Johnson (2004) has observed that, without oral arguments, the Court has little control over the information it obtains about a case. The oral argument is the one opportunity for justices, if they so choose, to gather the information that they want, not simply process information that others want them to have. For example, justices may use the oral arguments to raise issues not covered in the briefs from either party (Johnson, 2004). They may ask hypothetical questions in order to determine the breadth of a decision or unanticipated consequences of it (Biskupic, 2000; Prettyman, 1984). Furthermore, justices may observe what questions are asked by their colleagues and thus identify who will be voting which way at conference.

And some justices publicly welcome the oral arguments; Justice Brennan, for example, said: "Often my idea of how a case shapes up is changed by oral argument" (O'Brien, 2000, p. 254), and the same view was expressed in detail by Justice John M. Harlan II: "The view is widespread that when the Court comes to the hard business of decision, it is the briefs, and not the oral argument, which count. I think that view is a greatly mistaken one" (1955, p. 6).

A survey of Ninth Circuit judges (Wasby, 1981) supported the conclusion that in those cases that are complex or deal with novel issues of the law, it is especially helpful to have the opportunity to question attorneys orally. It is less helpful in simple cases, in "frivolous" ones, and—as one would expect—in "run-of-the-mill" cases. These conclusions reflect a fundamental psychological contribution to understanding judicial decision-making: the phenomenon of the person–situation interaction. The influential social psychologist Kurt Lewin (1951) proposed that behavior is a function of both the person *and* the environment; these interact together. Consider Chief Justice Rehnquist's response to the question whether oral arguments change any minds:

> In a significant minority of the cases of which I have heard oral argument, I have left the bench feeling differently about a case than when I came to the bench. The change is seldom a full one-hundred-and-eighty-degree swing, and I find it is most likely to occur in cases involving areas of law with which I am least familiar. (2001, pp. 243–244)

Justice Rehnquist's statement can be read as saying "On many issues, I already know enough about the case before hearing the oral arguments to form a firm opinion, but on those topics of which I am least knowledgeable, it is the environment (i.e., the points made in oral arguments) that affects my behavior." The effectiveness of any oral argument is interactionally determined. For some judges with strongly held positions, the best possible oral argument is still doomed to be ineffective. For others, whose opinions are not so solid or who may be less informed on the topic, the quality of oral argument may make a difference.

Judges also differ in how well prepared they are for the oral arguments. O'Brien (2000) reported that most of the current Supreme Court justices come armed with "bench memos" that note central facts, issues, and potential questions. Thus prepared, a judge is much more capable of probing the factual basis and the logical support for each side's oral arguments than is a judge who has only casually read the briefs. But, as Chief Justice Rehnquist noted, each justice may prepare for oral arguments in a different way; while chief justice, he described his own procedure as follows.

> Several of my colleagues get what are called "bench memos" from the law clerks on the cases. . . . I do not do this, simply because it does not fit my own style of working. When I start to prepare for a case that will be orally argued, I begin by reading the opinion of the lower court that is to be reviewed. I find this a good starting point because it is the product of another court which, like ours, is sworn to uphold the Constitution and the laws, and is presumably not biased against either party to the case. I then read the petitioner's brief, then the respondent's brief. Meanwhile, I have asked one of my clerks to do the same thing, with a view of our then discussing the case.
>
> I let my law clerks divide up the cases according to their own formula. Since there are around twelve cases in each two-week session of oral argument, this means that each clerk will end up with four cases for which that clerk is responsible. I think that most years my clerks have divided up the cases with a system something like the National Football League draft, in which those morsels viewed as most choice are taken first in rotation, with the cases left as the dregs at the end.
>
> When the law clerk and I are both ready to talk about the case, we do just that—sometimes walking around the neighborhood of the Supreme Court building, sometimes sitting in my chambers. I tell the clerk some of my reactions to the arguments of the parties, and am interested in getting the clerk's reactions to those same arguments. If there is some point of law involved in the case that doesn't appear to be adequately covered by the briefs, I may ask the clerk to write me a memorandum on that particular point. (2001, pp. 239–240)

Justice Rehnquist noted that at that point, he did not reach a final resolution of the case; rather, he would let it "percolate" in his mind. The actual oral argument served as a catalyst for generating further thought on the case.

The Judicial Conference

A judicial conference is held the same week as the oral arguments, usually on Friday. These conferences tend to last about an hour and one half. Only the nine justices are present. The chief justice keeps a record of the disposition of each case, and other justices may keep notes, but no record of the votes or decisions is announced to the public. However, some justices have kept extensive notes about what has happened at conference; those of Justice Powell and Justice Blackmun, available to scholars, have led to some conclusions about what transpired. For example, Johnson's analysis of Justice Powell's records led him to conclude that the justices "rarely discuss issues raised in legal briefs that they did not ask about during oral arguments" (2004, p. 77).

The Decision to Recuse Oneself

Whenever judges have a personal, financial, or other conflict of interest in the outcome of a case, they are expected to recuse themselves, but no fixed rules exist for judges to explain why they absent themselves from granting or disposing of cases. As O'Brien observed, "[s]ome Court watchers find this practice of unexplained judicial disqualification disturbing because of the large number of cases in which one or more justices recuse themselves" (2000, p. 189).

But of greater concern are the wide disparities in the decision to recuse oneself especially when, from the perspective of an outsider, a clear conflict of interest exists. (As of early 2004, the number of recusals per term ranged from 42 per term for Justice Breyer to 7 per term for Justice Ginsburg and Chief Justice Rehnquist [Mauro, 2004a].) (Most of the recusals by Justice Breyer—and also those by Justice O'Connor—reflected ownership of stock in one of the contesting companies [Mauro, 1997].)

In contrast, Justice Rehnquist did not recuse himself with respect to three 1972 cases in which he had been involved as an assistant attorney general prior to his appointment to the Court. As Rohde and Spaeth (1976) noted, all of these were emotionally charged decisions involving the legality of antiwar protests, and they were all decided in favor of the government. In each of these, Justice Rehnquist cast the deciding vote in a 5 to 4 decision.

Similarly, Justice Breyer did not recuse himself in October 2004 when a case challenging the federal sentencing guidelines came before the Court, even though he had helped prepare them in a previous job, and likewise Justice Scalia did not recuse himself in March 2004 from a case involving Vice-President Richard Cheney as the petitioner (*Cheney v. U.S. District Court of the District of Columbia*, 2004), even though he acknowledged Cheney as "a friend" and had recently gone on a duck-hunting trip with him. (In fact, he and his daughter had flown to the site of the Louisiana duck hunt on Air Force Two, which critics considered a "sizable gift" to Scalia.) Extensive media attention (and criticism) was directed to Justice Scalia, such that he prepared a 21-page defense of his decision that dismissed any concerns about a possible impropriety. He provided some examples in the past of justices having friendships with presidents, senators, and others high up in the other branches of the federal government (some of which were described in chapter 2). Chief Justice Rehnquist, in response to criticism of Justice Scalia from some members of

Congress, replied that it was "ill-considered" for members of the legislative branch to suggest how justices should behave (Mauro, 2004a). In fairness to Justice Scalia, it should be noted that he has recused himself 196 times in his first 18 years on the bench; most of these recusals—as with each of the justices—occurred at the initial review period rather than in situations, such as the *Cheney* appeal, in which the case has been scheduled for oral arguments and a decision. Justice Scalia eventually did vote with the majority in support of Vice-President Cheney's position, but his vote did not make the difference, as the Court voted 7 to 2.

In some cases, a decision to recuse oneself should be straightforward. Justice Thurgood Marshall recused himself from 98 of the 171 cases that were decided by the Supreme Court during the 1967–1968 term, but most of these were cases in which the federal government had been a party. Marshall, as the solicitor general of the United States prior to his Supreme Court appointment, had participated in the development of one side's position for those cases (Segal & Spaeth, 1993). Perhaps as a result of questions about self-determination of recusal, a law was passed in 1974 that prohibited federal judges from participating in the ruling in a case in which they had previously expressed an opinion. But this does not cure the problem entirely.

Justice Thomas recused himself from participating in a case in which the Virginia Military Institute was a party because his son was a student there. But Thomas was criticized for failing to recuse himself in a case (in which he eventually wrote the majority opinion) involving the pension benefits of an employee at Lockheed Corporation. The issue was how to interpret a law that required Lockheed and other employers to contribute to the pension plans of older workers without discriminating on the basis of age (Mauro, 1996). While chairing the Equal Employment Opportunity Commission (EEOC) in 1988, Thomas had concluded that the law should not be applied retroactively to benefit older workers who had already been the objects of discrimination, saying: "We think that substantively, we are absolutely correct" (p. 3A). The Internal Revenue Service disagreed and instructed companies to make such retroactive payments. In the June 1996 decision, Justice Thomas ruled against retroactivity, consistent with his EEOC position eight years before. He was joined in his ruling by six other justices.

Judges are not required to give reason why they recuse themselves or, more important, why they *don't*, despite a recommendation in 1993 by a federal commission that the Supreme Court establish some mechanism for reviewing justices' ethics. And it must be acknowledged that sometimes the decision to recuse can obfuscate the operation of justice (Lubet, 1995). If the issue before the Court is to decide whether to grant certiorari, the "rule of four" means that an abstention counts the same as a no vote. As described in chapter 1, the recusal of four justices in an appeal involving tax deductions for judges meant that the earlier decision had to stand. And in respect to the federal circuit courts, in which the initial decision is made by a three-judge panel, if one of the judges recuses himself or herself, it gives an additional responsibility to another judge.

Procedures at the Case Conference

At the conference to act on cases, the chief justice presides and summarizes each case and expresses an opinion. The other justices follow in order of seniority. (Even Oliver Wendell Holmes, Jr., at the age of 61 only a first-year justice, spoke last and had to serve as a doorkeeper.) In earlier times, apparently the vote was taken in reverse order of seniority, so that the most recently appointed justice would not be unduly influenced by his seniors. This ground rule recognized the possibility of conformity pressures. But recent accounts of the judicial conference procedure say that it no longer applies. In his book on the Supreme Court, Chief Justice Rehnquist wrote:

> For many years there has circulated a tale that although the discussion in conference proceeds in order from the chief justice to the junior justice, the voting actually begins with the junior justice and proceeds back to the chief justice in order of seniority. But at least during my thirty years on the Court, this tale is very much of a myth; I don't believe I have ever seen it happen at any of the conferences that I have attended. (2001, p. 254)

For some cases, a consensus emerges, and no formal vote is necessary. The important aspect is to determine which party's position has received the support of the majority.

Not much lobbying for votes occurs during the conference. Chief Justice Rehnquist has commented:

> When I first went on the Court, I was both surprised and disappointed at how little interplay there was between the various justices during the process of conferring on a case. Each would state his views, and a junior justice could express agreement or disagreement with views expressed by a justice senior to him earlier in the discussion, but the converse did not apply; a junior justice's views were seldom commented upon, because votes had already been cast up the line. Probably most junior justices before me must have felt as I did, that they had some very significant contributions to make, and were disappointed that they hardly ever seemed to influence anyone, because people didn't change their votes in response to their, the junior justices', contrary views. . . . Having now sat in conferences for nearly three decades, and having risen from ninth to first in seniority, I realize—with newfound clarity—that my idea as a junior justice, while fine in the abstract, probably would not have contributed

much in practice, and at any rate was doomed by the seniority system to which the senior justices naturally adhere. (2001, pp. 254–255)

Designating the Opinion Writer

After the vote, or the determination of the majority, one justice in the majority is assigned the task of drafting the Court's opinion. The votes during the conference are not binding, and there is a sense that, at least in complex cases, "some things will have to be worked out in the writing" (Rehnquist, 2001, p. 257). The broad outlines of a position of the Court emerge during the conference, but the eventual written opinion must clarify a number of issues that are often unresolved during the conference.

If the chief justice is in the majority, he or she assigns the task of writing the draft opinion; if not, the most senior associate justice who is in the majority does so. The opinion assignment in *Granholm v. Heald*, revealed when the decision was announced on May 16, 2005, instantly surfaced as a rarity. Of Chief Justice Rehnquist, the senior associate justice (Stevens), and the next most senior associate justice (O'Connor), none was in the majority; hence it fell upon the fourth justice in seniority (Scalia) to assign the opinion. He assigned it to Justice Kennedy. In actuality, the chief justice does the major part of the assigning—about 80 percent of the cases in the Burger and Rehnquist Courts, and about 95 percent back when William Howard Taft and Charles Evans Hughes were in charge (Epstein & Knight, 1998).

The assignment decision is not casually done, as many strategic considerations apply. For example:

> The author of the initial opinion draft can significantly affect the policy the Court produces because the opinion writer's first draft establishes the initial position over which the justices bargain. Depending on the writer's preference, the first draft can be crafted broadly or narrowly, can ignore or apply past precedents, and can fashion various kinds of policy. Moreover, the opinion writer is in a position to accept or reject bargaining offers from [his or her] colleagues. (Epstein & Knight, 1998, p. 126)

Some observers have argued that the justice holding the least extreme opinion should be the one who writes what serves as a binding opinion for the Court, but actual reasons for assigning an opinion to a particular judge depend on a variety of considerations. In highly important cases, the chief justice (if in the majority) has usually assigned himself as the author. Steamer (1986) observed that every chief justice since John Marshall (who wrote almost all of the important opinions of his Court) has assigned to himself the opinion writing in cases that dealt with critical constitutional issues. But like other decisions in the Court, the assignment reflects human considerations. Certainly politics plays a role, but many other considerations are also possible:

- To equalize workload
- To keep this justice in the majority
- To maximize the desired content of the opinion
- To give the opinion a political advantage
- To reward a justice who has a particular interest in writing the opinion, or to prevent another justice from placing his or her stamp on the opinion

An empirical study of assignments made by the three most recent chief justices concluded that they reflected a consistent attempt to encourage specialization by assigning opinions to those justices who had expertise on the topic under consideration (Maltzman & Wahlbeck, 1996a). Opinion writers were also selected on the basis of their ability to make the majority view palatable to outsiders, such as Congress, the president, and various influential organizations. The opportunity to select the opinion writer seems to be symbolically important as well. It has been noted that Warren Burger, while he was chief justice, sometimes "passed" at the initial voting or even changed his vote, to ensure that he was in the majority—just so he could be the one to assign the opinion writing (Woodward & Armstrong, 1979).

The Draft Opinion

Preparing opinion drafts can be time consuming. It is at this point that the Court once again resembles "nine small independent law firms," because each justice finds that writing his or her opinions is a solitary process, or at least a process done in conjunction only with his or her own law clerks.

After the opinion writer completes a draft, it is circulated to the other justices, who indicate whether they are willing to concur. They may want changes—some minor, but some major. This leads a period of exchanges of memos, lobbying, and negotiations, completely unseen by the public.

Negotiations

Often, many drafts have to be prepared so as to meet the wishes of others in the majority. The reasoning may be altered to accommodate other viewpoints, especially those justices who waver or threaten to go over to the other side. The attempts to persuade are more intense during this period than at the judicial conference. The situation is rife with the type of pressures that operate on any group that must form an opinion or take an action, including pressures toward uniformity and opinion change. Baum observed:

Once that opinion is completed and circulated, it often becomes a focus of negotiation. Ordinarily the assigned justice wishes to obtain the support of as many colleagues as possible for the opinion. The writer will seek to convince justices in the minority to change positions, and it may also be necessary to discourage allies in the conference from leaving the fold. (1985, p. 115)

As the foregoing quotation implies, some justices may shift from the majority to the minority; what was originally the "losing" side may become the winner. In the highly important abortion case *Planned Parenthood of Southeastern Pennsylvania v. Casey* (1992), Chief Justice Rehnquist circulated the draft of a majority opinion that overturned *Roe v. Wade*, but Justices Kennedy, O'Connor, and Souter met privately and drafted a substitute opinion that restricted abortions but maintained the central aspect of the *Roe* opinion. It became the majority decision for the Court.

The Majority Opinion

Eventually an opinion draft is agreed upon by the majority of the justices (although some may concur with only parts of it). This has been referred to as the "report vote," to distinguish this final decision from the earlier, tentative conference vote. Justices who disagree with the majority opinion may prepare dissents.

The Function of Dissents

Why prepare a dissent, rather than simply registering one's vote to disagree with the majority? Dissents are discussed more extensively in chapter 4, but it can be noted there that one purpose is to try to persuade, if not one's colleagues now, perhaps those in the future. Also, expressing one's opinion in writing may have a cathartic value for the justice, just as it does for the rest of us.

Announcement of the Decision

The Court does not announce in advance when it will present its decision. Interestingly, on those "decision days," when several cases are decided, the justices go in reverse order of seniority in announcing the decisions for which they were the opinion writer. When the Supreme Court began more than two hundred years ago, it followed the English practice, with every justice delivering an individual opinion on every case. But now, when the decision is announced, the justice who authored the opinion has the option of reading a summary or a portion of it to the press and public. Because of time constraints, justices are discouraged from reading their entire opinion. Thus, some justices may take only a few minutes (O'Brien, 2000). Regardless, this opinion "speaks for the Court." As this chapter has tried to illustrate, it is an individual's opinion, in the sense that the words in it have come from the office of one justice, but it is also a group opinion, in that it is responsive to discussion and comments from the other justices. Those in the minority may express their dissent when the decision is announced.

4

Day to Day in the Life of the Court

The fact is that the Court functions less as one deliberative body than as nine, each justice working largely in isolation except as he [*sic*] chooses to seek consultation with others.—Justice Robert Jackson, "The Supreme Court as a Unit of Government" (1961)

As we seek to understand the decision-making of the Supreme Court, it is helpful to gain a sense of what the day-to-day life is like in the massive Supreme Court building. The purpose of this chapter is to concentrate on some specific aspects that give elaboration to a description of the activities of the justices and those around them.

The Extent of Interaction between Justices

How much do the justices interact? And what is the nature of their interaction? The public sees posed photographs of the justices, robed and sitting together; in addition, television accounts of important cases, while the taking of photographs is not allowed inside the courtroom, may show artists' sketches of the justices seated at their massive bench. Is this how they are usually attired? Is this how they spend most of their time? The short answer is no.

"Nine Separate Law Firms"

Although the public has access to the Supreme Court building and can attend the Court's oral arguments, that portion of the building that houses the offices of the justices and their staff is closed off. Only occasionally do justices speak about their day-to-day existence, but the reminiscences of their former law clerks are sometimes more voluble. This chapter's attempt to portray what their everyday life is like is based on a sampling of observations by specific justices and their law clerks, as well as the known constraints on the justices' activities resulting from their scheduled meetings.

The Supreme Court building houses a self-sufficient organization. Lazarus described it as follows.

> The Court is a remarkably small place considering its profoundly important function, employing fewer than 300 persons, most of whom stay for many, many years. Moreover, the Court building, though by no means posh except for the public rooms, houses a cafeteria, snack bar, gymnasium, wood shop, police force, custodial staff, barbershop, seamstress, print shop, library, nurse, in house-law office, gift shop, and curator. As a consequence, from the beginning of the workday to its end—whether that day be a marshal's assistant's standard shift or a law clerk's fourteen-hour grind—the Court's employees virtually never venture outside its walls. (1998, p. 26)

The "gymnasium" mentioned by Lazarus is on the top floor and contains a basketball court ("the highest court in the land"); when Byron White was a justice, he would play intense games of basketball there with some of the clerks.

A number of observers have described the justices as resembling "nine separate law firms," and it is true that most of the time they are in their separate offices, along with their office staff and their law clerks (whose duties may resemble those of the associates in law firms). Most justices spend more time interacting with their law clerks than with the other justices.

The Routine

So how much time *do* the justices spend together? The answer depends upon which weeks are considered. From the first Monday in October through late April (with a month-long recess around the holidays) the Court holds oral arguments every other two weeks; on those weeks, the justices are together for six hours of oral arguments (two hours each on Monday, Tuesday, and Wednesday), lunches during the week, and case conferences to discuss these cases on Friday. Also, on these Fridays, the justices review the certiorari list. Recently, only six oral arguments or fewer have been scheduled for each week, meaning a maximum of 84 hours of oral arguments (and 84 cases) for the whole term. (The Court does not meet on national holidays, and recently it has not scheduled oral arguments on days that are Jewish holy days.) The length of the discussion of the week's cases is less predictable, but for the weeks when oral arguments are scheduled, the justices are together, at most, for around 15 hours during a standard 40-hour work week.

In the alternate two-week periods, the Friday meetings to discuss recent petitions for certiorari are held, but the justices have much more time on their own. By no means are they free of all other obligations; they have briefs and summaries of petitions to read, opinion drafts of their own to write, and opinion drafts of other justices to consider. But during this two-week period each month, they have somewhat more latitude to travel, give speeches, or visit law schools, which some justices frequently do (during 2004, Justice O'Connor took 28 trips, and Justice Scalia took 15). Toward the end of the term, pressure mounts to concentrate on the cases at hand. No oral arguments are scheduled for the months of May and June, and the chief justice monitors the progress of each case in order to reach the goal of having all decisions announced by the end of June.

Thus the relationship of the justices may be characterized as reflecting both isolation *and* interaction. Business-type matters are handled through memoranda and e-mails; there seems to be little of the "walk down the hall and chat" as a form of discussing or resolving differences. Some justices—Souter and Thomas for example—apparently do not socialize with the other justices very much, away from the workplace. (Justice Souter even retreats to his native New Hampshire for the entire summer.) Exceptions do exist, however; Justices Rehnquist and Scalia were in the same poker-playing group; Justices Breyer and Kennedy play bridge, and Justices Ginsburg and Scalia and their spouses spend New Year's Eve together.

Justice Stevens in Florida

The extreme example is Justice Stevens, who has spent much of the winter—at least those weeks in which oral arguments are not scheduled—in his condominium in Florida. Sometimes referred to as the "Fed-Ex judge" (Lazarus, 1998), he dispatches his comments on certiorari petitions and opinion drafts expeditiously during those weeks that he is away, but the point is that he *is* away.

Conflict or Collegiality?

What is the relationship among the justices? Can a small group of people, whose decisions affect the lives of millions, who are highly motivated, educated, and articulate, whose opinions are well thought out but often in disagreement with those of their colleagues, exist in a collegial relationship?

The odds would seem to be against it. A whole book has been written about the now-famous conflicts between earlier justices, such as those between Justices Jackson and Murphy or between Justices Black and Frankfurter in the 1950s and 1960s (Cooper, 1995). How can collegiality exist when one of the nine justices is as contentious as Justice Scalia? He is notorious for what several other justices refer to as "Ninograms"—each is generally "a one- or two-page, single-spaced, and always colorful legal polemic on a pending case. Hand-delivered, usually without warning, in innocuous manila envelopes, these diatribes would provoke consternation and anger from Scalia's adversaries, amusement and appreciation from his allies" (Lazarus, 1998, p. 42). He has attacked his colleagues individually and as a group; in the *Cruzan* case described in chapter 3, he asserted that the justices were no better qualified to rule on the right to die than nine people selected at random from the Kansas City phone book (Vitullo-Martin, 2004).

Yet whenever a current justice is asked in public about relationships among the justices, the response is very favorable. Justice Thomas's comments usually bear upon his experiences in each of the three branches of the federal government; he has said that the atmosphere in the Court reflects more civility than that within either of the other two branches, and he has said that he has never heard a word spoken in anger during the conferences (Thomas, 1996). Justice Breyer has noted the ritual of shaking hands before every conference or set of oral arguments (instituted by Chief Justice Melville Fuller) and proposed that it contributes to the atmosphere of collegiality. He also has said: "I have never heard one member of the Court say something insulting about another, even as a kind of joke" (Associated Press, 2003, p. 6A). Even after the rancor of the *Bush v. Gore* (2000) decision, those justices who were willing to be quoted insisted that collegiality continues to prevail.

It is clear that the current justices value civility. Justice Thomas has used this term as an organizing theme for one of his speeches. Justice Kennedy, in an address to the ABA, called civility the "mark of an accomplished and superb professional" (Willing, 1997, p. 3A). Even when things get heated, the justices try to maintain their closeness; Justice O'Connor, in a television interview, said: "When you work in a small group of that size, you have to get along, and so you're not going to let some harsh language, some dissenting opinion affect a personal relationship" (Cushman, 2003, p. A9).

An example of this manifestation of civility is described in Linda Greenhouse's (2005b) biography of Justice Blackmun. Shortly after Clarence Thomas became a justice, one of his supporters, an economist and conservative columnist named Thomas Sowell, denounced Justice Blackmun as a "vain and shallow old man whom that media have puffed up for their own ideological reasons . . . a tawdry symbol of what has gone wrong in American law over the past few decades" (pp. 238, 240). Justice Thomas sent Blackmun a handwritten note: "It is upsetting to me to see any friend of mine cause you such distress. I will speak with him. In the meanwhile, please know that you have had a profound, positive influence on me during my brief tenure on the Court. With great respect, Clarence" (p. 240).

Institutional considerations may contribute to a pressure toward collegiality. The justices know that they will be working with each other for years, even decades. They realize that they may differ—they *will* differ—on issues, but they also realize that the system cannot work without their interdependence.

The Justices' Workload

The public may have the perception—if it has any perception of the Court at all—that the justices do not work very hard. They seemingly have the summer off, from late June to the beginning of October; their clerks are sometimes perceived as doing much of their work for them; and, as noted, during those weeks when no oral arguments are scheduled, they may travel and give speeches.

But it is also true that the justices put in long hours, usually arriving early in the morning and not leaving until 7 or 8 p.m. Some are in the office on Saturdays. They may be called on during weekends and the summer for emergency decisions. The importance of their decisions carries a heavy burden, and the sheer weight of the material they are expected to read is literally staggering. Justice Jackson (1961) noted that the briefs and records for some cases consumed five feet of shelf space. Justices describe the workload as relentless, and it is hard to dispute the claim that the job is one in which closure is impossible to achieve.

It has been noted that in recent terms, the Court has reduced the number of cases that it takes on; in the 1970s and 1980s, it handed down as many as 170 rulings per term (Epstein, Segal, Spaeth, & Walker, 1996, table 3-1, p. 194). For the terms ending in June 2002, 2003, 2004, and 2005, the number of cases decided was in the low or mid-seventies. Does this mean the workload is less than it used to be? Certainly the justices would say no, and perhaps their actions verify Parkinson's law that "work expands to fit the time allotted for it." But it is noteworthy that lawyers trying to get the Court to grant certiorari have started to argue that their cases should be heard simply because the justices have the time to! A brief filed by General Motors said:

> We are not here arguing that the Court's relatively lighter work load justifies granting a petition that does not otherwise warrant the Court's review. . . . Rather, our point is that the clear absence of a crushing workload for the next term eliminates any need to pass over a petition . . . that raises important and recurring issues of constitutional law. (quoted by Biskupic, 1996, p. J-3)

The Role of the Law Clerks

While each justice's interaction with the other justices is dependent on the schedule of oral arguments and conferences, the interaction with his or her law clerks is usually an intense hands-on experience. As Hoeflich (1996) noted, judges and their clerks come to form close professional and personal ties. The law clerks do legal research on pending cases; most draft opinions for their judges. All the recent justices, except Justice Stevens, have participated in a "certiorari pool," in which their clerks review the never-ending flow of certiorari petitions and draft summaries of them for their bosses' review.

The Origin of the Use of Law Clerks

Given the volume of material, it is hard to conceive of the justices doing their jobs without the aid of law clerks (although in 1889 the Court turned out 265 opinions without them [Rehnquist, 1987b]). The first Supreme Court justice to have a law clerk was Justice Horace Gray, who, in 1882, hired a recent Harvard Law School graduate at his own expense. But the phenomenon of the judicial clerkship was given prominence by Justice Oliver Wendell Holmes, Jr. Each year he would invite a new graduate of Harvard Law School to work with him as a combination of secretary, research assistant, and personal assistant (Hoeflich, 1996). The idea caught on; now almost all federal judges and some state judges have such clerks. Each Supreme Court justice now has four, if he or she wishes to.

As Posner (1996) has observed, people wondered what, if anything, Justice Holmes's clerks did "besides balancing his checkbook, listening to his anecdotes, reading to him at night and doing other valet-like services for this elderly and quite infirm man (Holmes retired at the age 90)" (p. 16). But the publication of Justice Holmes's voluminous correspondence with Justice Frankfurter (edited by Mennel and Compston, 1996) proved that Holmes sought out and occasionally followed the clerks' criticisms of his opinion drafts. Judge Posner noted in his review: "There was more give and take between justice and clerk than I had suspected, even on matters far from the law" (p. 16).

While Justices Gray and Holmes paid clerks out of pocket, it took 40 years for Congress to get around to appropriating money for each justice to have one clerk (at a salary of $3,600 a year, in 1922). Clerks are now paid more than 10 times that salary, but one of the extra benefits is that most law firms hiring the clerks after their time (usually one year) at the Supreme Court add a hefty bonus (perhaps $35,000) to the lawyer's initial corporate salary (Amon, 2001). Incidentally, recent law clerks are prohibited (for two years) from arguing a case before the Supreme Court, reflecting concern about a possible conflict of interest (Biskupic, 1994).

How Are Clerks Selected?

More than one thousand neophyte lawyers apply to be clerks each year (Biskupic, 1994), but only about 35 are chosen. Most justices select their law clerks with great care. A year's experience as a law clerk with another federal judge is a requirement for some justices (Thomas 1996); certainly a record of outstanding performance, such as a position on the law school's law review, is essential.

A "feeder system" exists, in which law professors at elite schools and lower court judges—mostly white males—suggest candidates to the justices (Mauro, 2000, 2004b). For example, in the first 12 years that Judge Laurence Silberman was on the U.S. Circuit Court for the District of Columbia, 20 of his clerks moved up to clerk at the Supreme Court (Bossert, 1997). In recent years, concern has been expressed about the resulting lack of diversity in the cohort of law clerks, both with regard to race and gender and with respect to the small percentage trained at non–Ivy League law schools (Mauro, 1999b, 2004b). For example, with respect to women as law clerks, few justices chose them until the 1980s; by the time he had retired from the bench in 1994, Justice Blackmun had hired more female law clerks than had all the other sitting justices combined (Greenhouse, 2005b).

The last decade has seen other changes; for the 2003–2004 term, 16 of 35 clerks were white males (including all four of Justice Scalia's clerks), but 19 had graduated from non–Ivy League schools. Yale and Harvard continued to lead (with eight and seven clerks, respectively), but the University of California's Boalt Hall had four, and the University of Texas two. The Court does not keep records or release demographic information on the clerks, but *Legal Times* has estimated that 8 of the 35 for the 2003–2004 term were from minorities (Mauro, 2003c, 2004b). Most of these were Asian American; only two were African American, and none were Hispanic. No Native American has ever served as a law clerk on the Court (Mauro, 2004b). Incidentally, during the term (2002–2003) that had the record of nine minority law clerks, seven of these were on the staff of the five justices who voted in the majority in the case of *Grutter v. Bollinger* (2003), which upheld the affirmative action program in the law school of the University of Michigan.

Are clerks who reflect the ideology of the justice more likely to be chosen? Edward Lazarus (1998) was a law clerk for Justice Blackmun for the 1988–1989 term; he has written a "tell-all" book about that year in the Court, which has received stinging criticism from those who believe he violated confidences and the ethics of the Court (Garrow, 1998; Rubin, 1998). Lazarus would say yes, that ideology plays a major role in selection. He noted that Justice Kennedy, for example, tends to choose members of the Federalist Society, a nationwide group of conservative law students and graduates. Certainly general compatibility is important. This is how Justice Rehnquist expressed it:

> Naturally I want clerks who get along with me and with whom I will get along, but this is not much of a problem; very few employees would fail to get along with their boss when the job lasts only one year. I also want clerks who will get along with my secretaries and aide, since the total population of our chambers is seven, and we all have to work together to be productive. I like clerks who seem to have a sense of humor, and who do not give the impression of being too sold on themselves. I ask the new clerks to begin work about the first of July, just at the time the Court will have recessed for the summer. One of the former law clerks stays for ten days to help break in the new ones, and the Court also conducts orientation sessions for them. I like to have mine come aboard in early July because for the next two months they really need to address themselves only to petitions for *certiorari* and not to preparation for argued cases or drafting of Court opinions or dissents. (2001, p. 232)

The Law Clerk's Duties

Clerks are usually hired by the spring before their term officially begins in October. However, all the clerks come on board in the summer, because the certiorari petitions inexorably arrive each week of every season. Lazarus described the clerk's initial summer as follows.

> For most clerks, this is the time for an orientation—to the extent that there is one. Immediately upon arriving in July, you begin to get the feel for your co-clerks, the justice's messenger, and the vitally important secretaries. This group, together with the justice, constitutes a "Chambers," the Court equivalent of a nuclear family, with all the risk of dysfunction that entails. At best, these are the people you will come to rely on, trust, and even love as you help support one another through a long year at close quarters. At worst, some become slackers, or rivals, or even enemies to be overcome as you try to do your own work as well as you can. Most Chambers, like most families, find some middle ground. (1998, p. 27)

The summer's work culminates the week before the official beginning of the Court's term, when the justices meet in a marathon session to dispose of the vast majority of the thousand or so petitions that have accumulated over the summer. In doing so, for most cases the judges follow the law clerks' recommendations.

The other important duty of the law clerks is to assist in the preparation of draft opinions or dissents. Here, how much of a role is played by the clerks is less clear, and partially dependent on the proclivities of the individual justice. Edward Lazarus, on the basis of his experience as one of Justice Blackmun's clerks, viewed the clerks as having a great deal of influence here. He boldly said: "Justices yield great and excessive power to immature, ideologically driven clerks, who in turn use that power to manipulate their bosses and the institution they ostensibly serve" (1998, p. 6).

What was most disturbing to Lazarus was the existence of what he called an influential "cabal" of law clerks who were motivated to use the proximity to their judges to achieve certain politically conservative goals, including the elimination of abortion rights and affirmative action, along with a more expeditious review of death-penalty appeals. Lazarus also described "the guerilla war that liberal and conservative clerks conducted, largely out of sight of those justices, to control the course of constitutional law" (p. 261). He wrote of the process as follows.

> Every year the behind-the-scenes commencement of the new fall term is a cocktail party for justices, clerks, and senior Court staff held roughly two weeks before the first oral argument in October. As clerks, we had already been at work for two months when Chief Justice Rehnquist, partway though the evening, gave us an official welcome and admonished us about our clerkly duties. . . .

I remember looking around the room and thinking how quaint such lofty abstractions sounded. By the time that Rehnquist spoke to us, the clerks of the October 1988 Term already were divided into two well-entrenched and hostile camps. Across the room we glared at each other, eyes hooded with distrust or outright contempt. . . . We had been through one execution and nearly came to blows over others narrowly averted. Preparation for the first set of argued cases was far enough along for us to know each other's policies and how cleverly we could pursue our respective views. Our thoughts were not on the "public trust" but of private strategies for the coming battle over the future of the Court. (p. 263)

Lazarus's book made two major claims about the law clerks: that they come to the Court with political biases and self-serving goals and that their actions significantly influence decisions purportedly made by their mentors. The first is easier to evaluate; certainly many clerks have already developed political orientations and, in fact, have been socialized to a particular point of view by exposure to influential law professors or having served as a clerk for a federal district judge or circuit court judge before clerking at the Supreme Court.

But what of Lazarus's second claim? Justice Louis D. Brandeis, back in the days when each justice had only one clerk, was asked why the public had such respect for the Supreme Court. "Because we do our own work here," was his response (Taylor, 1988, p. 22). Do justices still do their own work? Do clerks "spoon-feed" opinions to their justices, or do they merely suffer from an exaggerated sense of their own importance? It is true that clerks spend huge amounts of time on drafts that are acted upon by their justices, and often the first draft—in its selection of words, materials, and structure—sets the tone for the final one (Mauro, 1998). Lazarus reported the oft-told tale that during his last years on the Court, Justice Thurgood Marshall watched soap operas while in his chambers and let his clerks do almost everything other than cast his votes. Lazarus claimed that "rarely do the justices disassemble the drafts they've been given to examine" and that some judges function as nothing more than "editorial justices" (1998, p. 273). Justices would respond that these are the exception rather than the norm. For example, many justices have already given detailed instructions to their clerks about what should go into these drafts, and the negotiation and back-and-forth memoranda between justices during the opinion-drafting period reflect how involved each justice is on a day-to-day basis.

The issue of the impact of the clerks on opinions resurfaced in the spring of 2005 as a result of the opportunity for scholars and journalists to peruse the massive files of Justice Blackmun, made available by the Library of Congress in March 2004. In a cover story in *Legal Affairs* magazine, the Pulitzer Prize–winning historian David Garrow accused Blackmun of "a scandalous abdication of judicial responsibility" (2005, p. 34). His criticisms of the justice centered on two issues—that, in Garrow's view, "he ceded to his law clerks much greater control over his official work than did any of the other 15 justices from the last half-century whose papers are publicly available" (p. 28) and that he condoned written comments by his law clerks that disparaged other justices. Garrow's observations led to heated reactions by many of Justice Blackmun's former law clerks and by scholars who are intensively studying Blackmun's files (Mauro, 2005a). They note that just because his files do not involve instructions and responses by Blackmun to clerks' memos, it does not mean that the justice abdicated responsibility. Every day Blackmun had breakfast with his clerks and discussed his position on the current appeals; one of his former clerks, Dean Howard Koh of the Yale Law School, said that he "directed his clerks orally through myriad conversations each day" (p. 8). These conversations were not transcribed and hence do not appear in the judge's files (Kobylka, 2005). As Blackmun biographer Joseph Kobylka sees it, "[c]lerks add *input* into the process, but they *weren't the process*" (p. 60, italics in original).

Do clerks affect decisions? It depends. It depends on the justice, the clerk, the case, and even the time left in the term.

The Clerk's View versus the Justice's View

Not surprisingly, the justices view the importance of the clerks in a somewhat different light—really, a more nuanced light. Chief Justice Rehnquist (2001) described the opinion-writing process as follows.

> When I assign a case to myself, I sit down with the clerk who is responsible for the case and go over my conference notes with him. These notes are unfortunately not as good as they should be, because my handwriting, always poor, has with advancing age become almost undecipherable to anyone but me. But the combination of the notes and my recollection of what was said at conference generally proves an adequate basis for discussion between me and the clerk of the views expressed by the majority at conference, and of the way in which an opinion supporting the result reached by the majority can be drafted. After this discussion, I ask the clerk to prepare a first draft of a Court opinion and to have it for me in two days or two weeks. (2001, p. 261)

It is relevant at this point to note that in recent terms, the Court has provided written opinions for only 75 or so cases; thus each justice, on the average, is responsible for writing no more than nine majority opinions during the term. With four clerks, that means each clerk may be the point man or point woman on only two majority opinions during the term. (However, this analysis does not take into account concurrences or dissents, which can account for a significant part of opinion-writing time.)

Chief Justice Rehnquist also commented upon the nature of drafts by law clerks:

> I know that [the aforementioned two-week] deadline seems onerous to the new crop of law clerks when, after the October oral argument session, they undertake the first drafting of an opinion for me. I am sure that every clerk coming to work for a justice of the Supreme Court fancies that the opinion he [*sic*] is about to draft will make an important contribution to jurisprudence, and in the rare case he may be right. But with this goal in mind the clerk is all too apt to first ponder endlessly, and then write and rewrite, and then polish to a fare-thee-well. This might be entirely appropriate if his draft were a paper to be presented in an academic seminar, or an entry in a poetry contest. But it is neither of these things; it is a rough draft of an opinion embodying the views of the majority of the Court expressed at conference, a draft that I may very well substantially rewrite. It is far more useful to me to get something in fairly rough form in two weeks than to receive after four or five weeks a highly polished draft that I feel obligated nonetheless to substantially revise. (2001, p. 261)

Justice Rehnquist indicated that the opinion writing is truly an interactive process, and at least for him and his clerks, one in which his views and goals always remained salient:

> When I receive a rough draft of a Court opinion from a law clerk, I read it over, and to the extent necessary go back and again read the opinion of the lower court and selected parts of the parties' briefs. The drafts I get during the first part of the term from the clerks require more revising and editing than the ones later in the term, after the clerks are more accustomed to my views and my approach to writing. I go through the draft with a view of shortening it, simplifying it, and clarifying it. A good law clerk will include in the draft things that he might feel could be left out, simply to give me the option of making that decision. (2001, pp. 261–262)

Justice Rehnquist was aware of the criticisms regarding the use of law clerks to draft opinions:

> The practice of assigning the task of preparing first drafts of Court opinions to clerks who are usually just one or two years out of law school may undoubtedly and with some reason cause raised eyebrows in the legal profession and outside it. Here is the Supreme Court of the United States, picking and choosing with great care less than one hundred of the most significant cases out of seven thousand presented to it each year, and the opinion in the case is drafted by a law clerk! I think the practice is entirely proper;

the justice must retain for himself control not merely of the outcome of the case but of the explanation for the outcome, and I do not believe this practice sacrifices either.

I hope it is clear from my explanation of the way that opinions are drafted in my chambers that the law clerk is not simply turned loose on an important legal question to draft an opinion embodying the reasoning and the result favored by the clerk. Quite the contrary is the case. The clerk is given, as best I can, a summary of the conference discussion, a description of the result reached by the majority in that discussion, and my views as to how a written opinion can best be prepared embodying that reasoning. The clerk is not off on a frolic of his own, but is instead engaged in a highly structured task that has been largely mapped out for him by the conference discussion and my suggestions for him. (2001, p. 262)

Justice Rehnquist reflected on the complex nature of the relationship and the task:

This is not to say that the clerk who prepares a first draft does not have a considerable responsibility in the matter. The discussion in conference has been entirely oral and, as I previously indicated, nine statements of position suffice to convey the broad outlines of the views of the justices; but these statements do not invariably settle exactly how the opinion will be reasoned through. Something that sounded very sensible to a majority of the Court at conference may, when an effort is made to justify it in writing, not seem so sensible, and it is the law clerk who undertakes the draft of the opinion who will first discover this difficulty. The clerk confronting such a situation generally comes back to me and explains the problem, and we discuss possible ways of solving it. It may turn out that I do not share the clerk's dissatisfaction with the reasoning of the conference, and I simply tell him to go ahead. If I agree with the objection or difficulty he sees, we then undertake an exploration for alternative means of writing the same passage in the draft. Similarly, the conference discussion may have passed over a subsidiary point without even treating it; it is not until the attempt is made to draft a written opinion that the necessity of deciding the subsidiary question becomes apparent. Here again, we do the best we can, recognizing that the proof of the pudding will be the reaction of those who voted with the majority at conference when they see the draft Court opinion.

After I have finished my revisions of the draft opinion, I return it to the law clerk, who then refines and on occasion may suggest additional revisions. We then print the finished product with the correct formal heading for the opinion. (2001, p. 263)

In summary, it is difficult to make a statement about the clerks' role that applies equally to every justice. Some justices, according to their former clerks, do much or all of their own first drafts; Justices Scalia and Stevens are examples (Savage, 2004; Taylor, 1988). Justice Kennedy has said that he likes "to talk through the cases with my clerks" in detail as he considers different arguments (Taylor, 1988, p. 22). Justice Blackmun once suggested that Justice Stevens often outlines his opinion, gives it to his clerks, and tells them "You put the footnotes in" (p. 22). But whatever the input, the justice has the bottom-line responsibility; it is the justice who determines the rationale for his or her vote and opinion, and the justice who receives the plaudits or takes the blame for the final opinion.

The "Freshman Effect"

Inevitably, when a new justice is appointed, as John Roberts was for the term that began in October 2005, he or she is faced with new challenges. Some are intimidated by it. For example, even though Harry Blackmun had been a federal circuit court judge for more than a decade, when he moved to the Supreme Court he wrote a friend: "In my few short days in Washington it is very apparent that the technique and the pace and the attitudes are different. I do not know whether I shall be able to survive" (Greenhouse, 2005b, p. 54). How much of an adjustment process is there? And does the system help neophytes adjust?

What Is the "Freshman Effect"?

Some observers of the Court have speculated that a "freshman effect" operates on new justices (Dorff & Brenner, 1992; Maltzman & Wahlbeck, 1996b); in its most extreme form, the theory of the "freshman effect" proposes that, in learning the rules of the game, new justices initially rely on the opinions of others on the Court, and even emulate them. Walter Murphy observed:

> Once on the Court, the freshman justice, even if he [*sic*] has been a state or lower federal court judge, moves into a strange and shadowy world. An occasional helping hand—a word of advice about procedure and protocol, a warning about personal idiosyncrasies of colleagues, or the trustworthiness of counsel—can be helpful and appreciated. Particularly, if a new justice comes to Washington in mid-term, aid in securing clerical assistance and law clerks can be a means of establishing goodwill—with the new justice as well as his staff. (1964, p. 50)

New justices may be the recipients of attempts by more experienced justices to ingratiate themselves. As Murphy has noted, a gracious note of welcome might cause the new justice to be more willing to trust the elder's judgment in an upcoming vote. Murphy noted the following examples.

When Wiley Rutledge was appointed, Felix Frankfurter, who, along with Stone, had been reported as working for Learned Hand's promotion, wrote the new justice:

"You are, I am sure, much too wise a man to pay attention to gossip even when it is printed. And so I depart from a fixed rule of mine—which even Lincoln's life has taught me—not to contradict paragraphs. I do so not because I think for a moment that the silly statement that I am 'opposed to' you for a place on this Court has found any lodgement in your mind but to emphasize it as a striking illustration of sheer invention parading as information. The fact of the matter is that the opposite of that baseless statement could much more plausibly be asserted." (1964, p. 49)

Murphy also noted that when, three years earlier, Justice Frankfurter's nomination was confirmed by the Senate, Chief Justice Hughes, despite the fact that his work on the Court had been sharply criticized by Frankfurter, immediately wrote a welcoming note, as follows.

"Let me extend to you a warm welcome to collaboration in our work—for which you are so exceptionally qualified. We need you and I trust you will be able to take your seat at the opening of our next session on January 30th. If there is anything that I can do to aid in making your arrangements here, command me.

"With kindest regards, and looking forward with the greatest of pleasure to the renewal, in this relation, of the association with you that I had when you were with the Department of Justice many years ago." (1964, pp. 49–50)

Supposedly, the helping hand will lead to emulating the voting habits of the helper. It has frequently been noted that on his first term on the Court, Clarence Thomas voted that same way as Justice Scalia did on all but one of 81 cases (and the one deviation was on a very technical case). But Justice Thomas has now been on the Court for over a decade, and in the 2004–2005 term he voted the same way as Justice Scalia in 88 percent of the cases, so there is little evidence for an emulation effect solely from being a novice on the Court. The most parsimonious explanation is that on most matters before the Court, these two justices see things the same way.

One suggested example of this type of freshman effect was Harry Blackmun. Assigned the task of drafting the opinion for *Roe v. Wade* during his second year on the Court (in late December 1971), Blackmun agonized for months and months before distributing a draft (on May 18, 1972). And even that product troubled supporters of his viewpoint, including Justices Brennan and Douglas, who felt it failed to address the core issue. But this delay is not proof of a freshman effect; Blackmun agonized over almost all of his opinions, and throughout his long time on the Court was notoriously slow to produce his assigned drafts.

Another conception of the "freshman effect" was posited by Howard, who emphasized instability rather than emulation as its core; that is, "unstable attitudes that seem to have resulted from the process of assimilation to the Court. It is not uncommon for a new justice to undergo a period of adjustment, often about three years in duration, before his voting behavior stabilizes into observable, not to mention predictable, patterns" (Howard, 1968b, p. 45). Justice Thomas called his first five years his 'rookie year," saying: "In your first five years you wonder how you got there. After that you wonder how your colleagues got there" (O'Brien, 2000, p. 264). As described in chapter 8, Justice O'Connor seemingly took a period of time before she found her niche, and the drifting away from Justice Burger's views that is reflected in Justice Blackmun's later decisions can be considered an example of Howard's "adjustment to the Court."

Evidence for or Against

But a number of studies discount the freshman effect, as defined by Howard (Heck & Hall, 1981; Melone, 1990; Rubin & Melone, 1988; Scheb & Ailshie, 1985). David O'Brien's review gives several examples:

> Justice Antonin Scalia recalls his "biggest surprise" on arriving at the Court was "the enormity of the workload. I don't think I worked as hard in my life," he adds, "including first-year law school, as I did my first year on the Court." Yet Scalia did not give any indication of experiencing a freshman effect; far from being circumspect, he quickly staked out his sharply conservative positions. Nor did Justice Anthony Kennedy give any evidence of experiencing a freshman effect during his first few terms on the Court. He quickly aligned himself with other conservatives on the bench and wrote his fair share of opinions, including some important non-unanimous opinions dealing with such vexing issues as mandatory drug testing and racial harassment in the workplace. (2000, pp. 264–265)

In summary, the "freshman effect" appears to be present in some justices more than in others. Like many other phenomena described in this book, it is also influenced by the nature of the case. And if the justice has had previous experience as a judge, it is diminished somewhat.

Assignment of Cases to a New Justice

Nevertheless, it is plausible to expect some effects from the first year of service. For example, it is assumed that the chief justice assigns cases, partially, on the basis of the justices' ability to complete the task on schedule (Brenner & Palmer, 1988), and thus the chief justice may temper his assignment of cases to first-year justices.

When a freshman justice does draft an opinion, the reaction of the other justices may take his or her novice status under consideration. Maltzman, Spriggs, and Wahlbeck speculated: "Freshman authors, we suggest, are likely to receive different responses from justices than their senior colleagues. . . . [J]ustices may seek to establish a cooperative relationship with the new justice through their responses to the new justice's majority drafts. Deference is one way of accomplishing such a goal" (2000, p. 74).

Dissenting Opinions

The Court strives for unanimity. Chief Justice Warren felt the urgency of a unanimous decision in the *Brown v. Board of Education* (1954) case and finally achieved it through Herculean efforts to persuade the laggards. But unanimity is achieved in only 30–40 percent of the decisions. Both concurring and dissenting opinions may weaken the impact of the majority. Concurrences, in effect, say the majority decision is correct but for the wrong reasons; dissents, of course, even reject the wisdom of the majority.

What determines that a justice will write a dissenting opinion? The reasons are many, beyond his or her basic disagreement with the outcome. Among the determinations are the following.

1. *The seriousness of the issue at hand.* If a justice disagrees with the majority, he or she is more likely to write a dissent if the issue at hand is an important one than if it is minor. Justice Brennan, in his last years on the Court, was more frequently in the minority, but he chose to avoid the acrimony of a dissent in some cases in order to preserve the goodwill he had. The decision whether to dissent is related to the process of strategic voting described in chapter 6.

But sometimes issues are so important that dissents cannot be avoided. Justice William O. Douglas wrote: "When justices do not agree, it is a sign that they are dealing with problems on which society is itself divided. It is the democratic way to express dissident views" (1961, p. 54).

2. *The relative clarity or ambiguity of the issue at hand.* In the case of *Chicago v. Morales* (1999), dealing with an ordinance about loitering by gangs in Chicago, the Court held oral arguments in December 1998 but did not distribute its decision until June 1999; even then, the Court announced a majority opinion, three concurring opinions, and two dissents. Thus six of the nine justices had a different take on the issues involved; the ordinance not only unleashed fundamental values about individual rights versus society's need for protection but was ambiguous and subject to a variety of interpretations.

3. *The time in the term.* The pace gets more frantic as the term comes to an end. With three weeks left in the 2004–2005 term, approximately 25 cases still needed to be resolved before the term recessed. In June 1982, Justice Rehnquist sent a note to Justice Marshall, who was preparing the majority opinion in a child welfare case: "If this were November rather than June, I

would prepare a masterfully crafted dissenting opinion exposing the fallacies of your . . . discussion. Since it is June, however, I join" the majority opinion (Biskupic, 2004, p. 2A).

4. *The composition of the Court.* The frequency with which a given justice publishes dissents is a function of the ideological balance of the Court, as will be illustrated in a later discussion concerning Justice Rehnquist.

5. *The personality of the individual justice.* Among current justices, Justice Scalia is the one whose dissents get the most attention, and his rationale for writing dissents will be discussed later in this section. But the justice who wrote the most dissents during the 11–year period from 1994 through 2005 that saw no replacements on the Court was Justice Stevens, who has said that he writes dissents because they expose holes in the thinking of the majority, they strengthen the conviction of those who disagree, and they further widen debate (Associated Press, 2001b).

Dissents are increasingly a part of the day-to-day life of the Court. Interestingly, those justices who historically were labeled the "Great Dissenters" disagreed publicly with the majority much less often than some of the more recent justices; for example, Oliver Wendell Holmes, Jr., dissented an average of 2.4 times per term, Brandeis 2.9, and the first John Harlan 3.5. These may be compared with Justice Stevens, who routinely dissents from 20 to 25 times a term, even though the number of cases is much smaller (O'Brien, 1999). Dissents are not determinative; the majority rules. But dissents may provide a key to what is happening beneath the surface; they can be harbingers of majority decisions in the future, and later majority opinions may quote them, even though they lack the force of law (Greenhouse, 1990). David O'Brien amplified this point:

> The author of a concurring or dissenting opinion, by comparison, does not carry the burden of speaking for the Court. Comparatively speaking, the dissenter, in Justice Cardozo's words, "is irresponsible. The spokesman of the Court is cautious, timid, fearful of the vivid word, the heightened phrase. . . . Not so the dissenter. . . . For the moment he is the gladiator making a last stand against the lions." Dissenting opinions, in the view of Hughes, one who rarely wrote dissents, appeal "to the brooding spirit of the law, to the intelligence of a future day, when a later decision may possibly correct the error into which the dissenting judge believes the Court to have been betrayed." A dissenting opinion is a way of potentially undercutting the majority's opinion, but also a potentially useful tactic in negotiating with other justices: for the threat of a dissent may persuade the majority to narrow its holding or tone down the language of its opinion. Some cases, of course, are "small fish," and a justice may not write a dissent in the hope of persuading the case-author to side with him in some future case. Justice Pierce Butler, for instance, once wrote

to his colleague: "I voted to reverse. While this sustains your conclusion to affirm, I still think reversal would be better. But I shall in silence acquiesce. Dissents seldom aid in the right development of the law. They often do harm. For myself I say: 'I lead us not into temptation.'" (1997, p. 46)

Of course, on many occasions, judges cannot accommodate their views to the majority. The decision to dissent is illustrative of the centrality of the person–situation interaction. During his early terms of the Court, Justice Rehnquist was known as "the Great Dissenter" by his law clerks because of the number of times he was in the minority. But with the ideological shift in the Court's membership, the number of his dissents diminished, and as he neared the end of his years as Chief Justice, his views on federalism dominated in decisions involving acts of Congress and states' rights.

Individual Justices' Views on Dissents

The decision whether or not to write a dissent is an individualized one. In the last decade of their service on the Court, the triumvirate of Justices Brennan, Marshall, and Blackmun were increasingly in the minority with respect to cases involving conflicts between individual rights and state power. Justice Blackmun often wrote strong and emotional dissents; Justice Brennan kept trying to win majority support; and Justice Marshall seemed to be resigned to the unwanted outcome and shifted his influence attempts to the public. One former law clerk described Marshall's reaction as follows: "Unable to exert much influence beyond casting his vote, Marshall reacted as many proud people would: instead of futilely trying to influence his colleagues inside the Court, he concentrated on making sure that his views reached the public through the pages of the *United States Reports*" (Tushnet, 1992, pp. 2109–2110).

The decision to write a dissent, rather than simply signing on to someone else's dissent, may reflect a number of motives. Justice Stevens is "an enigmatic independent jurist" (Smolla, 1995, p. 12) who feels the need to provide a separate opinion when he is in the minority, or even when he is in the majority. In contrast, Justice Scalia's dissents often reflect attacks on the logic or conclusions of the majority opinion; he rarely reflects a desire for compromise or conciliation. Often, his dissents explicitly reflect his values and clearly take sides on issues that divide the country; in his dissent to the decision in *Lawrence v. Texas* (2003), which threw out laws criminalizing homosexuality, he declared himself to be on the side of those "who do not want persons who openly engage in homosexual conduct as partners in their business, as scoutmasters for their children, and teachers in their children's schools, or as boarders in their homes" (Broder, 2003, p. 10B). In the Michigan law school affirmative action case (*Grutter v. Bollinger*, 2003), he sarcastically wrote that "the non-minority individuals who are deprived of a legal education, a civil service job or any job at all by reason of their skin color will surely understand" (Broder, 2003, p. 10B). In a very candid article Justice Scalia made his satisfactions clear:

> To be able to write an opinion solely for oneself, without the need to accommodate, to any degree whatever, the more-or-less differing views of one's colleagues; to address precisely the points of law that one considers important and *no others*; to express precisely the degree of quibble, or foreboding, or disbelief, or indignation that one believes the majority's disposition should engender—that is indeed an unparalleled pleasure. (1994, p. 42, italics in original)

Justice Scalia, in dissents, has described one of Justice O'Connor's opinions as "irrational" and several of Justice Kennedy's as "incoherent" or "terminal silliness." Once, as Scalia dominated oral arguments—as is his custom—Justice Powell turned to Justice Marshall and asked: "Do you think he knows the rest of us are here?" (Cooper, 1995, p. 47).

The case of *Lee v. Weisman* (1992) also reflected Justice Scalia's outrage when things don't go his way. This case dealt with the legality of including a prayer as a part of a public school graduation ceremony. A court action (a temporary restraining order) had been initiated by the father of 14-year-old Deborah Weisman four days before her graduation from middle school; he sought to bar the school board from the practice of inviting members of the clergy to give invocations and benedictions at the high school and middle school ceremonies. The Constitution, of course, prohibits the establishment of a state religion. But do these actions reflect that?

The case eventually made its way to the Supreme Court, which ruled that prayer in the public schools carries an acute risk of indirect and subtle coercion and that high school students who wished to abstain would suffer real injury if forced to pray in a way antithetical to their consciences; in fact, the majority decision bolstered this "common assumption" (*Lee v. Weisman*, 1992, p. 2659) with three research articles from prominent psychological journals, claiming that the articles showed that "adolescents are often susceptible to pressure from their peers toward conformity, and that the influence is strongest in matters of social convention" (p. 2659). The majority opinion, after a 5 to 4 vote, was written by Justice Kennedy.

In his dissenting opinion, Justice Scalia had some sharp remarks for the majority's opinion about what he called "psycho-coercion" (p. 2685). Calling it a "jurisprudential disaster" (p. 2685), he felt that Justice Kennedy completely misunderstood the nature of religious coercion . He argued that historically coercion meant requiring colonists to adopt a particular religious orthodoxy and to provide financial support to a state church under threat of penalty (p. 2683). That brand of coercion, he added, "is readily discernible to those of us who have made a career of reading the disciples of Blackstone rather than of Freud" (p. 2684). Thus, he concluded, the majority's coercion test "suffers from the double disability of having no roots whatever in our peoples' historic practice, and being as infinitely expandable as the reasons for psycho-therapy itself" (p. 2685). (This was not the only time that Justice Scalia has gratuitously attacked psychology.)

Many would agree with Justice Jackson's position that "each dissenting opinion is a confession of failure to convince the writer's colleagues, and the true test of a judge is his influence in leading, not in opposing, his court" (1961, p. 28). If this is the case, Justice Scalia is often a failure. Certainly Justice Scalia's position on dissents is in keeping with his avoidance of coalition building. Law professor Rodney Smolla has offered this analysis of Scalia:

> In the end, his color and candor may at once define Justice Scalia's strengths and limitations. He does not appear to build coalitions easily among his colleagues. With the possible exception of Justice Clarence Thomas, who often does join with him, Scalia has not formed lasting or consistent alliances with others on the Court who might be thought to share his general inclination toward conservatism, such as Chief Justice Rehnquist or Justice Kennedy. His willingness to attack his colleagues in dissenting opinions with bitter derision might, some Court watchers argue, interfere with his ability to work behind the scenes to create solid voting blocs on the Court. (1995, p. 11)

Minority Opinions and Degree of Cognitive Complexity

Are dissenting opinions, like the aforementioned one by Justice Scalia, simple and sincere? Writings can be analyzed on the basis of whether they are cognitively simple or complex. *Conceptual complexity* (also called *integrative complexity*) is defined on the basis of two cognitive structural variables: dif-ferentiation and integration. Philip Tetlock and his colleagues explained:

> Individuals at the simple end of the complexity continuum tend to rely on rigid, one-dimensional, evaluative rules in interpreting events, and to make decisions on the basis of only a few salient items of information. Individuals at the complex end of the continuum tend to interpret events in multidimensional terms and to integrate a variety of evidence in arriving at decisions. (Tetlock, Bernzweig, & Gallant, 1985, p. 1228)

Thus, a person reflecting differentiation recognizes that multiple per-spectives on an issue exist, and the person's use of integration refers to his or her recognition of conceptual relations among differentiated dimensions (Gruenfeld, 1995).

For example, a judge analyzes a case in an undifferentiated manner when he or she focuses all attention on one issue or theme. For Tetlock and colleagues, a more differentiated approach is reflected in a judicial opinion that recognizes the existence of reasonable arguments on both sides of a controversy. They wrote:

"Integration refers to the development of complex connections among differentiated characteristics. Differentiation is thus a necessary condition for integration" (1985, p. 1231).

The published opinions of Supreme Court justices can be "scored" on the basis of integrative complexity, and that is what Tetlock and his associates did. They selected the 25 justices who served on the Court between 1946 and 1978; eight opinions authored by each justice were analyzed. Four dealt with economic issues, and four with civil liberties issues. Most of the justices' opinions came from their first term on the Court.

What qualities might be associated with differences in integrative complexity in judicial opinions? As noted earlier, dissenting versus majority opinions is one possibility. This position argues that majority opinions need to be more integratively complex because they must represent viewpoints that are partially in conflict. Thus, one of their functions is strategic; the eventual majority opinion is a collaborative enterprise; the opinion writer responds to and incorporates responses from other justices. An implicit goal is to be encompassing, even if the decision is a narrow one. Furthermore, the majority opinion is a policy-making one; the author feels accountable for the positions espoused. In contrast, dissents reflect strongly held beliefs that justice has not been rendered. In a comment about senators, but applicable to dissenting justices, Tetlock and his colleagues wrote that those in the minority "had the rhetorical freedom to take strong, unqualified stands in opposition to the majority" (1985, p. 1235).

An example of this difference between the majority opinion and a dissent may be found in the case of *Yarborough v. Alvarado* (2004), dealing with the interrogation of a 17-year-old suspect who was not read his *Miranda* rights. The majority concluded that although he had been brought to the police station by his parents and had been questioned in a small room in the police station for two hours, he was free to leave at any time. Toward the end of the questioning he confessed his role in a carjacking that led to a murder. The majority opinion, by Justice Kennedy, acknowledged that there were arguments on both sides, and "fairminded jurists could disagree over whether Alvarado was in custody" (Greenhouse, 2004c, p. A17). But his conciliatory tone was not persuasive to Justice Breyer, who wrote an impassioned dissent, asking, "What reasonable person in the circumstances . . . could have thought to himself, 'Well, anytime I want to leave I can just get up and walk out'?" (Greenhouse, 2004c, p. A17).

Tetlock and his associates also proposed a second determinant: political ideology. Previous research, using speeches by legislative participants in the United States Senate and the British House of Commons, had concluded that advocates of right-wing causes were more likely to think in simple, value-laden, and absolutist patterns than were advocates of moderate or left-wing causes (Tetlock, 1983). According to this argument, right-wing political beliefs serve one of the functions of attitudes described in chapter 5, the ego-defensive function; they are a means of simplifying things and imposing order on a threatening external world and of dealing with unacceptable inner feelings. Although a tendency existed for extremists at either end of the spectrum to be lower in integrative complexity, the rigidity-of-the-right hypothesis was verified by the analysis of Supreme Court opinions done by Tetlock and his colleagues (1985). Both the liberals and the moderates on the bench wrote more integratively complex judicial opinions than did the conservatives. (The differences were substantially greater on economic than on civil rights issues.)

But majority opinions also differed in complexity from dissents. The latter were less integratively complex.

Gruenfeld (1995) has pointed out that during the period from which Tetlock's data were drawn, the Supreme Court was dominated by liberals and moderates. In the last three decades, the balance has shifted. Would the relationship between ideology and integrative complexity still hold? She sought to control for such factors. In her first study, Gruenfeld examined two majority and two minority opinions authored by each of the eight most liberal and the eight most conservative justices during the period from 1953 to 1990. She found that individual justices expressed lower levels of integrative complexity when writing minority opinions than when writing majority opinions. But, contrary to the findings of Tetlock and colleagues (1985), liberal and conservative justices did not differ in overall integrative complexity. As predicted from the foregoing discussion on the motives for dissents, more emotional intensity (measured through the use of verb modifiers, italics, and punctuation) was present in minority opinions, regardless of ideology.

The function of inclusiveness in majority opinions was examined in Gruenfeld's second study, which compared majority opinions in unanimous versus nonunanimous decisions. The latter had a higher level of integrative complexity. Unanimous decisions, as expected, were lower in complexity than nonunanimous decisions; the lack of dissent rendered differentiated cognitive processing less necessary. Overall, Gruenfeld's analysis found support for the conclusion that opinion status (majority versus minority) was more strongly related to integrative complexity than was political ideology.

Summary

In some ways, the justices of the Supreme Court resemble the faculty in a small department at a prominent academic institution. The justices have their law clerks, who emulate and often idolize them, just as the faculty have their graduate students; in both settings, there is much collaboration and interaction between the mentor and his or her apprentices. Close personal as well as professional ties are formed from both types of unions. The faculty members may or may not socialize with each other, just like the justices, but much information about them is transmitted between students of different faculty, just as the clerks for different justices may share gossip about their mentors. Like the justices, who are appointed for life, an increasing number of faculty are tenured, with the resultant job security. Faculty members are, in some respects, the final authority; they rule their classrooms, where they determine everything from curriculum to students' grades, and complaints about their performance have little recourse to a higher authority. They do spend time together in meetings, but more of their time is spent alone, or with their students, doing research or preparing reports on it. And they even nominally have summers off, just like the justices, although they will tell you—just as the justices will—that they are never fully free of their work responsibilities.

Even on the matter of collegiality, a small academic department may resemble the group of Supreme Court justices. Many departments may have their equivalents of Justice Scalia—a professor who makes intemperate comments at departmental meetings that often disparage his or her colleagues. But such comments are often tolerated—"That's just the way he is"—and the grant of tenure is like the justices' appointment for life, leading to a realization that the group is interdependent and its members have to live with each other for a long time.

So, in summary, justices are human beings who, like many other human beings, have their jobs as the central focus of their life, jobs that carry prestige and power but also exert a toll with respect to their pressure.

5

A Psychological Analysis
of Decision Formation

My fundamental commitment, if I am confirmed, will be to
totally disregard my own personal beliefs.—William H. Rehnquist
(November 3, 1972)

One Judge's Decision

Justice Clarence Thomas joined the Supreme Court under a cloud of controversy, and some of his decisions on the Court have perpetuated questions about
the desirability of his appointment. Perhaps his dissenting opinion in the case
of *Hudson v. McMillian* (1992), in his first term on the Court, received the
greatest number of raised eyebrows. His dissent in this case will be used to
illustrate one theory of how justices form their opinions.

Keith J. Hudson was an inmate at Louisiana's Angola State Penitentiary
in 1983. It was his claim that as he was being moved from one cell to another,
the prison guards beat him; one punched him in the mouth, eyes, chest, and
stomach, and a second officer restrained him but also kicked and punched
him. Hudson also alleged that a third correctional officer, the supervisor, did
nothing to stop the beating and, in fact, encouraged the other officers. An
examination revealed that Hudson's teeth were loosened, his dental plate was
partially cracked, and he received bruises and a swelling of his face, mouth,
and lips.

Given this report, the basic question would seem to be: Were his Eighth
Amendment rights to avoid cruel and unusual punishment violated by these
actions? However, when the Supreme Court granted certiorari, it limited its
review to a more specific question: whether the prisoner had to suffer a "significant" injury for the cruel and unusual punishment clause to apply. The
Court ruled, by a 7 to 2 vote that it is not necessary for a "significant" injury
to occur, that the Eighth Amendment was driven by a concern that even

prisoners be treated with decency, humanity, and civilized standards. The majority opinion was written by Justice O'Connor.

But Justice Thomas (joined by Justice Scalia) dissented. He noted that the magistrate judge who investigated the claims concluded that Hudson's injuries were "minor" and that the decision by the Fifth Circuit (rejecting Hudson's claims of cruel and unusual punishment) did not challenge the finding; thus he concluded that the "sole issue" in the case *was* the extent of the injury. His dissent even went further than that; as Gerber has noted, "the most significant aspect of Justice Thomas's dissenting opinion was his plainly stated view that the Eighth Amendment did not apply *at all* in the prison context" (1999, p. 120, italics in original). Justice Thomas argued that the original intent of the framers of the Constitution and the Eighth Amendment provision was to apply it only to torturous punishments meted out by statutes or judges' sentences; it was not until 1976 ("185 years after the Eighth Amendment was adopted" [*Hudson v. McMillian*, 1992, p. 20]) that the Court began to apply the claim to acts against prisoners while they were in prison. (In the 1976 case, *Estelle v. Gamble*, the prisoner had been denied medical treatment.)

Media publicity about Justice Thomas's dissent made him sound not only insensitive to the abuses of prisoners but also hypocritical, given his statement to the Senate Judiciary Committee at his confirmation hearing about observing prisoners from his EEOC office window and thinking "There but for the grace of God go I." A *New York Times* editorial criticizing him was titled "The Youngest, Cruelest Justice" (Thomas, 2001).

To be fair to Justice Thomas, it should be noted that his dissent stressed that such acts by prison guards were "immoral," "criminal," and "possibly remedial under other provisions of the Federal Constitution." The issue, to repeat, was the applicability of the Eighth Amendment; he wrote that this amendment "is not, and should not be turned into, a National Code of Prison Regulation" (*Hudson v. McMillian*, p. 22). His continued mentioning about what he felt was a misunderstanding of his position shows very human frustration on his part. As his biographer, A. P. Thomas, has noted,

> [y]ears later, Thomas still complained about the media's treatment of his *Hudson* dissent. He said in one speech, "I must note in passing that I can't help but wonder if some of my critics can read. One opinion that is trotted out for propaganda, for the propaganda parade, is my dissent in [*Hudson*]. The conclusion reached by the long arm of the critics is that I supported the beating of prisoners in that case. . . . How one can extrapolate these larger conclusions from the narrow question before the Court is beyond me, unless, of course, there's a special segregated mode of analysis." (2001, p. 479)

But in more recent dissents (in *Hope v. Pelzer* [2002] and in *Dcek v. Missouri* [2005]) Justice Thomas's image remained one of lacking sympathy for prisoners. The first of these cases dealt with the liability of Alabama prison guards who chained disruptive inmates to "hitching posts" and left them outdoors without food or water. In his dissent from a ruling of cruel and unusual punishment, Justice Thomas said that inmates were chained for a legitimate penological purpose, "encouraging compliance with prison rules while on work duty" (Associated Press, 2002, p. A6). The second case dealt with a Missouri procedure in which a defendant who had been convicted was brought in shackles and chains as the jury heard evidence about what sentence to give. While the Court ruled that this procedure should not be used unless there were "special circumstances," in a dissent Justice Thomas wrote: "My legal obligation is not to determine the wisdom or the desirability of shackling defendants, but to decide a purely legal question" (*Deck v. Missouri*, 2005, p. 2023).

The Legal Model

Do justices really pay attention to the intentions of the framers of the Constitution and to legal precedents in forming their opinions? Justice Thomas, along with Justice Scalia, is the prime proponent of what has come to be called the *legal model* of Supreme Court decision-making. In a speech at the University of Kansas in 1996, Justice Thomas said: "We are bound by the will of the people as expressed by the Constitution and the statutes." While he acknowledged that "reasonable minds can differ in their interpretation of the Constitution," he maintained that "there are right and wrong answers to legal questions" and "to be a judge is to exorcize the passions of a frail human being." One day after the *Bush v. Gore* decision was announced, he told a group of high school students that politics had played no role in the Court's decision (Lewis, 2000). Similarly, William Rehnquist expressed his position regarding whether justices ought to consider public policy needs in their decisions:

> The justices of the Supreme Court were not appointed to roam at large in the realm of public policy and strike down laws that offend their own ideas of what laws are desirable and what laws are undesirable. Justices of the Supreme Court have a great deal of authority, but it is not the authority to weave into the Constitution their own ideas of what is good and bad. (Weaver, 1990, p. 19)

The legal model assumes that the Court's decisions are based on the facts of the case, and that the justices consider these facts "in light of the plain meaning of statutes and the Constitution, the intent of the framers, and/or precedent" (Segal & Spaeth, 2002, p. 48). Thus, judges begin with a principle or rule of law as their premise and apply this premise to the facts and thus arrive at a decision (Frank, 1963). Note that adherents to the legal model describe not only how they see judges acting but how they *should* act; that is, they should interpret the law rather than *create* the law.

The legal model would suggest that in cases involving constitutional interpretation, the a decision usually has one of the following three bases.

1. *The intention of the framers of the Constitution.* The argument for originalism, as put forth by Justice Scalia (1997b), says that the Constitution is "an enactment that has a fixed meaning ascertainable through the usual devices familiar to those learned in the law" (p. 189). For example, when the majority of the Court ruled in *Maryland v. Craig* (1990) that the confrontation clause in the Constitution was not "absolute"—thus permitting children who had been sexually abused to testify via closed-circuit television so that they would not see their alleged attacker—Justice Scalia objected, claiming that the majority had read into the Constitution qualifications not intended by its framers.

2. *The meaning of the words.* This is akin to the first concern; the attempt is specifically to define the words of the Constitution according to the meaning they had when the document was written (Spaeth, 1972). For example, article 5 of the Bill of Rights declares that "no person shall be . . . deprived of life, liberty, or property, without due process of law"; Justice Scalia interprets this as a justification for the death penalty. That is, he interprets the statement that a person may be "deprived of life" by the state as reflecting the Founding Fathers' implicit endorsement of a death penalty.

3. *A logical analysis, or logical reasoning.* Benjamin Cardozo (1921), a Supreme Court justice from 1932 to 1938, wrote a book-length classification of factors that determine an individual judge's ruling. For him, logical analysis reflected the use of a rule or analogy and the use of precedents. Judges may ask: How does this case resemble past cases? What principle or rule applies? By studying rulings in previous cases, a judge may see something analogous in the case at hand. In such an approach, the place of precedent is central; according to Justice Cardozo, judges continually reaffirm the legal doctrine of *stare decisis*. Many are reluctant to overturn precedent—that is, to take completely new directions. It was widely recognized throughout the first half of the twentieth century that all-black schools in the South and elsewhere were not provided with the same resources as all-white schools, but the Supreme Court, in several decisions during this period, simply rejected those procedures on the basis that they were unequal, rather than overturning the *Plessy v. Ferguson* doctrine from 1896.

But Justice Cardozo also noted that in some cases precedent can be found to support both sides. For this and other reasons, justices may rely on additional factors for their decisions. For example, they recognize major changes in society, and these changes may make some precedents inappropriate. He used the term *sociological concerns* to refer to an awareness of changes in the predominant societal values that demand reinterpretations of the laws. For example, only in the decade of the 1990s was it articulated in this country that physically disabled people should have unfettered access to public buildings, elevators, and restrooms.

Political conservatives become upset when the legal model is not used as the guiding system for a judicial opinion. They fear that some judges have come to substitute their own values for the original intent of the authors of the

Constitution and the "plain meaning of the laws." In response to the majority decision in *Romer v. Evans* (1996), a decision that clarified the rights of homosexual persons, columnist Mona Charen wrote: "six members of the Court have obviously decided that they are free to legislate their preferences in the guise of applying legal principles . . . [but] courts are not supposed to interpret the law based on changing political and social fashions" (1996, p. 7B). Similarly, in his endorsement of a dissent by Justice Scalia, columnist George Will expressed his view that there were only two choices in interpreting the Constitution: "The meaning given it must either be decisively shaped by history—by the framers' intent, as illuminated by national traditions—or it must be determined by something other than the Constitution, meaning the justices' personal preferences" (1996, p. C11).

In the middle of the first decade of the twenty-first century, criticism by conservatives of judicial activism and of a lack of adherence to legal precedents increased, partly as a result of decisions that, in the opinion of critics, gave more attention to the laws in other countries than they did to the U.S. Constitution. Especially singled out for criticism were *Lawrence v. Texas*, in 2002, expanding gay rights, and *Roper v. Simmons*, in 2005, overturning the death penalty for adolescents. Capitalizing on a phrase coined by Judge Douglas Ginsburg in an obscure book review a decade earlier, some observers claimed the criticisms coalesced into what came to be called "the Constitution in Exile" movement. Regardless of whether an organized movement existed or not (Greve, 2005), the phrase became a convenient label for beliefs that recent decisions by some justices had failed, for example, to recognize religious practices in public life, to respect the autonomy of states, and to give adequate protection of property rights. Advocates of the movement wished to restore the Constitution to the position it purportedly held in the Supreme Court's decision-making before the Court acceded to President Roosevelt's New Deal. Interestingly, the height of publicity about the movement occurred right before the announcement of decisions in three cases, all of which were relevant to the goal of "returning the Constitution from exile." One dealt with property rights and eminent domain (*Kelo v. City of New London*, 2005), the other two with displays of the Ten Commandments in, or in the environs of, public buildings (*Van Orden v. Perry*, 2005; *McCreary County v. ACLU*, 2005).

This desire to return to bases for decisions prior to the New Deal certainly was congenial with that of the "originalists" on the Supreme Court, as Justices Scalia and Thomas want to interpret the Constitution to mean what they believe it meant when it was ratified in 1787.

Some justices (not Justices Thomas or Scalia) believe that the Constitution must accommodate to changing times and circumstances. Advocates of a "living Constitution" note that for the framers of the Constitution, the term "persons" referred to—and only to—white males who owned property. But advocates of the legal model see the adaptive approach as reflecting "nonoriginalism," and Justice Scalia sees the latter as an invitation to apply current societal values (1997b). Many judges, he believes, while searching for the original intent of the Constitution, have in fact imposed their own preferences onto the decisions they make. They may even disregard the "plain meaning" of the Constitution; for example, Justice Scalia noted: "No fewer than three justices with whom I have served have maintained that the death penalty is unconstitutional, *even though its use is explicitly contemplated in the Constitution*" (1997a, p. 46, italics in original).

But even Justice Scalia (1997b) acknowledges that even for those committed to originalism, avoiding the intrusion of one's own values is the hardest part of being a conscientious judge and that perhaps no judge succeeds entirely.

Questioning the Legal Model

The legal model aspires for judges to be objective and unprejudiced, and it assumes that they will be. Justice Felix Frankfurter, dissenting in the case of *West Virginia State Board of Edcuation v. Barnette*, wrote:

> As a member of the Court I am not justified in writing my private notions of policy into the Constitution, no matter how deeply I cherish them or how mischievous I deem their disregard. . . . It can never be emphasized too much that one's own opinion about the wisdom or evil of a law should be excluded altogether when one is doing one's duty on the bench. (1943, pp. 646–647)

But is it humanly possible to do so? Yes, but it depends on the case and the person. Some cases may not trigger prejudices or private notions of policy, and for these the legal model may effectively represent the jurist's approach. For example, consider the case of *Kansas v. Colorado*, which the Supreme Court decided to resolve in 2001. A dispute between these two states over diversion of water from the Arkansas River had seemingly been ameliorated by the passage of the Arkansas River Compact by Congress back in 1949. But for a number of years, Kansas had complained that Colorado had violated the compact. After the Court had so ruled in 1995, it remanded the case to a special master. But Kansas claimed that Colorado continued to violate the rules. In 2001, the Court again sided with Kansas, including a judgment that Colorado should pay interest on the damages accrued. While the question of an interpretation of the Eleventh Amendment was part of the issue at hand, the Court ruled unanimously, and the case appears to be a straightforward one reflecting an application of the law.

But most cases are not so clear-cut. Lawrence Baum has suggested that hard cases—those where the Constitution and precedents are less consistent—"give judges free rein to justify whatever decision best accords with their policy views" (1997, p. 66). An additional concern about the legal model stems from the fact that this model assumes that the intent of the framers is clear and discernible. Not all judges agree. Each article of the Constitution is remarkably succinct. What did the framers mean when they wrote that "life, liberty or property" could not be withdrawn "without due process?"

Some justices have acknowledged their human limitations (Simon, 1998). Speaking of the Court, Justice Robert Jackson once said: "We are not final because we are infallible, but we are infallible only because we are final" (Schwartz, 1996a, p. x). For Justice Oliver Wendell Holmes, Jr., law was nothing more than "the prophecies of what the courts will do in fact" (1897, pp. 460–461). That is, the institution and its statutes are not clear about what is permitted and prohibited; it is up to the judges to decide what they may say and may not do (Segal & Spaeth, 1993, p. 241).

For cases dealing with the interpretation of statutes, the legal model emphasizes either an analysis of the legislative history of the statute or analysis of its "plain meaning." Again, the possibility of bias many enter. Critics of the legal model emphasize the theme of this book: judges are human beings, hence not free always to be objective. Alan Barth expressed this point eloquently:

> Judicial judging is not encompassed by general expressions of principle and theory. Intuition, personal experience, surges of human sympathy are also influences upon decision. And, in the end, judges, like other human beings, are certain to be swayed by what they think, and feel, is *right*. The Supreme Court may be a court of law, but it is a court of justice, too. For justice must be the end of law. And law is but a reflection of ethical values. (1974, p. 192, italics in original)

A More Radical View: Decisions as Rationalizations

Jerome Frank was never a Supreme Court justice, but he served as a judge for many years and wrote extensively on the law. At the trial level, he proposed that "facts" are not objective; "they are what the judge thinks they are" (1963, p. xviii). At the appellate level, he questioned the legal model's view that the judge begins with some rule or principle of law as his or her premise. He wrote:

> Since the judge is a human being and since no human being in his [*sic*] normal thinking processes arrives at decisions (except in dealing with a limited number of simple situations) by the route of any such syllogistic reasoning, it is fair to assume that the judge, merely by putting on the judicial ermine, will not acquire so artificial a method of reasoning. Judicial judgments, like other judgments, doubtless, in most cases, are worked out backward from conclusions tentatively formulated. (p. 109)

That is, a judge may first arrive at a decision intuitively and only then "work backward to a major 'rule' premise and a minor 'fact' premise to see whether or not that decision is logically defective" (p. 184). Judge Frank's observations received support from a statement Chief Justice Hughes once made to Justice Douglas: "You must remember one thing. At the constitutional level where we work, ninety percent of any decision is emotional. The rational part of us supplies the reasons for supporting our predilections" (Douglas, 1980, p. 8).

Judge Frank proposed that judges were far more likely to differ among themselves on questions of fact than on questions of law. He quoted the comments of Supreme Court justice Samuel Miller, who served on the Court from 1862 to 1890: "In my experience in the conference room of the Supreme Court of the United States, which consists of nine judges, I have been surprised to find how readily these judges came to an agreement upon questions of law, and how often they disagree in regard to questions of fact" (Frank, 1963, p. 115).

An Example: What Are the Facts?

At the appellate level, it is presumed that the facts of the case are not at issue. But facts can intrude and take on a life of their own and thus influence judicial decisions. The case of *Ake v. Oklahoma* (1985) illustrates how two different justices can have different readings of the same set of "facts."

The Case

Glen Burton Ake had been convicted of the 1979 murder of an Oklahoma minister and his wife. Ake and an accomplice, Steven Hatch, had gained entrance to the couple's rural home on the pretext of needing to use the phone. They immediately pulled out guns, bound the family members with heavy twine, and terrorized them for several hours. Then, as the woman begged for mercy, Ake shot and killed both her and her husband. He also wounded the two children, shooting each in the back. At his trial, the prosecution was permitted to introduce testimony from a psychiatrist who concluded that Ake was sane, but Ake was denied a court-appointed psychiatrist for his defense. He appealed to the Supreme Court, claiming that due process required that the state provide access to a psychiatrist if a defendant using the insanity defense could not afford one.

Justice Marshall's "Facts"

At the judicial conference, Thurgood Marshall was assigned the task of writing the Court's opinion. Here is the section of his opinion in which he described the facts of the case:

> Late in 1979, Glen Burton Ake was arrested and charged with murdering a couple and wounding their two children. . . . His behavior at arraignment, and in other prearraignment incidents at

the jail, was so bizarre that the trial judge, *sua sponte*, ordered him to be examined by a psychiatrist "for the purpose of advising with the court as to [the psychiatrist's] impressions of whether the Defendant may need an extended period of mental observation." The examining psychiatrist reported: "At times [Ake] appears to be frankly delusional. . . . He claims to be the 'sword of vengeance' of the Lord and that he will 'sit at the left hand of God in heaven.'" The psychiatrist diagnosed Ake as a probable paranoid schizophrenic and recommended a prolonged psychiatric evaluation to determine whether Ake was competent to stand trial.

In March, Ake was committed to a state hospital to be examined with respect to his "present sanity," i.e., his competency to stand trial. On April 10, less than six months after the incidents for which Ake was indicted, the chief forensic psychiatrist at the state hospital informed the court that Ake was not competent to stand trial. The court then held a competency hearing, at which a psychiatrist testified: "[Ake] is a psychotic . . . his psychiatric diagnosis was that of paranoid-schizophrenic-chronic, with exacerbation, that is with current upset, and that in addition . . . he is dangerous. . . . [B]ecause of the severity of his mental illness and because of the intensities of his rage, his poor control, his delusions, he requires a maximum security facility within—I believe— the State Psychiatric Hospital system." The court found Ake to be a "mentally ill person in need of care and treatment" and ordered him committed to the state mental hospital.

Six weeks later, the chief forensic psychiatrist informed the court that Ake had become competent to stand trial. At the time, Ake was receiving 2000 milligrams of Thorazine, an antipsychotic drug, three times daily, and the psychiatrist indicated that, if Ake continued to receive that dosage, his condition would remain stable. The State then resumed proceedings against Ake. (*Ake v. Oklahoma*, 1985, p. 1090, italics in original, citations deleted)

Nothing in this description suggests the possibility that Ake was faking or malingering. We are led to believe that his symptoms are genuine, and the opinion cites the diagnosis, prior to medication, of Ake as a paranoid schizophrenic person. Justice Marshall's view, concurred with by the majority of the justices, was that Ake was entitled to the assistance of a state-paid psychiatrist when he claimed, at his trial, insanity as his defense.

Justice Rehnquist's "Facts"

Justice Rehnquist wrote a dissenting opinion in which he questioned both the breadth of the decision and the majority's interpretation of the facts: "I do not think the facts of this case warrant the establishment of such a principle;

and I think that even if the factual predicate of the Court's statement were established, the constitutional rule announced by the Court is far too broad" (p. 1098). Here is Justice Rehnquist's description of the facts:

> Petitioner Ake and his codefendant Hatch quit their jobs on an oil field rig in October 1979, borrowed a car, and went looking for a location to burglarize. They drove to the rural home of Reverend and Mrs. Richard Douglass and gained entrance to the home by a ruse. Holding Reverend and Mrs. Douglass and their children, Brooks and Leslie[,] at gunpoint, they ransacked the home; then they bound and gagged the mother, father, and son, and forced them to lie on the living-room floor. Ake and Hatch then took turns attempting to rape 12-year-old Leslie Douglass in a nearby bedroom. Having failed in these efforts, they forced her to lie on the living room floor with the other members of her family.
>
> Ake then shot Reverend Douglass and Leslie each twice, and Mrs. Douglass and Brooks once, with a .357 magnum pistol, and fled. Mrs. Douglass died almost immediately as a result of a gunshot wound; Reverend Douglass's death was caused by a combination of the gunshots he received, and strangulation from the manner in which he was bound. Leslie and Brooks managed to untie themselves and to drive to the home of a nearby doctor. Ake and his accomplice were apprehended in Colorado following a month-long crime spree that took them through Arkansas, Louisiana, Texas, and other states in the western half of the United States. (pp. 1098–1099)

Conclusions

Even Justice Rehnquist's description does not reflect the full extent of the criminal actions of Ake and Hatch. They stole $1,500 at gunpoint from another Oklahoma family, and two weeks after the Douglass murders, Ake shot two Texas surveyors after Hatch refused to do so. They were finally captured in northwest Colorado after they had driven a stolen car into a snowdrift.

In contrast to Justice Marshall's opinion (which did not even mention the attempted rape), Justice Rehnquist gave a description of the actual crime; he named the victims, thus personalizing them; and he used emotion-laden terms such as "brutal murders" and "month-long crime spree" (p. 1100). In contrast to the majority opinion, which is free of emotion, Justice Rehnquist's dissent—though within the bounds of legal commentary—struggled to suppress the outrage the writer felt over the perversion of justice resulting from the decision to permit Ake to have a court-appointed psychiatrist. For it is clear that Justice Rehnquist doubted the validity of Ake's claim of insanity; he noted:

- Three days before he was extradited from Colorado to Oklahoma on November 20, 1979, Ake gave the local sheriff a detailed statement about the crime which, when typed, ran to 44 pages. No suggestion of insanity is present in this detailed confession.
- Ake appeared in court, along with his codefendant, on December 11; at that time, Hatch was transferred to the state hospital for a 60-day observation period to determine his competency to stand trial. No such request was made by Ake or his attorney.
- It was not until the formal arraignment on February 14, 1980—almost three months after the extradition—that Ake began to be, in Rehnquist's description, "disruptive."
- During Ake's trial in June 1980, the prosecutor produced the testimony of a cellmate of Ake, who reported that Ake had told him that he was going to "play crazy." The jury was not allowed to hear the testimony of the cellmate.

Justice Rehnquist concluded his review by saying: "The evidence . . . would not seem to raise any question of sanity unless one were to adopt the dubious doctrine that no one in his right mind would commit murder" (p. 1100). But no justices concurred in Rehnquist's dissent, and the Oklahoma courts were told to give Ake a second trial. At this trial, in 1986, a court-appointed psychiatrist testified that he diagnosed Ake as a paranoid schizophrenic who had been hearing voices since 1973. Despite this testimony, the jury in the second trial also found him guilty, and Ake was sentenced to life in prison. Ironically, his accomplice, Steven Hatch—who did not commit any of the murders—was convicted in a separate trial and sentenced to death. He was executed in August 1996.

Explaining Differences through the Concept of Motivated Reasoning

How can two justices see one case in such different ways? The concept of *motivated reasoning* offers an explanation. Social psychologist Ziva Kunda proposed that motivation may affect reasoning through the reliance on what she called a biased set of cognitive processes. Thus motivation—defined as "any wish, desire, or preference that concerns the outcome of a given reasoning task" (1990, p. 480)—can affect the forming of impressions, the evaluating of evidence, and the making of decisions. That is, "[p]eople rely in cognitive processes and representations to arrive at their desired conclusions, but motivation plays a role in determining which of these will be used on a given occasion" (p. 480). Kunda wrote:

> People do not seem to be at liberty to conclude whatever they want
> to conclude merely because they want to. Rather, I propose that
> people motivated to arrive at a particular conclusion attempt to be

rational and to construct a justification of their desired conclusion
that would persuade a dispassionate observer. They draw the desired
conclusion only if they can muster up the evidence necessary to
support it. . . . In other words, they maintain an "illusion of objec-
tivity." . . . To this end they search memory for those beliefs and
rules that could support their desired conclusion. (pp. 482–483)

Can such an analysis apply even to Supreme Court justices, who are experts on the issue at hand and very involved in their task? Kunda's review
concluded that people can process information in depth yet be biased at the
same time. Confronted with the briefs in the *Ake* case, Justice Marshall drew
upon his lifelong commitment to the rights of defendants and minorities; he
was influenced by the fact that the prosecution had a psychiatrist while the
defendant did not. In contrast, the reports of Ake's "crime spree" and his intent to fake a psychosis jumped out at Justice Rehnquist as he read the briefs.

The Attitudinal Model

The legal model relies on precedents. But the decision whether a given precedent is applicable is a subjective one (Simon, 2002). For example, in the case
of *Lassiter v. Department of Social Services* (1980), the majority opinion concluded that a set of previous cases "speaks with one voice," whereas the minority felt they most certainly did not. The challenge to the assumption that
a judge dispassionately and objectively considers the issues is manifested in
its most detailed form in what has come to be called the *attitudinal model* of
judicial decision-making.

Attitude Formation

A book by Jeffrey Segal and Harold Spaeth, *The Supreme Court and the Attitudinal Model* (published in 1993 and revised in 2002), proposed that judges'
decisions are based on the facts of the case but only "in light of the ideological
attitudes and values of the justices" (1993, p. 32). Clayton has summarized
the essence of this book:

Analyzing Supreme Court decisions over a thirty-year period,
Segal and Spaeth found that justices' votes within a particular issue
or policy domains approximate a "unidimensional structure" (that
is, justices' voting patterns remain stable over time), and that
justices' voting patterns correspond closely to their *a priori* policy
preferences. (1999, p. 24)

Any comprehensive explanation of attitudes and values must deal with their
formation. Why that particular attitude or value? How was it formed? What
needs or motivations does the formation of that value or attitude satisfy?

A value may be thought of as a standard for decision-making; values are broad and do not have specific objects. In contrast, an attitude has generally been defined as an evaluative reaction to a denotable object. Here "object" may be specific and tangible or general and abstract. One's values with regard to automobiles may emphasize aesthetic values and appearance; thus, that person may have a specific, favorable attitude toward, for example, a Ford Thunderbird or a Corvette. But the object can be more general; judges can have attitudes about ideas, arguments, and conclusions. Although conceptual distinctions are sometimes made between the terms *attitude* and *opinion*, the usage here will be *attitude*—it is more general; and *opinion* will be reserved for the legal reference to the term. Thus a judicial opinion, the written statement of a judge's decision on the disposition of a case, may be partially based on that judge's attitude—his or her evaluative reaction to a stimulus object (legal briefs, in this context). In written form, the judicial opinion becomes the behavioral component of the attitude.

Functional Theories of Attitude Formation

Two rather similar functional theories of attitude formation have been developed by social psychologists, one by Katz and Stotland (Katz, 1960, 1968; Katz & Stotland, 1959) and one by Smith, Bruner, and White (1956; for a contemporary review of these approaches, see Eagly & Chaiken, 1998, pp. 303–309). Each theory has proposed that attitudes can serve one or more functions, as follows.

First, attitudes may serve an instrumental, adjustive, or utilitarian function. According to Katz, a person develops a positive attitude toward objects that are useful in meeting his or her needs. If an object thwarts the person's needs, he or she develops a negative attitude toward it.

Second, attitudes may serve an ego-defensive, or externalization, function. Here, Katz's theory is influenced by psychoanalytic considerations. An attitude may develop or change in order to protect a person from acknowledging central truths about himself or herself, or the harsh realities of the person's external world. For example, derogatory attitudes toward out-groups and minority groups may serve as a means of convincing oneself of one's own importance. Without utilizing psychoanalytic supports, Smith and colleagues (1956) see attitudes functioning in a similar way, permitting the externalization of reactions.

For example, with respect to the position of Justice Clarence Thomas on affirmative action, some observers see a paradox. In his professional and career advancement, Justice Thomas benefited from affirmative action policies; yet his Court decisions and votes have staunchly opposed these policies. Certainly he does not see affirmative action as the reason he has achieved these goals; he once said that the worst experience of his life occurred when white students at the Yale Law School told him that he had been admitted there only because of racial quotas (Thomas, 2001, p. 141). (At the time of his admission, Yale had set aside up to 10 percent of the places in the entering law school class for members of minority groups; they competed against each other, rather than whites, for these openings.) It was during this period at law school that he began to develop his views about the invidious effects of affirmative action upon its recipients; he has complained to his friends about the condescending way he was treated by white liberals. Is it possible that his adamant stance serves an ego-defensive function?

A third function is the knowledge appraisal or object appraisal function. Attitudes may develop or change in order to "give meaning to what would otherwise be an unorganized chaotic universe" (Katz, 1960, p. 175). This would especially happen when a problem cannot be solved without the information associated with the attitude. Smith and colleagues (1956) saw this function as a "ready aid in 'sizing up' objects and events in the environment from the point of view of one's major interests and going concerns" (p. 41). Thus, categorizing objects or events is done more efficiently, and no time is spent in figuring out afresh how one should respond. Object appraisal thus "stresses the role that gathering information plays in the day-to-day adaptive activities of the individual" (Kiesler, Collins, & Miller, 1969, p. 315).

Put simply, attitudes function to help us with our daily activities. Each of us needs to "size up" relevant stimuli. A judge, when presented with a brief, possesses a personal template of attitudes by which to evaluate it: What are the brief's major claims? Are they supported by logic, by precedent, by past experience? Are they articulated clearly? What will be the outcome if they are accepted? Similarly, some attorneys have appeared before the Supreme Court so many times—Professor Laurence Tribe of Harvard Law School has made 30 oral arguments before the Court—that the justices have some sense of what to expect when one of these experienced advocates surfaces, regardless of the type of case.

Fourth, there is the value-expression function. Katz theorized that individuals gain satisfaction from expressing themselves through their attitudes. A highly cynical person may focus on those reports in the media that he or she finds ridiculous and use every opportunity to lambaste them to friends and colleagues. Beyond this, the expression of attitudes helps form one's self-concept. Smith and colleagues (1956) diverged most widely from Katz on this point. To them, the expressive nature of attitudes does not mean that any need for expression exists but rather that a person's attitudes "reflect the deeper-lying patterns of his or her life" (p. 38).

Judges who inhabit the same bench can differ in their deeply held values, and this may help to explain some of their disagreements on decisions—for example, whether they are considered activist judges or not. Consider this statement by Chief Justice Warren: "The beginning of justice is the capacity to generalize and make objective one's private sense of wrong" (quoted by Menez, 1984, p. 2). Contrast it with the following statements by nonactivist (sometimes called "strict constructionist") judges:

"The Constitution is not a panacea for every blot upon the public
welfare" (dissenting opinion by Justice John M. Harlan II in
Reynolds v. Sims, 1964)

"The Constitution does not provide judicial remedies for every social
and economic ill" (opinion by Justice Lewis Powell in *San Antonio
Independent School District v. Rodriguez,* 1973)

An Example of Values in Conflict:
The Case of *Michael H. v. Gerald D.* (1989)

Decisions and dissents in some cases lay bare the differing values and attitudes
of justices. Consider the case of *Michael H. v. Gerald D.* In May 1976, Carole
D., an international model, and Gerald D., a top executive for a French oil
company, married in Las Vegas; they lived in Playa del Rey, California. In 1981
a child was born to Carole D., while she was married to and living with Gerald
D. But she had an ongoing affair with a neighbor, Michael H., and believed
him to be the father of her child. A blood test that year found a 98 percent
probability that he was the father.

From 1981 to 1984, Carole D. and her child, Victoria, lived in a "variety
of quasi-family units," including Michael H.'s home, occasionally with Gerald
D., and at other times with another man. In October 1981, six months after
Victoria was born, Gerald D. moved to New York City, but Carole remained
in California. In January 1982, she and her child visited Michael H. in St.
Thomas, in the Virgin Islands, where he had business interests and maintained
a residence. From March to July 1983, she lived with her husband in New York
City, but in August she returned to California and became involved with
Michael again. In June of 1984, she reconciled with Gerald and joined him in
New York; they later had two children.

In November 1982, Michael H. sued to establish his paternity and visitation rights; Gerald D. countersued. The courts in California rejected Michael
H.'s request, and Gerald D.'s motion was granted a summary judgment, based
on California's statute that provided "the issue of a wife cohabiting with her
husband, who is not impotent or sterile, is conclusively presumed to be the
child of the marriage." (This law had been adopted more than one hundred
years earlier, in 1872.)

Michael H. appealed this decision to the U.S. Supreme Court, which decided to take the case. The issue thus facing the Court was: Does an unmar-
ried (apparent) father have a due process right to prove paternity against the
wishes of the married mother and her husband?

The determining opinion, written by Justice Scalia, upheld the California law; Michael H. was denied visitation rights. Justice Scalia has written that
the purpose of the Constitution "is to prevent future generations from lightly
casting aside important traditional values" (quoted by Nagel, 1994, p. 149).
At six different places in his opinion, Justice Scalia described the relationship

between Michael and Carole as "an adulterous affair." For him, the family is a sacrosanct concept, and the family is not, in his words, "a relationship established between a married woman, her lover, and their child during a three-month sojourn in St. Thomas or during a subsequent eight-month period, when, if he happened to be in Los Angeles, he stayed with her and the child" (*Michael H. v. Gerald D.*, 1989, p. 114).

Justice Brennan wrote a strong dissent to this opinion by Justice Scalia, and the values reflected in his dissent were as explicit as those of Justice Scalia. He described the relationship of Michael, Carole, and Victoria as a "family" and noted that they had lived together and Victoria had called Michael "Daddy." Brennan felt that to give constitutional significance to the legal status of marriage is "pinched." In doing so, Brennan reflected views he had expressed in previous decisions; for example, in *Eisenstadt v. Baird* (1972), he wrote: "if the right of privacy means anything, it is the right of the individual, married or single, to be free . . . to bear or beget a child" (p. 453).

Evidence for the Attitudinal Model

Some observers argue that, compared to trial justices or other appellate judges, Supreme Court justices have greater discretion to base their decisions on their values or on public policy goals. One of the advocates of the attitudinal model has written: "For a number of reasons, the Supreme Court's rule structures are such that the justices are freer than other political actors to base their decisions solely upon personal policy preferences" (Spaeth, 1972, p. 63). For example, they are appointed for life, they can be removed from office only with great difficulty, they don't seek higher office (with very few exceptions), and they have no higher level of judicial authority that can overturn or even criticize their decisions.

One of the earliest empirical demonstrations of evidence supporting the attitudinal model was the work of C. Herman Pritchett (1948), who analyzed Supreme Court decisions during Franklin Roosevelt's administration and showed that certain pairs of justices consistently voted the same way, whereas other pairs of justices consistently voted in opposite ways. Pritchett concluded that justices are "motivated by their own preferences" (p. xii). This trend has continued throughout the years. For example, as noted earlier, in the term that ended in June 2004, Justices Scalia and Thomas agreed with each other in 90 percent of the cases (in 96 percent of the criminal cases) and Justice Breyer agreed with Justice Ginsburg in 92 percent of the cases (and 93 percent of the criminal cases). The predictability of particular judges was further demonstrated by the work of Glendon Schubert in *The Judicial Mind* (1965) and *The Judicial Mind Revisited* (1974). The point that it was public policy preferences that were reflected in the votes was made explicit by the work of Rohde and Spaeth (1976), who went so far as to conclude that the Supreme Court's structure gives justices great freedom "to base their decisions *solely* upon personal policy preferences" (p. 72, emphasis added).

Typical of this line of research is a study of the ideological values of all justices from Earl Warren to Anthony Kennedy, based on newspaper editorials from the nation's leading newspapers (Segal & Cover, 1989). These were content-analyzed and coded to reflect whether the justice's position was liberal, moderate, conservative, or not applicable. Based on the content analysis, Justices Fortas, Brennan, and Marshall came out as the most liberal; Justices Scalia and Rehnquist were classified as the most conservative. The values for each of 18 justices were correlated with their votes on civil liberties cases; the resulting correlation was .80, indicating a high degree of relationship. (Civil liberties issues were those involving criminal procedure, civil rights, the First Amendment, due process, and privacy. Those votes that reflected the following were considered to be liberal votes: prodefendant, pro–civil liberties or civil rights claimant, proindigent, pro–Native American, or antigovernment in regard to due process or privacy.)

The Theme of Consistency in Decisions:
Justice Rehnquist and Justice Blackmun as Examples

The Consistent Values of William Rehnquist

Implied in the attitudinal model is the assumption that justices have "deeper-lying patterns" of values that are established before they reach the Court, and that these values are manifested in attitudes that lead to a consistent set of decisions on their part (H. Schwartz, 1988). Partly because of the length of his time on the bench—more than 30 years—Chief Justice Rehnquist may serve as one example to demonstrate this claim. In the eyes of those supporting the attitudinal model, the writings of Justice Rehnquist, going back almost 50 years—long before he was appointed a justice—reflected steadfast emphasis on the values of *property rights* and *states' rights*.

In most of his decisions, Justice Rehnquist did not support the claims of rights by individuals and minorities. Typical were his votes in the 2001–2002 term; here, the Supreme Court decided nine cases dealing with defendants' rights; Chief Justice Rehnquist voted to deny individual defendants their rights in all nine cases. He ruled for the government and against individuals in all four cases dealing with Fourth Amendment rights, and he voted against prisoners in six of the eight cases dealing with prisoners' rights. Even while he was been an associate justice, he "consistently denied claims of discrimination brought by women, aliens, and illegitimate children, whether such claims were based on civil rights statutes or the equal protection clause of the Fourteenth Amendment. More often than not, he . . . also denied claims of racial discrimination" (Davis, 1989, p. 20). For example, he voted to make women in the U.S. military meet higher standards for obtaining spousal support allotments than married men in the service had to meet (Schwartz, 1988). Likewise, he has throughout his career rejected the rights of homosexual persons; a quarter-century ago he compared homosexual persons with those who are suffering from measles (and hence are quarantined) (Mauro, 2004d; Murdoch & Price, 2001, p. 203), and since then he has repudiated gay rights in every case before the Court.

The attitudinal model proposes that such votes reflect a long history in the individual's development of a specific ideological perspective. While he was a law clerk for Justice Robert Jackson in 1954, Rehnquist drafted a memorandum in defense of the 1896 *Plessy v. Ferguson* decision that had justified racial segregation. He wrote:

> To those who would argue that "personal" rights are more sacrosanct than "property" rights, the short answer is that the Constitution makes no such distinction. To the argument made by Thurgood, not John, Marshall that a majority may not deprive a minority of its constitutional rights, the answer must be made that while that is sound in theory, in the long run it is the majority who all determine what the constitutional rights of the minority are. (Fiss & Krauthammer, 1982, pp. 14–15)

At his confirmation hearings, Rehnquist denied that the foregoing words reflected his own personal feelings, saying that, instead, he was drafting a position for his boss, Justice Jackson, as the Court considered the 1954 *Brown v. Board of Education* case (Schwartz, 1989). But in that memorandum Rehnquist also wrote: "I realize that it is an unpopular and unhumanitarian position for which I have been excoriated by 'liberal' colleagues, but I think *Plessy v. Ferguson* was right and should be reaffirmed" (quoted by Adler, 1987, p. 44). Furthermore, Justice Jackson's longtime secretary, Elsie Douglas, denied Rehnquist's excuse. Richard Kluger, in his magnificent account of the desegregation cases, *Simple Justice*, explained further:

> Mrs. Elsie Douglas [was] Jackson's secretary and confidante for the nine years preceding his death in October 1954. She told the *Washington Post* that by attributing the views of a prosegregation memo to Jackson, Rehnquist had "smeared the reputation of a great justice." She challenged Rehnquist's assertion that Jackson would have asked a law clerk to help prepare the remarks he would deliver at a conference of the justices, especially in view of Jackson's acknowledged gift for spontaneous eloquence and his splendid oral performances before the Court while solicitor general and while serving at the Nuremberg war crimes trials. She told *Newsweek* that Rehnquist's account was "incredible on its face." (1976, p. 607)

In another memorandum to Justice Jackson, while he was his law clerk, Rehnquist wrote (with reference to a case dealing with a type of all-white primary in the South):

> It is about time that the Court faced the fact that White people [in] the South don't like the colored people; the Constitution restricts

them from effecting this dislike through state action, but it most assuredly did not appoint the Court as a sociological watchdog to rear up every time private discrimination raises its admittedly ugly head. (Yarbrough, 2000, pp. 2–3)

A decade after he was a law clerk, when Rehnquist was an attorney in Phoenix, he again demonstrated his values in several ways. In 1957 he wrote an article published in *U.S. News and World Report* (Rehnquist, 1957) in which he complained of the "liberal" biases of Supreme Court law clerks, claiming they showed "extreme solicitude for the claims of Communists and other criminal defendants, expansion of federal power at the expense of State power, [and] great sympathy toward any government regulation of business" (Yarbrough, 2000, p. 5). And during the turbulent 1960s, he opposed a local Phoenix ordinance designed to prevent discrimination in public accommodations. The issue, as he saw it, was whether it was right to "sacrifice" the freedom of the property owner in order to give minorities the freedom to eat at whatever restaurant they chose.

As an assistant attorney general and head of the Office of Legal Counsel in President Nixon's administration, he was an advocate of wiretapping, government surveillance, preventive detention, and other actions in keeping with Nixon's "law and order" aspirations. In 1970, he drafted a proposed constitutional amendment that would ban busing to achieve racial school desegregation (Kluger, 1976).

Justice Rehnquist has valued state autonomy and for states to be free of restrictions, and he has sought to impose strict limits on the powers of the U.S. Congress and the federal courts. Commentators have concluded that "in his devotion to state autonomy . . . [he] does not flinch from using the power of the judiciary to restrict the power of the elected branches, and particularly Congress" (Fiss & Krauthammer, 1982, p. 16). Justice Rehnquist wasn't troubled by a Texas law that imposed a life sentence on a man for obtaining $120.75 under false pretenses. (He had accepted payment for repairing an air conditioner but never did the job.) The individual had been convicted twice before, for frauds involving $80 and $28.36, and had received a life sentence under Texas's multiple-offense law. Rehnquist's reaction: "Some states will always bear the distinction of treating particular offenders more severely than any other state" (quoted by Fiss & Krauthammer, 1982, p. 21).

During the 1995–1996 term, Rehnquist authored an opinion (*United States v. Lopez*, 1995) that Congress had no basis for outlawing possession of a gun within 1,000 feet of a school because it was not a matter of interstate commerce. This decision was a harbinger of things to come. The impressive mass of decisions announced at the end of the 1996–1997 term was interpreted as reflecting Justice Rehnquist's goal to reestablish the rights of the states as fundamental. In an astonishing breadth of decisions, the Supreme Court— in one week—upheld two state laws that prohibited physician-assisted suicide, scolded Congress for instituting federal regulation of what was typically a state-regulated matter (gun sales), and upheld another state law that some observers believed challenged the due process rights of sexual predators. Saying that Congress had unlawfully usurped power from the states and the federal courts, the Court also struck down the Religious Freedom Restoration Act of 1993 (Carelli, 1997). Perhaps most illustrative of Justice Rehnquist's imprint on the Court was the ruling that invalidated a portion of the 1993 so-called Brady bill, which forced state and local police to make background checks on people seeking to buy handguns (*Printz v. United States*, 1997). As one expert noted, "[t]his is a Court more skeptical of federal authority than any Court in recent history" (Carelli, 1997, p. A16). Throughout Chief Justice Rehnquist's remaining terms, other acts of Congress were declared unconstitutional because they interfered with the rights of states.

A review of the book that Chief Justice Rehnquist wrote about the history of the Supreme Court, first published in 1987, observed that the book's contents focused on decisions that have upheld the exercise of governmental power and virtually ignored decisions by the Warren Court that extended individual rights and curtailed police actions (Adler, 1987). An analysis by political scientists David Rohde and Harold Spaeth (1989) concluded that attitudes and values underlying Justice Rehnquist's decisions did not change after he became chief justice in 1986. His influence upon his colleagues increased after he became chief justice, and, especially in the period between 1997 and 2003, he was able to marshal a majority for his views on cases involving the clash between acts of Congress and federalism. In the more-than-30 years he was on the Court, Rehnquist moved from being what his early law clerks labeled the "Lone Ranger"—he filed 54 *solitary* dissenting opinions in the 15 years that he was an associate justice, a record—to being a theme-setter on the Court.

He was explicit about his views. While reluctant to give interviews to the media, he did, on occasion, express his position, as follows. "I think I am a judicial conservative. . . . I'm a strong believer in pluralism. Don't concentrate all the power in one place . . . you don't want all the power in the federal government as opposed to the states" (quoted by Weaver, 1990, p. 18).

While Chief Justice Rehnquist tempered some of his views, especially on school segregation and women's rights, an analysis published 30 years ago still seems accurate:

> It remains to be said that William Hubbs Rehnquist has been,
> from the first dawning of political awareness, a forceful, outspoken
> conservative with a low threshold of tolerance for civil-liberties
> claimants and the civil rights of minorities. "The justice's views on
> the law, the Constitution, discrimination and crime seem indistin-
> guishable today from those [that] friends recall in his late adoles-
> cence," wrote veteran Washington correspondent Warren Weaver,
> Jr., in an article on Rehnquist in the October 13, 1974 issue of the
> *New York Times Magazine*. "While most people's views evolve and

shift as they grow older, Rehnquist's conservative outlook seems to have been adopted and then flash-frozen while he was an undergraduate at Stanford. . . . A law-school classmate at Stanford, an unabashed liberal, recalls: "Rehnquist was very consistently more than just conservative . . ." Another fellow student observed: "Bill was the school conservative. A lot of us had mixed views about him. He was very sharp, a brilliant student, but so far-out politically that he was something of a joke." (Kluger, 1976, pp. 608–609)

Although such conclusions appear to be generally accurate, two votes of Justice Rehnquist in recent and important cases raise questions about this consistency. Chapter 1 described his majority opinion in the case of *Dickerson v. United States* (2000), which upheld the use of *Miranda* warnings by police. On first blush, this decision would seem to be contrary to Justice Rehnquist's "law and order" orientation, but, noted in chapter 1, it appears that the issue of Congress's usurpation of the Supreme Court's role took precedence in forming his opinion. Second, Chief Justice Rehnquist's concurrence in the *Bush v. Gore* (2001) decision was seen by some as a rejection of his long-held belief in states' rights; I will reserve until chapter 7 my analysis of the explanation for the votes in this case.

Harry Blackmun: Inconsistent Votes but Consistent Values

Another example of a justice reflecting consistency of values is Harry Blackmun. This claim may surprise some, because Justice Blackmun's voting record over his 24 years on the Court shifted dramatically. But his deepest values did not. An example is his position on the death penalty. Even when he was nominated to be a circuit court judge, a decade before his appointment to the Supreme Court, he expressed his personal feelings of opposition to the death penalty, his "distaste, antipathy, and, indeed abhorrence" (Greenhouse, 2005b, p. 114). But he voted on the Court to support this penalty in several cases during his first decade on the Court, and his shift to a voting pattern consistent with his values was gradual. He went nearly 13 years before he dissented from a single decision upholding a death sentence, but by the end of his tenure he had written: "I feel morally and intellectually obligated simply to concede that the death penalty experiment has failed" (*Callins v. Collins*, 1994, p. 1144).

At the beginning of his time on the Court he supported the state's right to use death as a punitive measure. Just five months into his first term, he joined the majority opinion in *McGautha v. California* (1971) that concluded that the Constitution did not prevent a jury from sentencing a defendant to death. But in the 1980s, he began to find serious problems in the manner that the judicial system processed capital cases (Stewart, 1998). Typical was his dissent in *Barefoot v. Estelle* (1983). In this case, two psychiatrists, at the sentencing hearing, had testified that the defendant was likely to commit further criminal acts. In Texas, where the trial took place, a death penalty could be given by the jury if it concluded there existed a probability that the defendant "would commit criminal acts of violence that would constitute a continuing threat to society" (p. 884). Even the American Psychiatric Association disagreed with the two psychiatrists regarding the likelihood of their assessment. Justice Blackmun distributed a strongly worded dissent that condemned the use of what he considered to be faulty information that permitted a man to be sentenced to death. He wrote: "the Court today sanctions admission in a capital sentencing hearing of 'expert' medical testimony so unreliable and unprofessional that it violates the canons of medical ethics" (p. 924, n. 6).

Five years later, in his dissent in *Darden v. Wainwright* (1986), he wrote an even stronger condemnation: "Today's opinion . . . reveals a Court willing to tolerate not only imperfection but a level of fairness and reliability so low it should make conscientious prosecutors cringe" (p. 189). But at this point, in the mid-1980s, he focused on individual cases and had not yet condemned capital punishment as a whole. His final statement on the matter came in 1994, shortly before he left the Court. His strong dissent in *Callins v. Collins* said:

> From this day forward, I no longer shall tinker with the machinery of death. . . . It is virtually self evident to me now that no combination of procedural rules or substantive regulations ever can save the death penalty from its inherent constitutional deficiencies. . . . The problem is that the inevitability of factual, legal, and moral error gives us a system that we know must wrongly kill some defendants, a system that fails to deliver the fair . . . and reliable sentences of death required by the Constitution. (p. 1145)

Summary View of the Attitudinal Model

During the 1980s and the early 1990s, the attitudinal model became the preferred explanation used by most political scientists for judicial decision-making. As noted earlier, the culmination of this view that "judges vote their attitudes" can be found in Segal and Spaeth's book *The Supreme Court and the Attitudinal Model*, in which they said:

> Though attitudes may be said to have cognitive, affective, and behavioral components, our concern is with the votes of justices, and thus the behavioral component of attitudes. These attitudes and values with which they associate should cause a behaviorally predisposed justice to support certain legal claims and to oppose others, while other justices behave in an opposite fashion. (1993, p. 69)

It is unclear whether advocates of the attitudinal model are saying that attitudes and values are the *sole* determinants of justices' votes; though an occasional quotation seems to be saying this, we doubt that their position is that extreme. One of the main proponents put it this way: "No serious scholar of the judiciary denies that the decisions of judges, especially at the Supreme Court level, are at least partially influenced by the judges' ideology" (Segal, 1999, p. 237). Consistent with a moderated view, some justices acknowledge that their position on cases may be influenced by their own life experiences and background, but they don't subscribe to the attitudinal model completely. Justice Breyer told a group of students:

> I'm a human being. . . . Because I'm a human being, my own background . . . my own views, will of course shape me. They make a difference. Somebody with different life experiences has different views to a degree; that will influence the way that they look at things. But that's very different from saying, "Oh, I decide whatever I want." I understand that my background, outlook, values, and everything influence me. But I don't feel I'm free to choose any result I happen to think is good. It's a complicated answer because I want you to get a feeling for what I think goes on. (1997)

The attitudinal advocates, by focusing on justices' votes as their dependent variable, have taken on an ambitious assignment. It is true that justices' votes are observable and final, hence their determination is important to the justice, as well as to the country. But votes are behavior, and any complex behavior has many causes, many of them extending beyond attitudes, values, and ideology. Second, the attitudinal model has been criticized for limiting itself to the search for determination of voting behavior.

> By focusing narrowly on how attitudes correlate with decisions on the merits, the model misses such things as why justices review some cases but conclude that others are "meritless," or why the facts of previous cases affect the attitudinal driven decisions of future cases, or what drives the justices' opinion when the Court upholds (rather than reverses) a statute or a precedent. (Clayton, 1999, p. 25)

Because of these and other concerns with the attitudinal model, theorists have sought more comprehensive explanations of judicial decision-making.

The Rational Choice Model

Note, in the quotation from Segal and Spaeth's book, that the emphasis of the attitudinal model is on the *votes* of justices. But, as we saw in the example of Justice Blackmun, sometimes votes do not reflect attitudes; they may even go against the justice's desired value outcome. Why is this? One reason, according to a third view, is that justices operate according to a *rational choice* model of human behavior; they pursue multiple goals; they act in ways that maximize their goals, and the institutions within which they operate sometimes affect their goals. Thus, sometimes they must do things that fail, in the short run, to achieve their goals. However, these actions are assumed to be congruent with the achievement of their long-term goals. Thus, central to the rational choice model is the phenomenon of strategic voting by justices.

Consider the following description of Justice Brennan's decision-making, as reflected in Woodward and Armstrong's book *The Brethren*. (The issue was whether a man sentenced to life in prison deserved a new trial. Justice Brennan's vote would have been the fifth vote needed by Lyman A. "Slick" Moore to have a second chance.)

> One of [Justice] Brennan's clerks thought that if Brennan had seen the facts as [Justice] Marshall presented them, he would not have voted the other way. He went to talk to Brennan, and thirty minutes later, returned shaken. Brennan understood that Marshall's position was correct, but he was not going to switch sides now, the clerk said. This was not just a run-of-the-mill case for [Justice] Blackmun. Blackmun had spent a lot of time on it, giving the trial record a close reading. He prided himself on his objectivity. If Brennan switched, Blackmun would be personally offended. That would be unfortunate, because Blackmun had lately seemed more assertive, more independent of the Chief [Burger]. Brennan felt that if he voted against Blackmun now, it might make it more difficult to reach him in the abortion cases or even the obscenity case. (1979, p. 225)

There was no new trial for "Slick" Moore. In the rational choice explanation of justices' voting behavior, a vote can reflect allegiance to another justice rather than the merits of the case, *if* that allegiance pays off with votes on really important cases down the road.

The attitudinal model seems to treat the Supreme Court as an autonomous—even insular—institution, whereas the rational choice model emphasizes that outside forces, especially Congress and the public, are always a consideration in the votes of justices (Hall & Brace, 1999). According to the rational choice model, the preferences of Congress put a restraint on judicial choice. In the last 10 years, a body of research has accumulated to support the rational choice model as an equally legitimate explanation for judicial behavior; therefore, I devote the next chapter to this model and its explanation of voting patterns in the Supreme Court.

6

The Rational Choice Model
in Judicial Decision-Making

Because Supreme Court opinions are the product of the interdependent choices of nine justices, the ability of any one justice to establish laws she most prefers is in part a function of her ability to adapt to the choices of others.—Lee Epstein and Jack Knight, *The Choices Justices Make* (1998)

Chapter 3 discussed the issue of whether the Court has control over its agenda. Though some experts disagree, most social scientists conclude that the justices have a great deal of control; in fact, the term *agenda setting* is used to refer to the process by which the Court decides which disputes to resolve and which to ignore. The control and discretion may even go further; that is, "after [the justices] agree to decide a case, they may (and often do) neglect to resolve questions that the parties had raised in their briefs" (Epstein & Knight, 1998, p. 88). Capitalizing on their prerogative to pick and choose among the issues to address, the justices display issue suppression in about half the cases they decide (McGuire & Palmer, 1995).

The Limits of the Attitudinal Model

Nothing in the foregoing paragraph would be disputed by those social scientists who advocate the attitudinal-model explanation of judicial decision-making described in chapter 5. But to what extent do Supreme Court justices "vote their attitudes" or reflect their value biases in their votes? Some critics of the attitudinal model have seen it as viewing "justices as unconstrained decision makers who are free to behave in accord with their own ideological attitudes" (Epstein & Knight, 1998, p. xii). Can justices disregard the facts and the law if they desire to?

But even Segal and Spaeth, leading advocates of the attitudinal model, note that there are limits on the extent to which attitudes determine behavior;

if an appeal has no merit to it, for example, "no self-respecting judge would decide [it] solely on the basis of his or her policy preferences" (1993, p. 70). Their example, however, possesses an irony they did not anticipate when they published their book in 1993: "If Michael Dukakis filed a suit arguing that he should be declared the winner of the 1988 presidential election, and if the Supreme Court had to decide the case, we would not expect the votes in the case to depend upon whom the justices voted for in the election" (p. 70).

History of the Study of Rational Choice

Like all humans, judges have a variety of goals in their professional work. As Baum (1997, p. 16) noted, most scholars who study judicial behavior have focused on proximate goals, the ones most directly related to the judge's behavior on the bench, but in varying degrees, judges also seek popularity and respect in the legal community or in the community as a whole, power within the court, and improvement in their financial status. Although decisions may reflect the judge's desire to achieve an accurate interpretation of the law, responses may also reflect more personal, even self-centered concerns, such as maintaining good personal relationships with the other judges or limiting one's own workload.

In addition, the judge's goals may reflect a desire to satisfy a portion of the public. We should remember that every federal judge is a political appointee, and he or she may have drawn the attention of the president or those senators from the judge's home state because of a visible allegiance to a political party. Even though federal judges do not have to stand for reelection, the political nature of their appointment (and confirmation) means that the goal of being sensitive to the community's needs is not far away from their awareness.

Classifications of judges' goals reflect this mixture of personal and professional; for example, Eisenstein and Jacob (1977) described four kinds of goals sought by judges and their associates: rendering justice, maintaining cohesion, disposing of workload, and reducing uncertainty. This variegated conception of a judge's motives seems to be to be more in keeping with the reality of human behavior than does a conception of a judge as driven by a single purpose. The emphasis on multiple purposes is a theme of Lawrence Baum's sensible book *The Puzzle of Judicial Behavior* (1997). In fact, Baum has labeled as a limitation of the attitudinal model its image of justices as single-minded; he noted that proponents of the attitudinal model in its purest form take the position that "justices act only on their interest in the content of legal policy. They seek to achieve good policy rather than good law, and their votes on case outcomes are direct expressions of their preferences rather than deviating from those preferences for strategic reasons" (p. 25).

The Origins of Rational Choice Explanations

In 1964, Princeton political scientist Walter Murphy published a book that described justices' voting behavior as examples of rational choice. (It should be noted that "rational choice" has several meanings in the social sciences; Dennis Chong, a political scientist, has written that "individuals act rationally when they choose the best available means to achieve what they believe to be in their best interest" [2000, p. 12]. The definition used by Walter Murphy varied somewhat with the selfish interest implied in Chong's definition.) One of Murphy's goals was to demonstrate that justices are political beings, that they are not unlike elected officials in the other branches. Specifically, he proposed that judges have public policy goals, that they want to see certain policies established or affirmed, and that they act to achieve these goals.

In the 40 years since the publication of Murphy's book, it has on the one hand been acknowledged as a classic, ground-breaking piece of work and on the other has frequently been disparaged because of its methodology (Epstein & Wright, 1998, 2003). Murphy bolstered his claims by citing examples (anecdotes, his critics would call them) of the actual behavior of justices as they gave reasons for their votes or sought to influence the votes of other justices. As the field of political science became more behavioralistic, critics demanded more evidence than anecdotes. The scholarship of the decades of the 1970s and 1980s ignored Murphy's viewpoint, as many political scientists became captivated by the attitudinal model. Also, behaviorally oriented political scientists studying judicial decision-making began to use larger samples of cases and submitted the results to complicated statistical analyses. Some observers concluded that the fundamental tenets of Murphy's viewpoint "essentially were set aside to explore social-psychological models of judicial decision-making and to clash with the legalists [i.e., the advocates of the legal model]" (Hall & Brace, 1999, p. 282).

But the publication of two books, *The Choices Justices Make*, by Lee Epstein and Jack Knight (1998), and *Crafting Law on the Supreme Court*, by Forrest Maltzman, James F. Spriggs II, and Paul J. Wahlbeck (2000), has given new impetus to the rational choice approach. The first set of authors proposed that

> [justices] are not unsophisticated characters who make choices
> based solely on their own political preferences. Instead, justices are
> strategic actors who realize that their ability to achieve their goals
> depends upon a consideration of the preferences of others, of the
> choices they expect others to make, and of the institutional context
> in which they act. In other words, the choices of justices can best
> be explained as strategic behavior, not solely as responses to either
> personal ideology or apolitical jurisprudence. . . . The law, as it is
> generated by the Supreme Court, is a long-term product of short-
> term strategic decision making. (Epstein & Knight, 1998, p. xiii)

The second group of authors argued that strategic calculations dominate in the decisions of justices. The two books share an emphasis on the rules, procedures, and norms of the institution that is the Court and their effect to constrain the justices from simply translating their attitudes, values, and preferences into policy outcomes.

The basic assumptions of what is referred to as the rational choice model, as reflected in these recent writings, are as follows.

1. Social actors, including justices, make choices to achieve certain goals.
2. Social actors, including justices, act strategically in that their choices depend upon what they expect the other actors to do.
3. These choices are constrained by an institutional setting in which they are made (Epstein & Wright, 1998).

Rational Choice and Strategic Behavior

What is an example of strategic behavior on the Court? In 1990, the Supreme Court acted on the case of *Pennsylvania v. Muniz*; the Court's ruling was that although a drunk-driving suspect had not been given his *Miranda* rights to remain silent during questioning, the prosecution could present a videotape at his trial that showed his slurred speech as he answered questions. The majority opinion said that "the physical inability to articulate words in a clear manner" was like physical evidence, such as a blood test, rather than like testimony and hence was not covered by the Fifth Amendment's protection against self-incrimination. What was precedent-setting about the decision was that it provided, for the first time, a "routine booking question" exception to the Miranda rule (Maltzman, Spriggs, & Wahlbeck, 2000). In one sense, the decision was not surprising, because the Court in the last 35 years has allowed many erosions to the original application of the Miranda rule; in fact, since 1969, the Court's rulings on *Miranda*-related issues have favored the government 72 percent of the time (Maltzman et al., 2000).

But what was surprising was that the opinion was authored by Justice Brennan. As Maltzman and colleagues (2000) observed, the decision was quite inconsistent with Brennan's traditionally broad interpretation of Fifth Amendment rights not to incriminate oneself. For *Miranda*-related cases that the Court considered while he was a justice, Brennan had supported the government only 28 percent of the time. Why did Justice Brennan write an opinion seemingly against his preferences? Maltzman and colleagues suggested that

> [t]he answers become clear when we delve into the personal papers of the justices. In a letter to Marshall dated June 7, 1990, Justice Brennan informed Marshall that although "everyone except you and me would recognize the existence of an exception to *Miranda* for 'routine booking questions,' . . . I made the strategic judgment to concede the existence of an exception but to use my control

over the opinion to define the exception as narrowly as possible."
In this letter, Brennan admitted that even though he personally
opposed his newly created exception to *Miranda*, he voted with the
majority to control the breadth of the legal rule being developed in
the opinion. . . . In a subsequent letter Brennan sent to Marshall
after seeing Marshall's *Muniz* dissent, Brennan wrote: "Thanks,
pal, for permitting me to glance at your dissent in this case. I think
it is quite fine, and I fully understand your wanting to take me to
task for recognizing an exception to *Miranda*, though I still firmly
believe that this was the strategically proper move here. If Sandra
had gotten her hands on this issue, who knows what would have
been left of *Miranda*." (pp. 3–4)

Analysis of the Court's public records and the private docket books,
memoranda, and voting records of several justices (especially Justices Brennan,
Marshall, Douglas, and Powell) permitted these two sets of authors to provide
extensive data supporting their claims. Their findings are reflected in analyses
of certiorari decisions, the drafting of majority opinions, and responses to these
drafts. For example, on the basis of an analysis of cases from the 1983 term,
during the conferences to discuss those cases, 48 percent of the remarks reflected
policy concerns (Epstein & Knight, 1998, table 2–1, p. 30).

The Decision to Grant Certiorari

The rational choice model proposes that justices, as policy seekers, reflect their
goals in their decisions whether to accept an appeal for review. Given the
present ideological division on the Court, each justice has some cases he or
she would like to see granted, while some of the other members would not
like to see them granted. Epstein and Knight proposed that if the certiorari
vote reflected justices' policy goals, then they would take cases they want to
reverse, in accord with their policy preferences; in actuality, the Supreme Court
reversed 61.3 percent of the six thousand lower court decisions it reviewed
between the 1953 and 1994 terms (Epstein & Knight, 1998, p. 27). (In more
recent terms, the percentage of cases reversed has increased to more than
70 percent; see chapter 10.)

Of course, other reasons exist for the aforementioned preponderance;
Segal and Spaeth reasoned that:

Given a finite number of cases that can be reviewed in a given
term, the Court must decide how to utilize its time, the Court's
most scarce resource. Certainly, overturning unfavorable lower
court decisions has more of an impact—if only to the parties to
the litigation—than affirming favorable ones. Thus, the justices
should hear more cases with which they disagree, other things
being equal. (1993, p. 191)

Those justices whose policy preferences urge them to grant certiorari but who fail to achieve the requisite four votes may dissent from the Court's decision not to take the case. An analysis of records from the 1982 and 1983 terms identified 55 cases in which the initial vote was insufficient to grant certiorari and one justice (or more) circulated a written dissent. In 23 percent of these influence attempts, the justice persuaded a fourth colleague to grant certiorari. In the 1983 term, of approximately 150 cases that were eventually decided, nine started as denials of certiorari (Epstein & Knight, 1998).

One of these was another of the cases dealing with restrictions of *Miranda* rights, *New York v. Quarles* (1984):

> *Quarles* began in 1980 with a woman reporting to two New York police officers that she had been raped by a tall Black man who was armed. When the officers drove to the site they spotted the assailant, Benjamin Quarles, ordered him to stop, and asked him where his weapon was. Quarles responded, "The gun is over there." At this point the officers placed Quarles under arrest and read him his *Miranda* rights. But a trial judge excluded Quarles's statement concerning the gun because he had spoken before hearing his rights.
>
> The case made its way to the Supreme Court but on April 14, 1983, the justices voted to deny certiorari. In response, Burger filed a short statement saying he dissented from the denial and would prefer to reverse summarily the decision of the court below. About a month later, Rehnquist circulated a dissenting opinion in which he not only urged his colleagues to hear the case but offered his view on *how* the Court should decide it. Rehnquist believed that the state's argument, namely that the justices should adopt a public safety exception to the Miranda rule, was entitled to "careful consideration. If there are ever to be 'exigent circumstances' justifying a refusal to exclude evidence because of a technical *Miranda* violation, the circumstances of this case would seem to be as likely a candidate as any." (Epstein & Wright, 1998, p. 64)

The Psychology of Drafting an Opinion

The selection of the opinion writer is very important; chapter 9 describes some of the considerations in the chief justice's mind as the assignment is made. (As noted in chapter 3, if the chief justice is not in the majority, the most senior associate justice in the majority assigns the opinion. But the rational choice model would note that if the chief justice is not anticipated to be in the majority, the senior associate justice may vote in a certain way in order to have the opportunity to determine who writes the majority opinion. The *Muniz* case, described earlier, shows how Justice Brennan so orchestrated matters.)

Once a justice is assigned to draft the majority opinion for the Court, observers ask a number of questions about the process. Does the draft opinion writer "count votes'? If so, how does vote-counting influence how he or she crafts the opinion draft? Does the extremity of the initial vote affect what draft is written? Do designated draft writers often find that they cannot write a satisfactory opinion? Do majorities shift to minorities?

The draft opinion writer has the opportunity to be an agenda setter; this draft establishes a baseline over which justices subsequently negotiate. Furthermore, the designated opinion writer is the one who decides whether to accept or reject proposed changes offered by colleagues. As Maltzman and colleagues observed:

> The opinion circulated by the author is almost always the first move in the case. Other justices wait to circulate concurring or dissenting opinions until they have at least seen the majority opinion draft. By virtue of this position, then, the assigned author enjoys an agenda-setting advantage, given his or her ability to propose a policy position from the range of policy alternatives. This advantage is enhanced by the costs associated with writing a competing opinion. Because justices encounter time and workload constraints, a justice who disagrees with portions of an opinion may simply join to avoid the costs associated with writing an alternative opinion. (2000, p. 7)

The writers of draft opinions must always count votes, and thus they must be careful to draft opinions that do not jeopardize defections from the majority. Sometimes they must put aside their most preferred opinion to generate a definitive ruling for the Court. Epstein and Knight (1998, p. 97) described the following as "perhaps the quintessential example of sophisticated opinion writing," in the case of *Segura v. United States* (1984):

> After Burger circulated the first draft of his majority opinion, he watched as three members of the majority coalition defected to the other side and knew that a fourth (O'Connor) was considering a concurrence in judgment only. To keep a Court, he produced *two* new drafts—one that was close to the first version and another that advanced a theory "perhaps preferred by Sandra, with whom I have conferred"—that he circulated only to the remaining members of the majority. Although he said in his memo that he preferred Draft A, he also expressed the view that he was "willing to abide by the wishes of 'four.'" With some minor adjustments, Draft B became the judgment of the Court. (1998, pp. 97–98, n. dd)

Analyses of retired justices' files conclude that in more than 50 percent of the cases during the Burger Court era, significant changes were made from the first draft to the published version; in landmark cases, the percentage increased to 65 percent (Epstein & Knight, 1998, p. 98). Here are some examples:

1. *Ballew v. Georgia* (1978): The issue was the minimum size of a trial jury; Georgia had been using five-person juries. Justice Blackmun's original draft included a long section explaining why the Court's decision would not be applied retroactively. The final opinion deleted this entire section.

2. *H. L. v. Matheson* (1981): The issue was the constitutionality of a Utah law that required doctors "to notify if possible" the parents of a minor before performing an abortion. The draft majority opinion by Justice Marshall struck down the law, but a response by Chief Justice Burger, who had been in the minority, caused two of the original 5-to-4 majority to shift sides, so Burger's opinion upholding the law became the majority opinion.

3. *Tennessee v. Garner* (1985): A Memphis police officer, chasing a teenager who had apparently robbed a house, shot and killed the suspect as he was climbing a fence to escape. The issue was the legitimacy of a Tennessee law that permitted law enforcement officers to fire at fleeing suspects if they were armed with a lethal weapon or if there was probable cause to believe the suspects had committed a violent crime. Justice White's original opinion upheld the law, but the final opinion ruled the opposite, that a belief that a fleeing suspect is armed is not in itself sufficient grounds to fire at the suspect to prevent escape.

4. *United States v. Nixon* (1974): In the famous Watergate tapes case, the original draft by Chief Justice Burger implied that a president's claim of executive privilege might be upheld if "core functions" of the executive branch were at stake. The other justices would not go along with the qualification; in the final, unanimous opinion, the "core functions" notion was dropped.

5. *Roe v. Wade* (1973): Justice Blackmun's first draft struck down the Texas law on narrow grounds, specifically its vagueness. (The law's sole criterion for exemption, "saving the life of the mother," was, in Blackmun's view, insufficiently informative to the physician.) But as noted in detail later in this chapter, Justices Brennan and Douglas pushed Blackmun to discard the law because it infringed on the Fourteenth Amendment's concept of personal liberty.

These are not, of course, the only cases in which significant changes occurred between first drafts and final opinions. Bernard Schwartz (1984, 1987, 1996b) has prepared three useful books that reproduce first drafts of approximately 10 opinions each during the administrations of Chief Justices Warren, Burger, and Rehnquist. These books illustrate how (and sometimes why) the draft opinions get changed during the negotiation process.

Postconference Influence Attempts

Although the oral arguments for a given appeal may be held in December, the Court's decision sometimes is not announced until the following May or June. What transpires during this long interim? The first draft of a majority opinion may take only a few weeks (although some justices are quicker at this than others); from then on, the exchange of reactions and suggestions for change may take months. How does the rational choice approach conceptualize this process?

Compliance-Gaining Strategies

Communication theorists have used the term *compliance-gaining* to refer to the process of trying to get others to act in ways one desires; one definition refers to it as "the attempt of some actor—the source of communication—to affect a particular, preconceived response from some target—the received of the persuasive effort" (Schenck-Hamlin, Wiseman, & Georgacarakos, 1982, p. 92). Influence attempts can occur during oral arguments (questions posed to one of the attorneys may have as their real intent to influence another justice), or during the judicial conference (although in the Rehnquist-led court, such opportunities were discouraged), but more occur during the post-conference period (in which the exchange of memos or hallway conversations reflect the compliance-gaining attempts).

Compliance-gaining is obviously the goal of many social encounters in real life. Marwell and Schmitt (1967) posed a question: How do people generally go about trying to gain compliance? A list of 16 different tactics was generated, later to be reconceptualized by Miller and Parks (1982), along two dimensions:

- *Reward v. punishment.* For example, did the persuader try to use rewarding or punishing techniques to gain compliance?
- *Communicator-recipient onus.* That is, did the persuader try to manipulate rewards directly (the "communicator onus") or did he or she try to stimulate positive or negative self-persuasion techniques, or the "recipient onus"? (Perloff, 1993)

The latter dimension, exemplified by such statements as "You owe me one" or "You'll feel better about yourself if you vote my way" may seem beneath Supreme Court influence attempts. We will see.

Power Strategies

Another set of dimensions, potentially more applicable, emerged from the research of psychologist Toni Falbo (1977), who asked respondents to write paragraphs on "How I Get My Way." The 16 strategies that emerged included bargaining, deceit, compromise, hinting, persistence, reason, and simple persuasion. The factors that emerged from an analysis of responses were the following:

- Direct versus indirect (e.g., assertions and simple statements versus hinting and bargaining)
- Rational versus irrational (e.g., by use of reason and compromise or by use of evasion and threat)

It is important to realize that though seen as encompassing two independent dimensions, such influence tactics could be:

- Both direct and rational, or *persistence*
- Both direct and nonrational, or *threat*
- Both indirect and rational, or *bargaining*
- Both indirect and nonrational, or *deceit*

Persuasion is context bound; that is, different influence strategies are used in different situations (Perloff, 1993; Wiseman & Schenck-Hamlin, 1981). Situations differ with respect to the intimacy level between parties, relationship status (equals versus superior–subordinate), and degree of resistance encountered (Perloff, 1993). A subsequent section will illustrate the claim that many of these strategies—including nonrational strategies—can be found in exchanges between Supreme Court justices.

Individual differences are also reflected in the process of compliance-gaining. In general, women employ polite or negotiable compliance-gaining tactics more often than do men (Baxter, 1984; Fitzpatrick & Winke, 1979). Some people rely on manipulation and deceit; others avoid such tactics. *Machiavellianism* as a measurable interpersonal orientation was a concept developed by social psychologists Richard Christie and Florence L. Geis (1970) to reflect the ideology of a person who has a zest for manipulating others and will use any tactic to gain compliance from others.

Normative versus Informational Influence

Social psychologists Morton Deutsch and Harold Gerard (1955) made a distinction between two types of influence that can operate in decision-making groups, a distinction that is clearly applicable to any appellate court's deliberations. *Informational influence* is reflected by the behavior of a group member who uses facts, logic, and data to try to persuade; *normative influence* is demonstrated when a group member appeals to someone in the minority to conform because of the power of the majority and hence the implied correctness of the majority's opinion. Emotional appeals that disparage the minority are also considered to be examples of normative influence. The courts assume that informational influence predominates, but the following section includes some examples of justices attempting normative influence to persuade their colleagues.

An Analysis of Influence Attempts

It is impressive that the treatises by political scientists on influence attempts within the Court refer to these compliance-gaining strategies, although not by that term. For example, Murphy's 1964 book spent a chapter on such procedures; he wrote:

A justice has considerable opportunity to try to exercise influence over his [*sic*] colleagues. He could attempt to appeal to their interests—to convince them that their interests would gain from furthering his interests or that their interests would suffer injury if they opposed his; to . . . appeal to their personal and professional esteem for him; and to appeal to their concepts of duty and moral obligation. (1964, pp. 39–40)

Murphy went on to describe the range of procedures a judge might use, even including the Machiavellian ones:

First, he might try by force of . . . intellect and will to convince his colleagues not only that what he wanted was in the best interests of themselves, the Court, the country, humanity, or whatever goals they might wish to foster, but also that it was morally incumbent upon them to act in the manner that he was proposing. Second, a justice might plan so to endear himself to the other justices that they would be reluctant to vote against him in matters he considered to be vital. Conversely, he might try to capitalize on fear rather than affection and try to bludgeon his colleagues into agreement by threatening them with the sanctions available to him. Fourth, he might conclude that the only viable way to come near achieving his goal would be to negotiate: to compromise with those who were less intensely opposed to his policies. (1964, p. 40)

The following types of responses are reported by Murphy in his book.

1. *Substantive feedback,* or attempts to persuade on the merits of the argument. An example: "I doubt that we are very far apart in the *Cantwell* case, but in order that you might get exactly my views, I have written them out and enclose them herewith" (Justice Stone to Justice Owen Roberts, quoted by Murphy, 1964, p. 59).

2. *Ingratiation.* An example: "You know how eager I have been—and am—to have our *Milk* opinion reflect your specially qualified expert views. . . . Of course, I am open to any further suggestion. I am sending this to you and not circulating it to others" (Justice Frankfurter to Justice Frank Murphy, quoted by Murphy, 1964, p. 59).

In this brief message, Justice Frankfurter not only displays ingratiation and flattery but also deceit, for he had little respect for Justice Murphy. Frankfurter, the former Harvard Law professor, valued legal craftsmanship; he believed that Murphy had neither the critical legal skills nor the writing ability that Frankfurter considered essential for the job.

3. *Bargaining.* An example: "After a careful reading of your opinion in *Shotwell v. Moore*, I am very sorry to be compelled to say that the first part of it (especially in the passage which I have marked in the margin) is so contrary to my convictions that I fear, unless it can be a good deal tempered, I shall have to deliver a separate opinion on the lines of the enclosed memorandum" (Justice Gray to Justice Miller, quoted by Murphy, 1964, pp. 57–58).

Bargaining can occur at several stages in the decision-making process, even at the initial conference devoted to certiorari petitions. Epstein and Knight (1998) argued that the decision whether to grant certiorari encourages bargaining:

> [T]he *cert.* decision contains all the makings of a classic bargaining
> problem. First, justices want to reach an agreement over whether
> to hear a case; if they are consistently unable to reach such agree-
> ment, they will fail to attain their main goal of issuing policy
> proclamations. Second, justices often disagree over which agree-
> ment—to grant or deny—is better. Available data suggest that at
> least one justice votes to grant *certiorari* in nearly 50 percent of the
> cases the Court discusses and denies, and at least one votes to deny
> *cert.* in 98 percent that the Court grants. Finally, justices have
> various tools at their disposal to enable them to bargain with their
> colleagues, with a potentially powerful one being the threat to
> issue an opinion dissenting from a denial of *certiorari*. (1998,
> pp. 58–59)

As soon as the case conference is over, bargaining can be resumed, even before the draft opinions start to circulate. This is especially true when the conference has produced something short of a consensus (Epstein & Knight, 1998). A typical bargaining message is one that Justice Brennan sent to Justice White in December 1976; part of it follows.

> I've mentioned to you that I favor your approach to this case and
> want if possible to join your opinion. If you find the following
> suggestions . . . acceptable, I can, as stated in the enclosed concur-
> rence, join you. I'm not generally circulating the concurrence until
> you let me have your reaction. (Epstein & Knight, 1998, p. 69)

Bargaining can take different forms; for example, privately contacting the opinion drafter with a bargaining statement, as Justice Brennan did, or circulating a separate writing in hopes of having it incorporated in the final opinion. In the analysis of memoranda issued during the 1983 term of the Supreme Court, Epstein and Knight found that in only 16 percent of the cases were no memoranda circulated. The average case generated six memos; sometimes the proposed changes ran on for more than 10 pages. Of course, not all these memoranda conveyed an attempt at bargaining. Some reflected an intention of writing a separate opinion or dissent. But the impressive magnitude—one case generated 35 such memoranda—clearly reveals that, as Epstein and Knight put it, "justices respond to one another's opinions" (1988, p. 72) and "bargaining is a regular feature of the process by which the justices reach their decisions" (p. 74). An analysis of cases handled by the Burger Court (Wood, 1996) concluded that 85 percent of the requests to the opinion writer for a change in language indicated that the requester's joining the opinion was contingent on the change being made.

Justices are all aware of what is taking place and sometimes even use the language of bargaining in their memos, as the following memorandum from Justice Rehnquist to three others illustrates: "I have been negotiating with John Stevens for a considerable time in order to produce a fifth vote for my *Bildisco* opinion. I have agreed to make the following changes in the currently circulating draft, and he has agreed to join if I do" (Epstein & Knight, 1998, p. 74).

Important cases, as expected, generate more communication; Epstein and Knight concluded that "in more than two-thirds of the most important cases of the 1970s and 1980s, at least one justice attempted to bargain with the opinion-writer—with a good deal of the negotiation done through private memos" (1998, p. 73).

Milliken v. Bradley (1974), a school desegregation case, is an example:

> After the Court voted 5 (Burger, Stewart, Blackmun, Powell, and Rehnquist) to 4 (Douglas, Brennan, White, and Marshall) to strike down the district court's plan, the Chief Justice assigned the decision to himself. Even before he circulated his first draft, he began to receive private communications from some of the members of the majority. Powell, for instance, wrote to tell him of a story he "recalled" in the press recently "to the effect that Senator Ervin was then holding hearings of a subcommittee on the proposed anti-busing constitutional amendment." Powell wondered if the Chief might want to get a hold of some of the testimony from school officials who had experienced the effect of school desegregation programs. Then, after Burger circulated two drafts of his opinion, he was barraged with a flood of private memos. Powell's list of suggested changes ran more than ten pages; Stewart's six; Rehnquist's which was sent to the chief justice, with a blind copy to Powell, and Blackmun's, two pages each. It was apparently going to be difficult to keep the majority coalition intact. But, by the third draft, it became clear that Burger would pull it off. As Rehnquist put it in a memo sent to the Chief and carbon copied to Stewart, Blackmun, and Powell: "I think you have made very substantial changes to accommodate the view expressed by the rest of us who voted with you at Conference on this case . . . I sincerely hope that we can come out with an opinion for the Court." Yet, the four members of the minority saw none of the "accommodation";

all they received were the end results of the bargaining process—
the various opinion drafts. (Epstein & Knight, 1998, pp. 73–74)

The second procedure, the circulation of a separate writing, may also
communicate to the opinion drafter that he or she cannot count on support
unless changes are made. But two other possible goals exist for such separate writings: they may be a way to alert other groups to alternatives to the
majority's policy, and they may be leaving a record for future decisions, reflecting a belief that the resolution of the issue is not complete (Epstein &
Knight, 1998).

In summary, bargaining is quite frequent, occurring in more than half
the cases spanning the Burger and Rehnquist Courts. Furthermore, justices
approve of the process; they believe that "bargaining can lead to favorable
outcomes. If they thought that their bargaining statements never had an effect, there would be no reason to make them" (Epstein & Knight, 1998, p. 76).

4. *Threats and blackmail.* In the everyday world, when bargaining fails for
some people, threats may follow. But is blackmail beyond the pale for appellate judges? Apparently not. An example: When the conference on the case of
Roe v. Wade was completed in late December 1971, Chief Justice Burger asked
Justice Blackmun to write the opinion, even though it was not clear that the
chief justice was then a part of the majority. In a strongly worded but brief
memorandum, Justice Douglas protested this assignment, saying that because
the chief justice had argued the minority view, Burger should have asked him—
as the senior associate justice in the majority—to assign the opinion. Douglas threatened to publish the dissent; the following is part of this threat:

> [Your action is] an action no Chief Justice in my time would ever
> have taken. For the tradition is a longstanding one that the senior
> justice in the majority makes the assignment. . . . When, however,
> the minority seeks to control the assignment, there is a destructive
> force at work in the Court. When a Chief Justice tries to bend the
> Court to his will by manipulating assignments, the integrity of the
> institution is imperiled. (Schwartz, 1996a, p. 46)

Chief Justice Burger was not persuaded; he replied that "there were, literally, not enough columns to mark up an accurate reflection of the voting"
in his docket book, and therefore he had marked down no vote (O'Brien, 2000,
p. 8). He told Justice Douglas that this was a case that would stand or fall on
the writing, apparently meaning that the issues were so complex or fundamental or emotional that a majority opinion would not be decided until after
a further exchange of drafts.

The assignment of the case remains shrouded in some mystery (Greenhouse,
2005b). It is possible that the chief justice did not see this as an assignment to
write an opinion but as merely a memorandum dealing with a multitude of issues. At any rate, Justice Blackmun found it no small task. It was only his second year on the Court, but he was already known for being notoriously slow in

preparing drafts; what's more, this was his first major case and hence his biggest challenge. He did not circulate a first draft until May 18, 1972, almost five months later. Although his draft supported striking down the Texas antiabortion law—and Douglas was pleased with that—the senior justice was quite unhappy with Blackmun's rationale, for it said nothing about a woman's constitutional right to privacy, which Douglas, along with Justice Brennan, pointed out had been the *basis* for the majority's view at the December 1971 conference.

Meanwhile, another problem for Justice Douglas had surfaced. When the oral arguments had been held the previous December, two new appointees to the Supreme Court, Rehnquist and Powell, had not yet been confirmed by the Senate and hence did not vote. But now they were on the Court, and there was a movement to delay the decision and rehear the oral arguments the next term, before a full, nine-person Court. Justice Douglas saw his majority slipping away. He sent Chief Justice Burger another inflammatory message, threatening to publicize the way Burger had handled the matter and to document "the tragedy it entails" (O'Brien, 2000, p. 9). He would make public the secret inner workings of the Court and embarrass the chief justice, who treasured his own public image. He sent to his friend Justice Brennan a draft of his dissent, which said:

> The plea that the cases be reargued is merely a strategy by a
> minority somehow to suppress the majority view with the hope
> that exigencies of time will change the result. That might be
> achieved, of course, by death or conceivably retirement. But that
> kind of strategy dilutes the integrity of the Court and makes the
> decisions here depend upon the manipulative skills of a Chief
> Justice. (Simon, 1995, p. 103)

The threat was not consummated; cooler heads prevailed. Justice Brennan realized that the Douglas dissent, if published in that form, could do grievous damage to the Court. He urged Douglas to remove all references to the chief justice's motivations. When time came to decide whether to hold arguments anew the next term, Douglas noted his dissent from the majority but did not express what he had shared with Brennan. However, he insisted that Blackmun personally assure him that he would not change his position after the reargument. The decision to delay might in actuality have been consistent with Douglas's goals, as it gave Blackmun a summer to research the complex issues in the case. After the second round of oral arguments in October 1972, Blackmun produced a draft that was in keeping with the rationale that had been advanced by Douglas and Brennan at the initial conference. That rationale persisted in the final opinion that Blackmun read from the bench on January 22, 1973.

Did Douglas's threat succeed? Court observer James Simon believes that it did; he wrote:

> As it turned out, Justice Douglas was the biggest winner of all. His
> prolonged tantrum had produced a firm commitment from Justice

Blackmun to hold to his original position of voting to strike down the Texas and Georgia statutes. And seven members of the Court eventually endorsed a woman's fundamental right to privacy that was broad enough to cover her decision to have an abortion in the early stages of her pregnancy—a position Douglas had taken in his original draft in December 1971. (1995, p. 104)

How Do Justices Respond to Influence Attempts?

The most common reaction to an opinion draft is to agree to it, or in the rather backward language of the Court, to respond by saying "Please join me." Analyses of cases during the Burger Court era found that 79 percent of the time, justices in the majority coalition at the conference responded to the opinion draft by signing on to it. While in agreement, they may still request editing changes; for example, in response to a draft by Justice Arthur Goldberg, Justice Harlan asked that "desegregation" be substituted for "integration." He wrote: "Throughout the opinion, 'integration' brings blood to Southerners' eyes" (O'Brien, 2000, p. 288). In contrast, even though he agreed with the opinion's thrust, Justice Brennan sent Chief Justice Warren a 21-page list of revisions to his draft for *Miranda v. Arizona* (1966).

Sometimes justices simply agree to join the majority opinion even though they have some reservations. For example, a memo from Chief Justice Burger to Justice Black in a 1971 case said: "I do not really agree but the case is narrow and unimportant except to this one man . . . I will join up with you in spite of my reservations" (Maltzman et al., 2000, p. 22). The justices have a name for this, as illustrated in a communication from Justice White to Justice Marshall: "I was the other way, but I acquiesce, i.e., a graveyard dissent" (p. 7).

Effects of Conformity Pressures

Social psychologists make distinctions between two processes that occur when a person's response is consistent with an attempt to influence it: *compliance* and *internalization* (Kelman, 1958). Compliance is an overt, public acquiescence to achieve some instrumental gain, whereas internalization is an actual acceptance of the values or beliefs espoused in the influence attempt. Applied to decisions made after the assignment of an opinion writer, compliance would be reflected by a justice whose vote goes along with the majority because of some reason other than a deeply held belief, whereas internalization would be exemplified when a justice becomes internally convinced of the legitimacy of the draft writer's opinion. For example, Justice Brennan once told Justice Stewart: "I voted the other way at Conference but you've convinced me" (quoted by Maltzman & Wahlbeck, 1996b, p. 581). Similarly, Justice Stevens once wrote to Justice Blackmun: "Although I voted the other way at Conference and was asked by Bill Brennan to prepare a dissent, your opinion sent me back to the brief and I am now persuaded that you have the better part of the argument. I therefore expect to join you" (Schwartz, 1996a, p. 56). Assuming these expressions are genuine, attempts to influence can lead to shifts in votes that reflect internalization. But some shifts are not genuine in the sense of reflecting internalization, as we will see.

The Concept of Fluidity

Do conformity pressures exert a sizable influence on the votes of Supreme Court justices? One approach to answering this question is to determine just how often justices change their votes from the conference's tentative ones to the final votes that are published when the opinion is announced. J. Woodford Howard, Jr. (1968b), was apparently the first political scientist to advocate the study of vote shifts, or what has come to be called *fluidity*, on the Court. On the basis of his inspection of the available docket books and other records, he concluded that fluidity was "commonplace," and thus the study of judicial decision-making should focus on the *shifts* in decisions rather than assuming that decisions, once made, remain stable. Howard's article can be considered a "call to arms" (Silvia, 1997) to study fluidity, but he did not provide empirical data of any systematic nature. Other political scientists, notably Saul Brenner and his colleagues, have since generated convincing empirical support as well as a more refined analysis of fluidity. For example, these researchers have distinguished three types of vote shifts:

- *Conformity voting:* voting with the majority at the original conference vote and with the majority at the final vote (this assumes that the outcome of the two votes is the same; i.e., to affirm on both votes or to reverse on both votes)
- *Counter-conformity voting:* voting with the majority at the conference and with the minority at the final vote, when the Court favors the same outcome on both votes
- *Shifting* when the Court is also shifting; this kind of switching could involve either minority-minority or majority-majority voting (Dorff & Brenner, 1992)

The Frequency of Fluidity

The most basic question is: How often does fluidity occur? An initial answer is: At least half the time. Brenner (1980) first analyzed the docket books of Justice Harold Burton, who served on the Court from 1945 to 1958, and found vote shifts in 61 percent of the cases. He then looked at the docket books of Justice Tom Clark, who served from 1956 to 1967; fluidity was found here in 55 percent of the cases. The importance of the case, however, has an effect on the likelihood of vote shifts; in the Burton docket books, fluidity was found in 52 percent of the major cases but in 62 percent of the less important ones.

In the Clark dockets, the percentages were 44 percent for major and 56 percent for minor cases (Brenner, 1982a).

These figures confirm the hypothesis that the actual votes reflect a person-times-situation interaction. Justices may feel more accountable when they know a decision will be scrutinized by the media and by legal scholars, so they pay more attention to the briefs and the oral arguments, making their initial vote harder to dislodge. Furthermore, the salience of the case is probably related to what Silvia (1997) called its "ideological relevance." Few justices are passionate about taking on tax cases or patent controversies, hence such cases are rarely salient. In contrast, cases involving affirmative action, abortion, the death penalty, or federalism issues are usually ideologically important to both the conservative and the liberal justices. Justices are more resistant to social influence in those cases that are, for them, ideologically relevant. Furthermore, it is not the decision itself but the rationale for it that is of concern; judges care about the legal rules articulated in opinion drafts and may shift their votes when these are not congruent with their goals. In other cases, the judge's initial opinion may be uncertain, leaving the justice more susceptible to a vote shift and to persuasion by colleagues (Maltzman & Wahlbeck, 1996b).

In fact, Howard's ground-breaking work on the topic of fluidity suggested uncertainty as a determining factor: "Shifting perspectives appear to have been a function of additional thought and homework, by a clerk or a justice, into issues that were only partially perceived at first because of inadequate argument, briefs, or time" (1968b, p. 47). Not surprisingly, when justices describe how they reached viewpoints that were different from their original ones, they used terms like "mature reflection" or "research and labor" (Maltzman & Wahlbeck, 1996b, p. 584).

In summary, Baum has said: "Evidence gathered from justices' papers and other primary sources makes it clear that justices often change their positions in the process of moving toward a collective decision. In particular, it is standard practice to modify the language of opinions in an effort to win colleagues" (1997, p. 106).

The Direction of Shifts

Social psychologist Solomon Asch's (1958) classic work on conformity pressures has documented how a lone holdout will sometimes succumb to the majority, even when the holdout's opinion is correct and the majority's is wrong. Research on the direction of shifts in Supreme Court justices' votes reflects the power of the majority to attract the minority, although not all of the effects parallel the findings of social psychological research. Baum observed that the justices are "far more likely to abandon positions in the original minority than to leave the majority" (1997, p. 109). During Justice Burton's service, 78 percent of the strong fluidity votes were moves toward the majority position, and in 86 percent of these shifts, the majority already had enough votes to win before the justice shifted (Brenner, 1980). In the analysis of Justice Clark's docket, the figures were similar: 84 percent of the shifts were toward the majority. In an analysis of more than 24,000 pairs of votes from the 1945 term to the 1975 term, Dorff and Brenner (1992, p. 764) found that 2.2 percent of the justices in the majority shifted, while 26.9 percent of those in the minority did; that is, justices are 12 times more likely to shift from the minority to the majority than to reflect a counter-conformity shift. Analyses of conference and final votes over 15 terms by Maltzman and Wahlbeck (1996b) found that justices who initially voted with the majority switched only 4.6 percent of the time, whereas justices who initially dissented shifted 18.1 percent of the time.

What is the explanation for such a consistent pattern? Baum suggested that

> [t]he most credible explanation is that justices want to be a part of the majority (Brenner & Dorff, 1992). In turn, that interest could reflect a variety of motivations, from an interest in shaping the majority opinion to an interest in achieving a maximum clarity in the law. It is very difficult to distinguish empirically among these motivations, and we have little sense of their relative importance. (1997, p. 109)

This shift toward the majority is relevant to the question of whether justices' votes can be predicted in advance; chapter 10 presents data from recent terms reflecting how the pressures toward uniformity color the predictability of individual votes.

One motivation for shifting may reflect awareness of a norm against "minimum winning coalitions," or decisions that squeak through on a 5 to 4 vote. Murphy wrote: "In the judicial process a 5–4 decision emphasizes the strength of the losing side and may encourage resistance and evasion. The greater the majority, the greater the appearance of certainty and the more likely a decision will be accepted and followed in similar cases" (1964, p. 66).

A minimum winning decision fuels the fires of discontent and can damage the Court's image of authority. What Murphy wrote 40 years ago about the *Brown v. Board of Education* (1954) decision would also apply to cases involving presidential executive privilege and to controversial issues: "One hesitates to imagine how much more difficult implementation of the school desegregation decisions would be had there been a four or three or even two-judge minority willing to claim in public that 'separate but equal' was a valid constitutional doctrine" (1964, p. 66). Narrow decisions also do not fulfill the Court's purpose of resolving lower court conflicts and establishing precedent; as Brenner, Hagle, and Spaeth (1990) have observed, a 5 to 4 decision "is likely to result in an unstable precedent for the Court, which might be overturned if membership changes or if one of the justices in the majority changes his mind" (p. 309).

In summary, the norm of seeking to achieve unanimity in highly visible cases is a powerful one. A minimum winning coalition is seen as less definitive by the public and by those who face the task of implementing the decision; as Silvia put it, "[t]he desire to appear authoritative is not mere judicial vanity" (1997, p. 9).

Thus we would expect that if the possibility of a 5 to 4 vote creates fluidity among the minority, there should be greater evidence of vote shifts toward unanimity when the majority is tenuous. Brenner's (1980) analysis of Justice Burton's records supports this. When all the instances of fluidity were tallied, little in the way of shifts was found when the initial majority was seven or eight. But conformity was substantially more frequent when the initial majority was only five or six (Brenner, 1980, table 3). But only to a point: when the winning coalition was large enough to appear legitimate and authoritative, conformity voting tapered off.

One reason for this outcome is that the draft opinion writer may be less willing to revise if he or she already has a secure majority. In the case of *Ake v. Oklahoma* (1985), described in chapter 5, Justice Thurgood Marshall circulated a draft opinion that was joined by everyone except Justices Rehnquist and Burger. The latter sent a response that asked for the addition of only four words. Marshall's opinion insisted that the state provide a psychiatrist's assistance to those defendants who employed the insanity defense and could not afford a psychiatrist. Chief Justice Burger wanted to restrict this to only capital cases. But Justice Marshall refused; he sent the other justices a memorandum saying: "Since seven of us agree, my current plan is not to make the change suggested in the Chief's ultimatum" (Maltzman et al., 2000, p. 95). Eventually, only Justice Rehnquist was in the minority, with Chief Justice Burger writing a separate opinion that concurred with the Court's ruling in favor of Ake.

Regardless of the motivations—and these are specific to the justice and to the topic of the case—the conclusion remains that fluidity is not a random, unsystematic phenomenon but rather is reflective of group processes present in any decision-making group. A study by Maltzman and Wahlbeck (1996b), relying on votes in all the cases from 1969 to 1985, emphasized the situation-specific nature of fluidity. Vote shifts are strongly determined by the sets of opinions and coalitions that emerge during the case conference. Justices "who find themselves closer to the opposing coalition . . . are more likely to switch than those whose ideologies differ significantly" (p. 591).

A danger of the foregoing analysis is the impression it conveys that responses to influence within the Court are simply and always *passive* responses. It must be remembered that policy-oriented justices have their votes available as bargaining chips; they may side with the majority but want the opinion to be written in a certain way, as we saw earlier in Justice Douglas's position on *Roe v. Wade*. They may even switch their votes on less important cases to achieve results consistent with their long-term goals, as illustrated by Justice Brennan's action in the appeal of Lyman ("Slick") Moore, described in chapter 5.

Summary and Conclusions

The important books by Epstein and Knight (1998) and by Maltzman, Spriggs, and Wahlbeck (2000) expanded on the distinction, first introduced by Walter Murphy in 1964, between *strategic voting* and *sincere voting*. Murphy's theory of judicial decision-making capitalized on the rational choice model from political science and economics. He proposed that appellate judges often make their decisions—including which cases to hear and which decisions to join—with policy considerations predominant in their mind. (By *policy* is meant proposed courses of action or general plans the Court should advance.) Also, judges are social beings; they do not make their choices in isolation. They must pay heed to the preferences of others. Thus the decision and the vote are not straightforwardly determined, and not necessarily "sincere" in the sense of reflecting only what the judge prefers. Strategic voting can occur at any step in the Court's procedures—at the certiorari conference or the case conference as well as after a draft opinion is prepared. After Murphy's book appeared, other political scientists had mixed reactions to his proposal that voting by justices is often strategic in character. *Elements of Judicial Strategy* was recognized and cited for its intuitions based on detailed analyses of decisions in specific cases (usually landmark cases), but in the early 1960s little in the way of rigorous empirical work had been done on the issue (and, of course, few judicial records were then public).

The books published in the 1990s (and the research they cite) have given new life to Murphy's perspective by putting it in a modern, interdisciplinary-oriented context that is congenial with models of social cognition from social psychology. Perhaps more important, scholars have done extensive analyses of court dockets to support Murphy's claims. Epstein and Knight urged their colleagues to view justices *not* "as unconstrained decision-makers who are free to behave in accord with their own ideological attitudes, [but] rather . . . [as] the sophisticated actors Murphy made them out to be" (1998, p. xii). Political scientist James Gibson has expressed this view succinctly: "Judges' decisions are a function of what they prefer to do, tempered by what they think they ought to do, but constrained by what they perceive is feasible to do" (1983, p. 9).

A key aspect of the rational choice approach is to emphasize the interdependence behind strategic voting; individuals' actions are a function of their expectations about the actions of others. Sometimes these considerations lead judges to make choices that reflect their sincere preferences, but in other cases, strategic calculations lead a judge to act in a way that does not accurately reflect his or her true preferences. They would rather support "a ruling that comes close to their preferences than to see their colleagues take positions that move policy well away from their ideal and see another institution (Congress, for example) completely reverse [the Court's] decision" (Epstein & Knight,

1998, pp. 19–20). Bargaining and similar responses to opinion drafts are, in the view of the rational choice theorist, inherently strategic.

> Parties involved in a bargaining situation—whether they are the leaders of two nations attempting to form an alliance or employers and employees trying to hammer out a benefits agreement—must, in making their own choices, consider the preferences of the other relevant actors and the actions they expect them to take. (p. 58)

If we accept the proposal that strategic voting does exist, those justices who are swing votes take on a particular importance. Being a pivotal vote becomes an attractive option to some justices, possibly leading them to shift to the ideological center (Epstein & Knight, 1998, p. 128). Consider, for example, Justice O'Connor and her propensity, when she was on the Court, to be on the winning side in so many 5 to 4 majorities. Political scientist Nancy Maveety (Bradley & Maveety, 1992; Maveety saw this as an example of strategic voting: "The tactical maneuver of going along with the majority offers the advantage of influence through bargaining" (Maveety, 1996, p. 4).

Lawrence Baum, a longtime observer of the Court and author of several books about it, has concluded that judges employ sincere voting when they support the case outcome that they most prefer "without considering the impact of their votes on the collective result in their court" (1997, p. 90). Judges who vote strategically consider the effects of their choices on "collective results"; that is, their motivation is to achieve the most desirable results in their own court and in government as a whole (Baum, 1997). Two well-documented case decisions may reflect strategic voting on the part of some of the justices. In the 1954 *Brown v. Board of Education* decision, several of the justices initially did not think it was the Court's prerogative to outlaw segregated schools, but their realization that it was in the best interests of the country eventually led to the unanimous vote sought by Chief Justice Warren (Cray, 1997; Kluger, 1976). And, as noted earlier in this chapter, the final opinion in the *Roe v. Wade* (1973) case looked quite different from the original draft by Justice Blackmun.

Baum limited the use of the term "strategic voting"; he did not include, for example, a judge who voted in a way opposite to his or her preferences in order to get reelected. In another example, a judge may be willing to abandon a minority position that reflects his or her preference so as to avoid the time and effort to write a dissenting opinion; Baum did not term this decision "strategic," either.

Yet a number of tactics can fall under this label, "from arguments in an opinion aimed at winning a colleague's support to efforts at influence over appointments to other courts" (Baum, 1997, p. 92). As we have seen, threats are not beyond the pale; justices may refrain from joining an opinion until their wishes are met. Even concerns about the relationship of the Supreme Court to the other federal courts can come into play. For example, consider the decision whether to write a separate concurring opinion or to join the majority opinion. In a memo to Justice Powell, Chief Justice Burger urged his colleague not to publish a concurrence: "Would it not be better to try for a 'united front' instead of a cluster of concurring opinions—a practice of which I increasingly receive complaints from judges all over the country" (Epstein & Knight, 1998, p. 42).

As indicated, policy considerations are not always at the forefront for every justice in every case. But it is hard to question a claim that, at least for most justices, their reactions to a decision reflect an awareness that they operate within an institutional context. The rational choice theorists emphasize the institutional rules (for example, the Rule of Four in granting certiorari, the senior justice assigning the draft opinion, etc.) that serve as constraints on the justices' simply acting out their personal ideologies or policy preferences.

7

The *Bush v. Gore* Decision

It is a sad day for America and the Constitution when a court decides the outcome of an election.—James Baker, George W. Bush's chief lawyer, after the Florida Supreme Court ruled in favor of a recount on December 8, 2000

The decision by the Supreme Court in *Bush v. Gore* will forever be mentioned as one of its most significant. On December 12, 2000, it curtailed the recounting of votes in Florida, meaning that George W. Bush had been elected president. Democrats questioned the legitimacy of Bush as president, and the issue resurfaced in the presidential election campaign of 2004. But it was not just members of the losing political party who questioned the motives of those justices who agreed to hear the appeal and then decided in Bush's favor. Many, like Alan Dershowitz, were angry at the Supreme Court "not so much because of whom it elected, but because it took it upon itself to elect anyone" (2001, p. 11).

The decision was important in a second way: in its impact on the image of the Court. Was it, in the words of Vincent Bugliosi, a "betrayal of trust by an institution revered by Americans like no other"? (2001, p. 4). Did the decision permanently impair the image of the Court as a bastion of constitutional authority, as some critics prophesied it would? Apparently not; the Court continues with business as usual, and its decisions have the same degree of impact that they did before the *Bush v. Gore* decision. Certainly more was written about the decision in the days, weeks, and months after it happened than any other decision in the last 50 years; much of what was concluded was very critical of the decision, but it often reflected the biases of the writers, including law professors (in what Judge Richard Posner called "naked partisanship" [2001, p. viii]), so that it is difficult to find objective treatments regarding the justification of the decision. At any rate, the purpose of this chapter is to examine the decision in detail, before it recedes into historical memory, in the hope that such an analysis will inform us about the nature of Supreme Court decision-making.

The 36 tumultuous days from November 7, 2000, to December 12, 2000, were replete with on-again, off-again recounts, conflicting court opinions, and almost daily shifts in vote counts. So it is useful to present a chronology of events leading up to the decision. After doing so, the chapter summarizes the opinion, describes criticisms and other reactions, and seeks to explain the outcome from the different models of decision-making described earlier in this book.

A Chronology of Events Leading up to the Decision on December 12, 2000

The decision announced on December 12, 2000, cannot be fully understood without considering the sequence of events preceding it. There were at least 58 lawsuits leading to 30 separate proceedings in three federal courts and five state courts, which accumulated almost six thousand pages of legal documents. The following chronology summarizes the most important activities and decisions.

- November 7: Election Day
- November 8: An initial tally of votes indicated that Vice-President Gore led slightly in the popular vote (by about 200,000) but Governor Bush would win in the electoral vote, *if* he won Florida. However, his lead in Florida was only 1,784 votes out of almost 6 million cast, and numerous reports of election problems surfaced in that state. For example, the so-called butterfly punch-card ballot introduced in Palm Beach County was confusing, and after leaving the voting booth, many Democrats wondered if they had voted for Pat Buchanan by mistake. Buchanan received 3,407 votes in Palm Beach County, 20 percent of his state total. Palm Beach County is heavily Democratic, and it has been estimated that 3,000 of these votes were intended for Gore. Furthermore, more than 19,000 ballots in that county were "overvotes," that is, with two candidates punched for president.
- November 9: A machine recount required under the Florida Election Code reduced Bush's lead to 327 votes. (In actuality, 18 counties, accounting for approximately 1 million ballots, only checked their numerical totals and determined that their computer software was functioning properly, thus ignoring the requirement that the ballots be put back in the voting machine [Kaplan, 2001].) Democrats also asked for a manual recount in four counties. Two of the counties, Palm Beach and Volusia, agreed to do so immediately. Despite the Gore group's mantra of "Count all the votes," the Florida Democratic Executive Committee did not ask for a recount in all 67 counties, a decision that even some of their supporters criticized (Kaplan, 2001;

Toobin, 2001). The deadline for counties to submit their vote totals was a rapidly approaching November 14, and Florida's secretary of state, Katherine Harris, announced that she had no discretion to extend the deadline. (Harris had been an honorary state cochair for the 2000 Bush campaign.)

- November 11: Bush's lawyers filed a suit in federal district court in Miami to prevent the manual recounts in the counties with disputed tallies, claiming that they would be no more nearly accurate than automated counts.
- November 13: The district court of the Southern District of Florida refused the request to block manual recounts, concluding that it was a state matter, not a federal one. U.S. District Judge Donald Middlebrooks, in a thoughtful 24-page opinion, concluded that "federal judges are not the bosses in state election disputes" (Kaplan, 2001, p. 96). In so doing, he quoted Judge J. L. Edmonson, a member of the Eleventh Circuit, the appeals court that might be reviewing his decision. Edmonson, known as the "Scalia of the South," was an influential member of the conservative Eleventh Circuit. Meanwhile, Secretary of State Harris announced that the position of her office was that such recounts should not be allowed.
- November 14: Florida attorney general Bob Butterworth, a Democrat, issued an advisory opinion that manual recounts should be allowed. Volusia County (one of those cited by Gore's attorneys) completed its recount, with Bush's lead reduced to 300 votes. Judge Terry Lewis ruled that the secretary of state may exercise discretion in whether to accept returns for statewide certification after the deadline.
- November 15: The Florida secretary of state ruled that statements from Volusia, Palm Beach, Miami-Dade, and Broward Counties reporting late returns did not justify extending the deadline for filing. Bush appealed the district court's ruling of November 13 to the United States Court of Appeals for the Eleventh Circuit. The Florida Supreme Court denied the secretary of state's decision to maintain the deadline for recounts.
- November 16: The Florida Supreme Court ruled unanimously that manual recounts could continue in the three counties that had not completed them. Democrats asked Leon County Judge Lewis to find the Florida secretary of state in contempt because of her decision not to extend the deadline.
- November 17: Judge Lewis rejected the Democrats' petition submitted the day before. Overseas absentee ballots increased Bush's lead to 930 votes. (Florida, in contrast to most states, accepts absentee votes from abroad up to 10 days after the election.)
- November 21: The Florida Supreme Court ruled unanimously that manual recounts must be included, and set November 26 as the amended deadline for certification.

- November 22: Bush appealed the decision of the day before to the United States Supreme Court. The Miami-Dade County canvassing board cancelled its recount of the county's 650,000 votes, on grounds that it could not be completed by the new deadline.
- November 23: The Florida Supreme Court denied Gore's request that the manual recount continue in Miami-Dade County.
- November 24: The United States Supreme Court granted certiorari to Bush's appeal of the November 21 ruling by the Florida Supreme Court.
- November 26: Palm Beach County's request for more time to recount was denied. The Florida Elections Canvassing Commission certified the election results, with Bush winning by 537 votes out of 5,825,000 counted.
- November 27: Gore filed suit contesting certification and questioned voting in three counties.
- November 28: Judge N. Sanders Sauls rejected Gore's request.
- December 1: Oral arguments in the United States Supreme Court were held on the Florida Supreme Court's decision to extend the deadline for certification. The Florida Supreme Court rejected Gore's request for an immediate recount of the ballots from Palm Beach County.
- December 4: The United States Supreme Court, by a vote of 9 to 0, remanded Bush's appeal to the Florida Supreme Court for further consideration, after vacating the November 21 decision by the Florida Supreme Court. Judge Sauls rejected Gore's appeal, concluding that Gore had failed to prove a "reasonable probability" that the election would have turned out differently if ballot counting had been continued.
- December 6: The United States Court of Appeals for the Eleventh Circuit rejected Bush's request to bar manual recounts.
- December 7: The Florida Supreme Court heard oral arguments on Gore's appeal of Judge Sauls's decision.
- December 8: The Florida Supreme Court ruled 4 to 3 in support of Gore's appeal, and ordered the Leon County Circuit Court to hand-count 9,000 ballots from Miami-Dade County. It also ordered the secretary of state to include 383 votes for Gore from Palm Beach County. Bush appealed these rulings to the United States Supreme Court.
- December 9: Even though the manual recount had begun, the United States Supreme Court, by a 5 to 4 vote, stayed the Florida Supreme Court's ruling of the day before. Justice Scalia wrote that counting these votes would "threaten irreparable harm to petitioner [Bush] . . . by casting a cloud on what he claims to be the legitimacy of his election."
- December 10: Lawyers for both sides filed briefs with the United States Supreme Court.
- December 11: Oral arguments were held in the United States Supreme Court. The Florida Supreme Court, responding to the remand from the U.S. Supreme Court on December 4, reversed the ruling by Judge Sauls that it was acceptable for the secretary of state to reject late filings.

- December 12: The United States Supreme Court, in a *per curiam* decision (but by a 5 to 4 vote), reversed the Florida Supreme Court ruling of December 11 and barred further count in of disputed ballots. The Florida legislature appointed electors representing Bush.
- December 13: Gore ended his campaign and conceded the election.
- December 14: The Florida Supreme Court dismissed the case remanded by the United States Supreme Court, concluding that the Florida Election Code did not provide the procedures needed for the resolution of disputed issues.
- December 18: The Electoral College voted, with Bush receiving 271 votes (including Florida's 25) and Gore receiving 266.
- January 6, 2001: Congress met to count electoral votes and declared Bush the winner and next president. Gore, as vice-president, presided over the session.

The Briefs and Oral Argument for *Bush v. Gore*

The chronological listing illustrates the often partisan and conflicting nature of the actions and decisions leading up to the oral arguments before the Court on December 11. What were the basic arguments presented by each side in its briefs and oral arguments?

The Case for Governor Bush

A focus of the lawyers for Governor Bush was that article 2 of the Constitution said that state legislatures, not state courts, made the rules for presidential elections. As Toobin noted, "[a] decision based on this rarely invoked provision of Article II would allow the Court to rule for Bush without disturbing any settled precedents" (2001, p. 259). But Justice Kennedy, at the oral argument, responded to this claim by observing that courts interpret the words of legislatures all the time, and Theodore Olson, arguing the case for Governor Bush, conceded: "It may not be the most powerful argument we bring to this Court" (p. 259).

A second argument claimed a violation of the equal protection clause of the Fourteenth Amendment, which had been adopted after the Civil War to protect freed slaves. The brief suggested that the Florida order for a recount challenged the principle of "one person, one vote," because ballots in some counties were reviewed more than ballots in other counties. But the Bush brief devoted only 5 of its 50 pages to this argument.

The Case for Vice-President Gore

The briefs for Vice-President Gore responded that it would not be a violation of the goal of equal protection to make accurate counts of ballots that earlier were undercounted. But even many supporters of Vice-President Gore felt that his lawyers did not do a good job of responding to Governor Bush's brief. For example, only one page of the 51-page respondent's brief that was submitted December 10 dealt with an equal protection argument. Nor did it cite a single case; instead, Gore's brief curtly concluded that the claim of a lack of uniform standards violated the Fourteenth Amendment "simply finds no support in the law." Instead, the brief for Vice-President Gore argued that there is variation from state to state in procedures for counting disputed votes, and to embrace Bush's equal protection argument would mean that these practices in other states violated the Fourteenth Amendment. Furthermore, the rebuttal brief failed to ask whether any evidence existed that a lack of uniform standards across Florida was more likely to hurt Governor Bush than Vice President Gore.

The Oral Arguments

Neither side's attorneys distinguished themselves at the oral arguments. While Governor Bush's brief had hinted at an equal representation argument, Theodore Olson ducked explaining that at length at the oral argument, knowing that recently the Court had used the equal protection clause as a justification to strike down only those "laws that explicitly discriminated against groups the Constitution projected, most notably racial minorities" (Toobin, 2001, p. 259).

The low point in the oral arguments was achieved by Joe Klock, an attorney representing the Florida secretary of state, who was given 10 minutes to justify the state's decision to reject the recounts. After several questions from Justices Souter and Breyer, Justice Stevens posed a difficult hypothetical question to Klock, who replied, "Well, Justice Brennan, the difficulty is that under—" He got no further before the courtroom exploded with laughter. As that subsided, Justice Souter intervened: "they have to throw their hands up?" he asked.

"No, Justice Breyer, what I'm saying is that—"

"I'm Justice Souter. You've got to cut that out." Now the laughter was like a thunderclap. A minute later, another justice took center stage; "Mr. Klock, I'm Scalia," he said, and again the audience roared. Attorney Klock, facing the biggest challenge in his life, had flubbed twice.

The prominent trial attorney David Boies, representing Vice-President Gore, did little better. Toobin evaluated the interaction as follows.

> The heart of Boies's argument should have come when Justices Kennedy and Souter asked him about variation in counting standards between different counties. What if dimpled ballots were recognized as votes in one county but not in another? "There may be such variation, and I think we would have a responsibility to tell the Florida courts what to do about it," Souter said. "On that assumption, what would you tell them to do about it?"

Boies had a temporary mind freeze. It is perhaps the most important question of the argument, and he simply didn't have an answer. Weeks of little sleep, not to mention inadequate time to prepare, had taken their toll.

"Well, I think that's a very hard question," Boies said simply.

Justice Stevens tried to come to Boies's rescue. "Does not the procedure that is in place there contemplate that the uniformity will be achieved by having the final results all reviewed by the same judge?"

Boies grasped the life preserver. "Yes," he said. "That's what I was going to say, Your Honor."

It took Justice Ginsburg to give an even better reply to the equal protection argument. True, as Stevens and Souter both suggested, Judge Lewis served as a fairness check for the process, but in a larger sense, no court had ever required a state to give all its voters the same technology or to evaluate all its ballots by a single standard. When Olson rose to give his rebuttal, Ginsburg said, "Well, there are different ballots from county to county, too, Mr. Olson. And that's part of the argument that I don't understand. There are machines, there's the optical scanning, and there are a whole variety of ballots. There's the butterfly ballot that we've all heard about and other kinds of punch-card ballots. How can you have one standard when there are so many varieties of ballots?"

Time was up before Olson could give a complete answer. Both sides had made competent, if uninspired arguments. . . . The vote on the stay had been five to four in Bush's favor, and nothing in the oral argument suggested that any of the justices had changed their minds. (2001, pp. 262–263)

The Decision of December 12, 2000

With the oral arguments completed at half past noon on December 11, the participants didn't have long to wait before a decision was announced. It came slightly before 10 p.m. on the evening of the next day. But it reflected several unconventional aspects, both procedurally and substantively. For example, it was not announced from the bench of the imposing courtroom, as is *always* done—in fact, the justices had gone home. Rather, the Court placed multiple copies of the 65-page document in the press room and left them for the media to grab, digest, and try to disseminate as rapidly as possible. But little help was given; the document even lacked the traditional "head note," the summary of the decision that, again, *always* came at the beginning of the printed opinion.

The Nature of the Decision

The essence of the decision was, in the words of one observer, "that the standardless recounts were an unconstitutional violation of equal protection and there was no time left for Florida to do anything about it" (Kaplan, 2001, p. 274). But who wrote the 13-page majority decision, and which justices subscribed to it? It was an unsigned, *per curiam*, decision, which carried with it five other opinions: a concurrence by Chief Justice Rehnquist (agreed to by Justices Scalia and Thomas) and four dissents, one each by Justices Stevens, Souter, Ginsburg, and Breyer. Only thus could it be concluded that the determining opinion reflected a bare 5 to 4 conservative-versus-liberal majority. Unsigned decisions are called *per curiam*, or "for the Court." Ordinarily, they are short opinions on uncontroversial cases and hence reflect unanimous votes; as they are unsigned, the opinion cannot be attributed to one justice as the sole author. But not here.

It eventually became the common wisdom that Justice Kennedy was the author of the opinion, with significant input from Justice O'Connor. Ironically, these two were the only justices whose names *do not appear* in any of the six separate opinions in this historic document.

Normally, in a case of this magnitude, as mentioned earlier, the chief justice would author the opinion for the Court. But Justice Rehnquist's draft never received support from the two swing voters, only from his conservative stalwarts, Justices Thomas and Scalia. Those who observed the process at close hand and were later willing speak to reporters anonymously—apparently some of the law clerks for the losing justices—noted that early on, Justice Kennedy began to focus on the claim of a failure in equal representation (Margolick, Peretz, & Shnayerson, 2004).

The Limited Applicability

Equally unconventional was the disclaimer in the determining opinion that the Court's decision was "limited to the present circumstances." (The reason given was that "the problem of equal protection in election processes generally presents many complexities" [*Bush v. Gore*, 2000, p. 532].) As Kaplan put it, "This isn't the way the Court does business." He wrote:

> Because it is the top court in the nation and because it decides fewer than one hundred cases a year, it both has to select appeals that will have broad application to other litigation and has to write opinions that will guide judges in the lower courts (as well as the Supreme Court itself). Rulings that are confined to a single moment and one set of litigants—in "the same class as a restricted railroad ticket, good for this day and train only," as Justice Owen Roberts put it in a famous 1944 dissent—not only squander the Court's time, but open it up to attack that its decision-making is unprincipled and result-driven.

Scalia could have told Kennedy all that. "The Supreme Court of the United States does not sit to announce 'unique' circumstances," he thundered in the lone dissent from a ruling that made the Virginia Military Institute co-ed. "Its principal function is to establish precedent—that is, to set forth principles of law that every court in America must follow. . . . That is the principal reason we publish our opinion." Yet *Bush v. Gore*, the Court instructed, had no precedent-making, as opposed to president-making, value. (2001, p. 282)

How can the Court on the one hand establish a new constitutional right and on the other limit it to only the present case?

The Dissents

Each of the four relatively liberal justices wrote a dissent. Others of the four joined in the dissent written by each (for example, Justices Ginsburg and Breyer joined in Justice Stevens's dissent), but each felt it important to express his or her own specific commentary.

Justice Stevens's Dissent

Justice Stevens argued that the Supreme Court should not have intervened; "the federal questions that ultimately emerged in this case are not substantial" (*Bush v. Gore*, 2000, p. 539). He wrote: "The Florida Supreme Court's exercise of appellate jurisdiction therefore was wholly consistent with, and indeed contemplated by, the grant of authority in Article II" (p. 540).

Justice Stevens did acknowledge the concern that different counties using similar voting systems had different standards for determining voters' intent. But he believed that these concerns would be alleviated, "if not eliminated," by the actions of an impartial magistrate who would adjudicate objections. The final paragraph of Justice Stevens's dissent has been widely quoted by critics of the Court's decision:

What must underlie petitioners' entire federal assault on the Florida election procedure is an unstated lack of confidence in the impartiality and capacity of the state judges who would make the critical decisions if the vote count were to proceed. Otherwise, their position is wholly without merit. The endorsement of that position by the majority of this Court can only lend credence to the most cynical appraisal of the work of judges throughout the land. It is confidence in the men and women who administer the judicial system that is the true backbone of the rule of law. Time will one day heal the wound to that confidence that will be inflicted by today's decision. One thing, however, is certain. Although we may never know with complete certainty the identity of the winner of this year's Presidential election, the identity of the loser is perfectly clear. It is the Nation's confidence in the judge as an impartial guide to the rule of law.

I respectfully dissent. (*Bush v. Gore*, 2000, p. 542)

Justice Souter's Dissent

Justice Souter noted in his dissent that he agreed with the three other dissenting opinions but wrote separately "only to say how straightforward the issues before us really are" (*Bush v. Gore*, 2000, p. 543). He believed that the interpretations by the Florida Supreme Court raised no substantial problem under article 2 of the Constitution. Only one issue in the petition was of merit, he wrote: The charge of unjustifiably disparate standards in different counties. Different standards for interpreting a voter's intent created a problem. But Justice Souter's solution was to remand to the Florida courts with instructions to apply uniform standards, and he was confident that Florida could do so and count the votes by the date set for the meeting of electors, December 18.

Justice Ginsburg's Dissent

The dissent by Justice Ginsburg began by focusing on Chief Justice Rehnquist's concurrence that acknowledged that Florida's Election Code "may well admit of more than one interpretation" (*Bush v. Gore*, 2000, p. 546). But she found no cause to question the Florida Supreme Court's interpretation of the law, noting that "not uncommonly we let stand state-court interpretations of federal law with which we might disagree" (p. 546). She even quoted from an article by Justice O'Connor supporting the ability of state court judges to litigate federal constitutional questions. Ordinarily, the Supreme Court has "accorded respectful consideration and great weight to the views of the State's highest court" (p. 547).

She noted that it was rare for the Supreme Court to reject outright the interpretation of state law by a state supreme court; she pointed out the chief justice's "casual citations" suggested that the three such instances cited by Justice Rehnquist are rare "and hardly comparable to the situation here"; in fact, they came from the Jim Crow South (*Bush v. Gore*, 2000, p. 548).

Justice Ginsburg also questioned the majority opinion's view that it was impractical to expect that a recount could be completed before the deadline; such is "a prophecy the Court's own judgment will not allow to be tested. Such an untested prophecy should not decide the Presidency of the United States" (*Bush v. Gore*, 2000, p. 550).

Interestingly, Justice Ginsburg ended her opinion with "I dissent," not the traditional "I respectfully dissent." Some have interpreted this as a rebuke of the majority, but Linda Greenhouse (2001a), who has reported on the Court for the *New York Times* for many years, has pointed out that Justice Ginsburg frequently does this for "an economy of style" rather than as an expression of anger.

Justice Breyer's Dissent

Justice Breyer's opening statement was explicit: "The Court was wrong to take this case. It was wrong to grant a stay. It should now vacate that stay and permit the Florida Supreme Court to decide whether the recount should resume" (*Bush v. Gore*, 2000, pp. 550–551). He felt that the majority's remedy to the issue of inconsistency in counting dimpled ballots—to halt the recount entirely—was an overreaction; there is no evidence, he said, that a recount could not be done before the deadline.

What Was the Decision-Making Process and Rationale?

The Court's deliberations, as always, were private. But Court-watchers have pieced together a likely scenario for the positions and developments. Joan Biskupic, who covers the Court for *USA Today*, summarized it effectively:

> The five conservative justices fractured into two camps: Rehnquist, Scalia, and Thomas, who continued to say that the Florida court had acted illegally and infringed on legislative power; and O'Connor and Kennedy, who agreed that any recounts would be improper but for a different reason—the different standards that Florida counties had been using for recounts. They believed this could violate the Constitution's guarantee of equal protection under the law. Meanwhile, those two justices were being pressured by two of the court's four liberals, Souter and Breyer, to adopt a compromise that would acknowledge the lack of standards for recounts but permit a review of the disputed ballots to continue under new rules.
>
> Kennedy, who was especially worried about the various county standards for determining voter intent, took on the responsibility for writing much of what became the Court's unsigned decision. But he was still torn about what to do. Kennedy has a slow, deliberate style and people close to the Court say at times he simply froze. In the Florida case, crafting a constitutional principle that spoke for any majority would have been difficult for the swiftest writer. What finally was released the night of December 12, two hours before a midnight deadline that would have raised the possibility of congressional intervention, was a thin mix of precedent and legal reasoning. The Court's decision stopping the recounts was a novel interpretation of the Constitution's guarantee of equal protection that included a declaration that the ruling shouldn't affect other cases.
>
> Supporting the opinion were Rehnquist, O'Connor, Kennedy, Scalia and Thomas—all ideological, if not political, conservatives. The liberals—Souter, Breyer, Stevens, and Ginsburg—dissented.

Souter and Breyer, who shared concerns about a statewide standard, had fought hard for a compromise. They wanted to avoid a ruling that would seem little more than a political calculation. More important, they believed that Florida's disputed ballots had to be tallied to make the election results credible. They tried to identify with the concerns of O'Connor and Kennedy. As time ran out, however, O'Connor and Kennedy said there was no practical way to swiftly set new standards. Rebuffed, Breyer and Souter left the courthouse in frustration. (2001, p. 2A)

The Reaction

Reactions to the decision varied and, for many, were predictable. As Renata Adler put it: "Outraged, gleeful, satisfied, resigned, the response seemed in almost every case to flow from the politics of the speaker. Republicans and 'conservatives,' for the most part, approved. Democrats and 'liberals' did not" (2001, p. 29). The decision provoked a multitude of op-ed pieces and articles by political scientists, law professors, and columnists, as well as letters to the editor by the public. Two useful, book-length compilations of commentaries have been published, edited by Dionne and Kristol (2001) and by Sunstein and Epstein (2001). Several very readable, chronologically organized books have described the events; those by Toobin (2001) and by Kaplan (2001) have been quoted in this chapter. Among the books by lawyers, two—by Alan Dershowitz (2001) and by Vincent Bugliosi (2001)—are extremely critical; Judge Richard Posner's (2001) is less so. But even those commentaries that can be linked to the political bias of their authors often raise provocative points and sharpen our understanding.

The Criticisms

This section attempts to separate each of the most frequent criticisms of the majority decision and evaluate them.

The Court Shouldn't Have Granted Certiorari

A number of critics have proposed that the Supreme Court should have simply rejected granting certiorari to Governor Bush's appeal. For example, law professor Elizabeth Garrett has written:

[The Supreme Court] should have left the matter to the political sphere. More specifically, it was the responsibility of Congress to resolve any disputes that might have risen from the election in Florida. Although the Court has a long history of involvement in the electoral process and in political matters, it often makes the situation it finds worse rather than better. Its rather undistinguished record in recent cases dealing with electoral issues results both from the limitations of case-by-case adjudication and from the Court's unsophisticated view of the political process. The Court should consider adopting a less intrusive stance in cases affecting the political process, intervening only to ensure free and equal access to that process. (2001, p. 39)

Critics support the position of the dissenting justices that the Court should have remanded the case back to the Florida Supreme Court with an instruction to establish a statewide standard that could be applied uniformly, and to continue the recount until the December 18 deadline. The December 12 deadline could be violated—it had in the past.

The Court Should Have Recognized That Its Own Image Would Suffer If It Became Involved

The justices had to be aware that their decision would decide the election and hence open them up to charges of partisanship. The specific impact of their decision made it different from the other election law cases and political process cases in which the Court had intervened (Garrett, 2001). The justices should have been aware that their decision could cause irreparable harm to the Court's image of being above the fray. Law clerks for some of the liberal justices were astounded; "it was just inconceivable to us that the Court would want to lose its credibility in such a patently political way," one was quoted as saying (Margolick et al., 2004, p. 312).

The Basis for the Decision Was Wrong

Critics claimed that the use of the equal protection clause as a rationale was, in the words of Bugliosi, a "legal gimmick" (2001, p. 23). Normally, claims of violation of equal protection are brought by aggrieved parties who have been discriminated against. Professor Erwin Chemerinsky noted: "The Rehnquist Court almost never uses equal protection jurisprudence except in striking down affirmative action programs" (quoted in Bugliosi, 2001, p. 45). As noted in Justice Ginsburg's dissent, the cases cited by the Court as legal precedent bear questionable application in the Florida situation. No Florida voters brought suit claiming they had been disenfranchised because of the different recounting standards that were being used. Instead, Governor Bush claimed he had been wronged by the procedure.

Some critics even questioned whether Governor Bush had legal standing to raise the equal protection claim. As he did not vote in Florida, he could not claim that he personally suffered an injury. Surprisingly, lawyers representing Vice-President Gore did not raise this issue.

The Decision Was Inconsistent with the Court's Recent Federalism Decisions

The founders of the nation envisioned two political capacities, one state and one federal, and this principle of dual sovereignty has remained central in the Court's reasoning. As noted in several previous chapters, the Supreme Court in recent years, under the stewardship of Chief Justice Rehnquist, has ardently favored the rights of states over the federal government. This is the Supreme Court that has permitted the execution of state prisoners who have exhausted their appeals, even when evidence surfaced for their innocence. In contrast, here, to quote a severe critic, the same five justices who "chose to intrude on Florida's election process . . . always claimed to be champions of the rights of states and foes of 'judicial activism' and 'judicial overreach'" (Dionne, 2001, p. 288).

Justice Ginsburg's dissent in *Bush v. Gore* reflected this criticism:

> Federal courts defer to state high courts' interpretation of their states' own law. This principle reflects the core of federalism with which we all agree. . . . Were the other members of this Court as mindful as they generally are of our system of dual sovereignty, they would affirm the judgment of the Florida Supreme Court. (2001, p. 549)

Some Justices Should Have Recused Themselves

Chapter 3 described the issue of recusal; as noted, the Court is reluctant to intervene if justices fail to recuse themselves when the facts seem to warrant doing so. Issues were raised especially in regard to three justices.

Justice O'Connor

Justice O'Connor and her husband, the night of the election, were watching the election returns with friends. When the networks incorrectly placed Florida in Gore's victory column—along with two vital states that Gore did win, Michigan and Illinois—it meant to her that the election was "over," and she exclaimed, "This is terrible." Two witnesses reported to *Newsweek* magazine that her husband said she was upset because they wanted to retire to Arizona, and a Gore win meant they've have to wait four more years (Thomas & Isikoff, 2000).

It is not against the law for Supreme Court justices to vote in presidential elections, and Justice O'Connor's allegiance to the Republican party was well known. (She had been a leading Republican state legislator in Arizona.) But if her use of the evaluation of "terrible" meant terrible for the country, as some have speculated (Dershowitz, 2001), then a sufficient conflict of interest was present. However, it should be noted that even though a Republican *did* become president in 2001, Justice O'Connor did not retire during the first four years of

George W. Bush's presidency. (And when she did retire, in 2005, an overriding reason was her need to care for her ailing husband.) Perhaps, as Dershowitz suggested, she needed the time to "rebuild her tarnished legacy" (p. 162). Others suggested that it would not look good for the justices who were rumored to be leaving—O'Connor and Rehnquist—to do so, thus letting "the man they anointed select their replacements" (Margolick et al., 2004, p. 358).

Justice Thomas

During the time of the November election campaign and the month of appeals, Justice Thomas's wife, Virginia Thomas, was employed at the Heritage Foundation, a conservative organization with close relationships to the Bush election campaign. Her job was to gather resumes for the Bush transition team (Dershowitz, 2001). She previously had been a staff member for the Republican Conference at the House of Representatives. So Justice Thomas's spouse had a substantial interest in the outcome of the election.

Justice Scalia

Two of Justice Scalia's sons are attorneys who worked for law firms that represented Governor Bush in his appeals.

Alan Dershowitz's (2001) book on the election goes into detail on the issue of recusal; he also questioned possible conflicts of interest by Justices Rehnquist and Kennedy. In fact, the detailed analysis returns us to an earlier criticism: If five of the justices had serious conflicts of interest, should the Court have taken the case?

Support for the Decision

While more commentators have been critical than supportive, justifications for the decision do exist. Three are discussed here.

The Need to Resolve the Conflict

One justification for the Court's decision was that the nation needed to be relieved of its state of ambiguity, that the United States was approaching a constitutional crisis that only the Court could resolve. Judge Posner's book justified the actions of the Court as "a pragmatically defensible series of responses to a looming political and constitutional crisis" (2001, p. ix). A poll taken by the *Washington Post* and reported on the day of the oral arguments found that almost half (43 percent) wanted the Court to discontinue manual recounting (*Washington Post*, 2000).

In 1876, when a similarly controversial presidential election dispute had occurred, it was not resolved until early March of the next year (Morris, 2003;

Rehnquist, 2004). What some have called "the Five Week Recount War" of 2000 (Dionne & Kristol, 2001, p. 2) needed to end. Supporters of the decision felt that by its prompt action, the Court provided resolution to the dispute and closure to the nation.

The Decision by the Florida Supreme Court Exceeded Its Authority

Supporters of the Court's decision in *Bush v. Gore* were highly critical of the Florida Supreme Court, claiming that it disregarded the opinions of the Florida secretary of state (the constitutionally designated chief election officer), two state court judges, and a previous cautionary opinion from the United States Supreme Court. Furthermore, they claimed that the Florida court exceeded its authority by setting a new date for certification. Judge Posner, for example, concluded that the state supreme court "had violated the requirement of Article II of the Constitution that each state's presidential electors be appointed in a manner directed by the state's legislature" (2001, p. 3).

Equal Representation Had Not Been Achieved

At its most basic level, the equal representation clause seeks fairness. Supporters of the Court's decision believed that the manual recount was flawed in several respects; it was to be done in only some counties (the most heavily Democratic), the standards for allocating partially perforated ballots were inconsistent, and undervotes were to be counted but not overvotes.

Claims of Loss of Prestige for the Court

Was the reputation of the Court for remaining above partisan politics immensely damaged by the decision? The Court has made unfortunate decisions before: *Dred Scott, Plessy v. Ferguson,* the decisions upholding the incarceration of 110,000 Japanese American citizens during World War II, the *Clinton v. Jones* decision, but for some, this decision was in a class by itself, because here the Supreme Court arrogated to itself a power the Constitution allocated to the states and to Congress "and specifically *not* to the federal judiciary" (Adler, 2001, p. 30).

Even Judge Posner has acknowledged that "the majority opinion . . . damaged the Court's prestige, at least in the short run" (2001, p. 175), although he also concluded that the dissents "did the Court no service" by accusing the majority of impairing public confidence in the judiciary's impartiality (p. 175). But the one study that was able to compare the public's view of the Court *before and after* the decision showed no net effect (Kritzer, 2001). In this study, public approval of the Court was measured a number of times, starting in May 2000 and ending in February 2001. In actuality, Democrats expressed more disapproval, but Republicans expressed more approval, and the net effect, in the words of the study's author, was "essentially nil" (p. 36).

The Impact of the Decision on Relationships within the Court

Journalists who observe the Court every day and have full-time careers writing about it have felt that the tenseness among the justices took some time to dissipate, despite efforts to do so (Biskupic, 2001). "When the justices returned to the bench [in January] for the first round of oral arguments since the decision, they seemed both wearier and testier. O'Connor . . . has at times been visibly impatient with her fellow justices" (p. 2A).

But despite the importance of the decision and the immediate frustration reflected in the wording of the dissents, the justices—at least those willing to speak about it—denied that any acrimony was long-lasting. Justice Breyer, speaking at the ABA convention eight months later, said that all decisions are met with "widespread acceptance of the final decision even where we may wholeheartedly believe the decision is completely wrong" (Associated Press, 2001a, p. 7A). Justice Scalia told a group of law students: "If you can't disagree without hating each other, you better find another profession other than the law" (Greenhouse, 2001a, p. A1). Less than three weeks after the decision, Justice Ginsburg and her husband Martin joined Justice Scalia and his wife Maureen for New Year's Eve dinner, a tradition the two couples have shared for years (Greenhouse, 2001a).

The institutional norm at the Court is compatibility; "there is a philosophy among the justices that rehashing a case or holding a grudge is useless and counterproductive. As lifetime appointees they cannot avoid each other's company" (Biskupic, 2001, p. 2A).

Explaining the Decision

Several of the earlier chapters in this book explicated different models for judicial decision-making. How would each explain the decision is this case?

The Legal Model

Chapter 1 described Justice Thomas as an advocate of the legal model—that cases are decided on the basis of the law, the Constitution, and legal precedents. And in keeping with his position, he responded to a question from a group of Washington high school students on the day after the Court's ruling by saying that the decision had nothing to do with politics.

The concurring opinion offered by Chief Justice Rehnquist offered several precedents to support a basis of a violation of equal protection. But, as noted, these precedents seemed a stretch. Furthermore, the Court had previously ruled in several cases, beginning with *Atkins v. Texas* in 1945, that the equal protection clause can only be applied if discrimination was intentional. Even as recently as 1996, in a case in which Chief Justice Rehnquist wrote the majority opinion (*United States v. Armstrong*), the Court concluded that just because the defendant showed that a policy had a discriminatory effect was not enough; the policy had to be motivated to harm. The Court even ruled similarly in a case involving voting. In 1980, in *City of Mobile, Alabama, v. Bolden*, the Court evaluated the procedure of electing city commissioners at large rather than from individual distracts, thus, it was claimed, diluting the voting strength of black citizens. The Court ruled that a violation of equal protection occurred only if there was *purposeful* discrimination.

The Attitudinal Model

Perhaps the strongest test of the applicability of the attitudinal model is to ask, as some observers have (see Adler, 2001; Dershowitz, 2001; Posner, 2001), if Al Gore had been the petitioner, rather than George W. Bush, with the same set of facts and arguments, would the Court have decided as it did? Adler concluded that "not a single justice would have agreed to hear the case" (2001, pp. 29–30).

It does appear that Justice Scalia, at least, had made his mind up, prior to the December 11 oral arguments, that Governor Bush had won the election. In his support of a stay on further recounts (written before the oral arguments of December 11), he gratuitously added a concurrence that said: "The issuance of a stay suggests that a majority of the Court, while not deciding the issues presented, believe that the petitioner has a substantial probability of success" (*Bush v. Gore*, on Application for Stay, December 9, 2000, p. 1).

Some commentators went so far as to endorse the attitudinal model as the way matters *should* be decided. Tom Bethell, senior editor of the *American Spectator* magazine, wrote in its February 2001 issue: "And we salute Supreme Court Justices Sandra Day O'Connor and Anthony Kennedy, who proved to be good Republicans when their votes were essential" (p. 14).

The Motivated Reasoning Model

The motivated reasoning model assumes that rationalization often occurs. At a conscious level, actors are sincerely shocked when a negative spin is put on the reasons for their actions. Did the majority of the Supreme Court wake up on December 12 and say to themselves "I'm going to do whatever I can to make George W. Bush president?" No; Justices Kennedy and Thomas have said in public that they regretted having to decide the case, but that it was their responsibility. But their underlying values caused them to perceive the actions of the Florida Supreme Court in a certain way, and they came upon a solution that would not only ensure they outcome they wanted, but to justify it in their own minds. As one insider observed about the justices, "people are amazing self-kidders" (Margolick et al., 2004, p. 358).

The conclusion of Judge Posner, quoted here, seems to support a motivated reasoning explanation:

> Do I believe, therefore, that *Bush v. Gore* would have been decided the same way if the parties had been reversed, that is, if Bush had been challenging the certification of Gore as the winner of the popular vote in Florida? I doubt that any of the justices has so debased a conception of the judicial office as to try *deliberately* to swing the election to his preferred presidential candidate. But the undeniable interest that a judge, especially a justice of the U.S. Supreme Court, has in who his colleagues and successors will be is likely to have alerted the justices to features of *Bush v. Gore* that might otherwise have eluded them. The conservative justices may have been more sensitive to arguments based on Article II and the Equal Protection Clause than they otherwise would have been, and the liberal justices more sensitive to the weaknesses of those arguments than they otherwise would have been. It is because judges who have different values and experience are sensitive to different features of a case that diversity of backgrounds is a valid consideration in judicial selection. (2001, p. 180)

The Rational Choice Model

According to the rational choice model, judges may decide to vote on the basis of their strategic goals. Professor John You of the University of California at Berkeley reflected this position in his interpretation of the outcome: "We should balance the short-term hit to the Court's legitimacy with whether . . . it was in the best interest of the country to end the electoral crisis" (Bugliosi, 2001, p. 47).

Conclusions

This book consistently emphasizes the human nature of judicial decision-making. Justices inevitably possess ideological positions on many issues, and as this book attempts to document, these ideologies color the justices' reactions to the facts and claims of many appeals. Chapter 10, in particular, documents the impact of liberal and conservative ideologies on the votes of justices, especially in cases involving defendants' and prisoners' rights, search-and-seizure cases, and civil rights claims. But the majority's opinion in *Bush v. Gore* was a *political* decision that extended beyond mere ideology.

8

How Individual Justices Affect Decisions

I'm a mule at the Kentucky Derby; I don't expect to distinguish myself but I do expect to benefit from the associations.—Justice William Brennan, to a friend, on October 1, 1956, when he was appointed to the Supreme Court

Similar Backgrounds but Different Personalities

In some important ways, each Supreme Court justice shares similarities with every other. All recent justices have been college educated and have law degrees. Whether their prior experience was primarily in a law firm or in the judiciary or in elected office, they internalized a professional identity as lawyers. Clearly, these experiences bring a specialized focus to their judicial decisions. In addition, as noted earlier, the similarities in the recent members of the Court are even more specific, in that all but one of those justices completing the term ending in June 2005 had prior experience as a judge before being chosen for the highest court. Furthermore, all are political, in the sense that they have been actively involved in one of the major political parties, even if they have not held an elected office.

But each justice has a unique personality, and it is a theme of this book that the justice's idiosyncratic background and temperament contributes to his or her effectiveness on the Court. "Effectiveness" can refer to many things— the quality of his or her votes, the lasting importance of the justice's written opinions, the ability of the justice to be a collegial member of the Court, or simply how the person adjusts to the challenges of a high-pressure job. In this chapter, I consider effectiveness to be the ability to influence, in two senses. First is the ability to write opinions that are of significance to the country. I accept the view of the rational choice theorists described in chapter 6 that justices act to achieve public policy goals (Murphy, 1964; Epstein & Wright, 1998). To what degree are their goals reflected in the corpus of decisions by the Court? Second, I consider the ability to influence one's colleagues on the Court. Can the justice bring others to his or her position? While "persuasiveness" might seem central to this quality, ability to influence certainly also reflects a number of the ideal qualities described in chapter 2, including ability to think clearly, good working habits, a strong intellect, and good mental health.

Throughout history, scholars and experts have classified justices as among the "best" or the "worst," mostly on the basis of their effectiveness; while such judgments are admittedly subjective, some agreements emerge. Why do some justices do a better job? Did they happen along at "the right time"? Or do they possess personal qualities that encourage success? I propose that even among the "great" and "nearly great," some justices have been more effective in influencing their colleagues than others.

This chapter presents an analysis of six justices who served during the last half of the twentieth century; these six have been chosen because they reflect different personalities and styles brought to judicial decision-making. Among the 27 associate justices who served during this period, I have not chosen these at random; rather, I think these six could be placed on a continuum of relative effectiveness on the Court, and I have included in the six the ones that, in the opinion of scholars, have been the very least and very most effective of those 27. One of the six was such a misfit that he resigned after only five years on the Court; the other was so effective that he was able to achieve his policy goals even when most of his conferees held values contradictory to his own. (I have not included any who served as chief justice, as the responsibilities are somewhat different, and the role of chief justice is examined in chapter 9.)

The Misfit: Charles Whittaker

I begin with an extreme, a justice who clearly was not able to cope with the demands of the job. Charles E. Whittaker, the only native of Kansas to serve on the Supreme Court, was a justice for only five years, from 1957 to 1962, before he left the Court because of a disability. When Stanley Reed retired from the Court, President Eisenhower appointed Whittaker, who had been serving as a federal judge in the Western District of Missouri for two years (1954–1956) and as a judge of the United States Court of Appeals for the Eighth Circuit for less than a year. (He thus became the first person to serve as a federal district judge, a judge at the circuit court of appeals, and a Supreme Court justice [Miller, 2002].) He was 56 years old when he was appointed, and was the fourth of five appointments that President Eisenhower made. Only 17 days after the president's announcement, the Senate confirmed Whittaker's appointment unanimously. Whittaker fit all of the criteria the president had established subsequent to his first appointment to the Court (Earl Warren); Eisenhower was adamant that each future candidate be under 63 years of age and have had judicial experience; furthermore, the person preferably would have moderate to conservative views. Whittaker also had a reputation that, as a lawyer, he worked hard and was always well prepared (Miller, 2002). Unfortunately other—more important—criteria were not considered, including intellect. Blaustein and Mersky (1978) rate him as a "failure." In Comiskey's (2004) recent survey, which asked legal scholars to rate the 52 justices appointed during the twentieth century, Whittaker received a rating of 1.11 (on a scale of 0 to 4), the lowest of any justice. In his *Book of Legal Lists* (1997), prolific legal scholar Bernard Schwartz listed his "10 worst Supreme Court justices," and Whittaker emerged as number 2. Schwartz wrote that Whittaker "may have been the dumbest justice ever appointed" (p. 30); he concluded that "there is not one Whittaker opinion that decides an important case or stands out from the humdrum" (p. 31). (Most of Schwartz's "worst list" nominees served on the Court before 1950; in addition to Whittaker, only one associate justice, Sherman Minton, who served from 1949 to 1956, and one Chief Justice, Fred Vinson, who served from 1946 to 1953, had terms extending into the last half of the twentieth century.)

Henry Abraham's admirable book on the first 108 justices noted that Whittaker started out as a farm boy without a college education and described him as a "rags-to-riches figure, who, on the basis of background and experience, gave every promise of being an outstanding justice" (1999, p. 203). But Herbert Brownell, Eisenhower's attorney general, and William Rogers, a trusted advisor, were both lukewarm about Whittaker, whom they viewed as a good judge but not outstanding (Yalof, 1999). Whittaker benefited from having a strong advocate in Roy Roberts, the influential publisher of the *Kansas City Star* and a close friend of the president. Besides, few federal judges fit Eisenhower's multitude of criteria, and being from Missouri, Whittaker offered the added plus of geographical balance to a Court that had representatives of states spanning from New England to California but skimped on the Midwest.

But for the newly named justice, the move was not a happy one, from the very beginning. When he joined the Court in March 1957, Justice Black asked him, "Well, how do you feel about being here as a justice?" Whittaker replied, "Mr. Justice, I am scared to death" (Atkinson, 1999, p. 128). Within a month of beginning the job, he felt it had been a mistake, and he never adjusted to life on the Supreme Court, despite his previous judicial experience. Some of the brethren, especially Justices Douglas and Frankfurter, he found to be intimidating, especially with regard to their facile ability to decide the law. Even working until midnight every night, he was not able to keep up. Clearly his values differed from some of the other justices; he seemed to be obsessed with following the principle of *stare decisis*, and his decisions—in keeping with the types of clients he had had as a private attorney, such as the railroads—"consistently favored company managers who were challenged by workers" (Miller, 2002, p. 21).

As a justice, Whittaker persisted in displaying some of his unfortunate habits tracing back to his days as a private attorney. He micromanaged and refused to delegate. In his law-firm days, he had "even refused to let his secretary affix

stamps on envelopes—he insisted on determining the proper postage himself, and insisted on personally mailing letters" (Miller, 2002, p. 28). He used
his law clerks only for the most trivial of activities; "even when he told a clerk
to look up a question of law, Whittaker might soon be at the clerk's side examining the same set of volumes" (p. 38).

On one occasion Whittaker asked his law clerks to critique an opinion he
had written.

> [T]hey took him at his word. One clerk pointed out excessive
> length of sentences and a need to tighten the relation of facts to the
> legal principles Whittaker had used to reach the opinion's conclu-
> sion. Whittaker became so indignant about a staff member daring
> to proffer invited criticism that he threw the pages at the clerk,
> exclaiming, "If you think you can do better, take a crack at it." In
> protest over his outburst, Whittaker's secretary walked out of the
> office and went home for the day. (Miller, 2002, p. 54)

He reportedly saw his job as a prison sentence; he agonized over writing
opinions. Justice Whittaker even struggled over voting on cases; in the landmark case of *Baker v. Carr* (1962), Justice Frankfurter lectured to him for five
hours during the case conference; Whittaker switched his vote several times
and ended up abstaining. Justice Douglas's diary presents a poignant example:

> Whittaker would make up his mind on argument, only to be
> changed by Frankfurter the next day. In Conference, Whittaker
> would take one position when the Chief or Black spoke, change his
> mind when Frankfurter spoke, and change back again when some
> other justice spoke. This eventually led to his "nervous break-
> down" and his retirement for being permanently disabled in 1962.
> No one can change his mind so often and not have a breakdown.
>
> Whittaker was duck soup for Frankfurter and his flying
> squadrons of law clerks. In one case when the vote was five to four,
> Whittaker was assigned the opinion for the majority. I had already
> written the dissent and went to his office to discuss a wholly
> different matter. When I entered he was pacing his office, walking
> around his desk with pursed lips as if possessed. I asked him what
> was wrong. He said, referring to the five-to-four decision, that he
> had been trying to write the majority opinion but simply could not
> do it.
>
> "That's because you are on the wrong side," I said.
>
> "Not at all. Not at all. I am right but I can't get started."
>
> "Would you like me to send you a draft of the majority
> opinion?"
>
> "Would you, please?"
>
> Within an hour the draft was in his office, and when the
> opinion came down (*Meyer v. United States*, 364 U.S. 410, 1960) it

was one of the few in which the majority and minority opinions were written by the same man. (1980, pp. 173–174)

On one occasion, in 1957, as the Court faced one of its first pornography cases, Justice Frankfurter decided to circulate a satire. He had his clerks prepare a fictitious case, with the decision draft supposedly written by Frankfurter. Shortly after it was circulated, Frankfurter received a note from Whittaker that he joined Frankfurter's decision (Schwartz & Lesher, 1983). One observer concluded that Whittaker found it impossible to adjust to life on the Court. He wrote:

> As a lawyer Whittaker had simply adopted his client's point of view; it usually had not been necessary for him to decide between competing positions. But as a judge, making decisions was what he had to spend much of his time doing, which was a continuous problem for him. He once said, speaking of the weekly conferences in which cases were decided, that as a junior justice he was obliged to speak last and vote first. It was an arrangement that "put the monkey on the junior's back." He was very uncomfortable as the tiebreaker. (Atkinson, 1999, p. 128)

Furthermore, when Whittaker was assigned to draft the majority opinion, he would not modify his draft to incorporate the comments of the other justices. "Once he had revealed his stance, other justices could take it or leave it" (Miller, 2002, p. 61).

Only five years into his service, in March 1962, he collapsed with what was at that time described as a nervous breakdown. Actually, only a few months after Whittaker had begun his time on the Court, Justice Burton had made the prescient observation in his diary: "Justice Whittaker has been on the edge of a nervous breakdown but hopes to finish the term to recuperate" (Atkinson, 1999, p. 128). In actuality, Whittaker had struggled with depression his entire life, although it had been kept a secret from the public (Miller, 2002).

The hospitalization at Walter Reed Hospital was less than satisfactory. According to his son, at one point Whittaker became suicidal (Atkinson, 1999). On March 29, 1962, only five years after he began service, he retired from the Supreme Court; he was the first justice to do so because of a claimed disability.

After recovering a year later, he returned to Kansas City, but no longer practiced law. He lived until 1973. Despite his having served as a district judge and—briefly—as an appellate judge, life as a Supreme Court justice was simply beyond his ability to cope. In retrospect, it is easy to see why he failed. His opinions at the district court level show him to be simply a "legal technocrat" (Miller, 2002, p. 46) with a provincial worldview. He had no feel for cases; he examined the facts of each case and the Constitution mechanically; he made decisions on the narrowest grounds possible. His Supreme Court opinions were pedestrian, without legal justification for their conclusions (Miller, 2002). He was able to write only seven opinions for the Court in each of his terms, a much-below-average level of productivity At the high-powered level of Supreme Court processing of ideas, his limited intellect and his propensity toward depression were too difficult to overcome. He must be considered as the least successful justice of the last half-century.

The Frustrated Professor: Felix Frankfurter

In retrospect, at least, it can been seen that Charles Whittaker lacked some of the essential personality and intellectual traits necessary to succeed as a Supreme Court justice. But if there ever was a newly appointed justice who was seen as possessing the traits necessary to lead the Court, it was Felix Frankfurter. Harold Ickes, advisor to Franklin Roosevelt, the president who appointed Frankfurter to the Court, told the president: "If you appoint Frankfurter, his ability and learning are such that he will dominate the Supreme Court for 15 or 20 years to come. The result will be that probably after you are dead, it will still be your Supreme Court" (1953, pp. 539–540). Both Robert Jackson (then solicitor general but later a justice himself) and Harlan Fiske Stone, then an associate justice, stressed to the president the extent of Frankfurter's ability to compete intellectually with the magnificent Chief Justice Charles Evans Hughes (Mason, 1956, p. 482).

A distinguished law professor at Harvard, Frankfurter had trained many lawyers who later became eminent judges. (William Brennan and Harry Blackmun were among his students at Harvard Law School; shortly before he died, Justice Blackmun described Frankfurter as one of the two best professors he had at Harvard.) As a young man, Frankfurter had sought out Justices Oliver Wendell Holmes, Jr., and Louis Brandeis as mentors and soaked up their tutelage. He made sure that many of his best students received appointments as Supreme Court law clerks. Professor Frankfurter was so highly regarded that before he was named to the Court, Chief Justice Harlan Fiske Stone had called upon him to instruct a new justice, Hugo Black, in the proper way to behave. "Do you know Black well?" Stone asked Frankfurter early in 1938; "You might be able to render him great assistance. He needs guidance from someone who is more familiar with the workings of the judicial process than he is" (quoted by Urofsky, 1991, p. 45).

Furthermore, while at Harvard, Frankfurter had been a longtime advisor, behind the scenes, to Franklin Roosevelt, beginning when the latter was governor of New York and continuing after he was elected president. In his role as informal counsel, he served Roosevelt as the teacher and the expert, but on topics far beyond narrow legal issues (Hirsch, 1981). When Roosevelt was elected in 1932 to his first term, Frankfurter provided names of persons to staff essential New Deal positions. As one biographer pointed out, "[i]n time, scores of his former students and proteges would find their way to Washington, creating a network of influence for Frankfurter that extended into virtually every crevice of the growing bureaucracy" (p. 103).

Roosevelt, always thirsting for new ideas, was captivated by Frankfurter. He even arranged for the Harvard professor to live in the White House for much of the summer of 1935; he told an associate: "Felix has more ideas per minute than any man of my acquaintance. He has a brilliant mind but it clicks so fast that it makes my head spin. I find him tremendously interesting and stimulating" (Lash, 1975, p. 46). By the middle of the 1930s, Frankfurter was "perhaps the most important non-elected official in the national government" (Hirsch, 1981, p. 99). And this was before he was a member of the Supreme Court; Roosevelt had wanted to appoint him to the Court but was, for several years, stymied from doing so. His first opportunity to appoint anyone at all did not come until 1937, his fourth year in office. And then he passed over Frankfurter to appoint Hugo Black, his loyal spear-carrier in the Senate. Frankfurter would not be appointed until 1939, and even then, after Roosevelt had been in office for more than six years, he was only Roosevelt's third appointment. Filling the seat once held by distinguished occupants such as Joseph Story, Oliver Wendell Holmes, Jr., and Benjamin Cardozo, he served as a justice for 23 years, from 1939 to 1962. He wrote many opinions, made extensive comments, and remained a significant influence on the development of American law. But he never had the impact that was expected on the basis of his intelligence, energy, experience, and credentials. Certainly no one would consider him a failure, and some experts regard his contributions quite highly. Bernard Schwartz (1997) did not include him in his list of 10 "greatest" justices, but did include him in a small "also-ran" category. Comiskey's (2004) sample of scholars gave him a rating of 3.27, or 12th among the 52 twentieth-century justices.

Why Was Frankfurter Not More of a Success?

Biographers have described Frankfurter as "a vibrant personality; witty, charming, warm, energized, sparkling" (Hirsch, 1981, p. 4). Yet he was also possessed of less desirable qualities: he could be intense, arrogant, and domineering. One of his biographers observed that he could not accept "serious, sustained opposition in fields he considered his domain of expertise; he reacted to his opponents with vindictive hostility" (p. 4).

Given the extended number of years that he was in the limelight and the massive amount of material written by him and about him, no dearth of speculation exists about why Frankfurter was not a more effective justice. Two reasons stand out for me. First, Frankfurter failed to adapt to new surroundings. For the first time in his life, he could not dominate his colleagues by the force of his intellect and his undeniable energy. One observer wrote: "The Supreme Court . . . was an environment unlike the ones in which Frankfurter had triumphed; he was [forced into] sharing power with strong-willed individuals who had ideas of their own. Frankfurter would not lead the Court and, much to his surprise, found himself faced with an opposing 'bloc'" (Hirsch, 1981, p. 6). He no longer could function effectively in his capacity as a freelance advisor.

The second reason for Frankfurter's less-than-anticipated level of effectiveness on the Court is related to the first. Throughout his adult life, Frankfurter had relied on ingratiation and flattery to facilitate his achievement of influence. When, as a young man, he served in private and government jobs as an assistant to Henry Stimson (who later became Roosevelt's secretary of war), Stimson became one of the first recipients of Frankfurter's flattery. In 1908, when Frankfurter was 28, he wrote:

> My dear Mr. Stimson:
> Others have given expression to the appreciation universally felt for your public service and professional achievement in securing the conviction of Morse. But no one can testify so appropriately as I to your disinterestedness and tender fairness, but above all, your thoughtfulness, generosity and loyalty towards your subordinates. These stand out all the brighter in the perspective now that the glow and fury of the conflict have passed away.
> An experience such as has been my rare fortune during the last few months becomes a life possession—it is at once humbling and inspiring.
> Very gratefully yours,
> Felix Frankfurter (reprinted by Hirsch, 1981, p. 28)

He constantly praised Oliver Wendell Holmes, Jr., when the latter was on the Court. "My dear Justice," he wrote, when he was in his 30s,

> I have often ventured to say to my colleagues that all the "modern" tendencies in legal writing—"sociological jurisprudence," "the functional approach" and the rest of the jargonic [sic] language— are indicated, if not expressed, in your essays of forty or fifty years ago. . . . Yes—much of our labor these days is bringing bricks to the building of the structures for which you long ago sketched the blueprints. (reprinted by Hirsch, 1981, p. 42)

As he advised Roosevelt, his style of ingratiation continued. One biographer concluded:

> In their 772 pages of published correspondence, there is an almost unbelievable amount of flattery heaped upon the President by Frankfurter. After speeches he would send telegrams, comparing FDR to Lincoln. After a difficult decision, Frankfurter would praise the president's statesmanship and courage. In a difficult period of stress, he would strive to bolster his friend's ego. (Hirsch, 1981, p. 106)

Those who witnessed this behavior became upset with its excessiveness. The editor of the Frankfurter-Roosevelt correspondence (and an admirer of Frankfurter), Max Freedman, acknowledged that Frankfurter "was an artist in adulation, and sometimes, forgetting the artistry, he laid on flattery with a trowel. Sometimes the flattery, it must be admitted, may seem excessive and repugnant" (1967, p. 27). And, tellingly, although Frankfurter would often criticize the president in his letters to others, he never made one criticism directly to Roosevelt.

Once Frankfurter joined the Court, his flattery did not work. He deluged his brethren with suggestions and compliments (and also, on occasion, with criticisms) but his colleagues—strong-willed and competent people like William O. Douglas, Hugo Black, Charles Evans Hughes, and later, Earl Warren, William Brennan, and John Marshall Harlan II—perceived themselves as his equals and of no need for help from the former professor. In fact, "former" is rather superfluous in the foregoing sentence; Frankfurter continued to play the role of all-knowing professor to a group of what he saw as eight students in need of elucidation.

However, his flattery did apparently work on the less confident, less capable Whittaker. Even as he disparaged Whittaker behind his back, Frankfurter wrote him gushing notes like the following: "Were I to retire tomorrow, one of the most gratifying memories I would carry with me my whole judicial life would be your behavior in *Yancy* [a Communist party case]. It was judicial behavior at the finest" (Schwartz & Lesher, 1983, pp. 136–137).

As one clerk later recalled, "It was clear to everybody on the Court—with the exception of Whittaker—that he was being used by Frankfurter and that Frankfurter was ingratiating himself in order to secure Whittaker's vote" (Schwartz & Lesher, 1983, p. 137).

As he failed to exert his expected influence on the bench, he often turned from excessive commendation to hostile criticism of his peers. As one biographer concluded, "[h]e would flatter them as long as they agreed with him, but at the first sign of independent thought, he would explode. During his tenure on the bench, no one—with the possible exception of Robert Jackson—escaped his scorn" (Urofsky, 1991, pp. 62–63). When his ridicule and browbeating turned to Whittaker, it was, according to Whittaker's son, "a major factor" in causing his father's nervous breakdown (Newman, 1994, p. 518). And when Justice Wiley Rutledge drafted an opinion that went against his advice, Frankfurter wrote: "If I had to explain all your fallacies I would have to write a short book on (1) federal jurisdiction (2) constitutional law (3) procedure generally" (Fine, 1984, p. 255). He came to alienate almost all of his colleagues at one time or another. Justice Douglas—who at one point decided not to participate in conferences as long as Frankfurter was there (Ward, 2003)—wrote what several of his colleagues also thought:

We had become pretty well separated from Frankfurter. This is nothing that happened overnight. It was an evolutionary thing. Frankfurter just lost the respect of Black and myself and Murphy, just generally speaking. We learned that he was utterly dishonest intellectually, that he was very, very devious. None of us had known him very well, but he spent his time going up and down the halls putting poison in everybody's spring, setting, trying to set one justice against another; going to my office and telling me what a terrible person Reed was or Black, going to Reed's office telling Reed what a stupid person somebody else was, and so on. So, we got a full measure of the intrigue of the man and of the manner of his operations. (p. 297)

Certainly his intellectual style and his rigidity were not the only reasons for his failure to have the impact that Ickes had promised President Roosevelt. His philosophy of judicial restraint increasingly was out of touch with the needs of a society that changed dramatically in the 1940s, 1950s, and 1960s. Justice Douglas wrote:

We began to realize that here was a man who instead of being a friend and a champion of civil liberties was using his position on the Court to line up allies for a constitutional doctrine that we didn't, we couldn't go with. . . . So the explosions in the conference had become more and more frequent, particularly between him and Black, and between him and me, and we had become more and more suspicious of the good faith of the man, his intellectual honesty. (Newman, 1994, p. 297)

The summary by one of his biographers, while perhaps downplaying the effect of his tactics, reflects a comprehensive view of the reasons for his underachievement:

It was not that Frankfurter lacked vision, but rather that time outran his vision: he would have been the perfect judge a generation earlier. Once on the bench he seemed ignorant of the tides of history, of the country's changing social and political climate—the same sins for which he, as an academic commentator, had lambasted the conservative judges of the 1920s and 1930s. He remained consistent, but consistency is not always a virtue.

Frankfurter's failure to gain the leadership on the Court was due not just to his abrasive personality. Black, Douglas, Murphy, Brennan, Warren and other strong-minded justices resented his patronizing tone and schoolmasterish lecturing. They also believed that the Court had a special obligation to do justice in protecting the rights of racial minorities and of those with dissident points of view. . . . [They] reflected the general sentiment that the Court ought to be the guardian of the Bill of Rights. (Urofsky, 1991, p. 178)

Although Justice Frankfurter wrote many important opinions during his long tenure on the Court, and the evaluations by the experts were often favorable, on the criterion of effectiveness he ranked as increasingly unsuccessful.

The Politician: Frank Murphy

If Charles Whittaker was a misfit for the Court and Felix Frankfurter was a worse-than-expected fit, Frank Murphy might be characterized as someone who was a square peg forcibly fit into a round hole. No recent member of the Court could be labeled a "politician" in its narrowest meaning of a person whose career has mostly been served in elected office. "Judicial temperament" is now—as it always has been—expected of Supreme Court justices, and each of the current crop of justices has had plenty of opportunity to develop that orientation.

But in the past, presidents have, on occasion, chosen to appoint to the Court men who would clearly fit the label "politician." Earl Warren was, of course, one example. For some, the shift from the political to the judicial orientation did not come easily. Frank Murphy, who served on the Court from 1940 to his death nine years later, is an example. Murphy earned a law degree at the University of Michigan but entered politics soon thereafter. Prior to his appointment to the Court, he practiced law for less time than almost any other justice. He was elected mayor of Detroit and later governor of Michigan. In 1939, President Roosevelt named him to his cabinet, as attorney general. When the president decided to appoint him to the Supreme Court only a year later, many questioned the wisdom of the appointment.

Even Murphy had doubts about his technical competence. His biographer wrote: "Accustomed to the rough and tumble of politics, he had no pretense to intellect or learning" (Howard, 1968a, p. 215). To make the challenge even worse, he was to occupy a seat among some of the most intellectual power-wielders—Douglas, Black, Frankfurter—the Court had ever known.

It has been argued that President Roosevelt displayed a lack of concern for the Court and often used his judicial appointments to solve other problems he was facing, and this may be true in Murphy's case (Abraham, 1999; O'Brien, 2000). Murphy had not done a good job of running the Department of Justice; White House press secretary Stephen Early saw him "as a complete washout" (O'Brien, 1993, p. 99). Assistant Attorney General Robert Jackson warned the president that Murphy lacked the temperament of a judge. But Murphy not only was loyal to the president's policies but also fit Roosevelt's demographic criteria; he was a Roman Catholic—an altar boy at age seven—and from the Midwest, just as was Pierce Butler, whose death created the vacancy. Murphy himself rejected the demographic criteria:

> As I see it, the view that one of a certain faith should be succeeded by another of like faith is entirely unworthy. . . . Members of the Supreme Court are not called upon or expected to represent any single interest or group, area, or class of persons. They speak for the country as a whole. Considerations of residential area or class interest, creed or racial extraction, ought therefore to be subordinated if not entirely disregarded. (Howard, 1968a, p. 216)

But Murphy was appointed and confirmed, much to his regret. Once appointed, his self-assessment seemed self-fulfilling. And it is true that in many ways he failed to live up to the ideal standard of a judge. He had his law clerks write most of his opinions, to such a degree that his clerks were derisively referred to as "Mr. Justice Huddleson" and "Mr. Justice Gressman" (Fine, 1984, p. 161). (The latter clerk, contrary to the practice of other justices, was retained by Justice Murphy as one of his clerks for six years.)

Even in his life outside the Court, Murphy was different from the typical manifestation of the "judicial temperament." While most justices relish their anonymity and privacy, Murphy—throughout his adulthood—was seen at parties, restaurants, the theater, always accompanied by an attractive, flirtatious woman. (He never married.) His entourage often included secretaries, advisors, and newsmen. While he was in the Roosevelt administration, one New Deal luminary marveled at how he managed to know so many pretty women at one time (Howard, 1968a). As he held one political office after another, he became "acutely conscious of the value of favorable publicity" (Fine, 1979, p. 28) and held frequent press conferences.

Felix Frankfurter—who had an opinion about everything and everyone—saw Murphy as too emotional in his opinions; he believed that Murphy voted with his heart in cases involving the poor and minorities; writing to another justice, Frankfurter opined: "the short of the matter is that today you would no more heed Murphy's tripe than you would be seen naked at Dupont Circle at high noon tomorrow" (Schwartz & Lesher, 1983, p. 132). His reputation among other justices—especially their perceptions of his being lazy and unsophisticated in the law—meant that Chief Justice Stone and, later, Chief Justice Vinson, gave him few opinions to write, especially with respect to important cases. Murphy once complained to Vinson, when turning in his "sole assignment to date": "I have done my best to write an opinion acceptable to the majority who voted as I did at conference. I have failed in this task and a majority has now voted the other way" (O'Brien, 2000, p. 282).

Even his biographer, J. Woodford Howard, Jr. (1968a), described his record as a justice as "mixed." He wrote: "Neither legal scholar nor craftsman, he was criticized for relying on heart over head, results over legal reasoning, clerks over hard work, and emotional solos over team play" (Howard, 1992, p. 568). This is not to say that Justice Murphy was one of the worst justices of the last century; his rating in Comiskey's (2004) survey was 2.63, slightly above the 2.46 for all justices; he did not make Bernard Schwartz's "worst 10" list, and he had values and a jurisprudence that in some ways resembled those of Earl Warren, who was to lead the Court only four years after Murphy's death. (Purists would say that Warren, too, lacked a "judicial temperament.") Abraham's assessment was as follows: "Very likely because his concerns and his productivity on the Court were essentially one-dimensional, no matter how noble and hortatory, Murphy was accorded, with considerable justice, only an 'average' rating by the Court watchers" (1999, p. 174).

For all his limitations, Murphy deserves recognition beyond his usual rating because he championed the rights of individuals and especially members of politically impotent minorities, and he should never be forgotten because of his ringing dissent in the case of *Korematsu v. United States* (1944), in which the majority of the Court (including Justices Black, Douglas, and Frankfurter) found constitutional the relocation and internment of more than 110,000 Japanese American citizens, a decision Justice Murphy, in his dissent, called a "legalization of racism" (pp. 241–242). Murphy died in 1949, but a number of his dissents served to presage the shift in the Court 10 to 15 years later, with the advent of decisions recognizing the rights of minorities and criminal defendants.

The Scholar: John Marshall Harlan II

John Marshall Harlan II served on the Supreme Court from 1955 to 1971; appointed by President Eisenhower, he was Republican whose view of the Court's function was in a minority during most of his time on the Court. Yet he was able to develop and maintain a prestigious—and sometimes influential—reputation because of the scholarly and well-thought-out nature of his judicial opinions (Bourgignon, 1980). When reviewing cases during his time on the Court, scholars look to see if he wrote the majority opinion, a concurrence, or a dissent, because he always provided an intellectually rewarding analysis of the issues. Of all the incumbents in the last half-century, he was "the jurist's jurist." Furthermore, he assumed the role of spokesperson for judicial restraint after Frankfurter's retirement in 1962 (Abraham, 1999). For those reasons, he can be classified as an effective justice. In fact, in Comiskey's survey of legal scholars, published in 2004, Justice Harlan's rating of 3.55 puts him above everyone but Holmes, Brandeis, and Brennan among twentieth-century justices.

Harlan came from a patrician background—a wealthy family, private schools, and then Princeton and Oxford, leading to a position with a large Wall Street law firm at the end of his training period. Prior to his appointment to the highest court, he served briefly as a judge on the U.S. Court of Appeals for the Second Circuit. His grandfather, the first John Marshall Harlan, had served as a Supreme Court justice for 34 years, from 1877 to 1911.

Reminiscences by his law clerks (collected by Dorsen & Newcomb, 2002) are consistent. One of them, Norbert A. Schlei, said: "The work of the Court was to Justice Harlan not just important but sacred. No amount of effort was too much to get the opinion just right—to make sure each sentence hit the mark and contained nothing inadvertent" (p. 146). Another said: "From the beginning of my clerkship I was struck by Justice Harlan's courtly manner, which reflected his background. He treated all people, whatever their station, with consummate politeness and consideration" (p. 147).

Woodward and Armstrong's book *The Brethren* is based on insiders' comments by the justices' law clerks (and apparently at least one of the justices); they described Harlan as follows.

> Like his grandfather, Harlan viewed the law as almost a religious calling. Despite—and also because of—his near-blindness in the last few years, Harlan was the Court's hardest working member. He read almost 150 words per minute, bent over, his eyes nearly touching the paper. Yet he was the Court's most prolific writer. No matter how insignificant the disagreement or how minor the case, Harlan felt compelled to spell out his views for the sake of intellectual honesty. (1979, p. 45)

When asked who were the most outstanding justices with whom he served during his record-breaking 36 years on the Court, William O. Douglas (1980) listed seven, including Harlan. Even Justice Brennan, who certainly differed with him on most issues, liked to tell his law clerks that Harlan had been the "only real judge" on the Court during his time, that Harlan was the only justice "who weighed the legal issues with sufficient dispassion" (Woodward & Armstrong, 1979, p. 223).

In some ways, Harlan served as a conscience for the Court, even when the other justices did not follow his moral imperative. He held the separation of powers to be essential, and avoided all expressions that might imply endorsement of a sitting president. For example,

> Harlan declined to vote in presidential elections (or any others) and never applauded the President's State of the Union address. In 1967, Harlan refused to continue a tradition in which the justices in top hats and tails annually paid their respects to the President at the White House at the opening of the Court's term. . . . Harlan persuaded the others [except for Justice Fortas] to abandon the practice of calling on the President, lest Johnson try to use them to legitimate his war effort. (Woodward & Armstrong, 1979, p. 127)

Shortly after Richard Nixon became president, he faced the opportunity to name a new chief justice, with the resignation of Earl Warren. Pat Buchanan, then an advisor to the president, urged him to elevate Harlan to the post. But Buchanan's motivations apparently went beyond Harlan's impeccable credentials; Harlan was then 69 years of age and reportedly in poor health. His anticipated demise, reasoned Buchanan, would thus give President Nixon the opportunity to name two chief justices in his first term (Yalof, 1999, p. 244).

But instead, Warren Burger was appointed chief justice by President Nixon, in 1969, and Harlan remained on the Court for two more years. As a purist, he was disturbed with Burger as Chief, as he discovered that Burger paid less attention to legal reasoning than Harlan felt was required. Harlan apparently told his law clerks that Burger was willing to decide cases without exploring the logic or their constitutional basis. In one case Burger wrote a majority opinion draft that, in Harlan's view, reflected the correct result but failed to address most of the fundamental questions. After careful review, he prepared a concurrence. Burger then revised his draft, borrowing much from

Harlan's concurrence by paraphrasing, but he ignored Harlan's citations from prior Court decisions and his careful review of the past legislative history and relevant administrative decisions. Harlan, upon receipt of the Chief's revisions, shortened his concurrence but insisted on distributing it, despite the fact that Burger did not like concurrences (and especially concurrences tacked on to majority opinions he had written). But Harlan had to keep "his standard of meticulousness" (Woodward & Armstrong, 1979, p. 59).

Justice Harlan was, according to his clerks, horrified when he learned that Chief Justice Burger had decided that the Supreme Court could tell a state how to interpret its laws without providing a constitutional reason. But Burger told him: "We are the Supreme Court and we can do what we want" (Woodward & Armstrong, 1979, p. 61).

Even as he was diagnosed with terminal cancer of the spine, Harlan continued to run his chambers from his hospital bed. Woodward and Armstrong, relying on descriptions by his clerks, described the scene:

> Nearly blind, he could not even see the ash from his own cigarette, but he doggedly prepared for the coming term. One day a clerk brought in an emergency petition. Harlan remained in bed as he discussed the case with the clerk. They agreed that the petition should be denied. Harlan bent down, his eyes virtually to the paper, wrote his name, and handed the paper to the clerk. The clerk saw no signature. He looked over at Harlan.
>
> "Justice Harlan, you just denied your sheet," the clerk said gently, pointing to the scrawl on the linen. Harlan smiled and tried again, signing the paper this time. (1979, p. 157)

When he concluded that he could do the job no longer, he postponed his retirement so as not to draw attention away from the retirement of his friend-yet-adversary Hugo Black. Harlan wrote Black's son:

> I am going to have to retire. But I do not want to do anything to detract from the attention your father's retirement will get. I don't have to tell you. He is one of the all-time greats of our Court. He has served with over one-third of the justices who ever sat on the Court. Nobody's judgment ever exceeded his—his is just the best. . . . Holding up until your father's retirement is recognized and commented on is the right thing to do. (Atkinson, 1999, p. 145)

Justice Harlan retired in September 1971 and died three months later, on December 29, 1971.

The Swing Voter: Sandra Day O'Connor

Sandra Day O'Connor will forever have the unique distinction in American history as the first woman to be named a justice of the Supreme Court. But on her last terms on the Court, she filled an equally distinctive—though not unique—niche; she was "the ideological midpoint among the nine" (Donahue, 2002), a swing voter among a divided group of justices, and her vote was often the one deciding which faction triumphed. For example, in the 1996–1997 term, of 18 5-to-4 votes, she was on the winning side in all but one. In the term that ended in June 2002, she was the deciding vote in at least two-thirds of the 5-to-4 decisions (Greenhouse, 2002a). Whether that was her goal or not, she became an exemplar of strategic voting; "the tactical maneuver of going along with the majority offers the advantage of influence through bargaining" wrote political scientist Nancy Maveety (1996, p. 4), referring to Justice O'Connor.

Can this attribute be related to Justice O'Connor's background, her personality, or the fact that she is a woman? Sandra Day was raised on a 250-square-mile cattle ranch in Arizona; her parents' house had no indoor toilets, electricity, or running water, and the nearest town was 35 miles away; she had to commute long distances to go to school. Her joint autobiography, written with her younger brother (O'Connor & Day, 2002), described how she rode horses from an early age and during her childhood counted the ranch's cowboys (who slept on the house's screened porch) as her best friends. Her father was a demanding perfectionist; conservative by nature, he was committed in his opposition to government restrictions on ranchers (Perry, 1999b). Did his constant battles with the Bureau of Land Management over its land and water restrictions affect his daughter's attitudes toward the power of the federal government? Very likely. Certainly her book portrays the ability of ordinary people, through the use of hard work and common sense, to take care of themselves. In an interview in conjunction with the publication of the book, Justice O'Connor said: "We just learned from a very early age to admire the ability in someone to take care of a problem as it arose, and we tried to learn how to do it ourselves" (Donahue, 2002, p. 2D).

Entering college at the age of 16, Sandra Day completed her undergraduate work and her law degree at Stanford University. During law school, one of her classmates was William Rehnquist, whom she dated briefly. (However, she married another lawyer-to-be, John Jay O'Connor III.) Despite her exemplary record and law review honors at Stanford, her applications to law firms were rejected because of her gender. (One firm did offer her a position as a legal secretary!) So she took what was available, mostly jobs as a government lawyer, and she even worked part-time while her three children were small.

Active in Republican politics in Arizona (as was William Rehnquist), she served as a state senator (she was the first woman to be elected the majority leader of any state senate in the nation) and was later appointed to the Arizona Court of Appeals. Thus she had some judicial experience when she was nominated to the Supreme Court in 1981 by President Reagan. During a period of turmoil in American life, the newly nominated justice had an opportunity to have an impact on how laws affected women and minorities. Yet as a possible advocate, she was something of a conflicted figure. Scholars noted that her personal judicial agenda did not emphasize gender issues but instead consisted of federalism and judicial restraint (Cook, 1991). Despite her rejection by major law firms, her own property interest in her family's ranch and her husband's prosperous law practice meant that she had a comfortable living, within a traditional family, and she did not experience the financial deprivations faced by many women in the workplace.

As one observer noted, "no evidence suggests that O'Connor went through a conscious-raising period like so many of her age cohort did in the 1960s. At the nomination hearings O'Connor admitted that job and pay inequities concerned her but explained the discrepancy between men's and women's wages by women's acceptance of lower-paying jobs" (Cook, 1991, p. 244). Her response to a request for examples of her "commitment to equal justice" led to her mentioning her success, as a state senator, in some minor accommodations dealing with sexist language and women's working hours.

Her rather ambiguous image was also reflected in the reactions of interest groups to her nomination to the Court. Feminists were pleased to see a woman chosen (and a woman who had endorsed the Equal Rights Amendment [ERA]) but were well aware that she had been chosen by a president who opposed the ERA and was by no means supportive of the general goals of feminists. (And feminists noted that when Arizona failed to ratify the ERA, O'Connor took no action to try to get the legislature to reconsider.) Prolife supporters welcomed another conservative to the Court but were unclear on her commitment to overturning *Roe v. Wade*. During her confirmation hearings, she refused to indicate whether she was committed to overturning this abortion decision. She expressed her personal view that abortion was offensive and repugnant, but abortion had not been a salient issue when she was in the Arizona legislature, and so her voting record provided few clues. In the eyes of one observer, her balance between reticence and candor was "an extraordinary political performance" (Cook, 1991, p. 244).

After she was confirmed, her impact on the Court was slow to appear. From 1981 to 1986 she was not assigned by Chief Justice Burger to write the majority opinion in any significant case (Cook, 1991). Her impact was revealed more in her voting patterns than in her majority opinions, at least during the early years of her tenure on the Court. During her confirmation hearings, she had described her agenda as treating each case before her as a unique set of facts. To a large extent, she later came to operate that way, in that her votes became less predictable than those of justices with finely developed policy positions. But some of her preferences showed through; for example, on federal–state court relationships, she advocated that the federal courts defer to state courts (except in *Bush v. Gore*) and that state court judges were equal in competence to federal judges (O'Connor, 1981). She also reflected the doctrines of her Stanford and Phoenix colleague Justice Rehnquist regarding federalism, and especially the Supreme Court's right to reserve for itself "the exclusive authority to decide what counts as illegal and impermissible in America" (Rosen, 2001).

Her early votes (1981–1986) reflected the conservative tone of the Court, including issues of abortion and affirmative action. But she tried to position herself in the center. For example, she distanced herself from some of the harshest opinions of Justice Scalia; when she wrote a concurring opinion in *Webster v. Reproductive Health Services* (1989) that refused to reexamine the *Roe* decision, Justice Scalia characterized her thinking as "irresponsible," "irrational," and "not to be taken seriously" (Gottlieb, 1996). In a later case also involving the legality of abortion, *Planned Parenthood of Southeastern Pennsylvania v. Casey* (1992), O'Connor met with Justices Kennedy and Souter to plan a compromise that would preserve the core of the *Roe* decision, while permitting some restrictions on abortion (Simon, 1995).

In Comiskey's survey, her rating was 2.66, barely above the average, but I expect her rating will rise over time. Some scholars have even concluded that among recent justices, Justice O'Connor has been the most influential member of the Court, able to craft standards that achieve a majority in case after case (Coyle, 1999). "Her narrow opinions have the effect of preserving her ability to change her mind in future cases" (Rosen, 2001); one of her former law clerks told an interviewer: "She tries very hard to avoid broad rules, for fear that if you speak too broadly, you might bind yourself down the road" (Rosen, 2001). During her final complete term on the court, 2004–2005, her approach to judging, 20 years after what she said at her confirmation hearings, remained a "pragmatic, case-by-case decision making in which facts and details are extremely important to outcomes" (Coyle, 1999, p. A14). For example, even though she voted with the majority in the Nebraska partial-birth abortion case decided at the end of the 1999–2000 term (*Stenberg v. Carhart*, 2000), she noted in her concurrence that other states' statutes regulating partial-birth abortions were acceptable.

The Coalition Builder: William J. Brennan, Jr.

William J. Brennan, Jr., was an anomaly on the Court. A Democrat appointed by a Republican, he was a liberal on an increasingly conservative Court. Yet he was able to craft coalitions such that his policy preferences were often achieved, despite the Court's predominant conservative ideological bias. Brennan served as justice for 34 years, from 1956 to 1990. He was part of the liberal majority on the Warren Court of the 1960s that generated more rights to minorities and criminal defendants, but by his retirement in 1990, only two Democratic-appointed justices remained on the Court, and one of these, Byron White, usually voted with the Republican appointees.

What were Brennan's background and personality, and how did they prepare him to become the ultimate persuader on the Court?

William Brennan was born in Newark, New Jersey, in 1906; his father was an Irish Catholic who had immigrated to the United States in 1896 and become a labor organizer. Thus, as a child, William Brennan, Jr., witnessed at close hand the suffering and social unrest present in a largely immigrant population. Brennan earned a scholarship to law school at Harvard (where one of his professors was Felix Frankfurter) and then joined a law firm in his hometown. He was appointed to the state trial court and later to the New Jersey Supreme Court. As mentioned in chapter 2, when Sherman Minton retired in 1956, President Eisenhower sought to appoint a Catholic, who was a Democrat, had judicial experience, and was relatively young (Brennan was 50 at the time). Brennan was one of the few people—not that the administration did a systematic check—who was qualified. It has been speculated that Eisenhower and Brownell were misled by the conservative nature of a speech given by Brennan while he was a New Jersey Supreme Court judge; Brennan had not written the speech but was simply delivering it for the ailing New Jersey chief justice Arthur Vanderbilt (Friedelbaum, 1991).

What made Brennan so successful as a justice? (Bernard Schwartz rates him as one of the 10 best justices ever, and Comiskey's survey placed him third among twentieth-century justices, at 3.56.) Over the years, Brennan wrote 428 opinions for the Court and 258 concurrences. While the liberals were dominant in the 1960s, Brennan wrote some of the Court's most influential decisions, including *Baker v. Carr* (1962) on reapportionment, *Cooper v. Aaron* (1958) on school desegregation, and *New York Times v. Sullivan* (1964) on First Amendment protections against libel. But although he was in the liberal majority, he was not at its extreme; his more cautious approach was to pay off later on, especially when other liberals were replaced by conservative justices. During his later years on the bench, when he was the senior associate justice, he assigned the opinion writer in those cases in which the chief justice was in the minority. When Warren was chief justice, Hugo Black was a dominant force in the decisions of the Court. But "because of Black's intransigence and insistence on an 'absolutist' construction of constitutional language, it often fell to Justice Brennan to serve as an intermediary between opposing blocs" (Friedelbaum, 1991, p. 100). In the words of one biographer, he possessed "an uncanny gift of forging consensus among his brethren of differing, if not warring, views" (Clark, 1995, p. 6).

Justice Brennan sought to avoid absolutes as the bases for his decisions; he sought to resolve a "balancing" of competing interests; thus he was seen, even by adversaries, as more open-minded. His personality was perhaps his greatest strength in building coalitions; he was "friendly and buoyant in spirit" (Warren, 1966) and treated everyone with genuine interest and concern. Amiable to all, he never used his clout to get his way.

Schwartz and Lesher (1983) begin their book about the Warren Court by describing Brennan's famous red Volkswagen square-back sedan; it seemed to fit the seemingly carefree, unpretentious man. A biographer described his style as follows.

Best of all, Brennan was easily the warmest and most natural of the justices. In conversation, Brennan moved in close, LBJ style. He talked with his hands and frequently touched whomever he was engaging. He got to know not only the clerks but the elevator operators and security guards. An inveterate note writer, Brennan sent letters of thanks or appreciation to almost everyone he met. He had inherited many of his father's natural political instincts. Just as he had an uncanny memory for cases, Brennan never forgot a name. Those were some of the sweet qualities that initially led D.C. Circuit Court of Appeals judge David Bazelon to his conclusion that Brennan was full of "blarney." After he had gotten to know Brennan better and even steered the justice into some business deals and real estate investments, Bazelon decided his initial impression had been totally wrong. Brennan was the same to everyone and treated everyone equally. There was nothing false about him, Bazelon concluded. (Eisler, 1993, p. 102)

However, Brennan also possessed two other qualities that were crucial in determining his success on the Court: intellectual discipline and a willingness to consider the opinions of others. His own opinions were scholarly and closely reasoned; recall from chapter 1 that his dissent in *DeShaney v. Winnebago County* (1989), in contrast to Justice Blackmun's "Poor Joshua," argued logically that the failure of social workers to act was indefensible.

Brennan always remained aware of the bottom line; "five votes can do anything around here," he was often quoted as saying (Schwartz & Lesher, 1983, p. 224). He displayed remarkable willingness to negotiate, as well as skill in revising his drafts to accommodate the comments of his colleagues (including those more conservative than he). Typically, he would write personal letters to the other justices about cases, rather than using face-to-face confrontation (Clark, 1995). He would write and revise draft after draft, to incorporate the views of potential dissenters. His achievement of a majority decision in *Texas v. Johnson*, in 1989, when conservatives dominated the Court, is perhaps the most remarkable example of his ability to form successful coalitions. As noted in chapter 1, Gregory Lee Johnson had burned a flag in public during the 1984 Republican convention in Dallas, to protest policies of the Reagan administration. A Texas law made it a crime to intentionally desecrate a state or national flag. After he was convicted and sentenced to a year in prison, Johnson appealed.

Brennan concluded that the conviction of Johnson was in violation of First Amendment rights to the free expression of ideas, even those that were offensive or disagreeable to the majority of citizens. He was able to write an opinion that could attract the support of Justices Scalia and Kennedy, in addition to the more predictable defenders of free speech, Marshall and Blackmun. (Justices Rehnquist, White, Stevens, and O'Connor dissented, but Brennan had his 5 to 4 majority.)

How much he accommodated his own views to achieve long-term goals is a legitimate question. Chapter 5 provided, in Justice Brennan's vote on the appeal by "Slick" Moore, an example of his willingness to vote in ways that sacrificed justice in a specific case for the sake of maintaining a relationship with a wavering colleague. Even at his confirmation hearings, in 1956, Brennan deflected Senator Joe McCarthy's penetrating questions with less than complete candor. Senator McCarthy, it should be conceded, began his questioning with a bias against confirmation of Brennan; he told the committee:

> "I have never personally met Mr. Brennan. Anything I say here is not motivated by personal feelings. I have asked to appear before this committee for one reason and one reason only. As the committee is well aware, the Supreme Court will have a number of cases before it in the months ahead concerning the Communist conspiracy and concerning congressional efforts to expose the conspiracy. Whether Congress will be able to pursue its investigations of communism will depend, in a very large measure, upon how those cases are decided. I think therefore that it is of the utmost importance for this committee, for the Senate, and for the American people to know if the judges that will decide those cases are predisposed against congressional investigations of communism. On the basis of that part of the record that I am dealing with, I believe Justice Brennan has demonstrated an underlying hostility to congressional attempts to expose the Communist conspiracy. I can only conclude that his decisions on the Supreme Court are likely to harm our efforts to fight communism. I shall therefore vote against his confirmation unless he is able to persuade me today that I am not in possession of the true facts with regard to his views. I shall want to know if it is true that Justice Brennan, in his public speeches, has referred to congressional investigations of communism, for example, as 'Salem witch hunts' and 'inquisitions,' and has accused congressional committees of 'barbarism.'" (Eisler, 1993, p. 109)

Brennan responded as follows.

> "Not only do I approve [of such congressional investigations], Senator, but personally I cannot think of a more vital function of the Congress than the investigatory function of its committees, and I can't think of a more important or vital objective of any committee investigation than that of rooting out subversives in government." (Murphy & Pritchett, 1961, p. 96)

But he refused to comment on any issues that were in any ways related to possible cases to come before the Supreme Court.

In keeping with the rational choice model of judicial decision-making, it can be argued that Justice Brennan was the ultimate game player, even though, in an interview, he claimed his role was not that of what he called a "play maker" (Friedelbaum, 1991, p. 122). He used his highly effective interpersonal skills to advance his policy goals (Eisler, 1993). In doing so, he counted votes, wrote opinions that maintained fragile majorities, and incorporated the viewpoints of others into his drafts. Furthermore, he avoided writing an excessive number of dissents and, whenever possible, joined in those opinions that were agreed upon by most of his colleagues. In one term, incredibly, he wrote not a single dissent. Yet at the same time, he never wavered from allegiance to the nationalization of the Bill of Rights, opposition to the death penalty, and the vitality of the First Amendment. He was strong-willed; despite enduring radiation treatments for throat cancer in 1978 (at the age of 72), he remained on the Court for 12 more years.

An observer has summarized his contributions as follows.

> Justice Brennan became the foremost social reformer and critic on the Court, an astute and avid advocate who was responsible for an unusual progressions in a moderate, sometimes conservative, tribunal. If any section of the Constitution served as his guide in spirit as well as substance, it was the Fourteenth Amendment's equal protection clause. Brennan's attempts to advance the cause of the underprivileged, of those who seek representational equality, of proponents of affirmative action, and of victims of discrimination were prolific. His unrelenting opposition to capital punishment was part of the same social agenda, designed to ameliorate the effects of poverty and injustice. In a commencement address, Brennan expressed his views with exceptional candor as he challenged the "establishment" to make sacrifices to eliminate the "legal inequities" in society—to demonstrate real efforts rather than "meaningless tinkerings which do little more than salve our own consciences." To do otherwise, he warned, might cause the disadvantaged to be tempted by the "apostles of violence and revolution." (Friedenbaum, 1991, p. 123)

The Impact of Different Personalities on the Court

The foregoing minibiographies illustrate the conclusion that which individuals are chosen as justices has great impact on the process of deciding as well as the outcomes. Had President Eisenhower appointed someone other than William J. Brennan in 1956, certainly the law of the land, in some specific respects, would be different today. The impact of the personality of the justice is increased when that justice is also the chief justice, the topic for examination in chapter 9.

9

The Chief Justice

More Influential Than Other Justices?

Tell the chief justice that I don't work for him.—Associate Justice James McReynolds, in response to a message sent by Chief Justice Charles Evans Hughes regarding his being late for the Court's oral arguments

Inaugurations of second-term presidents possess the usual pomp and circumstance but generally lack much suspense. But for inveterate Court-watchers, the beginning of George W. Bush's second term—Inauguration Day, January 20, 2005—was different. Would the chief justice of the United States show up? After it was announced in late October 2004 that Chief Justice Rehnquist had been diagnosed with thyroid cancer and was undergoing intensive treatment, he had made no public appearances (although he had occasionally been working in his office and attending case conferences). He did not preside over oral arguments held in November and December, nor did he attend the annual Christmas party held at the Court, and it had been announced that he would not participate in the voting on cases heard in November. However, he had promised to perform the duty of the chief justice of administering the oath of office to the President on Inauguration Day. And he did. The last to arrive, he appeared using a cane, and spoke in a clear but husky and uncharacteristic voice as he administered the oath. And then he left, after being there for only 13 minutes (Greenhouse, 2005a).

The 2004–2005 term would be his last as chief justice. In mid-July 2005, Rehnquist surprised everyone by announcing that he would continue as chief justice as long as his health permitted him to do so. But he died two months later.

The Power of the Chief Justice: Real or Imagined?

From 1789—when John Jay became the first—through the year 2005, only 17 persons served as chief justice of the United States. John Marshall held the post for an astounding 34 years, but others (Roger Taney, 28 years; Melville Fuller, 22 years; Warren Burger, 17 years) served for impressively long periods, including William Rehnquist, for whom the 2004–2005 term was his eighteenth.

Acknowledged by scholars as the greatest chief justice, John Marshall established the power of the judiciary as a third "coequal" branch of the federal government. But the role of the chief justice has changed significantly since Marshall's death in 1835. Back then, the Court had a much lighter workload, and the chief justice had the opportunity to do most of the opinion writing. Marshall chose to do so, and his colleagues acquiesced; furthermore, they wrote few dissents or concurrences. Since then, the types of cases before the Court have changed, the number of divided votes and dissents has increased, and the need for the chief justice to serve various functions has similarly grown. Like any executive, the ideal chief justice needs to employ a multitude of human relations skills as well as administrative ones.

It has become the common practice to identify the Court by the name of the then current chief justice (e.g., "the Warren Court," "the Rehnquist Court"); such a convenience implies that the chief justice exceeds his colleagues in power as well as prestige. Is this really the case? Some would say no. Like each of the other justices, the chief justice has only one vote. The Chief cannot hire or fire other justices, or even determine their salary raises. The Chief's office staff is quite limited, and barely more than that of any other justice (an administrative assistant's duties involve mostly responsibilities other than the Supreme Court).

Nonetheless, in presiding over the Court, the chief justice has two responsibilities that give the person occupying that position additional power: chairing all the conferences and oral arguments and, if in the majority at the conference vote, deciding who drafts the majority opinion for the Court. (In addition to being in charge of the Supreme Court, the chief justice has other responsibilities; actually, the title is not chief justice of the Supreme Court but chief justice of the United States. The Chief's duties also include chairing the Judicial Conference of the United States, which is the governing body for the federal judicial system that includes all federal judges; chairing the four annual meetings of the Federal Judicial Center, which serves as a research and training agency; supervising the administrative office of the United States Courts; and serving as a member of the boards of trustees of the National Gallery of Art, the Hirschhorn Museum and Sculpture Garden, and the Smithsonian Institution. Despite all these additional time-consuming duties, the chief justice's current salary is only $8,700 higher than that of other justices.)

But if we consider only the supervision of the Supreme Court, it is legitimate to ask: Do the functions of chairing meetings and assigning opinions give the chief justice a heightened power, as well as a heightened prestige? In the sense that a change in the incumbent can change the atmosphere of the Court, yes, the Chief does have heightened impact. But does the leader have a greater opportunity to persuade the other justices? Former Justice Abe Fortas was only one of many advocates of the view that the position carries additional clout: "This prestige not only affects the public, the bar, and the bench generally, but it also makes possible for the chief justice to influence the output of the Court, to a much greater degree than colleagues of equal or superior personal and professional caliber" (1975, p. 405). Steamer noted that "it has almost routinely been accepted among the scholarly fraternity of Court watchers to refer to the chief justice as *primus inter pares*, or first among equals" (1986, p. 10). In short, the Chief sets the tone and, in many subtle ways, significantly influences the output and atmosphere of the Court.

Separating the impact of the office and the incumbent is sometimes hard to do. But even in the case of an executive with limited position power, as the chief justice's position is, some incumbents have been able to exert effective influence, not only on the other justices but on the country as a whole. As one commentator wrote, "[a] Chief must get his real eminence not from the office but from the qualities he brings to it. He must possess the mysterious quality of leadership" (Cray, 1997, p. 268). The office does have an impact; as the first among equals, the chief justice elicits special attention (O'Brien, 1997); pronouncements, messages, and actions of the chief justice are considered more noteworthy than those of other justices by the media and by scholars. Chief Justice Hughes explained it this way:

> Popular interest naturally centers on the chief justice as the titular leader of the Court. He is its executive officer; he presides at its sessions and its conference, and announces its orders. By virtue of the distinctive function of the Court he is the most important judicial officer in the world; he is Chief Justice of the United States. (p. 47)

Even by the other justices the chief justice is treated differently; justices informally refer to each other by their first names, but whoever is the chief justice is always called "the Chief."

Why are some incumbents able to capitalize on the office and bring about changes in society, while some incumbents fail to do so? As illustrated in chapter 8 with regard to associate justices, every chief justice has been different from his predecessors in ways that have had an impact on his effectiveness. Only a few achieve eminence. Polls of legal scholars have found 3 of the 16 chief justices to be deserving of the label "great"—John Marshall, Charles Evans Hughes, and Earl Warren. (Bernard Schwartz's "10 greatest" justices—associate or chief—include these three chief justices plus a fourth, Roger Taney.) But when President Eisenhower appointed Warren chief justice in the fall of

1953, few expected him to be one of the three most influential to hold this position. He was not even the president's first choice; John Foster Dulles and Thomas E. Dewey, among others, received earlier consideration. Certainly Warren possessed a distinguished career in public service in California, first as a district attorney, then as attorney general, and later governor. He ran for vice-president of the United States unsuccessfully on a ticket with Thomas E. Dewey in 1948. In many ways, his background was similar to that of associate justice Frank Murphy, whose experience as a politician made it challenging for him to adjust to the demand to reflect "a judicial temperament." Like Murphy, Warren was not considered an intellect; he had never authored any law review articles or significant policy analyses. Furthermore, he had not engaged in legal practice, or even been in a courtroom, in many years. When John Gunther, a prominent journalist, published his widely read chronicle of American life, *Inside U.S.A.* (1947), a short six years before Warren moved to the Court, he wrote of then governor Warren: "He will never set the world on fire or even make it smoke; he has the limitations of all Americans of his type with little intellectual background, little genuine depth or coherent political philosophy, a man who probably never bothered with abstract thought twice in his life" (1947, p. 18). Even when Warren was named chief justice, some observers saw his function as mainly a healer of quarrels, a competent but colorless manager thrown among intellectual heavyweights such as Felix Frankfurter, Hugo Black, and William O. Douglas, who dominated the Court at that time (Steamer, 1986, p. 49).

President Eisenhower expected Warren to make decisions that would reflect his moderate Republican background, decisions that would not rock the boat; instead, he led a major shift in Court decisions toward a reinterpretation of the Bill of Rights. He created a unified court and capitalized on the strengths of each justice. He was a "great" chief justice because he shaped Court decisions that continue to influence American life today, 50 years later. His appointment could legitimately be considered the most influential act of the Eisenhower presidency.

Before Warren's appointment, the Court was split on the issue of school desegregation. Fred Vinson, the chief justice who died suddenly and was replaced by Warren, had polled the justices and found that the three southerners had strong reservations about outlawing segregated schools. A fourth justice, Felix Frankfurter, had expressed concerns about the activist nature of any such decision, writing: "However passionately any of us may believe that such a policy of segregation . . . [is] both unjust and short-sighted, he travels outside his judicial authority if for this private reason alone he declares unconstitutional the policy of segregation" (Cray, 1997, p. 282). Despite his intellectual limitations, Warren had a sense of himself, as well as an ability to communicate his authority that generated loyalty and respect from his colleagues. He lobbied the holdouts, as he sought a unanimous vote to reject racially separate schools. Within one year, he brought this contentious group of justices to a position of unanimous agreement on one of the most momentous decisions in Supreme Court history.

In contrast, three of the six most recent chief justices have failed in important aspects. Harlan Fiske Stone, as I will describe in detail later, was not able to administer the case conferences effectively, leading to not only inefficiency but frustration among his colleagues. Fred Vinson, appointed by President Truman in the hope that he could coalesce a Court filled with contentious prima donnas, was unable to do so. Warren Burger, appointed by President Nixon to move the Court away from its decisions favoring civil liberties and defendants' rights, was not as successful as Nixon had hoped; the title of a prominent book provocatively referred to Burger's administration as "the revolution that wasn't" (Blasi, 1983).

This chapter examines how the recent chief justices have varied in their response to the challenges of the position, and then considers a psychological analysis of the nature of the job. It should be apparent that not all chief justices brought the same skills to the job, and even taking into account the changing nature of the job's demands over the last 200 years, we can evaluate just how well each incumbent fulfilled the leadership functions of the job.

The Chief Justice as Chair at Oral Arguments and Conferences

The chief justice presides over all the meetings of the Court. At oral arguments, the Chief announces the case, initiates the presentation of each side, and terminates the presentations when they reach their time limits. Often such termination is abrupt; it is claimed that Chief Justice Hughes called time on an attorney in the middle of his uttering the word "if" (O'Brien, 2000, p. 259). However, the chief justice does not necessarily dominate the questioning of attorneys. Just how much each justice participates at oral arguments is dependent upon his or her personal style and agenda. But certainly the chief justice, as the symbolic leader, has an added impact, and thus the Chief's interactions with attorneys receive extra attention. And on occasion, for example, Chief Justice Rehnquist would forsake his usual gracious style when he felt that an attorney had not fulfilled his or her responsibilities during an oral argument. The following is an example.

> The February 1995 exchange between the Chief and an embarrassingly under-prepared attorney, Robert Moxley, occurred in the vaccine liability case. . . . Moxley, representing the family of a young girl allegedly injured by a vaccine, had responded inconsistently to the same question addressed to him by several different justices. Finally, an exasperated Rehnquist blurted out, "How can you stand up there at the rostrum and give these totally inconsistent answers?"

Moxley's response, "I'm sorry, Your Honor," only further infuriated the Chief Justice, who chastised him with, "Well, you should be." Moxley tried to placate the seething Chief by saying, "I don't mean to confuse the Court." Rehnquist, all the more enraged, pounced on the wilting counsel, "Well, you haven't confused us so much as just made us gravely wonder . . . how well-prepared you are for this argument." As Moxley attempted to extricate himself from the hole he had dug, Rehnquist abruptly and angrily declared, "Your time has expired." Tony Mauro later reported that Moxley's earthy description of how it felt to be publicly humiliated at the Supreme Court was, "I felt like I dropped out of a tall cow's ass." Not surprisingly, the justices eventually voted 9–0 against Moxley's weakly-argued position. (Perry, 1999a, p. 109)

At conferences to review certiorari petitions, the chief justice has done prior work, determining which petitions are worthy of considering; chapter 3 described this small sample of the multitude of submissions as the "discuss" list. At all the conferences, the chief justice must monitor the use of time, and various incumbents have differed in how tight a ship they have run. Chief Justice Hughes is reported to have sought to limit the discussion of each certiorari petition to 3½ minutes and was largely successful in doing so, because, according to Justice Owen Roberts, "so complete were his summaries that in many cases nothing needed to be added by any of his associates" (O'Brien, 1997, p. 39).

At conferences held after the oral arguments, the chief justice introduces each case and begins the discussion by giving an opinion. Chief Justice Burger described the procedure as follows:

The Chief Justice gives a brief summary of what the case is about, as he sees it, what the issues are, and perhaps in some of them indicating his view on the matter; that is not always the case because as the discussion goes around the table then, from chief justice to senior [associate] justice and in seniority, it is not uncommon for a justice to say he would like to hear the full discussion before he comes to a conclusion. This might mean that he waits until the junior justice has expressed his views, and then a general discussion may take place. (O'Brien, 1997, p. 43)

One of the reasons that Charles Evans Hughes is considered one of the "greats" was his style in leading the case conferences. Observers raved about his intellectual abilities and his command of arguments:

Indeed, with his marvelous process of concentration (he would inhale a page), his incisive intellect, his imposing presence and an impish wit that erupted unexpectedly . . . Hughes could dominate any gathering . . . Justice Hugo Black told a biographer that

Hughes was the "perfect presiding officer. . . . [Y]ou could be sure that [when he stated a case] it was correctly stated. He might identify four or five possible decisions and then assert, "I think we should follow the first line. It will keep us away from the troublesome problems opened up by the others." (Newman, 1994, p. 281)

While he lacked Hughes's meticulous cognitive abilities, Chief Justice Warren, at these conferences, laid out the issues of the case simply, and ran the meetings briskly. According to his biographer, he preferred not to argue when one of the other justices disagreed with him. Similarly, Chief Justice Rehnquist maintained "a no-nonsense timetable at conferences" (Perry, 1999a, p. 109). But he would give other justices the opportunity to dissent, and even those justices who disagreed with him applauded his fairness and openness.

Among recent chief justices, Warren Burger has received the most criticism for his handling of case conferences. As noted earlier, instead of following the prerogatives of the chief justice to vote first he would—on occasion—delay his vote to see which side was attracting the majority, and then he would vote with that majority so that—according to his critics—he would get the opportunity to determine who would draft the majority opinion. Later in this chapter, I will demonstrate other ways Chief Justice Burger usurped the power of other justices to participate in decision-making.

Assignment of the Draft Opinion Writer

It can be argued that the chief justice's most important function is the assignment of a justice to write the majority opinion. Writing about Chief Justice Warren, Cray noted:

> The Chief, as long as he was in the majority, could pick a man who would seek to broaden the impact of the decision, or one who would narrow it. He could tap the justice whose opinions were closest to his own. He could pick a man given to compromise, or to unbending doctrine. He could give a case to a man expert in the area, or one whom the chief hoped might become an expert. He could cultivate alliances or drive a wedge into the philosophical opposition with a desired assignment. He could assign the most important cases to the favored few, including himself, or he could give each an opportunity for judicial fame. The wise chief justice also watched for political implications when making assignment—for the Court could never be far from the political. (Cray, 1997, p. 268)

The chief justice also has to assess the skills of the designated draft writer, because an inadequate draft—too broad in scope, too poorly written—can cost votes, and even contribute to the majority shifting to the other side.

Furthermore, justices pay attention when they are ignored in opinion assignments, especially on important cases—or when the Chief keeps assigning them only the "dogs" of the cases.

What *Is* Leadership?

Each chief justice is a unique personality, and we have already seen some indications that their differences contributed to their effectiveness on the job. But what makes one person a successful leader while another fails in the same position? Early efforts in the scientific study of leadership, in the 1920s and 1930s, sought to discover internalized traits that were present in all leaders to a greater degree than in those who did not become leaders. This approach turned out to be of limited value in understanding what made a particular chief justice "great." First, every chief justice is already a leader by having been appointed to that office. More basically, this approach did not produce much in the way of consistent findings; only a few traits consistently appeared across leaders in a variety of settings. Just four—intelligence, initiative, extroversion, and a sense of humor—appeared often enough to be labeled "general traits of leadership" (Bird, 1940, p. 380).

But it is illuminating to compare these four traits with those that are common to the most eminent chief justices. While the three designated "great" chief justices lived at different times and came from different backgrounds, they had some traits in common. Steamer (1986) evaluated the traits shared by Chief Justices Marshall, Hughes, and Warren as follows.

> All had a commanding physical appearance; all had robust health and all were capable of hard work, Hughes by nature, Warren and Marshall by necessity, the latter only in spurts. All were exemplary patriots with a deep respect for the American system and a mission to preserve it. They were basically conservative in outlook, but all were willing to stretch judging—in different degrees—to accommodate their own convictions, a not uncommon trait in American appellate judges generally. All had a certain natural dignity. Marshall and Warren liked most people and were liked in return, but each had a reserve which only the intimate might penetrate. Hughes' reserve was closer to the surface, very much so in fact, and he was generally characterized as personally aloof, a human icicle, but many of those close to him found him charming and warm and not at all like the public image he projected.
>
> All were strong self-disciplinarians, Hughes sternly so, Marshall and Warren less rigid than Hughes but concerned with regulating their lives in order to accomplish the tasks at hand. All had an ability to see the irony and fate in life; they were serious

men who did not take themselves seriously, men who were never impressed with any self-importance, a trait that enabled them to discern the superficial and shallow among them. John Randolph wrote that John Marshall was the "most unpretending and unassuming of men" and the same can be said of Earl Warren and Charles Evans Hughes. Perhaps more important, all were straightforward, moral men, personally, professionally and publicly incorruptible. Justice Story said of Marshall that he could never be an "intriguer," and again the same may be said of Hughes and Warren. None of them was a scheming, petty politician; none was an aggressive office seeker. Although there is a difference in degree from the reluctant participation of Marshall in public affairs to the seeking of the presidency by both Hughes and Warren, neither of the latter was an enthusiastic political self-starter but was borne on the winds of circumstance in pursuing elective office. (1986, pp. 37–38)

Several explanations exist for the small number of demonstrable "leadership traits." Situational factors can override personality factors in influencing how effective a leader is; by situational factors I mean the resources available to the group, the difficulty of the task, the nature of the working relationship between group members, and other aspects that often go beyond the control of the leader. For example, a new chief justice may find a Court composed of associate justices with differing ideologies. I explore this issue in detail in the next sections, first by looking at psychological approaches that take into account the quality of the environment in which the leader operates, and second by applying this concept of person–situation interaction to different chief justices.

Leadership Functions

Leadership is composed of a mixture of functions. Refinements in the definition of leadership reflect this awareness. Beginning in the middle of the twentieth century, studies centered on the functions of leaders; influential work was done by R. F. Bales at Harvard University and by John Hemphill, Ralph Stogdill, Carroll Shartle, and others at the Personnel Research Board at the Ohio State University. The result of these efforts was a new focus upon *influence* as the single most important aspect of leadership. For example, Stogdill defined leadership as "the process (act) of influencing the activities of an organized group in its efforts toward goal setting and goal achievement" (1950, p. 3). An emphasis on goal-oriented functions of leaders led to various analyses of the group's tasks and the leader's tasks. Lists of the dimensions of a leader's behavior were generated, sometimes seven dimensions, sometimes nine or another number. But a factor analysis of leaders' actions led to a conclusion that two qualities of leadership—determinants of the ability to influence, if you will—accounted for most of the variance between successful and unsuccessful leaders (Halpin & Winer, 1952). The first aspect was labeled *consideration.* This quality represents the extent to which the leader shows behavior that is "indicative of friendship, mutual trust, respect, and warmth" in relationships between the leader and other group members (Halpin, 1966, p. 86). Genuine consideration by the leader reflects an awareness of the needs of each group member. In Halpin and Winer's analysis, consideration accounted for almost half of the variance in leaders' behaviors.

The second quality of leadership was called *initiating structure,* which was later defined as "the leader's behavior in delineating the relationship between himself and members of the work group, and in endeavoring to establish well-defined patterns of organization, channels of communication, and methods of procedure" (Halpin, 1966, p. 86). Thus, initiating structure refers to the leader's ability to get the group moving toward its designated goal. This quality accounted for about one-third of the variance in leaders' behaviors.

A focus on the leader's functions produced similar divisions into two primary dimensions. Bales (1953) concluded that leadership functions may be differentiated into *task orientation* (achievement of the group's goals) and *group-maintenance orientation,* in which a leader is concerned with establishing or enhancing the group members' morale and cohesiveness. Because of independent confirmations by Bales (1958) and others (Fleishman, Harris, & Burtt, 1955), we may conclude that initiating structure and consideration are two major dimensions of leadership behavior and not simply mutually exclusive leadership patterns (Gibb, 1969).

Is it possible for a leader to be skilled in both initiating structure and consideration for others? Yes, it is possible, but some leaders find it difficult to fulfill both these functions simultaneously. The impact of pressures from the job situation may preclude the achievement of both at the same time, and some people simply lack the desire or ability to do both. The workload of the chief justice is tremendous and may get in the way of fulfilling group maintenance functions. For example, the memoirs of Chief Justice Warren described his schedule and workload:

> We accepted practically no invitations to private homes because
> that called for reciprocation, and that would crowd our evenings
> and so could not be accommodated to my work. I worked almost
> every night to some extent, even on nights when we attended a
> White House or embassy dinner. Even at that pace, I never felt that
> I was abreast of my reading. I am not a fast reader of important
> materials, and the amount of such reading at the Court is colossal.
> When I first came to Washington, I wondered how I would ever
> get through it. At that time the Court met at noon, recessed for

lunch for thirty minutes at 2:00 p.m. and then sat until 4:30. This was the procedure Monday through Friday while hearing the cases argued. Then on Saturday morning at 10 o'clock, we would convene in conference and, with the exception of thirty minutes for lunch, would continue until our work was completed—until five, six, or even seven o'clock. (1977, p. 345)

Thus, although Justice Warren was able to simultaneously accomplish goals of initiating structure and consideration, his personal life and family time were sacrificed to do so. In his memoirs, Chief Justice Warren also labeled his schedule "backbreaking;" his mornings were consumed with administrative tasks, including the management and board activities listed earlier. He took home briefs and memoranda every night, usually reading them until midnight. He awakened early and read for an hour and a half before departing for the Court. In his 16 years as chief justice, he missed only one day at work because of illness.

If a chief justice is not able to achieve both functions, another justice may emerge as the leader concerned with consideration, sometimes called the socioemotional leader of the group. Sometimes this is the best liked of the judges on the panel; it is usually someone who dislikes conflict and seeks to avoid it on the Court (Danelski, 2002). On rare occasions, the chief justice may become the socioemotional leader and another judge the task leader. Danelski's analysis of the Supreme Court led him to conclude that this was the case during William Howard Taft's chief judgeship:

Taft was the social leader and his good friend and appointee, Van Devanter, was task leader. Evidence of Van Devanter's esteem and task leadership is abundant. Taft, time and time again, asserted that Van Devanter was the most able justice on the Court. . . . At times, Van Devanter's ability actually embarrassed Taft, and the chief justice wondered if it might not be better to have Van Devanter run the conference himself. (pp. 663–664)

Some leaders have difficulty achieving both goals because they find achievement and consideration to be in competition with each other. The achievement-oriented leader may become intolerant of the "relaxed" work pace of other group members; a leader with this orientation must constantly turn the members' attention toward the goal, when they digress into some diversionary activity or superfluous conversation. Often the leader reports that it is difficult to be task-oriented and considerate at the same time. Hence another group member may become the group-maintenance expert, concerned with arbitrating task-oriented disputes, relieving tension, and giving every member a chance to be heard or a pat on the back. But sometimes a given action may facilitate the achievement of both functions; a leader who helps a group solve a difficult problem may, by this action, develop solidarity and better morale (Cartwright & Zander, 1960, p. 496).

Applications to the Functioning
of the Chief Justice

Different chief justices can be contrasted with respect to their degree of success in each of the two activities: initiating structure and consideration. Consider the contrasting styles of two chief justices in processing certiorari petitions: Chief Justice Charles Evans Hughes came to the conference fully prepared; he had not only read all the petitions but had rejected those that, in his opinion, were the frivolous ones. He barely tolerated debate and discouraged efforts by the other justices to have more time to study the matter. In contrast, Chief Justice Harlan Fiske Stone presented his own ideas in a casual manner and encouraged full discussion and debate; he "allowed himself to be freely interrupted, and invariably granted extensions [of time]" (White, 1978, pp. 226–227).

Chief justices can demonstrate their skill in initiating structure and their concern for consideration in numerous ways. With regard to initiating structure, one indication—as shown in the aforementioned contrast between Hughes and Stone—is the ability to move the justices expeditiously through the agenda of cases. Steamer has observed that Chief Justices Edward Douglass White and Harlan Fiske Stone were each the intellectual equals of other justices but each was incapable of orchestrating a cohesive Court. He wrote:

> Chaos is the only word to describe the Court after Stone succeeded
> Hughes. The conference became a debating society with tempers out
> of control and tensions running high as the justices bickered almost
> endlessly, with honest intellectual differences escalating into
> personal antagonisms. Rather than concluding the conference in a
> few hours, Stone permitted it to go on for days. White, a genial,
> well-liked man, did not [and] could not give the conference firm
> leadership. Encountering a difficult case, he was known to say:
> "Here's a baffling case. I don't know what to do with it. God help
> us!" Clearly such prefatory remarks to the discussion of a case give
> wide berth to the brethren to debate *ad infinitum* until one of them
> assumes the leadership role abandoned by the Chief. (1986, p. 28)

One possible reason that Stone was ineffective in initiating structure was that after he became chief justice, he still kept acting like an associate justice (Danelski, 2002). Not only did it appear that he was struggling for a solution when he presented cases but also he participated in the evaluative reactions of the associate justices during discussion; he would say, "Jackson, that's damned nonsense" or "Douglas, *you* know better than that" (p. 665). Eventually, it fell upon Associate Justice Hugo Black to provide task structure during the period of Stone's chief judgeship.

But characteristics of the other justices can also affect success in initiating structure; one example is the degree to which the other justices agree with the chief justice's view of a case. According to this conception, the more frequently the chief justice is in the minority, the less effective he is. If dissents do indicate an inability to lead, once again Chief Justice Stone had the worst record, having been in disagreement with the majority of his colleagues in almost half the cases. John Marshall was the opposite, with only a minuscule six dissents in his 34-year term. (Marshall authored more than half of the thousand opinions during his time on the Court.) As chief justice, Earl Warren dissented, either with or without a written opinion, about a quarter of the time, but on major cases he was almost always in the majority (Steamer, 1986).

But it is dangerous to put too much emphasis on the dissent rate as an indicator of inability to initiate structure, because it fails to recognize the situation in which the chief justice operates, or the types of cases considered. For example, in the 2001–2002 term, Chief Justice Rehnquist dissented in several highly publicized criminal law and First-Amendment cases, but in every case involving federalism, he was in the majority. Steamer observed:

> The Chief is always a prisoner of the times in the sense that some issues are so controversial—affirmative action, abortion, integration of the schools through busing, capital punishment—that the most charismatic leader in the nation could not persuade eight independent colleagues to adopt a single view. (1986, p. 8)

Increasingly, the Court is divided. The split court may have reached the ultimate in complexity at the end of the 1995–1996 term, as exemplified by two of the decisions in June 1996. One struck down as unconstitutional three Texas congressional districts. The vote was recorded as 5-to-4. Justice Sandra Day O'Connor wrote the determining opinion, but only two other justices (Rehnquist and Kennedy) joined. Justices Thomas and Scalia voted for the same result but for different reasons, as expressed in a concurring opinion by Thomas.

The second decision, dealing with indecent programming on cable television, produced six separate opinions and generated 118 pages. The vote may be summarized as follows. Justice Breyer announced the judgment of the Court and delivered the opinion of the Court with respect to Part III in which Stevens, Kennedy, Souter, and Ginsburg joined; an opinion with respect to Parts I, II, and V in which Stevens, O'Connor, and Souter joined; and an opinion with respect to Parts IV and VI in which Stevens and Souter joined. Stevens and Souter filed concurring opinions. O'Connor filed an opinion concurring in part and dissenting in part. Kennedy filed an opinion concurring in part, in which Ginsburg joined. Thomas filed an opinion concurring in the judgment in part and dissenting in part, in which Rehnquist and Scalia joined.

An important aspect of initiating structure is the chief justice's intellectual leadership. If the incumbent chief justice lacks the highest of intellectual skills, he needs to be able to capitalize on the abilities of ideologically similar colleagues. As effective as he was in rallying justices to his view, Earl Warren was—as noted earlier—not seen as an intellectual giant. Rather than analyzing the legalistic ramifications of an issue, he would ask: "What is fair?" A colleague, Justice Potter Stewart, described Warren as deciding cases in favor of "widows or orphans or the underprivileged" (Howard, 1997, p. 33). When it came to jurisprudence, he would defer to Justices Black or Frankfurter.

Robert Steamer's comprehensive review of the office of Chief Justice concluded that only two occupants, John Marshall and Charles Evans Hughes, "approximate the ideal in the simultaneous exertion of personal and intellectual leadership" (1986, p. 27). He said:

> We do not know the precise ways in which John Marshall dealt with his Court, but we do know of his warmth, his magnetism, the respect, affection and esteem in which he was held by his colleagues, and of, course, the brilliant results of his labors. The Hughes record is well documented. At one time or another, virtually all of the brethren paid tribute to Hughes' leadership generally and to his conduct of the conference specifically. Hughes' penchant for order and his photographic memory brought him to each conference almost formidably prepared. After summarizing a case accurately and comprehensively, he would then suggest how the case ought to be decided, and in some instances that was the only discussion the case received as the justices proceeded to vote for the disposition suggested by the Chief. When a justice did want to speak, he did so in order of seniority and without interruption, which meant that interchange of views was with the Chief and not with the other justices. (pp. 27–28)

The second quality of leadership, consideration, can be manifested in many ways. The Chief Justice, like any leader, has to settle petty disputes and make everyday decisions in a manner that avoids charges of favoritism or arbitrariness. When Justice Reed retired in 1957, Chief Justice Warren was informed that Justice Frankfurter preferred Reed's office to his own. Before acceding to this request, the chief justice consulted with Justice Black, who was senior to Frankfurter. He then wrote the other justices that he had assigned Reed's office space to Frankfurter, adding: "Unless one of you wishes to move into the rooms vacated by Justice Frankfurter, that suite will be assigned to the new justice" (memorandum from Chief Justice Warren, February 8, 1957, quoted by Steamer, 1986, p. 21). Earl Warren's procedure contrasted with that of Warren Burger. During the summer, when the other justices were not around, he decided to convert the longtime conference room, where the justices met in secret to decide cases, into his own ceremonial office and private dining room (Woodward & Armstrong, 1979).

Sometimes such "little things" that a chief justice does (or fails to do) are the strongest indicators of the presence or absence of consideration. According to one of his law clerks, Chief Justice Warren had an operating principle: "If you want to talk to somebody, don't ask them to come to your office. . . . Go to theirs" (Cray, 1997, p. 283). This policy of relinquishing power and a willingness to meet on the other's "turf" reflected Warren's sensitivity to the needs of others. Also, Warren for several years tried to persuade Congress to appropriate the money for cars and drivers for each of the justices (the chief is the only justice with this "perk"). Warren argued that Frankfurter, at age 70, and Reed, Black, Burton, Minton, and Jackson in their sixties, should not have to negotiate themselves through the traffic congestion of Washington. While his efforts were not successful, they were appreciated by his colleagues, who recognized a basic concern for the needs of others.

Similarly, when Justice Douglas was in the hospital in 1947 but insisted on doing his share of work, newly appointed Chief Justice Fred Vinson tried to be aware of Douglas's workaholic tendencies but still act in his better interests, as noted in the following letter.

> Dear Bill:
> Received your note relative to No. 715, State of Oklahoma vs. The United States.
> I also have your note of the 11th, insisting on some more work. I am saving some cases without assignment, but with the understanding that they will be ready for you if you are ready for them. Actually, old-timer, I hesitate to assign any cases to you for a week or so unless you are dead certain that you can do it without the slightest danger from it. So, hold your horses and get well. That bug innervates, and not a one of the Brethren wants to retard your speedy recovery.
> Missed you at Tom Clark's party, and Mildred didn't act like she was having a good time at all.
> Harold [Burton] did a good job for you in the rate case. . . .
> So, again, hold your horses, and get back in trim. If you are in fit form, we will enter you for the home stretch; otherwise, you will not even get to the paddock.
> Affectionately,
> Fred (quoted by Steamer, 1986, p. 20)

A Contingency Theory of Leadership

In my review of psychological approaches to the understanding of leadership, I have shown how the search for basic personality traits produced little in the way of consistent results. This disappointment led to a shift—toward analyzing the functions or dimensions of a leader's behavior, along with documenting the relationships between the leader's effectiveness and the ratings the leader received from supervisors, coworkers, and subordinates. But a functional analysis was not enough. Not until the work of social psychologist Fred E. Fiedler (1967, 1969, 1971) was the trait approach meaningfully combined with a functional analysis.

Fiedler defined the leader as the individual in the group who is given the task of directing and coordinating task-relevant activities. Fiedler's theory is called a *contingency theory of leadership* because it relates the leader's degree of success to aspects of the situation in which the group operates. Specifically, the theory predicts that the leader's contribution to group effectiveness is dependent upon both the characteristics of the leader and the favorableness of the situation for the leader. To Fiedler, there is *no one* successful type of leader; task-oriented leaders may be effective under some circumstances but not others. A permissive leader who is oriented toward human relations and who has been successful with one group may not be successful in another group where the situation differs.

What did Fiedler mean by "the favorableness of the situation for the leader?" He proposed that three qualities of the situation are central in determining favorableness; these are the leader's personal relations with the members of the group, his or her position power, and the degree of structure in the group task. The relevance of each to leadership by the chief justice is examined hereafter.

The Leader's Personal Relations with Members of the Group

This first situational determinant refers to the atmosphere in the group and the degree of confidence and attraction the group members have for the leader. Relationships between the leader and the group can range from very good to very poor; they are partially determined, of course, by the leader's personality, *but there may be aspects of the relationship that are beyond the control of the leader.* The leader may have become the replacement for someone who was quite popular and well liked by the group. For example, when Warren Burger replaced Earl Warren, resentment over the replacement was directed at the new leader. Linda Greenhouse's (2005b) absorbing book on the lifetime relationship between Justices Burger and Blackmun revealed that Justice Burger had many desirable personality attributes; he worked well under pressure, he thought well on his feet, he was able to express his feelings. But Burger began his tenure in a less desirable position because he was replacing such a revered leader. Fiedler concluded that the leader–group relationship is the single most important factor in determining the leader's influence in a small group (Fiedler, 1964, p. 159). If the atmosphere is positive and members trust and get along with the leader, the leader–member relations are defined as *good*; to some extent, leaders with good relationships can overcome the limitation of being weak in the second component, or the degree of their *position power*.

Recent chief justices have certainly differed in their personal relations with the other justices. William Rehnquist was appreciated for his sense of humor by the other justices, whether they agreed with him or not. Earl Warren was a considerate and diplomatic leader; one of his colleagues noted that he "was never divisive, impatient, short-tempered or abusive. He created an atmosphere of comradeship, even within strongly felt and sometimes sharply stated disagreements" (Fortas, 1975, p. 412). He was so highly esteemed that the label "Super-Chief"—bestowed on him by Justice Douglas—reflected a genuine respect and admiration from his colleagues (Fortas, 1975).

In contrast, Warren Burger had—in Fiedler's framework—"poor" relations with the other justices. First, as noted earlier, he replaced the highly regarded Warren; moreover, he made some early decisions that were quite unpopular; and, as noted in chapter 8, some justices (including John Harlan and other conservatives) viewed him as a pretentious intellectual lightweight.

Chief Justice Burger's imperious way of running case conferences and assigning opinions reflected a lack of consideration for his colleagues, and his actions sometimes drew rebukes from the other justices. Even his long-term friend Harry Blackmun complained to the chief justice that the latter was not assigning him enough opinions to write; Justice Blackmun wrote that he felt humiliated, both personally and publicly (Greenhouse, 2004b, 2005b). In another example, Justice Thurgood Marshall wrote in April 1972 to his colleagues:

> I am deeply disturbed as a result of the conference on argued cases being held in my absence. I know that this has not occurred during my few years here except where the justice involved was ill and unable to be present and, even then, it was with the consent of the justice involved. I had assumed that this was the usual practice here.
>
> I am not worried so much about this particular conference as I am that it may become a precedent for some future time. Like the late John Harlan, I, for one, am worried about changing some of the time-honored practices of the Court. (Cooper, 1995, p. 43)

Burger's way of assigning opinions was unique. On several occasions, Justice Douglas asserted that the chief justice simply miscounted conference votes so that he could determine the opinion assignment (Cooper, 1995, p. 43). On one occasion, Douglas, who was the senior justice in the majority at the conference, found that Burger had assigned the opinion on his own—to another justice. Douglas chided the chief justice as follows.

> You apparently misunderstand. *Lloyd* is already assigned to Thurgood and he's at work on an opinion. Whether he will command a majority, no one knows.
>
> Under the Constitution and Acts of Congress, there are no provisions for assignment of opinions. Historically, the chief justice has made the assignment if he is in the majority. Historically, the senior in the majority assigns the opinion if the chief justice is in the minority.
>
> You led the conference battle against affirmance and that is your privilege. But it is also the privilege of the majority, absent

the chief justice, to make the assignment. Hence, *Lloyd* was assigned and is assigned. The tragedy of compromising on this simple procedure is illustrated by last term's *Swann* [decision]. You who were a minority of two kept the opinion for yourself and faithfully wrote the minority opinion which the majority could not accept. Potter wrote the majority view and a majority agreed to it. It was not circulated because we thought you should see it. After much effort your minority opinion was transformed, the majority view prevailed, and the result was unanimous.

But *Swann* illustrated the wasted time and effort and the frayed relations which result when the traditional assignment procedure is not followed.

If the conference wants to authorize you to assign all the opinions, that will be a new procedure. Though opposed to it, I will acquiesce. But unless we make a frank reversal in our policy, any group in the majority should and must make the assignment.

This is a two-edge sword. Byron might well head up five members of the Court, you, Bill Brennan, Potter Stewart and I being the minority; and we might feel strongly about it. But in that event it is for Byron to make the assignment. It is not for us in the minority to try to outwit Byron by saying "I reserve my vote and then recast it to control the assignment." That only leads to a frayed and bitter Court full of needless strains and quarrels.

Lloyd stays assigned to Thurgood. (pp. 44–45)

Later, I examine other examples of different chief justices on the dimension of the leader's personal relations with members of the group. Not only is it usually the most important of the three factors in determining the leader's influence but it is the factor that has the more capacity for differentiating between chief justices. Much less variation seems available for the second situational component, position power.

The Leader's Position Power

How much power and authority are provided the leader by the position he or she holds? Does the leader have the authority to hire and fire; can the leader reward persons by giving raises in pay or status; or is the leader quite limited in regulating the behavior of other members? Leaders with high position power carry some kind of separate rank or status and have "clout," whereas leaders low in position power cannot punish their coworkers by altering their rank or status. Fiedler considered position power to be the least important of the three components of a leader's effectiveness because group success can often result from a structured task or a popular leader even if the leader lacks authority and power.

How much position power does the chief justice have? Conventional wisdom would say, with respect to regulating the behavior of the other justices, not much. Steamer has speculated that if an advertisement were to appear in the Help Wanted section of the *New York Times* with a job description for the chief justice, it would include:

> Although the chief justice will be responsible for assigning the writing of opinions among eight associate justices, he [or she] will have no legal authority to discharge or take minimal disciplinary action against any of the associates for any reason whatsoever. If any of them is slothful, senile, abrasive, or downright impossible, the Chief's ability to cope with such an exigency must depend solely on his powers of persuasion. (1986, p. 3)

As noted, the chief justice neither hires nor fires colleagues (although the Chief may work behind the scenes to encourage an aging justice to retire). The associate justices have ultimate job security and a salary fixed by Congress; they choose their own law clerks and office staff. If an associate justice delays in getting an opinion drafted, the Chief cannot capitalize on the customary devices of bosses to get the task done.

When it comes to making judicial decisions, the chief justice's vote counts no more than any other justice's. About the only influence-bearing example of the leader's position power is the prerogative in assigning authorship of opinions in cases in which he is in the majority; a chief justice can use this power to reward or punish other justices. As Justice Douglas noted earlier in his reaction to a writing assignment, the chief justice can been seen by other justices as usurping even that limited power.

But it should not be overlooked that the chief justice has this position for life. While the Chief cannot fire associate justices, they cannot fire him, in contrast to many organizations in which the leader's low position power also implies a fragile job security. Chief justices tend to serve for a long time; if we disregard the length of time of the first three—before the Court was defined—the average tenure of the next 13 is 15 years.

Task Structure

The amount of structure in the task that the group has been assigned to perform is the third situational determinant of the leader's effectiveness, according to Fiedler. How well does the leader know how to proceed? Some types of tasks possess a great deal of *goal clarity*; for most types of sports teams, the requirements of the task for each player are clearly known or at least learnable. To the contrary, tasks of ad hoc committees, policy-making groups, and creative groups often lack goal clarity and structure—no one knows what the group's purposes are, much less how the group should proceed. A second element of task structure is its degree of *solution specificity*; that is, there may or may not be more than one correct solution for the group's task. A third aspect is the degree of *decision verifiability*; once a decision has been made, how clearly does the group know that it is a correct one? All these aspects of a task's structure play a role in determining the effectiveness of different types of leaders. The theory proposes that those tasks that are completely structured tend to give more control to the leader. However, task structure clearly interacts with position power. If the task is clearly structured, the leader needs less position power to get the job done because everybody's responsibilities have already been specified.

How much structure is there to the task facing panels of appellate judges? The requirements of the task are clearly stated and known to every individual in the group, the path to accomplishing the task has few alternatives, and only a limited number of correct solutions to the task exist. Furthermore, in the case of the Supreme Court or any appellate court, the group has been in operation for a long period of time, procedures have been developed to handle the process, and the justices are aware of how to proceed. The one aspect of Court responsibilities that varies from the ingredients of a highly structured task is the verifiability, in that there is no one correct solution to the task. *Decision verifiability* may be thought to vary from case to case. Sometimes the language of the Constitution or the statute is clear; as we have seen, more than one-third of the cases are settled by a 9 to 0 vote. But in cases that result in a 5 to 4 or 6 to 3 vote, it would seem that, by definition, decision verifiability is lower.

But an established way of doing things can work to an innovative leader's detriment. Those leaders who try to change firmly established procedures—even momentary or trivial changes—find out just how little position power they have. Shortly after William Rehnquist became chief justice, he permitted an oral argument to extend 15 minutes beyond its allotted hour, so that it intruded into the justices' lunch hour of noon to 1 p.m. Two of the justices were so outraged that they walked out while the attorney was still making her oral argument, and the others grumbled about the deviation in procedures. Chief Justice Rehnquist later let his colleagues know that he would never again permit intrusions on their lunch hour (O'Brien, 1993).

For purposes of simplification and analysis, Fiedler considered each of these three aspects of the situation a dichotomy. Leader–member relationships are either good or poor; position power is either strong or weak; and task structure is either clear or unclear. As there are two categories in each of three aspects, we may conceive of a system of eight classifications (2 x 2 x 2) that would encompass all the possible combinations of these aspects. Fiedler has done this in order to see what leadership style works best in each situation. In fact, he has added a ninth category to cover instances in which the leader–member relationships are extremely poor.

The major hypothesis of Fiedler's contingency model is that the leader's effectiveness is a function of both the leader's style and the three situational components. With regard to leadership style, he distinguished between *task-oriented* and *relationship-oriented* leaders. Task-oriented leaders get their satisfaction and self-esteem from the group's completion of its tasks, even if the leader must suffer poor interpersonal relationships in order to do so; an example would be a football coach whose players all hate him but whose teams win all their games. In contrast, for relationship-oriented leaders, satisfaction comes from happy, collegial group relationships, and "success," as measured by productivity, is less salient.

Fiedler hypothesized that the degree to which the conditions are favorable to the leader interacted with leadership style. Favorable conditions emerge from situations that permit the leader to exert a great deal of influence on the group. Fiedler proposed that the task-oriented leaders are most effective under conditions that are either very favorable or very unfavorable to the leader; that is, in cases in which the leader has a great deal of influence and power or in cases in which the leader has no influence and power. On the other hand, relationship-oriented leaders are most effective under conditions that are moderately favorable or unfavorable and where the leader's influence and power are mixed and moderate.

Several metaanalyses have led to a generally positive conclusion about the validity of Fiedler's contingency theory, and Fiedler has extended his theory to cognitive factors of the leader and other situational factors such as the stress of the job (Fiedler & Garcia, 1987; Peters, Hartke, & Pohlmann, 1985; Strube & Garcia, 1981). The conditions under which task-oriented versus relationship-oriented leaders were most effective were more salient in studies of groups created in the laboratory; in contrast, in real-life groups, the relationship was less clear-cut. However, the contingency theory perspective has become the predominant one by which to evaluate leadership effectiveness (Chemers, 1997). Does it have heuristic value for the Supreme Court?

Applications of a Contingency Theory to the Supreme Court

How may a contingency theory of leadership be applied to the workings of the Supreme Court? With regard to the three situational characteristics, the following conclusions seem warranted. The position power of the chief justice is *poor*, with little "clout" to get other justices to behave as the Chief wishes. The group's task structure is mostly *clear*; there is a longstanding tradition about how to proceed; the agenda for the group is generated by the petitions submitted to the Court, and the "outcome" is determined by a vote of the members of the group. As noted earlier, decision verifiability is the one ingredient that clouds the clarity of the task structure; in fact, the correctness of a group's decision is the major issue of dispute. Occasionally a justice will later disclose that he or she erred in an earlier decision. Four years after his vote was the determining one in the case of *Bowers v. Hardwick* (1986) that criminalized homosexual acts, Justice Lewis F. Powell announced that he had "probably made a mistake" in doing so (Jeffries, 1994, p. 530).

It is on the dimension of leader–member relations that the possibility of variability exists from one chief justice to another. If we can say that the chief justice's job is one in which the position power of the leader is *weak*, the task structure is *clear*, and the leader–member relations can range from good to poor, depending on the chief justice, we find that the Supreme Court reflects Fiedler's combinations of factors—"mixed or moderate," to use Fiedler's terms—creating situations in which Fiedler finds that the relationship-oriented type of leader is more effective than the task-oriented leader.

Task Orientation and the Chief Justice

But aren't all chief justices task oriented? Would a person have attained that prestigious position without expecting colleagues to follow orders and be productive? Yes, but only to a degree. That is, variations exist in the backgrounds, eminence, and probably even the task orientation of those who have become chief justice. I mentioned Earl Warren's record as a political office-holder, and clearly he was innovative and task oriented in his behavior. His background seems in contrast with that of Morrison Waite. When he was appointed chief justice by President Grant in 1874, Morrison Waite was a national nonentity, mostly an unknown quantity outside of his home state of Ohio. His only national recognition came from serving as one of the three U.S. representatives to the Geneva Arbitration Tribunal, convened to settle the U.S. *Alabama* claims. He had held only three minor elected positions within his home state, had never sat on a court of any kind, and was mostly content to be a successful lawyer in Toledo. When one of the then current justices on the Supreme Court, Stephen Field, heard of Waite's appointment, he wrote: "He is a new man that never would have been thought of for the position by any person except President Grant" (Steamer, 1986, p. 115). Ironically, it was only because he was President Grant's seventh choice for the job that he was confirmed by the Senate; Grant first offered it to two of his closest friends and associates, but the Senate opposed them. After four prominent politicians—including three senators and the secretary of state—declined the offer, President Grant in desperation turned to Waite, and the Senate confirmed him with relief (Steamer, 1986).

Morrison Waite served as chief justice from 1874 to 1888. His entry into the job reflects perhaps the nadir in leader–member relations; as Steamer (1986) observed, he came to the Court with three strikes against him; he was appointed by President Grant, known for his cronyism and the haphazard nature of his appointments, he had no national reputation, and he joined a Court on which several of the incumbent justices had actively sought the appointment as chief justice and clearly considered themselves to be superior to the new appointee. Despite the tough entry, Waite became an adequate chief justice—not a great one, but a generally satisfactory one. He was not brilliant, or especially talented—his writing style was quite pedestrian—but he worked hard, he assigned opinions fairly and sensibly, and he wrote more than his share of opinions. Even though at least one associate justice, Samuel Miller, never quite accepted being passed over for chief, Waite showed diplomatic skill in achieving a smoothly running court (Magrath, 1963).

Differences in Relationship Orientation

Perhaps what most distinguishes between different chief justices is their degree of relationship orientation. As noted earlier, Warren Burger, when he became chief justice, made a number of decisions about Supreme Court procedure without consultation with the other justices; he took over the judicial conference room as his own office; he changed the structure of the table in the courtroom from rectangular to boomerang-shaped, and he even tried to standardize the justices' chairs. His pattern of unilateral decisions does not imply a person overly concerned with his relationships with others. In contrast, Chief Justice Taft, as mentioned earlier, was the socioemotional leader of the Court. He wanted to be liked, and he valued the friendship of each justice with whom he served, even that of Justice James McReynolds, whom he described as a "grouch." Taft wrote to one of his sons after an altercation with McReynolds that "the best way to get along with people with whom you have to live always is to restrain your impatience and consider that doubtless you have peculiarities that try other people" (Danelski, 2002, p. 663).

The Taft court is an example of the conclusion that the chief justice does not have to be the task-oriented leader if he is successful at being the relationship-oriented leader and someone else is effective in provide structure and task leadership. Even critical justices such as Brandeis were pleased with the conferences. And the tasks got done; for the first time in more than 50 years, the Court came close to clearing its docket while Taft was chief justice.

Summarizing the Conclusions of Contingency Theory

In a speech before the ABA, Chief Justice Rehnquist recalled being told of a Canadian chief justice who, during oral arguments, would tap his pencil on the bench whenever he wanted his fellow judges to stop asking so many questions. Rehnquist wistfully confided, "I have occasionally wished that I had similar authority in our court" (Associated Press, 1996, p. 7A).

A contingency theory of leadership is sensitive to just such kinds of complaints by a leader. As applied to the role of the chief justice, the theory makes two contributions to understanding the leader's effectiveness:

1. Some types of leaders are more effective in certain situations; other types in other situations. In the situation at hand, with clear task structure and limited position power, the nature of the leader's relations with the group members largely determines his or her effectiveness.

2. Leaders who are liked and respected do not need formal position power; they can achieve compliance with their goals even under challenging circumstances.

Using the terminology of psychological theory, the position power—the "authority" of the chief justice—is limited. But the Chief remains a designated leader with sizable prestige, and if the incumbent's personal character and qualifications are of a certain sort, the chief justice can persuade the others to a degree beyond that expected from the position's weak position power. In short, just who is the incumbent can make a huge difference, as is illustrated in the Court's shift on *Brown v. Board of Education* when Warren replaced Vinson.

Ideal Qualities of a Chief Justice

The foregoing emphasizes that many factors contribute to the effectiveness of a given chief justice. Does the incumbent's appearance make a difference? Justice Felix Frankfurter wrote: "Supreme Court justices should be tall and broad and have a little bit of a bay window. They should look the way Stone looked" (Phillips, 1960, p. 62). Chief Justice Burger not only had the requisite looks but also a deep voice that commanded attention. But of the ten chief justices during the twentieth century, Burger and Stone were two of the least effective (White and Vinson were the others). It is better to turn to internal factors, which we can use to generate a kind of checklist against which to evaluate the leadership success of different chief justices. Qualities that contribute to the evaluation might include the following.

Being Willing and Able to Work Hard

It is essential that the chief justice do well at several activities: these include being ready for the conferences that discuss certiorari petitions and the briefs accepted for oral argument, as well as writing at least an appropriate share of the majority opinions. Chief Justice Charles Evans Hughes came to the certiorari conference fully prepared, having read all the petitions and having dispensed with those he considered without merit. His "blacklist" of merit-less petitions was rarely questioned. In contrast, when Harlan Fiske Stone was chief justice, he encouraged full discussion of the certiorari petitions, and his own analysis of them was offered in a most diffident manner (White, 1978). As a result, the Stone-led conferences went on relentlessly for hours, and often they needlessly extended into the weekend; the Court became the most contentious of the twentieth century.

Being Intellectually Capable

Experts look to a leader to be able to provide a perspective, a "vision." In the case of the chief justice, this includes putting a stamp on the Court's opinions, or persuading the other justices to adopt some ground-breaking principles. Effectiveness as a chief justice means a coherent jurisprudence that gives the lower courts reliable guidance. As chief justice, Warren Burger was not able to instill a consistent conservative impact; for example, on major issues such as abortion and affirmative action, his attempts at leadership were often insufficient (Greenhouse, 2005b, p. 157). In contrast, Chief Justice Warren provided an excellent example of effectiveness. Despite the disclaimers about his intellectual limitations, he had a consistent judicial philosophy that was implemented in a program of decisions that had long-reaching effects on the criminal justice system and on social policy in general. Even more important, while he was not the *first* chief justice, John Marshall (who was the fourth, serving from 1801 to 1835) established the role of the Court as a result of his vision that the provincialism of the state legislatures required the discipline of the federal laws if the American republic was to survive (Smith, 1996). Chief Justice Marshall's perspective led to the establishment of guidelines for the challenging task of allocating power between the federal government and the states.

Assigning Opinions Sensibly

An astute chief justice can capitalize on the office's limited power to assign opinions in order to influence the Court (Murphy, 1964). But this process is delicate; it has been claimed that "opinion assignment represents the greatest test of a Chief Justice's administrative skill" (Magrath, 1963, p. 262).

We are aware that the chief justice has great discretion in the assignment of opinion writing. Playing favorites and attempting to sabotage the process are to be avoided. Chief Justice Warren once said:

> if assigning opinions wasn't done with regard to fairness, it could well lead to great disruption in the Court. During all the years I was there . . . I did try to see that we had an equal work load . . . Everybody, regardless of the length of time they were on the Court, had a fair opportunity to write important cases. (Rohde & Spaeth, 1976, p. 173)

(However, an analysis by Ulmer, 1970, indicated that Justice Frankfurter was consistently slighted by Chief Justice Warren, perhaps because of his argumentative nature and the deteriorating relationship between the two [Schwartz, 1981].)

Chief Justice William Howard Taft, in making his assignments, relied heavily on three factors: his estimate of the judge's ability; his concern for the judge's views; and his understanding of the judge's temperament and knowledge of the judge's state of health (Steamer, 1986). When one of the other justices was not in good health, Taft would lighten his load and take on the resulting extra writing assignments himself.

Some chief justices, including Fuller, Taft, Hughes, and Warren, would assign the dullest and most boring cases to themselves (Menez, 1984). But also, assignments are often made on the basis of the expertise of the particular judge. Warren would consult with Justice Hugo Black in assigning opinions (Cray, 1997). In the Taft court, Justice Brandeis was assigned tax and rate litigation cases, Van Devanter land claims and Indian litigation cases, and Sutherland cases involving boundary lines, water rights, and irrigation projects. Patent cases were especially burdensome, because they were so technical and complicated, and justices sought to avoid them (Mason, 1965). Tax cases have apparently have replaced them as the current "dogs" of the Court; Baum has noted Justice Souter's joke that he willingly responded to Chief Justice Rehnquist's request to sing carols at the Court's Christmas party because "I have to. Otherwise, I get all the tax cases" (1997, p. 114).

Running an Organized Ship

One of the major goals of the Court is disposing of cases. This can be done efficiently or in a too casual or leisurely manner. Chief Justice Edward Douglass White had an easygoing nature that allowed for prolonged debate; this elevated the tension between the justices as well as delaying the disposition of cases. Noted earlier was the opposite extreme, Chief Justice Charles Evans Hughes, whose skill as a presiding officer of the Court has never been equaled. Paul Freund wrote about him that

> [h]is Jovian figure seemed to occupy the central seat by natural right. His powers of concentration were total; he transfixed counsel with a piercing stare, at intervals betraying his purpose to intervene by a quickening movement of the eyelids. When he did intervene, he showed a remarkable capacity to bring an argument into focus, to go for the jugular. Not infrequently he rescued counsel as they suffered repetitive assaults from vantage points along the bench. (1967, p. 13)

In contrast to his immediate predecessor, Chief Justice Rehnquist "ran the Court efficiently; conferences were much shorter and more sharply focused, and opinion assignments were unambiguous. Re-arguments, almost an annual ritual under Burger, became rare" (Greenhouse, 2005b, p. 234).

Sensitivity to Others

Designated leaders are expected not only to be task leaders but to be concerned about the welfare of other members of the group and the maintenance of the continued positive atmosphere within the group. When Earl Warren was suddenly named the chief justice, he realized that he lacked appellate experience and that the other justices were veterans at it. Therefore, he asked Associate Justice Hugo Black to chair the judicial conferences until he learned the procedures. Warren also recognized that Justice Frankfurter was an inveterate law professor, and thus he was initially willing to let Frankfurter treat him as a promising but untutored student who needed to be brought up to speed (Howard, 1997).

Development and Maintenance of a Collegial Atmosphere

Before they begin each day of oral arguments or a judicial conference, the nine justices on the Supreme Court shake hands with each other, a tradition begun by Chief Justice Melville Fuller in the late 1880s (King, 1950). This act recognizes the ties between the justices, despite whatever ideological conflicts may be present. But chief justices differ in the degree to which they implement this appearance of collegiality; the example of Chief Justice Burger's impetuous procedures serves as one unfortunate illustration of an obstacle to the maintenance of collegiality.

A Spirit of Conciliation

The chief justice, in seeking to maintain an atmosphere of goodwill between participants, must often take the lead in reducing tensions—that is, the Chief must go more than halfway—when conflict emerges. While chief justice, Rehnquist was often gracious and complimentary to the majority opinion writer even as he dissented. After Morrison Waite became chief justice in 1877, his assignment of an opinion writer in one of the first major cases drew the ire of another justice who had expected to have been given the task. Chief Justice Waite answered in a conciliatory manner, leading the upset justice, Stephen Field, to retract some of his original harsh language but to insist that the assignment still should have been given to him. At that point Waite responded:

> "No one appreciates your vigorous style more than I do, and, but for these considerations [that the opinion should be written by a justice who was not so close to one of the parties involved in the case], I should have been glad to have had its use in the case—And while I regret that you do not look on the matter as I do, I cannot but think that my judgment was for the best interest of us all. . . . I certainly intend to treat all my brethren fairly in this most delicate and at the same time important part of my work. If I do not, it is the fault of the head and not the heart. I am glad to know that I misunderstood some of the expressions in your former note, and that I may hope to retain your friendship and respect if my conduct shall be such as to merit it." (Steamer, 1986, p. 131)

Although a task orientation and a relationship orientation can be identified as separate concerns for a chief justice, each contributes to the effectiveness of the incumbent. That is, each has an impact on the chief justice's ability to achieve majority decisions that are congruent with policy goals.

William Rehnquist as Chief Justice

When President Nixon was suffering through a string of rejections of his nominees for the Supreme Court, William Rehnquist was in charge of the White House Office of Legal Counsel. Well before he became the president's eventual choice for a nominee, Rehnquist told a reporter he had "no chance at all" of being nominated, because "I'm not from the South, I'm not a woman, and I'm not mediocre" (Dean, 2001, p. 191). As chief justice, Rehnquist showed that he truly was not "mediocre." How will William Rehnquist compare with the few "greats" among the 15 previous chief justices? A chapter published only five years after he became chief justice was prescient:

> The differences between Chief Justice Burger and his successor
> may be significant as well in moving the Court toward a new
> constitutional era. Rehnquist possesses greater leadership potential
> because of his greater analytical skills, coherent judicial philoso-
> phy, lucid writing style, and warm personable manner. Beyond
> that, he has a more conservative majority to lead. Referring to
> the Supreme Court from 1969 through 1986 as the "Burger
> Court" is little more than a convenient and perhaps arbitrary label
> for identifying a chunk of history; that may be less true of the
> Rehnquist Court. Chief Justice Rehnquist may have the skills and
> allies necessary to move the Court into a new constitutional era.
> (Lamb & Halpern, 1991, p. 447)

If the essence of leadership is exerting an influence, then in the 2001–2002 term Rehnquist showed the peak of his leadership. The veteran court observer and reporter for the *New York Times*, Linda Greenhouse, wrote:

> If there is one phrase that best describes the Supreme Court term
> that ended late last week, it is this: the triumph of William H.
> Rehnquist. In the term that marked the chief justice's 30th
> anniversary on the bench, the Court moved far toward accom-
> plishing his long-term goals, lowering the barrier between church
> and state and elevating states' rights through expanding the
> concept of sovereign immunity. (2002a, p. A1)

Since that term, not all of the major cases went Chief Justice Rehnquist's way; major examples include the *Lawrence v. Texas* (2003) case on gay rights described in chapter 10 and one of the University of Michigan affirmative action cases. But as Chief Justice Rehnquist's service on the bench moved toward its end, he received substantial consideration as the fourth of the "great" chief justices. For example, law professor Jeffrey Rosen (2005b), writing in the *Atlantic Monthly*, titled his article "Rehnquist the Great?" and listed these as among his attributes:

1. "He was essentially a pragmatist who believed in certain core conservative values—primarily states' rights and convicting criminals—but didn't fuss too much about how he achieved his aims" (p. 79).
2. He was able to get along with this ideological opponents. He was fair, good-natured, and sensitive to the needs of his colleagues.
3. He had "unparalleled organizational skill: he got opinions out quickly and made the arguments run on time both in and out of court" (p. 80).

In summary, Rosen concluded:

Rehnquist will always take half a loaf over no loaf at all, and as chief justice he has proved far more willing than most of his colleagues to support, for the good of the Court, opinions with which he disagrees.

Rehnquist's successes as chief justice provide an object lesson for future holders of the office: having a judicious temperament is far more important than having a consistent judicial methodology. (2005b, p. 90)

Others, whether they agree with Rehnquist's views or not, acknowledge his impact. Walter Dellinger, former solicitor general under President Clinton, called him "one of the dominant chief justices of American history" (Garnett, 2005, p. 34). Cass Sunstein, a distinguished professor of law, has said that

Rehnquist must be counted as one of the giants of American law, because he has presided over and greatly contributed to a Supreme Court that has radically revised previous understandings of the Constitution. . . . [While] the Rehnquist Court has not always acted in accordance with the views of William Rehnquist . . . it has moved dramatically in his preferred directions. (2004–2005, pp. 32–33)

10

Can the Court's Decisions Be Predicted?

I play a game with my [law] clerks. . . . They are *so* smart. I let them guess the votes [at the case conference]. They are rarely right.—Justice Clarence Thomas (1996)

Deja Vu All Over Again

Late in the year 2002, the Supreme Court agreed to hear the case of *Lawrence v. Texas* (2003), and many Court-watchers with long memories doubtless responded with a reaction of "What? Again?" As we will see, the facts of this case bore an uncanny resemblance to those of a case decided by the Court 16 years earlier. Police in Houston, Texas, received a report—later proved phony—that an armed man in a neighboring apartment was "going crazy." (The caller was later convicted for filing a false report.) Sheriffs' officers entered the apartment and encountered two men having sexual relations. John Geddes Lawrence and Tyron Garner were arrested because they had violated Texas's law that prohibited sodomy between two persons of the same sex. Each man was held overnight, charged with a misdemeanor offense under Texas's Homosexual Conduct Law, and after pleading no contest, fined $200. They appealed first to the Texas Court of Appeals, which ruled that the Texas statute did not violate equal protection rights because it barred all persons from engaging in this behavior and because homosexual persons were not a protected class.

After the state's highest court refused to review the case, the two men appealed to the U.S. Supreme Court, claiming that the law violated Fourteenth Amendment guarantees of equal protection as well as their right to privacy. (As of the beginning of the year 2003, 13 states banned sodomy—four of these restricted sodomy only between same-sex partners, but nine other states also criminalized sodomy in heterosexual couples.) The Court's decision in the case of *Lawrence v. Texas* was announced at the very end of its 2002–2003 term; it found for the two men, ruling that state laws that criminalized sodomy only among same-sex couples were discriminatory.

Two Similar Cases—Would They Have Similar Outcomes?

The reason for the experience of *deja vu* is that the aforementioned facts and the applicable state law were remarkably similar to those in a case decided by the Supreme Court in 1986, *Bowers v. Hardwick*. In this earlier case, the facts were as follows. On the morning of July 5, 1982, Michael Hardwick left a gay nightclub in Atlanta; he had worked there all night and he was tired and thirsty. As he left, he grabbed a beer and took some swigs as he walked along the sidewalk. A police officer spotted him and wrote out a ticket for drinking in public. Hardwick later paid the $50 fine, but the paperwork on his appearance in court never caught up with the police officer, who had threatened him: "I'm counting on you to show up in court. If you don't, I will take it that you're laughing in my face. And I'll come find you. And I will lock you up" (Harris, 1986, p. C4).

Thinking he had been ignored, the police officer sought to find Hardwick, and like the two law enforcement officers in the Texas case, he went on a mistaken mission, only to discover two men *in flagrante delicto*. Someone met him at the door of Hardwick's house and permitted him to enter. The police officer went down the hall; a bedroom door was ajar, the room lit by a candle. Inside, he saw Hardwick and another man engaged in oral sex. Both were arrested and charged with sodomy; each faced a possible sentence of 1 to 20 years in prison.

The American Civil Liberties Union encouraged Hardwick to challenge the Georgia sodomy law on the behalf of all homosexual persons, and he agreed to. In May 1985, a three-judge panel of the U.S. Court of Appeals for the Eleventh Circuit ruled 2 to 1 that the Georgia law infringed on Hardwick's rights to privacy. The state appealed, and the Supreme Court agreed to take the case. Amicus briefs for Hardwick made several basic arguments:

1. Same-gender sexual orientation is not pathological, nor is oral-genital sex.
2. Criminal punishment has harmful psychological consequences for people who engage in the proscribed conduct. Fear and threat of criminal prosecution hurt the development of mental health among gay people by fostering detrimental labeling, by themselves and by society. Lesbians and gay men become stigmatized as "deviants" and are viewed as possessing undesirable stereotypes.

But the majority opinion of the Court disregarded these; on June 30, 1986, again in one of its last announced decisions for the term, the Supreme Court ruled that the Constitution did not protect homosexual relations between consenting adults, even in the privacy of their own homes. Georgia's statute was upheld. In the narrow 5 to 4 majority were Justices White, Burger, Rehnquist,

O'Connor, and Powell; dissenting were Justices Blackmun, Brennan, Marshall, and Stevens. Justice White's majority opinion stressed the "ancient roots" in English common law of those statutes that criminalized homosexual relations. He wrote: "The Court is most vulnerable and comes closest to illegitimacy when it deals with judge-made constitutional law having little or no cognizable roots in the language or design of the Constitution" (*Bowers v. Hardwick*, 1986, p. 2846).

With regard to previous rulings, Justice White acknowledged that the various "fundamental rights" not specified in the Constitution could not be deprived without "due process of law," but he also concluded that fundamental rights were limited to those that are "deeply rooted in the nation's history or tradition" or "implicit in the concept of ordered liberty" (Taylor, 1986, p. A19). Apparently homosexuality was such an anathema to Chief Justice Burger that he wrote a concurring opinion that didn't add anything other than to reaffirm that the restriction of same-gender sexual conduct was "firmly rooted in Judeo-Christian moral and ethical standards" (*Bowers v. Hardwick*, 1986, p. 2847).

While the majority opinion in *Bowers v. Hardwick* rejected the arguments provided by mental health experts, the minority opinion written by Justice Blackmun endorsed them; one observer (Melton, 1989) concluded that Blackmun's dissent relied heavily on an amicus brief prepared by the American Psychological Association. Justice Blackmun wrote that

> despite historical views of homosexuality, it is no longer viewed by mental-health professionals as a "disease" or disorder. See Brief for American Psychological Association and American Public Health Association as *Amicus Curiae* 8–11. But obviously, neither is it a simple matter of deliberate personal election. Homosexual orientation may well form part of the very fiber of an individual's personality. (*Bowers v. Hardwick*, 1986, p. 2850)

The majority decision in *Bowers v. Hardwick* was obviously a disappointment to gay rights activists and to many liberals and mental health professionals, but the resulting protest may have had a subtle and slow-acting effect. (The frustration and disappointment increased when, several years later, Justice Powell, who had been the deciding vote for the majority, acknowledged that he had made a mistake.) A decade after the *Hardwick* decision, the Court again considered the issue of the rights of persons with a homosexual orientation. The decision in the case of *Romer v. Evans* (1996) was not only inconsistent with the earlier decision—it did not even cite it. It is true that the specific issues of the two cases were not similar, but did the outcome in the *Romer* case portend the outcome in the *Lawrence v. Texas* case?

The Temptation to Predict Outcomes

When the Supreme Court granted certiorari in the *Lawrence v. Texas* case, inveterate Court-watchers immediately began to speculate about the possible votes and outcome. Two justices who were among the majority in *Bowers v. Hardwick*, Chief Justice Rehnquist and Justice O'Connor, were still on the bench, along with one dissenter, Justice Stevens. Longtime Court-watcher Joan Biskupic offered the following observation.

> The justices who have joined the Court since then probably fall into two camps. Antonin Scalia and Clarence Thomas have suggested they would uphold a sodomy ban. David Souter, Ruth Bader Ginsburg, and Stephen Breyer have indicated that they are more likely to strike down such a law. Justice Anthony Kennedy probably falls somewhere in the middle and could be a key vote in the Texas case.
>
> Kennedy wrote a 1996 decision [the aforementioned *Romer v. Evans*] that struck down a Colorado constitutional amendment that barred cities from protecting lesbians and gay men from bias. In that case, however, the six-justice majority (which also included O'Connor) did not cite the 1986 ruling. (2002, p. 4A)

Did the fact that the Court granted certiorari to an appeal whose facts and law were very similar to an earlier case mean that the Court was likely—or even willing—to overturn its decision of 16 years earlier? Linda Greenhouse suggested:

> While there is of course no guarantee that the Court plans to strike down the Texas law, which defines "deviate sexual intercourse" to include oral and anal sex, the general sense today among lawyers who follow gay rights issues was that the Court would not have bothered to intervene in the case unless a majority of justices had concluded the time had come to revisit the issue. (2002c, p. A27)

The possibility of a ruling favoring the petitioners, Lawrence and Garner, raised several questions: How much does the decision to grant certiorari predict the future outcome of the case? Is the Court willing to admit it erred earlier, and under what conditions can it overrule itself? In *Planned Parenthood of Southeastern Pennsylvania v. Casey* (1992), the Court said that a reversal should be based on some special reasons other than simply the belief that a previous case was wrongly decided. The Court specified four factors for deciding whether to overrule itself:

- The workability of the rule
- The extent to which the public has relied on the rule
- Relevant changes in legal doctrine
- Changes in the facts or perceptions of the facts

Certainly, in the two decades since the *Bowers v. Hardwick* decision, perceptions of facts (if not the facts themselves) had changed. Recognition that a significant portion of the population possesses a homosexual orientation is commonplace. (Back in 1986, when the Court was considering *Bowers v. Hardwick*, Justice Powell told one of his law clerks that he did not even know any homosexual persons, and he asked the rather embarrassed clerk detailed questions about the nature and determinants of arousal of sexual behavior in those men who had a homosexual orientation.) A viewpoint that homosexuality is "wired" into the system rather than a matter of choice has received wide acceptance. Legislation has reflected the increased awareness; for example, in contrast to about half the states having outlawed sodomy in 1986, only 13 still did in 2003. (Ironically, the Georgia law that the Court upheld in 1986 was overturned by a state court's ruling in 1998, so consensual homosexual sex was no longer prohibited in Georgia.)

But *stare decisis* is a powerful force in some judicial decisions, and some justices may still subscribe to the views of Chief Justice Burger about the immorality of homosexuality. Prior to the announcement of the outcome, observers felt that it was very likely that the vote on this case would be a close one, probably 5 to 4 or possibly 6 to 3; the question was: In which direction?

The Outcome in *Lawrence v. Texas*: How Much a Prototype?

The actual vote in *Lawrence v. Texas* was 6 to 3, and in several respects, the outcome was accurately predicted by the Court-watchers quoted earlier. The four relative liberals, Justices Stevens, Souter, Ginsburg, and Breyer, all voted to overturn the state law; the three most conservative justices, Justices Rehnquist, Scalia, and Thomas, voted to uphold it. As predicted, the swing votes of Justices O'Connor and Kennedy determined the outcome.

If we were to use this case as a prototype, we would conclude that the votes of most justices are quite predictable, but that would be an oversimplification. The purpose of this chapter is to explore the actual degree of predictability of outcomes of cases, as well as the votes of individual justices.

The Role of Prediction in Understanding Outcomes

Lawrence v. Texas is not the only case for which experts seek to predict the outcome. Speculation about upcoming votes is inevitable. Lawyers arguing a case before the Court relentlessly count votes (Urofsky, 1997, p. 133, provides an example in one important case). Media mavens do it, law professors do it, and political scientists and psychologists are not free of such conjecture either. After all, aren't social scientists expected to be able to predict human behavior?

Should predicting votes be the main goal of those who seek to understand the workings of the Court? Probably not. But attempting to anticipate outcomes is legitimate, because these decisions have a huge impact on our daily lives. And every vote by a justice gives us further clues to understanding his or her basic orientation toward the law.

Difficulties in Prediction

You would think that predicting outcomes of votes in the Supreme Court would be easy. We have vast information on each of the justices' backgrounds, their voting records, and often their viewpoints off the bench, as illustrated in speeches, law review articles, or books. Chapter 3 reported on two recent surveys that, using a small number of cases, found that the outcome was usually predictable, based on a simple count of the number of questions the justices asked each side's attorney. But, as we will see, votes often are predictable, but only up to a point.

The Line-Item Veto Case:
Soliciting Predictions from Experts

The difficulty in making accurate predictions is illustrated in an important case from the 1990s. The *National Law Journal* asked three prominent constitutional law professors to predict the outcome of a case for which the Supreme Court had heard oral arguments in a special session in May 1997. The case, *Raines v. Byrd* (1997), dealt with the constitutionality of the Line-Item Veto Act of 1996, in which the Congress gave the president increased budgetary powers; specifically, the act gave the president the right to "cancel in whole" three types of budget items: dollar amounts of discretionary budget authority, new items of direct spending, and limited tax benefits (Coyle, 1997). To veto such specific provisions, the president had to act within five calendar days of signing the legislation.

Six members of Congress challenged the act's constitutionality the day after it became a law, creating one of the issues for the Court to decide: Did the persons who challenged the law have *standing*? That is, could they show that they had an injury or interest that was affected by the law? The issue was raised during the 70 minutes of oral arguments in the May 1997 special session. A second issue dealt with whether the Court should be required to decide on constitutionality even before the president had exercised the authority granted by the act (Coyle, 1997). President Clinton did not exercise his line-item veto until August 1997.

Needless to say, President Clinton supported the act, and the United States solicitor general argued for its constitutionality before the Supreme Court. But the members of Congress who challenged the act contended that it conferred on the president certain powers of "veto, revision, and repeal of federal law" that violated article 1 of the Constitution, dealing with the separation of powers. They claimed that they had standing because the act injured them by altering the "legal and practical effect" of their votes and by divesting them of their constitutional role in the repeal of legislation (Coyle, 1997, p. A22). The district court agreed, striking down the law—hence the appeal to the Supreme Court (*Raines v. Byrd*, 1997).

The Experts' Expectations and the Outcomes in the Line-Item Veto Case

In a speech at the ABA convention, Justice Stevens noted the fallibility of predicting how judges will decide and said that even his predictions about his colleagues' votes were often wrong. So how did these three experts do on the line-item veto decision? To use psychological terminology, they had no reliability; that is, no consistency existed from one predictor to another. Two of the experts expected the Court to conclude that the petitioners had standing, while the third thought that was uncertain, even doubtful. What about their validity? The actual decision was announced in late June 1997; the Court ruled 7 to 2 that the petitioners, in effect, did not have standing because they had not suffered any personal injury (Pear, 1997). Chief Justice Rehnquist wrote the majority opinion; he noted that a private plaintiff who suffered a loss of money or benefits as a result of a line-item veto would probably have the right to sue. The chief justice's opinion was signed by Justices O'Connor, Scalia, Kennedy, Thomas, and Ginsburg. Justice Souter voted with the chief justice but wrote his own opinion. Justice Breyer dissented, as did Justice Stevens, maintaining his reputation as a maverick. Justice Stevens even went so far as to conclude that the act was unconstitutional. Justice Breyer's dissent did not express an opinion on the ultimate issue.

In contrast, two of the three experts had predicted that the Court would conclude the petitioners had standing. Justice Breyer proved to be the most predictable justice for the panel of experts. For example, Professor Laurence Tribe was correct in predicting that Breyer might find the members of Congress had legal standing because he is "a pragmatist less concerned than his colleagues with formalism" (Berkman, 1997, p. A10).

The issue came before the Court a second time in April 1998; this time, New York City and an Idaho potato growers' group challenged the law. The case, when it went before the Supreme Court, was *Clinton v. City of New York* (1998). In June 1998, the Court announced its decision; by a 6 to 3 vote, it rejected the line-item veto act. Justice Stevens, in the majority opinion, concluded that the Constitution prohibited the president from—in effect—rewriting legislation via the veto of single spending items. Voting in the majority with Justice Stevens were Justices Thomas, Souter, Kennedy, Rehnquist, and Ginsburg; in opposition (i.e., supporting the statute) were Justices O'Connor, Scalia, and Breyer.

Two of the three experts were correct in their prediction that the line-item veto act would not be upheld. But their predictions of the votes of individual justices were off the mark, with the exception of Justice Breyer's, and partly Justice Scalia's.

If Justices Are Human, Aren't They Somewhat Predictable?

This book's thesis has been that justices are human beings and that even in their court decisions, they reflect many human qualities. The foregoing example may not give a fair test of the predictability of their votes, as it is not central to the conservative-versus-liberal classification that has become the main way of labeling justices. But that is the point of this chapter: justices are predictable only within limits. Legal philosophies and personal attitudes go only so far in predicting. Situational determinants may intrude. Can we find ways to increase the predictability, or is it impossible?

I believe that "predictability" needs to be analyzed in more detail, and I offer the three following hypotheses that will be assessed in this chapter.

1. Some justices are more predictable than others. That is, some justices hold deep-set ideologies that influence their votes in a broad spectrum of types of cases. Other justices treat petitions on a case-by-case basis.
2. Some cases are more predictable than others. Some cases raise issues that are more basic and straightforward, while others may deal with complex issues or specific but technical matters, such as the wording of bankruptcy laws.
3. Some methods for prediction are more likely to be accurate than others. The basic contrast is between an empirically based method that relies on past votes in similar case, and a more "clinical" or "seat of the pants" method that relies on impressions and speculation.

An Analysis of Votes in the 2001–2002 Term

This chapter will approach the matter of predictability of justices' decisions in several ways. One approach is to determine if the votes of the justices follow a reliable pattern.

To provide further information relevant to voting tendencies, Sarah Thimsen completed a senior honors thesis under my supervision (2003) that analyzed the 75 cases decided by the Supreme Court during the 2001–2002 term, to determine consistencies in response patterns. Of these 75 decisions, 27 or 36 percent were unanimous, the lowest rate in a decade. The Court split 5 to 4 in 21 cases, or 28 percent of the total; in 10 of these, the five-person majority was Rehnquist, Scalia, Thomas, Kennedy, and O'Connor, and in four it was Stevens, Ginsburg, Breyer, Souter, and O'Connor. As implied from the foregoing, Justice O'Connor was the justice who was most often in the majority in 5 to 4 votes—in 17 of the 21 cases. In keeping with this, Justice O'Connor wrote the fewest number of dissents (9), with Kennedy close, at 10. Justice Stevens wrote the most, 23, with Justice Scalia closest at 21. Assignment of majority opinion writing reflected a fairly even workload: Rehnquist, 10; Breyer and Ginsburg, 9; Thomas, 7, and everyone else, 8.

Distinctions between Conservatives and Liberals

Certain pairs of justices tend to vote the same way; for example, in the 2001–2002 term studied by Thimsen, Justices Thomas and Scalia agreed on 89 percent of the cases (and 94 percent of the criminal cases), while Justices Souter and Ginsburg agreed on 92 percent of the cases (including all of the criminal cases).

For Court-watchers, or even some members of the general public, these consistencies are not surprising. But Thimsen and I sought to determine not only the degree of consistency but also the topics where inconsistency occurred. We expected that the predictability of votes would be higher for some types of cases than others. For example, consider the typical classifications—Justices Scalia, Thomas, and Rehnquist as the conservatives; Justices O'Connor and Kennedy as the swing voters—in her review of the 2001–2002 term, Marcia Coyle called Justice O'Connor "clearly now the swing vote with whom to reckon" (2002, p. C1)—and Justices Stevens, Ginsburg, Breyer, and Souter as the relative liberals. We proposed that these distinctions would be more applicable in reactions to cases in which an individual is challenging the government and in criminal cases—especially defendants' rights and prisoners' rights—than for cases involving civil procedure, administrative law, or conflicts between states and the federal government. In making these distinctions, we capitalized on a detailed distinction between liberal and conservative positions on judicial issues developed by Lawrence Baum:

> In criminal cases, liberals are relatively sympathetic toward criminal defendants and their procedural rights, while conservatives give more emphasis to the effectiveness of the criminal justice system in fighting crime.
>
> Liberals are more supportive of personal liberties, such as freedom of speech, freedom of religion, and the right to privacy. Conservatives are more supportive of values that may conflict with these liberties, such as maintenance of public order and national security.
>
> Liberals more strongly support expanded rights and improved status for disadvantaged groups, such as Blacks, women, and the poor. Conservatives give relatively great weight to the costs of these expansions and improvements, such as encroachment on the freedom of action of private institutions and the monetary costs of public welfare.
>
> Liberals are more favorable to government regulation of business to achieve such goals as the protection of the environment, while conservatives are more protective of the autonomy of businesses.

In economic conflicts between businesses and individuals—
for example, a dispute between an insurance company and an
injured automobile driver—liberals are more likely to support the
individual than are conservatives. (1990, table 1.3, p. 13)

Specifically, we expected the greatest predictability in the following types
of cases—those we considered to be ideology driven:

1. Defendants' rights (of which there were nine cases in the 2001–2002
   term)
2. Prisoners' rights (eight cases)
3. Fourth Amendment cases (four cases)

For a second set of cases, we expected a moderate level of predictability.
These were the following types:

1. Cases in which an individual sued a government agency (11 cases)
2. Suits testing the limits of the Americans with Disabilities Act (five
   cases)

For the third and remaining grouping, we proposed that the ideological
distinctions between judges would not be applicable. This grouping included:

1. Federal jurisdiction cases (four cases)
2. Interpretations of federal or state laws (21 cases)

In summary, we analyzed the voting patterns of the justices in seven types
of cases. In the following sections we report the findings.

Voting in Cases Dealing with Ideology-Driven Issues

Defendants' Rights

With regard to the votes on the nine cases dealing with the rights of criminal
defendants and the eight cases dealing with prisoners' rights, we recorded
which justices voted in the majority and which dissented, and then classified
each vote as favoring the criminal defendant or prisoner or opposing the defendant or prisoner. In five of the nine cases, the decision went against the
defendant, and in four, it favored the defendant. One decision was unanimous
(*United States v. Ruiz*, 2002) and another (*United States v. Vonn*, 2002) was
all but unanimous, as Justice Stevens included a separate opinion that partly
concurred and partly disagreed. But three of the nine decisions reflected
5 to 4 votes; in two of these (*Kelly v. South Carolina*, 2002, and *Alabama v.
Shelton*, 2002), Justice O'Connor joined with the four relatively liberal justices to swing the decision in favor of the defendant. The other case with a
5 to 4 vote reflected a less characteristic pattern, with Justice Thomas siding
with the liberals but Justice Ginsburg siding with the conservatives. In this
case, *Harris v. United States* (2002), both the swing voters ruled in favor of

the government, so the defendant's appeal was rejected. In contrast, in the case of *Atkins v. Virginia* (2002), which struck down the use of capital punishment for mentally retarded criminals, the two swing justices sided with the liberals, creating a 6 to 3 majority.

For each of the nine defendants' rights cases, Chief Justice Rehnquist ruled against the defendant; Justice Scalia did so in eight, and Justice Thomas in seven. In contrast, Justice Stevens supported the claims of the defendant in all but one case.

A statistical procedure used in the assessment of attitude scales can be employed to determine if there is a reproducible pattern in the votes of justices. We capitalized on a procedure developed by Louis Guttman in 1944 to determine if a set of attitude statements is unidimensional; that is, can we reproduce a respondent's responses to each attitude statement on the basis of his or her scale score? An almost perfect pattern exists in cases dealing with defendants' rights. If we order the cases from the one in which the vote was most consistently against the defendant (*United States v. Ruiz*) to the one most consistently supporting the defendant (*Ring v. Arizona*), the justices can be clearly rank-ordered in the nature of their votes; their votes follow a perfect pattern with only three exceptions.

Guttman developed a simple formula to determine how reproducible a set of responses was; it is as follows.

Reproducibility = 1 – $\dfrac{\text{total number of errors}}{\text{total number of responses}}$

In regard to these cases, there are only three deviations, or "errors," leading to 1 minus 3/81 or 1 minus .04, or a very high coefficient of reproducibility of .96.

Another way to assess predictability is to compare the three ideological groups of justices with regard to how frequently they support defendants' rights:

> Justices Rehnquist, Scalia, and Thomas rarely supported defendants' rights, with only three votes (out of 27), or an average of one case out of the nine.
> Justices Kennedy and O'Connor supported defendants' rights somewhat more, with five votes (out of 18), or an average of two and a half cases out of nine.
> The four relative liberals supported defendants' rights most of the time, with 24 votes (out of 36), or an average of six cases out of nine.

Thus, on this issue, the pattern of the justices' votes is quite predictable.

Even though unidimensionality was present, based on this analysis, veteran Court-watchers were surprised at the outcomes of some of the death penalty cases. For example, in *Mickens v. Taylor* (2002), the Court ruled that a capital defendant was not entitled to a new trial even though the presiding judge did not question the conflict of interest resulting from the fact that the defendant's attorney had represented the victim a few days before his murder. Also, in *Bell v. Cone* (2002), the Court failed to grant relief to a capital defendant who claimed an ineffective counsel (his attorney had offered no mitigating evidence or a closing argument during the penalty phase).

Previously, Justices Ginsburg and O'Connor had both expressed public concerns about the flaws in the administration of the death penalty, and some scholars hoped that "these remarks would translate into majority Supreme Court decisions," but, as American University law professor Ira Robbins noted, "[w]e really didn't see anything like that" emerging in these opinions (Coyle, 2002, p. C4).

Given this degree of consistency, it is worth examining the three votes that deviated from the pattern. In the case that was the source of two of the discrepant votes, *Harris v. United States*, the majority concluded that a judge can increase the minimum sentence beyond statutory limits if certain factors are present (in this case, brandishing and discharging a gun). Here, Justice Thomas supported the claim of the defendant, in contrast to the other conservatives. But Justice Ginsburg's vote in the other direction counterbalanced his. The other "discrepant" vote was Justice O'Connor's in *Ring v. Arizona*, an important case that ruled that only juries, not judges, can decide a death sentence. Justice O'Connor was apparently concerned that since nine states at that time permitted judges to have a say in death sentences, the courts in those states would be flooded with lawsuits from the seven hundred death-row inmates challenging their previous sentencing.

Prisoners' Rights

The eight cases that involve prisoners' rights reflect a similar pattern. Justices Scalia and Thomas denied prisoners their claimed rights in all eight cases. Justice Kennedy did in seven, and Chief Justice Rehnquist in six. The opinion of the Court favored prisoners' rights in half of the cases and opposed it in half; five of the eight cases resulted in a 5 to 4 vote, with Justice O'Connor casting the deciding vote in all five. There are *no* deviations in the voting pattern to explain; the coefficient of reproducibility is 1.00, as high as it can be.

Differences in the three ideological groups reflect this predictability:

> The three conservatives supported prisoners' rights only rarely, with two votes (out of 24), or two-thirds of a case out of the possible eight.
>
> The two swing voters cast five votes (out of 16) favoring prisoners' rights, or an average of two and a half cases out of eight for each justice.
>
> The four liberals cast 28 votes (out of 32) for prisoners' rights, or seven cases out of eight cases per justice. Splits between the ideological groups were extreme.

Even though there are no deviations that need to be explained, the split in votes in a particular case can reveal something about justices' values and their reasons for voting as they did. The case of *Carey v. Saffold* (2002) is a good example; the votes seemed to revolve around the definition of the word "pending."

Fourth Amendment Rights of Individuals

The third type of case for which we expected a high degree of predictability dealt with Fourth Amendment rights of individuals. Only four cases fit this classification; they were:

1. *United States v. Arvizu* (2002), dealing with the constitutionality of the Border Patrol's stop-and-search of a van that yielded more than one hundred pounds of marijuana.
2. *United States v. Knights* (2002), resolving whether a warrantless search of a probationer that is supported by reasonable suspicion and has an investigatory, not a probationary, purpose violates the Fourth Amendment.
3. *United States v. Drayton* (2002), asking if it is constitutional not to require police officers to inform bus passengers of their right to refuse to cooperate and to consent to searches.
4. *Board of Education v. Earls* (2002), on the constitutionality of requiring those middle school and high school students who participate in extracurricular activities to submit to random drug tests.

In each of these four cases, the opinion of the Court was to deny Fourth Amendment rights to individual petitioners, a position consistent with the majority in recent terms. In two of these cases, the vote was unanimous; in a third it was 6 to 3, and in a fourth, 5 to 4. So, if the analysis is limited to this classification of cases, the reproducibility coefficient is once again 1.00, or perfect. But if the traditional liberal-versus-conservative classification is applied, it should be noted that Justice Breyer voted with the conservatives to deny Fourth Amendment protections and Justice O'Connor voted with the minority to grant Lindsay Earls these rights.

The three ideological groups can be compared as follows.

The conservatives restricted application of the Fourth Amendment rights in 12 of 12 votes; the swing voters did in 7 of 8 votes, and the liberals in 10 of 16 votes, or percentages of 100 percent, 87 percent, and 62 percent, respectively. The differences between the ideological groups are not as extensive as in the aforementioned types of cases, because here, even the liberals sometimes voted to deny petitioners the application of Fourth Amendment protections they sought.

Other Types of Cases

Results for the other two types of case found less ideology-based consistency in these types of case. In federal jurisdiction cases, little variability existed between justices with differing ideologies, as was the case in the multitude of cases involving interpretations of federal or state laws. When an individual sued a large organization—a business or a government agency—conservatives and swing voters supported the government about the same percentage of the time, 79 percent and 82 percent, but liberals did so less often (52 percent).

Conclusions from Analysis of 2001–2002 Term Cases

The analysis of votes during the 2001–2002 term leads us to conclude that justices' votes *can be placed on one dimension,* a conservative-liberal dimension, *if* one somewhat restricts the type of case. Ideology plays a greater role when the petitioner is a criminal defendant or felon seeking a favorable application of a constitutional principle to his or her case. In such types of cases, votes reach a 99 percent level of predictive accuracy. However, only 21 of the 75 cases in the 2001–2002 term fit these categories. For other types of cases, unidimensionality is less apparent, and the conservatives do not vote in ways that clearly differ from the other justices.

But this analysis does not answer the bottom-line question: What is the outcome of the case? Does the Court decide to affirm or reverse the lower court's ruling? Likewise, while this analysis gives some information about the relative likelihood of justices to vote in a certain direction, it does not specifically predict the votes or outcome in each case. For this, we need a different approach, which is described in the next section.

Predicting Decisions for the 2002–2003 Term

The Supreme Court Forecasting Project at the School of Law at Washington University in St. Louis has provided a fruitful set of data for anyone interested in predicting outcomes of Supreme Court appeals (Ruger, Kim, Martin, & Quinn, 2004). For all cases in the 2002–2003 term, the staff developed a prediction of the votes and decisions on the basis of a statistical formula employing only six generally straightforward variables. These were the following.

1. The circuit court of origin
2. The issue area of the case (using the 15 topic areas employed by Harold J. Spaeth (2003)
3. The type of petitioner (e.g., the federal government, an employer, etc.)
4. The type of respondent
5. The ideological direction (liberal or conservative) of the ruling by the lower court

6. Whether the petitioner argued that a law or practice is unconstitutional (Ruger et al., 2004, p. 1163)

This information was fed into classification trees and generated predictions for the votes of each justice and hence the outcome of the case. The classification trees differed from justice to justice; a variable that was prominent in the decision tree of one justice—such as the type of petitioner—might be "relatively unimportant or altogether absent in another" (Ruger et al., 2004, p. 1165).

The staff also identified a pool of 83 experts, 71 law professors, and 12 appellate attorneys (including 38 former Supreme Court law clerks) and for each case, asked as many as three who had a specialized knowledge in the type of case to predict the votes and outcome.

Experts were asked to predict the decisions in cases within only their areas of expertise. Like the predictions from the statistical formula, all predictions by the experts were made *prior to oral arguments*. Experts were provided with a copy of the lower court opinion and citations to the parties' Supreme Court briefs, but they were free to consider any sources of information they considered relevant.

The results of the analyses of these data were published in the May 2004 issue of the *Columbia Law Review*. The predicted votes and outcomes were also made available on the project's website (wusct.wustl.edu), and I used the information from the website to do some analyses prior to the availability of the law review article.

This section looks at outcomes; the next section focuses on the votes of individual justices. This section provides answers to the following questions.

1. In what percentage of cases does the Court reverse the previous lower court decision; what percent does it affirm? Does it matter which federal circuit's actions led to the appeal?
2. How well does the statistical model do in predicting outcomes? How well do the experts do? Is success influenced by the type of case?

The Sample of Cases

A total of 76 cases provided the beginning data base; these include all the signed opinions for the 2002–2003 term, with the exception of *McConnell v. FEC*; this case, while technically part of the O.T. 2002 term, had its oral arguments immediately prior to the beginning of the next term, and its decision was not announced until the late fall of 2003. The analysis by the Supreme Court Forecasting Project staff (Ruger et al., 2004) excluded eight cases from its pool, because they were dismissed, they resulted in equally divided votes, or they resulted in complex outcomes that could not be classified simply as "affirmed" or "reversed."

The Trend to Reverse Rather Than Affirm

If one stands back and asks whether the Supreme Court is more likely to affirm or reverse those cases for which it has granted certiorari, I suggest the sensible answer is to *reverse*. Some have referred to this as a "naive assumption," but I believe it merits more than that label. It reflects both logical and empirical bases. As noted earlier, the Supreme Court currently grants certiorari to less than 1 percent of the petitions it receives. Sometimes one of the reasons for taking a case is the belief, held by at least four of the justices, that the decision made at the lower level was an incorrect one. This is, of course, not the only reason to grant certiorari; many cases reflect a conflict in decisions between two circuit courts; constitutional issues demand resolution, as do matters of national importance. And just because a mistake was made at a lower level is not a guarantee that the petition will be viewed favorably. But it is one reason. The empirical data support this reasoning. In the last 10 terms, the percentage of cases in which the previous decision was reversed averaged around 70 percent. (In the 2001–2002 term, it was 75 percent; the term before it was 67 percent.) For the term analyzed in this section, the 2002–2003 term, it was 74 percent for the decided cases, including *per curiam* cases; for the 68 cases used by Ruger et al. (2004), it was 72 percent.

Thus, if someone is asked to predict the outcome, and knowing nothing else about the case, he or she should predict that the Court's decision will be to reverse. We can use the figure of 71 percent reversal rate from previous terms as a figure against which to compare predictions for different approaches. My analysis found that the statistical model predicted a very high reversal rate of 87 percent; it predicted that only nine cases would be affirmed. (Of the nine, it was correct on five.) In contrast, the experts as a group predicted reversals in only 58 percent of the cases. (The percentages for the three groups of experts were 55 percent, 61 percent, and 57 percent.) Thus, the statistical model overpredicts the frequency of reversals, while the experts underpredict it.

Which Circuits Provide the Greatest Number of Certiorari Petitions?

An interesting side question asks: Where do the petitions that are granted certiorari come from? The majority, all but nine, come from the federal circuit courts. Of the 13 circuits, almost 40 percent come from one circuit, the Ninth (California and the West), which has a reputation for being a liberal circuit. The Ninth Circuit is by far the largest circuit, as it includes nine states and one-fifth of the population of the United States, so the fact that it leads in certiorari decisions is not surprising. Of the 22 cases from the Ninth Circuit granted certiorari, the Supreme Court reversed 17, or 77 percent, not different from its overall reversal rate. No other circuit had more than seven of its decisions chosen for review by the Supreme Court, but the Ninth Circuit's liberal reputation does not seem to affect the Court's decision, once certiorari has been granted.

Comparing Models for Accuracy in Predicting Outcomes

Next we consider the bottom-line issue of the accuracy of prediction of outcomes. Overall, the statistical model correctly predicted 75 percent of the decisions in the 2002–2003 term, while the experts, as group, were correct only 59.1 percent of the time (Ruger et al., 2004, table 1, p. 1171). The Washington University project staff also did more detailed analyses, leading to the following findings.

1. One might expect an increase in accuracy of predicting outcomes on cases that ended up with unanimous votes. However, the statistical model's accuracy dropped very slightly, from 75 percent to 74.2 percent. The experts did improve, from 59.1 percent to 65.3 percent (based on 31 unanimous cases). As the staff noted, "unanimous decisions that in hindsight look like 'easy' cases are not obviously predictable prospectively" (Ruger et al., 2004, p. 1172).

2. The 59.1 percent accuracy rate for experts was based on the 171 individual judgments of experts in 68 cases (or 2.51 experts per case). What happens to the accuracy level of the experts if one uses the predictions of the majority of experts on each case as a consensus prediction? Use of this approach improved the accuracy rate of the experts substantially, from 59.1 percent to 65.6 percent, but still below that of the statistical model.

3. Those experts who had clerked at the Supreme Court did not display greater accuracy levels than the experts at large, averaging only about 60 percent correct (Ruger et al., 2004, p. 1178). But the 12 appellate attorneys were much more successful in predicting outcomes (92 percent) than were the 71 law professors (53 percent). The cases were not assigned randomly, and the appellate attorneys may have disproportionally been assigned to the more straightforward cases. But as was mentioned earlier, "straightforward" cases—at least those that led to unanimous verdicts—are not predicted much more successfully. As Ruger et al. observed,

> [it] is plausible that the two groups actually differ in their predictive accuracy. The practicing attorneys who participated in the project are appellate lawyers who appear regularly before the Supreme Court. Prediction of Supreme Court outcomes, in order to advise clients and develop litigation strategies, is an important element of their professional role. By contrast, for most legal academics, even those whose scholarship centers on the Supreme Court, forecasting cases is a minor component of their work—both in terms of time and importance. (pp. 1178–1179)

I chose to determine whether the difference between the statistical model and the experts would be consistent across types of cases, because Thimsen had found that it was not consistent in the previous term. The staff of the Supreme Court Forecasting Project also felt that certain types of cases were more likely to tap into the ideologies of justices and hence be more predictable. It should be noted that the classification of types of cases I employed here is not completely consistent with the classifications used by Ruger and colleagues or by the *National Law Journal* or other legal publications. For example, a case that I might include in the category "defendants' rights" might otherwise be classified under "constitutional issues" if it involved, for example, *Miranda* warnings. The analysis by Ruger and colleagues used more comprehensive categories but came to the same conclusion that I independently found; "the relative success of the two methods varies significantly depending upon the issue area" (Ruger et al., 2004, p. 1175). For example, the forecasting project had a category of "economic activity"; here the statistical model was accurate in 87.5 percent of the cases, compared to the experts' 51.3 percent. The statistical model was also more accurate by a wide margin in the categories of civil rights and criminal procedure, but the two were about the same (but only 60 percent accurate) in federalism cases. In "judicial power" cases, in contrast, the experts correctly predicted 73.7 percent of the outcomes, compared to 50 percent by the statistical model.

I used seven categories; these, with the number of cases, are as follows.

1. *Prisoners' rights:* five cases in the 2002–2003 term
2. *Defendants' rights:* 12 cases
3. *Civil rights (discrimination, racial issues, sexual preference, Indian cases, affirmative action):* nine cases
4. *Cases involving rights of ex-felons or aliens:* three cases
5. *Cases in which an individual was pitted against a large organization, such as a company or government:* 14 cases
6. *First Amendment cases:* four cases
7. *Intellectual property:* three cases

This total of 50 cases comprises about 70 percent of all the cases decided by the Court in the 2002–2003 term. Overall, the statistical model predicted the outcome correctly in 76 percent of these cases (very close to its 75 percent accuracy for the entire set of cases). The accuracy rate for the experts was 55 percent, slightly below their overall rate of 59 percent. (A chi square test produced a value of 6.31, indicating that the accuracy rate of the statistical model was significantly different from the experts' at the .05 level.) Of the seven types of cases, the statistical model does an excellent job in all but the category of "individual versus large organization," where it correctly predicted the outcome in only six cases and erred in eight cases. (In this type of case, the Supreme Court had less of a tendency to reverse than in the other types; six cases were affirmed, and eight were reversed—perhaps not unrelated to less accuracy in the statistical prediction here.)

Successes for the Statistical Model in Predicting Outcomes

In four of the seven categories, the statistical model predicted the overall outcome correctly in every case—in all five of the prisoners' rights cases, in all four of the First Amendment cases, in all three of the ex-felons' and aliens' rights cases, and in all three of the intellectual property cases. In the two remaining categories, it was successful in a majority of the cases—10 of 12 in defendants' rights and seven of nine in civil rights cases.

The Experts' Accuracy Rate in Predicting Outcomes in Different Types of Cases

Although the experts did less well overall, they did well in the prisoners' rights cases (11 of 13 experts were correct) and in cases involving ex-felons' and aliens' rights (six of nine experts correct); they did better than chance in cases involving defendants' rights, with 19 correct and 12 incorrect. They actually were more successful than the statistical model in predicting the outcome of cases involving an individual against a large organization (the statistical model was correct six times and wrong eight times, while 18 experts were correct, and 13 were not). But in three categories—civil rights, First Amendment, and intellectual property—only a minority of experts correctly forecast the outcomes (12 of 25, 2 of 10, and 1 of 7, respectively).

Predicting Outcomes in Intellectual Property Cases

In the intellectual property category, the greatest discrepancy emerged between the statistical model and the experts. Granted, this category had only three cases, but the statistical model was correct on all three, while only one of seven experts was. These three cases are worth examining; one of these is "the most closely watched intellectual property case in years" (Greenhouse, 2003a, p. A22), the second has broad implications, and the third, at the very least, has a titillation value.

Eldred v. Ashcroft: Is the Extension of the Copyright Retroactive?

Eldred v. Ashcroft (2003) affirmed a District of Columbia Circuit Court decision that the Sonny Bono (*sic*) Copyright Term Extension Act of 1998, which expanded the duration of copyrights by 20 years, applied retroactively to existing copyrights. The extension of 20 more years, which had been passed by Congress, was apparently instigated by the Disney Company, fearful that such classics as *Snow White and the Seven Dwarfs* and characters such as Mickey Mouse would soon become part of the public domain. (It also means that Sonny Bono's estate will receive royalties from "I've Got You Babe" until 2068.) Thus the standard copyright is now for the life of the author, plus 70 years. Eric Eldred, the petitioner in the case, wanted to put on his website a book of some poems by Robert Frost that first appeared in 1923. Despite arguments by the petitioner's attorney, the Supreme Court held that the act did not violate the First Amendment and was a rational exercise of the power of Congress under the copyright clause.

The statistical model correctly predicted that the Court would affirm, while each of two experts predicted a reversal. Justice Ginsburg wrote the opinion to affirm; also in the majority were Justices Rehnquist, O'Connor, Scalia, Kennedy, Souter, and Thomas. Justices Stevens and Breyer dissented. The statistical model correctly predicted the vote of each individual justice, except Justice Ginsburg. In contrast, the first expert not only predicted a reversal rather than an affirmance but incorrectly predicted the votes of seven of the nine justices, getting only Justices Rehnquist and Souter correct. The second expert did only a little better, predicting three justices' votes correctly (Rehnquist, Stevens, and Ginsburg).

Why did the experts err in the *Eldred* case? In the view of one observer, Justin Beck, a law school instructor on copyright law, the experts knew too much. He wrote:

> With hindsight, it is easy to see why the experts got *Eldred* wrong. They knew, and cared, too much about copyright law. In 1999, to honor the late Sonny Bono [who died while he was a member of Congress], and in response to intensive lobbying by Disney and other media giants, Congress extended the term of existing copyrights by 20 years. Copyright law academics, regardless of any affection for the memory of Sonny Bono, were generally outraged by this extension. No legal purist wants to see his or her specialty captured by lobbyists. Under long-established precedent interpreting the copyright clause of the Constitution, copyrights are granted for limited terms to encourage the creation of new works that will ultimately enrich the public domain. Reward of authors and artists (and media giants) is secondary to the public interest. Extending the term of already existing copyrights does not encourage the creation of new works and does not fit easily into what appeared to be a well-established constitutional framework. Unfortunately, few Supreme Court justices are copyright purists, and with no strong feelings one way or the other on the subject, the majority simply deferred to Congress and to the memory of the late Sonny Bono. The experts got it wrong because they knew too much about copyright law and erroneously assumed the Supreme Court would share their outrage. (2003, p. 19)

During the oral arguments for *Eldred*, some of the justices seemed to acknowledge that the 1998 act was a bad law (albeit, perhaps not unconstitutional). In fact, in her majority opinion, Justice Ginsburg wrote: "In sum, we find that the C.T.E.A. is a rational enactment; we are not at liberty to second-guess congressional determinations and policy judgments of this order, however debatable or arguably unwise they may be" (*Eldred v. Ashcroft*, 2003, p. 789). Furthermore, the Supreme Court in recent years has not been reluctant to strike down federal laws that, in its view, exceed the powers of Congress. (Since 1995, the Supreme Court has rejected more than 30 federal laws that it believes exceed Congress's enumerated powers.) So the experts had grounds to predict a reversal, but they were incorrect.

Dastar v. Twentieth Century Fox: Using Material in the Public Domain without Permission

The second intellectual property case, *Dastar v. Twentieth Century Fox* (2003), led to a unanimous decision, in which the justices reversed a Ninth Circuit Court decision and ruled that the Lanham Act—which prohibits the giving of a false designation of origin for goods and services—allows the copyrighting of material that is in the public domain without giving credit to the source. The Ninth Circuit panel had upheld a district court judgment that had imposed a penalty on Dastar of twice its profits from a set of videos, or about $1.6 million.

The case stemmed from Dastar's decision in 1998 to market a set of videotapes about World War II that included Twentieth Century Fox's 1949 television series *Crusade in Europe,* based on General Eisenhower's book of the same name, without giving credit to Fox for the work. Dastar called the package of videotapes "World War II Campaigns in Europe"; the Dastar tapes had a new opening sequence and did not use all the material from the television series, but did use quite a bit of it. The ending credits for the new tapes listed only Dastar employees. Although Fox's copyright had expired in 1977, it sued Dastar Corporation for "reverse passing off," or misrepresenting someone else's work as your own, which was a violation of the Lanham Act. Dale Cendali, who argued the case for Twentieth Century Fox, said that a decision in favor of Dastar would permit her to publish "Dale Cendali's War and Peace," thus claiming Tolstoy's masterpiece as her own (Greenhouse, 2003c).

But in the view of the Court, the meaning of the phrase "origin of goods" in the act applied only to tangible goods, such as a counterfeit watch, and not to the author of an idea or concept or communication embedded in that piece of goods. In the *Dastar* case, eight justices voted to reverse the Ninth Circuit's opinion and remanded the case for further review; Justice Breyer recused himself (his brother Charles is a federal judge who participated in the lower court decision). Justice Scalia wrote the majority opinion; he concluded that it would be impractical to require that credit be given to all originators of a product; he also observed that Fox could have protected itself by renewing the copyright, but it didn't. (Ironically, the *Eldred* decision by the Court five months earlier limited the public domain by extending current copyrights for 20 years.)

The statistical model correctly predicted the unanimous vote. One of the experts did predict the outcome correctly, and even was on target on each justice's vote, but the other expert predicted that the Court would affirm, not reject, with a vote of 7 to 2. Justin Beck's view of this case decision is as follows.

> The result in *Dastar* was predictable, even if one of the two experts
> got it wrong. The Supreme Court had no problem separating the

trademark and the copyright laws. The maker of the Dastar videotape was the person who made the copy, not the author under the Copyright Act. Correctly identifying the author of a work is not the same thing as correctly identifying the maker of a copy of the work. Because the defendant correctly identified itself as having made the videotape copies, there was no false designation of origin under the trademark laws. (2003, p. 19)

Moseley v. V Secret Catalogue: When Is a Copyright "Diluted"?

The third intellectual property case was also noteworthy, if for no other reason than one of the parties was Victoria's Secret. In *Moseley v. V Secret Catalogue* (2003), Victor Moseley, with his wife Cathy, in 1998 opened a retail store in a strip mall in Elizabethtown, Kentucky, which sold sex toys, adult videos, and similar merchandise. At first he called the store "Victor's Secret" after himself, only to have a local resident, offended by the store's "unwholesome, tawdry merchandise," send a copy of the store's advertisement to Victoria's Secret. The lingerie company, in a vigorously worded complaint, demanded a change in the store's name, so Mr. Moseley changed it to "Victor's Little Secret." The large business, Victoria's Secret, was not satisfied and filed a suit claiming an infringement of its trademark, under the Federal Trademark Dilution Act, passed by Congress in 1995. The Sixth Circuit Court, based in Cincinnati, issued an injunction barring the store owner from using the name Victor's Little Secret. We may assume that Mr. Moseley hoped that the association with the famous name would give recognition to his store and attract more customers, although he denies it. But when Victoria's Secret sued, did it have to show actual damages?

The Supreme Court granted certiorari to the petition because of a conflict between circuits regarding the elusive nature of the term "trademark dilution" and how much proof of dilution (for example, actual economic losses) a famous trademark-holder had to show to receive damages. (The statute defines dilution as a reduction in "the capacity of the famous [trademark] to identify the goods of its owner.") In another unanimous decision, the Supreme Court overturned the Sixth Circuit's ruling that "dilution" of a trademark occurs if the trademark is distinctive, even if no actual harm has been proved. (The Court remanded the case to the lower court for further review; meanwhile, the Moseleys have changed the name of their store to "Cathy's Little Secret."). The relatively brief decision (only 16 pages), written by Justice Stevens, concluded that the federal statute requires proof of actual harm, specifically, it "unambiguously requires a showing of actual dilution"—rather than mere "likelihood" of harm.

Again here, the statistical model was accurate not only regarding the outcome but also in predicting that it would be unanimous. The predictions of the three experts could hardly have been more wrong; each predicted that the Supreme Court would affirm the lower court, and two of the three predicted unanimity in a direction opposite that of the actual outcome. The third expert predicted a 7 to 2 vote in the wrong direction.

Why the discrepancy? Justin Beck suggested:

> The lower court found that the use of those names blurred and tarnished the Victoria's Secret trademark and that evidence of actual damage was unnecessary because blurring and tarnishing a famous mark was the essence of dilution. The experts predicted the lower court's ruling would stand because associating a famous [trademark] with a tawdry "adults only" business was clearly dilution. [But] the justices read the statute and concluded that the way it was written, evidence of lessening of the value of the famous [trademark] was required. Evidence that the junior user was freeloading off a mental association with the famous mark or that the holder of the famous mark did not like the association that consumers made, was, without more, insufficient. Where did the experts go wrong? Again, they knew too much. They clearly understood that anti-dilution statutes were aimed at free-riding. That the statute may have missed some free-riders was hard to accept. Particularly because it is difficult to prove actual injury to a famous mark in the absence of confusion, the experts naturally assumed that the statute provided an effective remedy against all free-riding. Unfortunately for the experts, the Supreme Court did not assume anything, but took the statute at face value. (2003, p. 19)

In addition, it should be noted that more than half the states have laws that permit damage awards if proof is made of a *likelihood* of injury, a more permissive standard than the "actual dilution" required by the Supreme Court (Kurz, Crowson, & Kurian, 2003). Perhaps these laws were at the forefront of the experts' predictions.

Predicting Individual Votes for the 2002–2003 Term

Each term a few cases draw intense attention from the media; one of these was the *Lawrence v. Texas* case on gay rights, described at the beginning of the chapter. The three intellectual property cases described earlier drew attention from the business community. Probably the most widely covered cases in this 2002–2003 term were the two University of Michigan affirmative action appeals. How accurate were the predictions in these publicized cases?

Predictions of Individual Votes
in Highly Publicized Cases

You may recall that the vote in the *Lawrence v. Texas* case was 6 to 3, with the two swing voters siding with the petitioners. The statistical formula predicted the outcome correctly, and missed on only one justice, expecting that Justice Kennedy would side with the conservatives. Two of the three experts also expected that the Court would reverse the lower court, and both of these had the votes of each justice pinpointed. However, the third expert saw Justices O'Connor and Kennedy siding with the conservatives and so predicted the outcome incorrectly. As mentioned earlier, the predictions in this case reflect an often-repeated pattern: the three conservatives on one side, the four relative liberals on the other, and Justices O'Connor and Kennedy deciding the outcome. But, as emphasized before, this model fits certain kinds of cases but not others.

The two University of Michigan affirmative action cases were *Gratz v. Bollinger* (2003), involving undergraduate admissions, and *Grutter v. Bollinger* (2003), involving admission to the law school. The Supreme Court rejected the procedure used for admission to undergraduates, by a vote of 6 to 3. The two swing voters sided with the conservatives, as did Justice Breyer. All four predictions of the outcome were correct. The statistical formula and one expert predicted the outcome correctly but missed on Justice Breyer's vote. The other two experts predicted a 6 to 3 vote, but were off in their expectations of the votes of other members of the minority, as well as Justice Breyer. In the law school case, the Court accepted the affirmative action procedure by a vote of 5 to 4, with Justice O'Connor once more in the majority, but this time siding with the relative liberals rather than the conservatives. The statistical model and two of the three experts missed on her vote and hence on the outcome. Only one expert got the outcome correct, because that expert had Justice O'Connor's vote correct. The results in this case dramatically indicate how one missed vote can affect the accuracy of the prediction of the outcome, as well as demonstrating, once again, Justice O'Connor's pivotal influence.

Which Justice Is Most Predictable?

Are certain justices more predictable? Do Justice Scalia's strong opinions lead him to be more accurately anticipated? Does the label "swing voter" make Justice O'Connor more difficult to predict? Do the incorrect expectations for Justice Breyer in the *Gratz* case reflect general difficulties in assessing his choices?

I took 50 of the 76 cases decided in the 2002–2003 term and tabulated the predictions made of individual votes by the statistical model and by the experts. (These 50 cases were classified into different types of cases, as was done in the earlier analysis by Thimsen.) Overall, the statistical model predicted 70 percent of the individual votes correctly, or 317 out of 450. The experts, overall, predicted 67 percent of the votes correctly, a total of 765 correct and 369 incorrect. (This total of 1,134 is less than 3 times 450, or 1,350, as the project was not able to obtain three experts for each case.)

The statistical model was more successful in predicting the voting patterns of some justices than of others: for Justices Thomas and Rehnquist, it was correct in 39 of 50 cases, or 78 percent, but at the other extreme, it was correct for Justice Ginsburg only 62 percent of the time (31 cases out of 50). Accuracy rates for the other justices by the statistical model were as follows: O'Connor, 74 percent; Scalia, 72 percent; Kennedy and Stevens, 70 percent; Souter, 66 percent; and Breyer, 64 percent. For what it is worth, the statistical model had a more difficult time predicting the votes of the relatively liberal justices (average of 65.5 percent) than the conservatives (76 percent).

The experts were somewhat different with respect to individual justices. They were most accurate in regard to Justice Stevens (77 percent, or 97 predictions correct and 29 wrong); thus they did a better job with this particular justice than the statistical model did. They were least accurate with Justices O'Connor and Souter, at 60 percent. Accuracy rates for the other justices by the experts were the following: Thomas, 75 percent; Scalia, 72 percent; Rehnquist, 70 percent; Ginsburg, 67 percent (better than the statistical prediction); Breyer, 63 percent; and Kennedy, 62 percent. Consistent with the statistical model, they were less accurate with the relatively liberal judges (66.75 percent) than the conservatives (72.3 percent).

So how good are the different approaches in predicting votes of individual justices? Only so-so. Granted, they are above 50 percent, or the level of guessing, but for a few justices, their success rate is 60 percent, or barely above. The average accuracies of 70 percent and 67 percent reflect a conclusion of accuracy only to a point.

In contrast to my use of those 50 cases that I felt dealt with ideologically relevant issues, the Supreme Court Forecasting Project based its analysis on 68 cases. The results are somewhat different; the experts were slightly more accurate in predicting justices' individual votes—67.9 percent—compared to the statistical model's 66.7 percent. This analysis led to several interesting conclusions:

1. Experts did better at predicting the justices at opposite ends of the ideological continuum; Justice Stevens at one end and Justices Rehnquist, Thomas, and Scalia at the other were all predicted with higher than 70 percent accuracy. In contrast, the experts' accuracy rate for the votes of Justice O'Connor was lowest, about 62 percent; Justices Souter, Kennedy, and Breyer were all around 65 percent.
2. Similar to my analysis, the statistical model was much better at predicting the votes of conservative justices than the relatively liberal justices (Ruger et al., 2004, p. 1174).

Do Pressures toward Unanimity Occur?

Among three-judge panels in circuit court cases, conformity exists, in the sense that the votes of the three judges are affected by the votes of their colleagues (Schkade & Sunstein, 2003). Does a similar phenomenon exist at the Supreme

Court level? I took the 72 cases from the 2002–2003 term for which the Supreme Court Forecasting Project had predicted votes from the experts and the statistical formula and I tabulated the number of cases in which 9 to 0, 8 to 1, 7 to 2, 6 to 3, and 5 to 4 votes were predicted. These were compared with the actual number of votes on these cases. Of the 72, a total of 31 resulted in unanimous decisions, but the statistical formula predicted that only 7 would. In actuality, there were only four 8 to 1 decisions by the Court, while the formula predicted there would be 20. A chi square analysis found these differences were statistically significant at the .0001 level.

The experts did a somewhat better job than the statistical formula in anticipating unanimous votes. While 43 percent of the actual decisions were unanimous (up from 36 percent in the previous term), experts predicted that about 22 percent would be unanimous, compared to the 10 percent expected from the formula. (Percentages for the three experts were 28 percent, 21 percent, and 17 percent, respectively.) But neither approach anticipated the finding that almost half of the decisions were unanimous. In fairness, my understanding of the statistical formula is that it focuses on each justice's vote, and does not build a "correction" for pressures toward uniformity. The degree to which each individual expert considered this possibility is, of course, impossible to ascertain.

A Replication of Sorts

The Washington University School of Law's Supreme Court Forecasting Project did statistical predictions of cases for the next term (2003–2004) also. However, slightly less than 50 of the cases were predicted, and no experts were used for this term. Still, these data permit a chance to determine whether the findings in the previous term are reliable over time. Generally, they are; for example:

- With regard to the outcome of the case, the statistical prediction was again correct in 75 percent of the cases; amazingly, this is exactly the same percentage as the term before.
- Once again, the number of 9 to 0 outcomes far exceeded the statistical prediction. The formula expected 11 out of these 46 cases; actually, 24, or more than half, were unanimous. The statistical procedure predicted that 18 cases would result in an 8 to 1 vote, while only 3 actually did. For the other possible vote combinations, the statistical model was close the actual figures.
- Also consistent with the previous term, the Court granted certiorari to far more cases from the Ninth Circuit than any other—a total of 22, or 30 percent of the 74 cases. But also consistent with before, the Court reversed this circuit close at to the same rate as the others, 77 percent of the time. (For six of the 13 circuits, the Court reversed *every* case it accepted.)

- In 35 of 46 cases, the statistical prediction was that the Court would reverse, or 76 percent, not as high as the term before. The Court did reverse in about 75 percent of the cases.
- The Court voted unanimously in 41 percent of the total number of 74 cases, a typical percentage.

The findings that the statistical model consistently outperforms the predictions of experts are consistent with the psychological literature's longstanding conclusion (first documented by Paul Meehl 50 years ago) that actuarial predictions (i.e., those that combine information based on prespecified, empirically based decision rules) do a better job than clinical predictions in which the decision-maker reviews a wealth of information and then combines it in an intuitive, or at least unspecified, way (Dawes, 1994; Grove & Meehl, 1996; Grove, Zald, Lebow, Snitz, & Nelson, 2000; Meehl, 1954; Westen & Weinberger, 2004). Similar to the limitations of the clinical approach found in psychologists' predictions, the problem here seems to be a base-rate problem; lawyer-predictors, considering individual cases, assume that the lower court's decision will be affirmed more often than it actually is.

Conclusions

Three hypotheses about the predictability of outcomes were offered in this chapter, and all were verified. Accuracy of predictions emerges much more strongly for cases involving ideology-driven issues; some justices (mostly the conservatives) are more predictable than others; and the statistical model fared fairly well in most types of cases, but the experts' predictions were not much higher than chance.

However, no system of prediction is perfect. Of 72 cases in the 2002–2003 term, in seven (or almost 10 percent), the decision of the Court was contrary to the prediction from the statistical model *and* that of every expert used by the Washington University Forecasting Project. Can we learn from these mistakes?

One of the seven was the decision in the case of *Nevada Department of Human Resources v. Hibbs* (2003). The facts of the case are these: William Hibbs was a social worker employed by the state who requested leave under the Family and Medical Leave Act (FMLA) to care for his wife, who had been injured in a car accident. He was fired after he failed to return to work after his employers had told him that he had exhausted his leave time. He claimed that this action violated the provisions of the FMLA, which provided additional leave time. The Nevada district court dismissed his case before it ever went to trial, concluding that Nevada had immunity, based on the Eleventh Amendment, which generally grants states immunity from suits brought by individuals using federal laws as the basis of their suits. But the Ninth Circuit reversed this action, so Nevada appealed to the Supreme Court.

The statistical model forecast a unanimous vote to reverse, to find in favor of the state. And all three experts also expected a reversal, although they each predicted 5 to 4 votes. Interestingly, each of the three experts expected the conservatives and the swing voters to side with Nevada, and the relative liberals to support the individual state employee. But the actual vote was 6 to 3 to affirm, with Justices O'Connor and Rehnquist siding with Mr. Hibbs, along with the expected four liberals. Chief Justice Rehnquist's vote was the most surprising—and more unanticipated was the fact that he chose to write the majority opinion—given that he had spearheaded a number of recent decisions that had expanded the scope of states' immunity and thus had restricted the power of Congress (Greenhouse, 2003b). Seemingly, for Justice Rehnquist, this consideration came in conflict with a series of opinions favoring equal treatment of men and women. Should the prediction models have anticipated this? That is a tough task. Some cases are just too complex to call.

11

Evaluating the Process

The great object of my fear is the federal judiciary.
—Thomas Jefferson, writing in 1821 to a friend

Thomas Jefferson was not the only president of the United States who was displeased with the Supreme Court. Earlier chapters have described Franklin Roosevelt's frustrated "court-packing plan," as well as rebukes by the Court of Presidents Nixon and Clinton. As noted, Theodore Roosevelt colorfully expressed his anger over the votes of justices he had put on the Court. Gerald Ford, before he was president, initiated an unsuccessful movement in the House of Representatives to impeach Justice William O. Douglas. And Harry Truman, not to mince words, once said to an interviewer about his own friend and appointee Tom Clark: "It isn't so much that he's a bad man. It's just that he's such a dumb son of a bitch" (Purdom, 2005, p. A1).

Although not so pungently, the legislative branch of the federal government has also vented its vexation. Republicans in Congress have decried "activist" decisions by the judiciary and have once again threatened retaliation in the form of impeachment of certain justices, or term limits, or restrictions on what types of cases could be decided by the Supreme Court. The two vacancies on the Court, occurring within a three-month period in mid-2005, and the subsequent confirmation hearings and Senate votes regarding John Roberts and Samuel Alito brought these matters before a public that is usually unaware of the conflict between the branches of government. Thus it is especially appropriate as we have experienced this time of heightened turmoil to stand back and evaluate how the Court goes about its business.

To put it succinctly, the purpose of this final chapter is to answer the question: Does the Supreme Court "work?" This term "work" covers a variety of aspects: the selection process by which justices are nominated and confirmed, the process by which judges leave the bench, the procedures for selecting the cases for review, the decision process in ruling on those appeals that are selected, and finally, the efficacy of the Supreme Court, once a decision is announced. Answers to questions about the effectiveness of each of these are admittedly subjective, but I believe that no book that seeks to understand the Supreme Court is complete without considering each of these aspects. The chapter also suggests reforms for those procedures thought by some scholars to be in need of revision.

The Nomination/Confirmation Process

Vacancies inevitably occur on the Court. Is the two-stage process of nomination and confirmation effective in getting the best candidates placed on the Court?

The Nomination Process

The Constitution gives no guidance in the selection of justices beyond the specification of nomination by the president and confirmation by a simple majority of the Senate. George Washington was the only president who had the luxury, and the power, to nominate persons for each position on the Court at the same time. Since Eisenhower no president has had the opportunity to fill more than four vacancies, and only a few have had the chance to fill two vacancies at the same time. But let us hypothesize that the current president has the opportunity that President Washington had, to start from scratch. Should the president select all nine justices from his or her own party? Perhaps the president reasons: I was elected because of the positions I have taken and the values I have expressed; thus it is legitimate to fill the Court with justices who share my perspective. Recall that in recent presidential election campaigns, some candidates have clearly expressed their preferences—so-called litmus tests—for the type of person they would appoint, if elected.

Perhaps the president should consider the nature of the electorate. Recent presidential elections have shown an evenly divided (some would say "highly polarized") country. If the president had the opportunity to nominate all nine justices, would a mixture of conservatives and liberals be best? Or should the president consider diversity and representativeness as goals? Would the president make sure to nominate some members of racial and ethnic minorities and some women? Is there a "Jewish seat" on the Court, as some have described it? Do emerging ethnic groups, such as Hispanics, have a guaranteed seat?

Should the president consider only those who have had experience as a judge in a lower court? Or should a politician be considered, as President Clinton did when he unsuccessfully tried to recruit Governor Mario Cuomo? And what about the temperament of the nominees, and how well they might work together? As Hirsch has observed, Franklin Roosevelt appointed to the Court "highly complex and extraordinary men—Hugo Black, William O. Douglas, Frank Murphy, Robert H. Jackson, and Felix Frankfurter—whose combined volatility made it impossible to achieve the judicial peace he sought" (1981, p. 4).

Chapter 2 described the procedures and criteria that different presidents have used, from Truman's casual "buddy system" to Eisenhower's criteria of age limitation, judicial experience, and diversity in religion and party identification, to Reagan's intensive review centered around a "litmus test," to Clinton's need to feel comfortable with the candidate. What is the best way to do it?

The decision should not, like Truman's, be made capriciously. After the announcement of Chief Justice Rehnquist's serious illness in October 2004, the Bush White House began preparing a list of nominees and apparently even approached some regarding their interest. This was done well before any justice's actual departure from the Court. (The resignation of Justice O'Connor on July 1, 2005, apparently caught the White House, like almost everybody else, by surprise, as the conventional wisdom was that it would be Chief Justice Rehnquist who would resign as soon as the term ended.) It is inevitable that when a vacancy appears imminent, names of potential nominees surface, but the Bush administration kept a fairly secure lid on its favorite choices before a vacancy actually was announced. Also, President Bush showed sensitivity to the "advise and consent" role of the Senate when he met with leading senators of each party before he expressed his preference. However, he did not go as far as President Clinton, who, when facing his first appointment, told the Republican who was the ranking minority member of the Judiciary Committee (Orrin Hatch) his possible choice. Senator Hatch told the president there would be great resistance toward that nominee, and President Clinton ended up nominating Ruth Bader Ginsburg, who was more acceptable to the Republicans (Hatch, 2002).

The Confirmation Process

How can the president maximize the possibility that the administration's nominee will be confirmed by the Senate? While we nowadays think the adversarial nature of reactions to judicial nominees is at its height, rancor over the president's nominations to the Court extends back to the beginning of the republic; one of President Washington's nominees for chief justice, John Rutledge, was accused by his enemies of being mentally ill. (He was despondent, and once attempted suicide, but despite that, Washington gave him a recess appointment to the Court.) All but one of President John Tyler's nominees were rejected by the Senate. But from the late nineteenth century to the middle of the twentieth century, Supreme Court nominees "enjoyed a virtual presumption of qualification, and nearly all of them were confirmed, rarely with a battle, often without a recorded vote" (Carter, 1994, p. 14). As mentioned in chapter 2, it was only after the Court's *Brown v. Board of Education* decision in 1954 (leading to an angry response by powerful Southern senators) that the Senate began to require nominees to appear before its Judiciary Committee. Since then, a number have received a grilling, including Thurgood Marshall, Robert Bork, William Rehnquist (especially when he was nominated to be chief justice), and Clarence Thomas. Judge Bork was rejected by the Senate by a vote of 58 to 42, and Justice Thomas was confirmed only by a bare four-vote margin.

While no nominee was presented to the Senate until more than a decade after Justice Breyer's nomination in 1994, the acrimony over presidential nominees to the lower courts of the federal system became manifest in the administrations of President Clinton and President George W. Bush (Epstein & Segal, 2005). Although both presidents saw *most* of their nominees to the lower federal courts eventually confirmed, the debate in the Senate Judiciary Committee often prolonged the process, and President Bush had to rely upon recess appointments to get some of his nominees temporarily seated on the circuit court before a compromise in mid-2005 permitted an up-or-down vote on several longstanding nominees.

Once such partisanship has accelerated, how can civility and reasonableness be reestablished? What can psychology, with its study of conflict resolution, offer? One guideline is for the president to nominate more middle-of-the-road judges; for example, both of President Clinton's nominees, Justices Ginsburg and Breyer, have reflected a less extreme voting record than some earlier nominees to the Court. If the president selects a nominee who is currently a circuit court judge, as most recent nominees have been, the nominee's record on the bench is relevant. A recent article by Choi and Gulati (2004) has offered a reasonably objective approach to evaluating which circuit court judges are most effective. The article suggests that if a circuit court judge is being considered for promotion to the Supreme Court, his or her opinions should be examined by collecting data that answer three questions:

1. How often are his or her opinions cited in later opinions?
2. What has been the workload of the judge?
3. Have the judge's opinions been independent of political ideology?

A recent book by Richard Davis (2005), concentrating on the nomination process, offered other suggestions:

1. Presidents should be careful not to articulate, prior to a nomination, that they require a "litmus test" of all candidates. While such campaign promises may rally the faithful, Davis felt they were counterproductive for two reasons: the nominee who is eventually selected may be judged against the previously stated criterion and found wanting, and such pronouncements—that the Court needs a certain type of person— damage the Court's prestige and role.

2. Presidents should avoid publicizing that they are interviewing a certain candidate or candidates. Interviews can be done in private, if needed. In fact, Davis argues that "[t]he presidential interview is overrated and should be discarded" (2005, p. 160).
3. When a justice resigns, the nomination of a replacement should be timely. The longer a president waits, the more lobbying by interest groups increases.

In his nomination of John Roberts for Sandra Day O'Connor's seat, President Bush followed several of Davis's suggestions. The announcement of the nominee's name came only 18 days after the announcement of the vacancy. Although the media and interest groups speculated about who the nominee would be, the White House did not release names of those on the "short list" to the public. In his statements prior to the announcement, the president restricted his criteria for selection only to candidates who, as judges, would "interpret the law, not make the law." President Bush's choice of John Roberts disappointed those (including his wife and Justice O'Connor) who wanted a woman, surprised Hispanic Americans who hoped for one of their own, but solidified his political base, as the choice was clearly a conservative. Furthermore, Roberts was exceedingly personable, he had clerked with Justice Rehnquist, he had argued 39 cases before the Supreme Court (and won 25 of them) when he was deputy solicitor general and a partner in a prestigious Washington law firm, he had friends in both political parties, and hence he was eminently confirmable.

Davis also suggested revision of the confirmation process. He concluded that the questions of many senators are repetitive, self-serving, and not at all useful. He argued that the major part of the questioning be done by the Judiciary Committee's majority and minority counsel rather than the senators themselves. Perhaps his most provocative reform was to propose that nominees "should be willing to express their personal views on issues" (2005, p. 167). This is not to say that they would indicate how they would vote on particular cases, but they would indicate their general values, ideologies, and points of view. This is a radical proposal; the most recent nominee to do so was Robert Bork, who was rejected by the Senate. At the same time, it is a pretense for a nominee to claim that he or she had never "discussed" a particular major issue, as Clarence Thomas did when asked his opinion on the *Roe v. Wade* decision.

Lifetime Appointments

The lifetime appointments given all federal judges—including Supreme Court justices—is, of course, a sound idea. It provides them with financial security (although, as chapter 1 noted, the current salary of justices of $194,000 does not compare with their earning potential in the private sector). More important, if their decisions offend the public, the president, or the Congress, they cannot be summarily removed from office. Article 3, section 1, of the Constitution says that federal judges "shall hold their offices during good behavior." Only one Supreme Court justice has been impeached—Samuel Chase in 1805. (Two others came close; Justice James Wilson died before the initiation of legal action because of indebtedness, and Justice Fortas resigned after publicity about his involvement with a financier who was under indictment.) Justice Chase was considered to be a brilliant (albeit opinionated) jurist, but the Jeffersonian Republicans in Congress became outraged, not over his acknowledged ability but over his activism and partisanship, especially his campaigning for Federalist candidates and his decisions that favored actions that had been taken by John Adams when he was president. After he had been impeached by the House of Representatives, Justice Chase faced a trial by the Senate (presided over by Vice-President Aaron Burr, who himself was fugitive from two states because of his killing Alexander Hamilton in a duel in the previous year). But his Senate opponents, despite having a chamber composed of 25 Republicans and 9 Federalists, were unable to muster the two-thirds vote necessary to convict Chase, and his acquittal was seen as a triumph for judicial independence (Bork, 1990; Presser, 1992). It is believed that had Chase been found guilty, the Republicans intended to impeach every other justice, including Chief Justice Marshall (Rehnquist, 2001).

Thus it is very difficult to remove justices from the bench, if they do not choose to leave. The problems are twofold: what mechanisms exist to remove incompetent judges, and who decides when a justice should retire?

Incompetent and Highly Disagreeable Justices

Clearly, Charles Whittaker was the one justice, at least in modern times, most ill equipped for the task at hand. (Chapter 8 detailed his difficulties on the bench.) Fortunately, he served only five years on the high court before the work pressures and his combination of mental exhaustion and depression caused him to retire prematurely.

A different kind of problem is illustrated in the case of Justice James C. McReynolds, appointed by President Wilson and on the bench for almost 30 years (from 1914 to 1941). No evidence exists that he was unable to perform his duties, but Justice McReynolds was a very disagreeable person; he was rude, impatient, and sarcastic; he was racist and anti-Semitic. He refused to shake hands with or even be photographed with the two Jewish justices, Brandeis and Cardozo. (For this reason, there is no official photograph of the 1924 term of the Court.) Justice McReynolds was intolerant and abusive of female attorneys. In his long tenure on the bench, he had 19 law clerks; the story around the Court was that his clerks served "as long as they could stand it" (Douglas, 1980, p. 169). McReynolds, a lifelong bachelor, died a lonely man; not a single one of the other justices attended his funeral.

We know more than usual about Justice McReynolds's relationship with his law clerks because of the publication (60 years after its writing) of the diary of one of his clerks, John Knox, who served Justice McReynolds in 1936–1937 (Hutchinson & Garrow, 2002). McReynolds hired Knox after checking out his handwriting and making sure he didn't use tobacco. He essentially treated Knox as a servant, and invited him only once to draft a Court opinion for him. After spending several days on the draft, Knox showed it to the justice. McReynolds glanced at it, tossed it in the wastebasket, and said, "We will now start writing an opinion as it should be written" (Greenfield, 2002, p. 81).

Justice McReynolds retired five years before he died, but not without unsuccessful efforts by others to replace him, or at least neutralize his impact. And he did have an impact, as he was one of the "Four Horsemen" who in the early days of the New Deal consistently overturned legislation aimed at getting the economy moving again.

Leaving the Bench

Some justices become physically disabled or even senile but refuse to retire. Justice William O. Douglas had a stroke on the last day of 1974 that left him partially paralyzed. His speech was impaired, and one arm and leg did not function. He missed much of the 1974–1975 term, returned in the fall of 1975, and was not at full strength. In fact, he was often confused and would refer to people by the wrong names, or not even be able to respond at all. Finally, after being hospitalized again shortly after the term began and after being advised that no hope existed for improvement, he submitted his resignation to President Ford in November 1975. But when he returned to the Court building a month later, he fully intended to vote on the appeals initiated before his retirement, and he refused to accept the fact that he was not allowed to (Simon, 1980).

Gabriel Duvall, who was a justice from 1811 to 1835, became so deaf that he was unable to enter into conversations, making his participation in oral arguments meaningless (Atkinson, 1999). But he refused to resign until he was assured that he would be replaced by someone of similar views. A book-length review of the issue of judicial longevity by Atkinson (1999) mentions several other examples of justices who served too long. Some, such as Duvall, Robert Grier, and Joseph McKenna, are no longer household names, but Atkinson believes that Thurgood Marshall as well as Justice Douglas (and possibly Hugo Black) are examples of eminent justices during the last half-century who stayed on the Court beyond their time. In contrast, several recent retirements reflect the justice's awareness that it was time to quit; Justices White, Burger, Blackmun, Brennan, and O'Connor are examples.

So what are the reasons for leaving the bench? Atkinson has listed the following: the threat of impeachment, an attractive pension (most justices retire at full pay), dissatisfaction, weariness, poor health or declining physical energy, mental decline, or family pressure (1999, p. 1). But despite the temptations of pensions and the pressures on the job, justices continue to serve into their seventies and even their eighties. Justice O'Connor was 75 when she retired; Justice Stevens was 85. When Chief Justice Rehnquist was diagnosed with thyroid cancer in October 2004, he had just achieved his eightieth birthday.

Is there any solution to the problem of justices who continue even though they have lost their effectiveness? On some occasions, fellow justices have gently urged the problem judge to relinquish the reins, and on occasion this has worked. For example, Justice McKenna, once he passed the age of 80, showed a decline in his mental abilities; "[h]e sometimes missed the point of what a case was about . . . [a]nd opinions had to be returned to him to be reworked, and even then they were seldom satisfactory and sometimes had to be reassigned to another justice" (Atkinson, 1999, pp. 93–94). Chief Justice Taft became increasingly frustrated; he wrote to his brother: "I don't know what course to take with respect to him, or what cases to assign to him. I had to take back a case assigned to him last Saturday because he would not write it in accordance with the vote of the Court" (p. 94). Taft met with McKenna on several occasions, and the justice initially denied that his mental powers had diminished; he finally agreed to resign, but the process took two years. He died only one year after his retirement.

Some have proposed mandatory retirement at a certain age, for example at 65, 70, or 75. But people differ with respect to the effect the aging process has on their competence; as Atkinson (1999) has suggested, some of the ablest justices have continued to make important contributions at an advanced age. Oliver Wendell Holmes, Jr., was 90 when he retired in January 1932. (A year later, Franklin Roosevelt, newly inaugurated as president, made a courtesy call on the eminent retired justice at his house. Finding him in his library, reading Plato, Roosevelt asked why. Holmes, now age 91, responded: "To improve my mind, Mr. President.")

Atkinson's review of every justice who left the court also concluded that "the danger of extended service on the part of a decrepit justice is today less than in the earlier periods of Court history" (1999, p. 169). While that is reassuring, it does not solve the problem. But a law that would establish term limits or a mandatory retirement age—proposals recently suggested by members of Congress—would, in my opinion, cramp the effectiveness of the Court.

The Size of the Court—Is It the Right Number?

We now move to a more procedural aspect: the size of the Court. People have come to assume that "nine justices" is somehow chiseled in stone, but nothing in the Constitution specifies a number. Congress set the Court at six justices; President Jefferson added a seventh in 1807; in 1837 it was increased to nine; and President Lincoln actually added a tenth justice in 1963. Three years later, President Andrew Johnson attempted to appoint his attorney general to a vacancy, and Congress responded by reducing the size from 10 to 7. Early in President Grant's administration Congress stabilized the size at nine, although, as described earlier, President Roosevelt's court-reorganization plan unsuccessfully tried to expand the size when the Court obstructed the implementation of his New Deal innovations.

So, is nine a good number? Certainly an odd number is better than an even number, to avoid ties. Again, obviously, the greater the number of justices, the more opportunity for representation of different political party identifications, racial, religious, and ethnic backgrounds, and genders. In that sense, a size of seven would be constricting. But what about a larger size—11 or 13? The greater the number, the less opportunity for the full sharing of ideas; the length of the oral arguments would have to increase, as well as the time in conferences. Nine appears to be a good compromise.

Reevaluating the Certiorari Process

Is the Court deciding the cases it should be deciding? Does the certiorari process "work?" These are challenging questions, first because they deal with value judgments, and second because the information necessary to answer these questions is not readily available. Most observers, I believe, would recognize that a majority of the eight thousand petitions received annually are frivolous or not worthy of the Court's review. But do legitimate appeals fall through the cracks? I am sure that if 10 knowledgeable observers carefully examined the discards, each would find some appeals that he or she considered worthy of Court review. And 10 different people might nominate 10 different types of cases.

The Process of Pruning

Over the decades, the justices have been forced to reduce the amount of personal attention they can give to petitions submitted for review. In 1925 Congress passed what is commonly called the Certiorari Act; it established that review of lower court decisions—previously mandatory—would occur only if the Supreme Court agreed to review them. At that time, the justices themselves reviewed the petitions, briefs, and printed record for every appeal, and each justice produced a memorandum for each. *Every* appeal was discussed at the weekly conference. But in the 1920s, only 350 to 400 appeals were filed each term, or seven or eight per week, a manageable number (Estreicher & Sexton, 1986). By 1947, however, the number had become too great, and the chief justice began to distribute a "dead list" that identified those appeals he felt were unworthy of discussion. Starting in 1950, a "discuss list" replaced the "dead list" (Provine, 1980).

If the Court receives eight thousand petitions a year, this is an average approaching 160 per week. The law clerks, with the exception of Justice Stevens's ones, divide these among themselves, which means that typically each clerk has five per week to review. (Justice Stevens's clerks would, of course, have more since they review all the petitions.) The clerks, we know, have other duties, but doing five or so each week seems reasonable, in the sense that the clerk can provide concentrated attention to each. A memo is prepared for each petition, and then these memos are sent to each of the eight chambers where clerks comprise the pool. Justices typically then ask their clerks to divide the memos and review them, with a goal of making a recommendation whether the petition should be granted or denied (Rehnquist, 2001).

Still, possible problems can emerge; as chapter 3 mentioned, the law clerks know what the fashionable topics are, and their values, just like those of the justices', may color what they choose to bring forward. The net result of this process is troubling; only two persons participate in the initial review of the petitions, the one clerk from the certiorari pool and one of Justice Stevens's clerks. How carefully do the justices review the memoranda from the clerks? Recall that 150 to 160 are processed each week (and at the beginning of the term, in one marathon session the justices decide about all of those—close to two thousand—that have accumulated over the summer). It *is* possible that something of importance is ignored, even though there is a further opportunity, as the next section indicates, for reconsideration.

The Chief Justice's Role

The chief justice plays a leadership role in organizing the conferences at which the justices consider the petitions for certiorari. While he was chief justice, Rehnquist sent out a list of the petitions he wished to have discussed; this list might include 15 to 30 of the 160 received that week. Each of the justices could add cases to this "discuss list." How often this happened, however, we do not know. Traditionally, if a petition is not discussed at the conference, it is automatically denied without any recorded vote. It would appear that approximately 80 percent, or 6,500 petitions a year, suffer this fate. Recall that several justices are on record that a significant percentage of the petitions are, to use Chief Justice Rehnquist's words, "patently without merit"; he has estimated that between a quarter and a half are (Rehnquist, 1987a, p. 264). But that leaves a large number per term that are not "without merit" but still are not even considered at the certiorari conference.

The "Rule of Four"

Four or more justices must vote at the conference in order to grant certiorari to a petition for it to be decided by the Court. This "rule of four" seems to be a good compromise, as noted in chapter 3. The number of important cases that don't meet this criterion is hard to determine. The list of cases to be discussed at each certiorari conference is public, and outlets such as *Legal Times* will periodically describe certain ones that would seem eligible to pass "the rule of four" but do not. And on occasion, but *rarely*, a justice who did not marshal the four votes will publicly express his or her disappointment or outrage.

Criticisms of the Process

In summary, two criticisms emerge about the certiorari process to this point: the law clerks have great power, and most cases are not even reviewed by the justices. Chief Justice Rehnquist had responses to each of these criticisms:

> I have on occasion described the *certiorari* process to groups interested in the work of the Court, and find occasional raised eyebrows at one or more of its aspects. I have been asked whether or not the use of the law clerks in a *cert.* pool didn't represent the abandonment of the justices' responsibilities to a sort of internal bureaucracy. I certainly do not think so. The individual justices are quite free to disregard whatever recommendation the writer of the pool memo may have made, as well as the recommendation of his [*sic*] own law clerks, but this is not a complete answer to the criticism. It is one thing to do the work yourself, and it is another thing to simply approve the recommendation of another person who has done the work. But the decision as to whether to grant *certiorari* is a much more "channeled" decision than the decision as to how a case should be decided on the merits; there are really only two or three factors comprised in the *certiorari* decision— conflict with other courts, general importance, and perception that the decision is wrong in the light of Supreme Court precedent. Each of these factors is one that a well-trained law clerk is capable of evaluating, and the justices, of course, having been in the *certiorari*-granting business term after term, are quite familiar with many of the issues that come up. (2001, pp. 234–235)

Chief Justice Rehnquist responded to the second criticism in the following way.

> Another criticism I have heard voiced is that the great majority of petitions for *certiorari* are never even discussed at conference and are simply denied without being taken up by the justices as a group. I do not think this is a valid criticism. For the sixty years since the enactment of the Certiorari Act of 1925, there have been significant ideological divisions on the Court, such that one group of justices might be inclined to review one kind of case, and another group of justices inclined to review another kind of case. When one realizes that any one of nine justices, differing among

themselves as they usually do about which cases are important and how cases should be decided, may ask that a petition for *certiorari* be discussed, the fate of a case that is "dead listed" ("dead listing" a case is the converse of putting a case on the "discuss list") is a fate well deserved. It simply means that none of the nine justices thought the case was worth discussing at conference with a view of trying to persuade four members of the Court to grant *certiorari*. It would be a totally sterile exercise to discuss such a case at conference since no justice would be a proponent of granting it and it would end up being denied in less time than it takes to write this paragraph. (2001, p. 235)

Determining Worthiness

Fewer than 1 percent of petitions are granted certiorari; in the term ending in June 2005, the Court decided 74 cases. Supreme Court Rule 17 says: "A review on *writ of certiorari* is not a matter of right, but of judicial discretion, and will be granted only when there are special and important reasons therefor" (Estreicher & Sexton, 1986, p. 42). But what are the "special and important reasons?" As Estreicher and Sexton observed,

> [v]irtually all agree that the modern Court can no longer serve as a tribunal of last resort, ensuring that justice is done in any given case. But this point is grudgingly acknowledged. Many . . . commentators persist in asserting that our system is fundamentally awry because the Court cannot or will not intervene in every case raising important issues of federal law. (1986, pp. 41–42)

As noted earlier, it is not the Supreme Court's purpose to correct every wrong that lower courts have committed. If two lower courts differ, Supreme Court Rule 17 says that the Court has the role of umpiring the dispute; likewise, acts of legislatures that seemingly conflict with the Constitution demand review. But even Chief Justice Rehnquist acknowledged that the task is challenging; "whether or not to vote *certiorari* strikes me as a rather subjective decision, made up in part of intuition and in part of legal judgment" (2001, p. 234).

But do all conflicts between circuits get accepted? No. Are all cases involving constitutional challenges granted certiorari? No, in the opinion of some, although it must be acknowledged that disputants will often claim a constitutional issue when none exists. The justices are human, and on occasion the Court has appeared "to be granting review largely out of intellectual fascination" with certain issues, or with a goal of resolving questions that are hypothetical (Estreicher & Sexton, 1986, p. 5). Reviewing cases from the 1982 term, Estreicher and Sexton concluded as follows.

- Nearly one-fourth of the cases granted review by the Court in the 1982 term had no legitimate claim to the Court's time and resources.

- Only 48 percent of the cases granted review during that term were cases that *had* to be heard by the Court that year. Thus, over half of the Court's docket was discretionary.
- Significantly less than 1 percent of the cases denied review during the 1982 term were cases that should have been heard by the Court that year. (1986, p. 6)

But in the 1980s, the Court reviewed as many as 170 cases, more than twice it has in recent years. Does this mean that the Court's choices of cases have become less discretionary?

Evaluating the Procedure for Deciding Cases

Deciding cases is the Court's most important activity. This section considers the adequacy of the procedure for deciding cases.

The Materials Available for Review

Within 60 days of the decision granting certiorari, the Court is provided with briefs, not to exceed 50 pages, by each party. Organizations wishing to submit amicus briefs need to do so by this deadline. The justices have access to prior decisions and may obtain copies of any published decision, federal or state, from the Supreme Court's library.

Prior to the oral arguments, most justices ask one of their clerks to prepare a memo on the case, and the justice may discuss the case with his or her clerk. From the evidence available, most of the justices are well prepared for the oral arguments.

The Usefulness of the Oral Arguments

If we were to design the procedures for oral arguments from scratch, what would the ground rules be? How long would they be? Or should the procedure be discarded entirely?

A survey by the Federal Judicial Center found that 100 percent of federal trial and circuit court judges would limit oral arguments to 15 or 20 minutes, and 90 percent of them would eliminate oral arguments entirely (Rehnquist, 1984). But the empirical findings described in chapter 3 show that oral arguments play a significant role in Supreme Court decision-making. Justices do seek information beyond that in the written briefs. The topics they raise in their questions in oral argument comprise a meaningful part of the conferences' discussions. When the outcome of a case is in doubt, the content of the oral arguments surfaces in the written opinions (Johnson, 2004). Furthermore, there is some evidence that the number and type of questions asked during oral arguments predict the eventual decision in the case.

That is not to say that the oral argument is without criticism. The bottom-line question is whether the oral arguments adequately serve two functions: first, to permit the justices to raise questions that they feel the briefs have not successfully answered, and second, to permit the attorneys for each side to summarize their arguments and answer the justices' questions.

The ground rules of the procedure, by which justices can interrupt at any time, theoretically seem to satisfy the first concern. But in actuality, the goal is not always achieved. The attorney may receive rapid-fire questions from some justices; plus there is the fact that the attorney may not have a chance to complete answering one justice's question before another interrupts with another, perhaps unrelated, question.

A second problem is that justices may ask questions not for the aforementioned purpose but instead to try to persuade another justice or even, in rare instances, to harangue or chide the attorney. While the justices emphasize civility in their interactions with each other, anything seems fair game in the questioning of attorneys, and only on rare occasions does the chief justice seek to restore decorum.

Chapter 3 discussed the question whether the oral arguments often change the minds of the justices. We need to back away from this issue and ask: Should the justices have formed an opinion before hearing oral arguments? I do not have a concern if they have—it seems a part of the human condition—as long as justices are open to shifting their views in the face of new evidence. The oral argument should account for only a small part of the variance in the decision; much more material—information, statutes, precedents, arguments—is contained in the briefs and prior decisions than in the 30 minutes of give-and-take for each side. Because they are public and the media are present, oral arguments are given an importance beyond their due. But they do serve an essential function.

The Case Conference

The conference to discuss the case usually occurs during the same week as the oral arguments for the case, typically on Friday. Only the justices are present; Chief Justice Rehnquist has described the procedure and the degree of preparation for it:

> If a justice is to participate meaningfully in the conference the justice must himself know the issues to be discussed and the arguments he wishes to make. Some cases may be sufficiently complicated as to require written notes to remind one of various points, but any extended reading of one's position to a group of only eight colleagues is bound to lessen the effect of what one says. (2001, p. 253)

The chief justice begins the discussion by reviewing the facts and the lower court's decision, "outlining his understanding of the applicable case law, and indicating either that he votes to affirm the decision of the lower court or reverse it" (Rehnquist, 2001, p. 254). The amount of time each justice takes to describe his or her position varies. Chief Justice Rehnquist has observed:

> The truth is that there simply are not nine different points of view in even the most complex and difficult case, and all of us feel impelled to a greater or lesser degree to try to reach some consensus that can be embodied in a written opinion that will command the support of at least a majority of the members of the Court. The lack of anything that is both previously unsaid, relevant, and sensible is apt to be frustrating to those far down the line of discussion, but this is one of the prices exacted by the seniority system. With rare exceptions, each justice begins and ends his part of the discussion without interruption from his colleagues, and in the great majority of cases by the time the most junior justice is finished with his discussion it will be evident that a majority of the Court has agreed upon a basis for either affirming or reversing the decision of the lower court in the case under discussion. (2001, p. 254)

Recently, little give-and-take has occurred during the conferences; while chief justice, Rehnquist proposed a reason:

> Each member of the Court has done such work as he deems necessary to arrive at his own views before coming into conference; it is not a bull session in which off-the-cuff reactions are traded, but instead a discussion in which very considered views are stated. We are all working with the same materials, dealing with the same briefs, the same cases, and have heard the same oral argument; unlikely as that may seem to the brand-new justice, the point that he seizes upon has probably been considered by some of the others and they have not found it persuasive. It is not as if we were trying to find a formula for squaring the circle, and all of those preceding the junior justice had bumblingly admitted their inability to find the formula; then suddenly the latter solves the riddle, and the others cry "Eureka! He has found it." The law is at best an inexact science, and the cases our Court takes to decide are frequently ones upon which able judges in lower courts have disagreed. There simply is no demonstrably "right" answer to the question involved in many of our difficult cases. (2001, p. 255)

Does the discussion change any votes? Chief Justice Rehnquist offered the following opinion.

> I do not think that conference discussion changes many votes, and I do not think that the impact of the chief justice's presentation is necessarily proportional to its length. I don't mean to give the impression that the discussion in every case is stated in terms of

nine inflexible positions; on occasion, one or more of those who have stated their views toward the beginning of the discussion, upon seeing that those views as stated are not in agreement with the majority, may indicate a willingness to alter those views along the lines of the thinking of the majority. But there is virtually no institutional pressure to do this; dissent from the views of the majority is in no way discouraged, and one only need read the opinions of the Court to see that it is practiced by all of us. (2001, p. 256)

Sounds like a well-working procedure, right? Perhaps. But the frequently expressed "collegiality" of the Court may exist at the sacrifice of completely free expression. Justice Rehnquist acknowledged that he valued the presence of a hierarchical and highly structured system; he wrote:

I think it is very desirable that all members of the Court have an opportunity to state their views before there is any cross-questioning or interruption, and I try to convey this sentiment to my colleagues. . . . On rare occasions questioning of a justice who is speaking by one who has already spoken may throw added light on a particular issue, but this practice carries with it the potential for disrupting the orderly participation of each member of the Court in the discussion. (1987a, p. 293)

The Conference Vote

At the end of the discussion on the case, the chief justice will record the vote of each justice, if it is clear. But often it is not clear . Justice Rehnquist has made the important point that such votes are not, and should not be, binding:

The upshot of the conference discussion of a case will, of course, vary in its precision and detail. If a case is a relatively simple one, with only one real legal issue in it, it will generally be very clear where each member of the Court stands on that issue. But many of the cases that we decide are complex ones, with several unrelated issues, and it is simply not possible in the format of the conference to have nine people answering either yes or no to a series of difficult questions about constitutional law. One justice may quite logically believe that a negative answer to the very first of several questions makes it unnecessary to decide the subsequent ones, and having answered the first one in the negative will say no more. But if the majority answers the first question in the affirmative, then the Court's opinion will have to go on and discuss the other questions. Whether or not the first justice agrees with the majority on these other issues may not be clear from the conference discussion. The comment is frequently heard during the course of a discussion that "some things will have to be worked out in the writing" and this is very true in a number of cases. (2001, p. 257)

This passage gives us another clue to the prevalence of collegiality on the Court. The justices offer their positions on the issues, but they know that this is only foreground; the draft opinion will serve as the real battleground for disagreement. As Justice Rehnquist wrote: "Oral discussion of a complex case will usually give the broad outlines of each justice's position, but it is simply not adequate to fine-tune the various positions in the way that the written opinion for the majority of the Court, and the dissenting opinion, eventually will" (2001, p. 257).

Does the procedure at the case conference meet its goals? Not surprisingly, Chief Justice Rehnquist expressed a belief that it does, but he also recognized some of the costs of the structured approach I described earlier:

Our conference is a relatively fragile instrument which works well for the purpose to which we put it, but also has significant limitations. As I have said, probably every new justice, and very likely some justices who have been there for a while, wish that on occasion the floor could be opened up to a free-swinging exchange of views rather than a structured statement of nine positions. I don't doubt that courts traditionally consisting of three judges, such as the federal courts of appeals, can be much more relaxed and informal in their discussion of a case they have heard argued. But the very fact that we are nine, and not three, or five, or seven, sets limits on our procedure. We meet with one another week after week, year after year, to discuss and deliberate over some of the most important legal questions in the United States. Each of us soon comes to know the general outlook of his eight colleagues, and on occasion I am sure that each of us feels, listening to the eight others, that he has "heard it all before." If there were a real prospect that extended discussion would bring about crucial changes in position on the part of one or more members of the Court, that would be a strong argument for having that sort of discussion even with its attendant consumption of time. But my years on the Court have convinced me that the true purpose of the conference discussion of argued cases is not to persuade one's colleagues through impassioned advocacy to alter their views, but instead by hearing each justice express his own views, to determine therefrom the view of the majority of the Court. This is not to say that minds are never changed in conference; they certainly are. But it is very much the exception, and not the rule, and if one gives some thought to the matter this should come as no surprise. (2001, p. 258)

Assignment of Draft Writer

One of the most important tasks, coming after the conference, is assigning a justice to draft a majority opinion, assuming that a majority has been discerned, albeit sometimes unclearly, at the case conference. The chief justice assigns about 85 percent of these, including all unanimous ones and all the others in which the chief justice was in the majority. (In the 2003–2004 term, the chief justice cast 15 dissenting votes in 74 signed opinions) The opportunity to write a majority opinion is important for every justice; "the signed opinions produced by each justice are to a very large extent the only visible record of his [or her] work on the Court, and the office offers no greater reward than the opportunity to author an opinion on an important point of constitutional law" (Rehnquist, 2001, p. 260).

Who gets assigned opinions? What considerations apply? An equal workload is one goal, and while the chief justice does not get to assign all the cases, he or she needs to monitor the assignments as the term progresses. Equality has been achieved in recent terms; for the 2002–2003 and 2003–2004 terms, each justice wrote between 6 and 9 opinions; in 2001–2002, the chief justice authored 10, Justice Thomas 7, and everyone else 8 or 9; in 2000–2001, 5 justices wrote 9, and 4 justices wrote 8.

Where the Court Fails

Every decision by the Court has its critics; it is, after all, an adversary system. But taking a broader view, we must ask if, on occasion, the Court fails to serve its function. On occasion the Court may choose to deal with an issue of major concern but fail to resolve it in a straightforward manner. In 1972, in the case of *Furman v. Georgia*, the Court dealt with the obviously important issue of the death penalty. While the majority of the Court ruled that the death penalty, as then exercised, was unconstitutional (it was reinstated four years later), the justices could not agree on the underlying rule of law. As noted earlier, the nine justices wrote nine different opinions, five in the majority and four in dissent. The nation deserved more clear-cut guidance. In 2003 a parent brought suit against his daughter's school because of the Pledge of Allegiance, which was a part of the school's daily ceremonies, contained the phrase "under God." After the Ninth Circuit had upheld his appeal, the Supreme Court agreed to hear the case, but then, in the spring of 2004, it decided that the father, Michael Newdow, did not have standing, because he was not the custodial parent of his school-aged daughter (*Elk Grove Unified School District v. Newdow*). The public was left asking: is the inclusion of "under God" in the Pledge of Allegiance constitutional or not?

Some critics believe that the Court, more often than it should, goes out of its way "to avoid dealing with important and controversial constitutional issues" (Kloppenberg, 2001, p. 1). Sometimes such avoidance results from a reluctance to rein in the acts of the politically responsive branches. On other occasions, the Court shies away because it wants to avoid claims of "activism." To compound the problem, critics see this avoidance not applied consistently; for example, in the *Bush v. Gore* (2000) decision, deference to the lower courts was rejected; this decision was clearly an "activist" one.

Similarly, the Court has been criticized for decisions that are quite limited in application. Cass Sunstein (1999, 2005), the distinguished professor of law, has called this *minimalism* and described it as follows.

> Many judges are minimalists; they want to say and do no more than necessary to resolve cases. Judicial minimalism leads in two different directions. First, minimalists favor shallowness over depth, in the sense they seek to avoid taking stands on the most deeply contested questions of constitutional law. They attempt to reach *incompletely theorized agreements*, in which the most fundamental questions are left undecided. They prefer outcomes and opinions that can attract support from people with a wide range of theoretical positions, or with uncertainty about which theoretical positions are best. In these ways, minimalist judges avoid the largest questions about the meaning of the free speech guarantee, or the extent of the Constitution's protection of "liberty," or the precise scope of the President's authority as Commander in Chief of the Armed Forces.
>
> Second, minimalists favor narrowness over width. Proceeding one case at a time, they seek decisions that resolve the problem at hand without also resolving a series of other problems that might have relevant differences. In the fashion of common law courts, minimalist judges prefer to focus on the particular question at issue, refusing to venture broader judgments that might turn out, on reflection, to be unwarranted. (2005, p. 48, italics in original)

Not all judges are minimalists, and not all recent decisions are minimalist, but it is true that some recent decisions have been so insufficient that the Supreme Court itself has had to make immediate remedies to clarify the situation. The issue of sentencing of defendants provides an example. In the case of *Apprendi v. New Jersey*, decided in 2000, the Supreme Court ruled that any fact that increased the "statutory maximum" sentence must be tried by a jury and proven beyond a reasonable doubt. In *Blakely v. Washington* (2004), decided four years later, it ruled that judges, in sentencing, could not rely on facts not presented to the jury during the guilt-determination phase, that is, that "any fact that increases the maximum lawful sentence must thus be tried and proven" by a jury, beyond a reasonable doubt (Stith, 2005, p. 222). The decision struck down the sentencing guidelines used by judges in the state of Washington. Thus the question arose: Did these decisions cast doubt on the applicability of the Federal Sentencing Guidelines? Under these rules, federal judges had rules calling them to calculate sentences on the basis of such facts as the amount of loss and the defendant's role in the crime. Experts and judges were left in the doubt, and the Court had to act quickly. Within two months of the announcement of the *Blakely* decision, the Court granted certiorari to two cases (later combined) dealing with the Federal Sentencing Guidelines, and the Court expedited the process so that oral arguments on these two cases were held the first day of the October 2004 term. The Court's decision was announced on January 15, 2005 (the combined case is *United States v. Booker*).

But the decision was, once more, a rather mixed one. On the one hand, the Court, by a 5 to 4 vote, concluded that the federal guidelines were in conflict with its *Blakely* decision that juries, not judges, should evaluate the facts that can be used to lengthen a sentence. But in another 5 to 4 vote, the Court also specified that the federal guidelines could be used by federal judges in an "advisory" manner so that they came up with "reasonable" sentences. The two parts of the decision were authored by two different justices (Stevens and Breyer, respectively) and the five justices in the majority in one part were not exactly the five who provided the majority in the second part. Sentencing disparity has been an issue for decades; should two people who committed the same crime be given the same punishment? It is unlikely that the Court's decision in *United States v. Booker* has provided the final answer.

Conclusions

The way the Supreme Court dealt with the sentencing issue reflected, once again, the human essence of the justices. When the media, scholars, and federal judges objected to the uncertain breadth of the *Blakely* decision, the Court reacted quickly with the goal of providing clarification. In addition to ideological preferences that reflected their individual beliefs about the role of punishment, some justices had special, personal preferences about the future of sentencing guidelines. Justice Breyer, for example, had been chief counsel to Senator Edward Kennedy on the Judiciary Committee and one of the authors of the legislation that created the Federal Sentencing Guidelines. Justice Breyer—in what has been described as "a remarkable act of judicial jujitsu" (Rosen, 2005a, p. 10)—was able to persuade his colleagues, the majority of whom voted to disenfranchise the mandatory nature of the guidelines, to keep them as "advisory" to federal judges.

The Supreme Court has begun a new era with two new justices, including a new chief justice of the United States presiding over the Court. As Mark Tushnet has noted, "writing about the Supreme Court is like shooting at a moving target" (2005, p. 347). With every new term—even with every new major decision—we learn more about how the Court decides its cases. And with new justices on the Court, more extensive changes are inevitable. (The changes may reside more in the way the Court operates than in its votes; it is noteworthy that with only about a dozen cases unsettled in the term ending in June 2005, Chief Justice Rehnquist had cast the deciding vote in only six cases.) But the human nature of its justices, and of the decisions they provide, will remain with us. That is the way it has been, and the way it always will be.

References

Abraham, H. (1992). *Justices and presidents: A political history of appointments to the Supreme Court* (3rd ed.). New York: Oxford University Press.

Abraham, H. (1999). *Justices, presidents, and senators: A history of appointments to the U.S. Supreme Court from Washington to Clinton* (Rev. ed.). Lanham, MD: Rowman and Littlefield.

Adamson v. California, 332 U.S. 46 (1947).

Adler, R. (1987). Coup at the Court. *New Republic, 214*(33), 37–48.

Adler, R. (2001). Irreparable harm. *New Republic, 228*(24), 29–35.

Ake v. Oklahoma, 105 S.Ct. 1097 (1985).

Alabama v. Shelton, 122 S.Ct. 1764 (2002).

American Civil Liberties Union v. Reno, 117 S.Ct. 554 (1996).

Amon, E. (2001, February 26). Texas messes with clerk perks. *National Law Journal*, p. A4.

Apprendi v. New Jersey, 530 U.S. 466 (2000).

Asch, S. (1958). Effects of group pressure upon modification and distortion of judgments. In E. E. Maccoby, T. M. Newcomb, & E. L. Hartley (Eds.), *Readings in social psychology* (pp. 174–183). New York: Holt.

Associated Press. (1996, May 18). Chief Justice bashes grandstanding lawyers. *Lawrence Journal-World*, p. 7A.

Associated Press. (2001a, August 5). Bush v. Gore demonstrates faith in courts, Breyer says. *Lawrence Journal-World*, p. 7A.

Associated Press. (2001b, November 18). Justice finds unity disagreeable. *Kansas City Star*, p. A20.

Associated Press. (2002, June 28). Prison "hitching posts" declared cruel and unusual. *Kansas City Star*, p. A6.

Associated Press. (2003, July 7). Supreme Court justices make rare TV appearance. *Lawrence Journal-World*, p. 6A.

Associated Press. (2005, January 25). Bush rallies abortion foes in annual protest. *USA Today*, p. 2A.

Atkins v. Texas, 325 U.S. 398 (1945).

Atkins v. Virginia, 122 S.Ct. 2242 (2002).

Atkinson, D. N. (1999). *Leaving the bench: Supreme Court justices at the end.* Lawrence, KS: University Press of Kansas.

Auchincloss, L. (2001). *Theodore Roosevelt.* New York: Times Books.

Bader, W. D., & Mersky, R. M. (2004). *The first 108 justices.* Buffalo, NY: William S. Hein.

Bailey v. Drexel Furniture Co., 259 U.S. 20 (1922).

Baker v. Carr, 369 U.S. 186 (1962).

Bales, R. F. (1953). The equilibrium problem in small groups. In T. Parsons, R. F. Bales, & E. A. Shils (Eds.), *Working papers in the theory of action* (pp. 111–161). Glencoe, IL: Free Press.

Bales, R. F. (1958). Task roles and social roles in problem-solving groups. In E. E. Maccoby, T. M. Newcomb, & E. L. Hartley (Eds.), *Readings in social psychology* (3rd ed., pp. 396–413). New York: Holt.

Ball, H. (1978). *Judicial craftmanship or fiat? Direct overturn by the U.S. Supreme Court.* Westport, CT: Greenwood Press.

Ballew v. Georgia, 435 U.S. 223 (1978).

Barbash, F. (1983, December 5). Brennan, Marshall keep vigil against death penalty. *Washington Post*, p. A10.

Barefoot v. Estelle, 436 U.S. 880 (1983).

Barth, A. (1974). *Prophets with honor: Great dissents and great dissenters in the Supreme Court.* New York: Random House Vintage Books.

Baum, L. (1985). *The Supreme Court* (2nd ed.). Washington, DC: Congressional Quarterly Press.

Baum, L. (1990). *American courts: Process and policy* (2nd ed.). Boston: Houghton-Mifflin.

Baum, L. (1997). *The puzzle of judicial behavior.* Ann Arbor: University of Michigan Press.

Baxter, L. A. (1984). An investigation of compliance-gaining as politeness. *Human Communications Research, 10*, 427–456.

Beauregard, E. (2001). In defense of President Harding's Supreme Court appointees. *Supreme Court Historical Society Quarterly, 22*(3), 1, 8–11.

Beck, J. (2003, November 3). Man vs. machine in the halls of justice. *Legal Times*, p. 19.

Bell v. Cone, 122 S.Ct. 1843 (2002).

Berkman, H. (1997, July 7). Experts miss their mark on line-item veto. *National Law Journal*, p. A10.

Berkman, H., & MacLachlan, C. (1996, October 21). Clinton's goals—not so liberal. *National Law Journal*, p. A10.

Bethell, T. (2001, February). The Bush clan's return. *American Spectator, 30*(2), 14.

Bird, C. (1940). *Social psychology.* New York: Appleton-Century-Crofts.

Biskupic, J. (1994, January 10–16). Clerking for the justices: Supremely rewarding. *Washington Post National Weekly Edition*, p. 32.

Biskupic, J. (1996, March 29). "The justices have nothing else to do." *Kansas City Star*, p. J3.

Biskupic, J. (2000, January 3). Masters of the hypothetical. *Washington Post*, p. A17.

Biskupic, J. (2001, January 22). Election still splits court. *USA Today*, pp. 1A–2A.

Biskupic, J. (2002, December 3). Supreme Court to review Texas anti-sodomy law. *USA Today*, p. 1A.

Biskupic, J. (2004, June 8). June is often time of compromise in court. *USA Today*, p. 2A.

Blackmun, H. A. (2004). Some personal reminiscences and what they mean to me. *Journal of Supreme Court History, 22*(3), 323–336.

Blakely v. Washington, 124 S.Ct. 2531 (2004).

Blasi, V. (Ed.). (1983). *The Burger Court: The counter-revolution that wasn't.* New Haven, CT: Yale University Press.

Blaustein, A. P., & Mersky, R. M. (1978). *The first 100 justices.* Hamden, CT: Archon Books.

Board of Education of Independent School District Number 92 of Pottawatomie County v. Earls, 122 S.Ct. 2559 (2002).

Bork, R. H. (1990). *The tempting of America: The political seduction of the law.* New York: Free Press.

Bossert, R. (1997, October 20). Clerk's route to top Court. *National Law Journal*, pp. A1, A13–A15.

Bourgignon, H. J. (1980). The second Mr. Justice Harlan: His principles of judicial decision-making. In P. B. Kurland & G. Casper (Eds.), *The Supreme Court review, 1979* (pp. 251–308). Chicago: University of Chicago Press.

Bowers v. Hardwick, 106 S.Ct. 2841 (1986).

Boy Scouts of America v. Dale, 120 S.Ct. 554 (2000).

Bradley, R. C., & Maveety, N. (1992). Reductionist conservatism: The judicial ideology of Sandra Day O'Connor. *Quarterly Journal of Ideology, 15*, 45–62.

Brenner, S. (1980). Fluidity on the United States Supreme Court: A reexamination. *American Journal of Political Science, 24*, 526–535.

Brenner, S. (1982a). Fluidity on the Supreme Court: 1956–1967. *American Journal of Political Science, 26*, 388–390.

Brenner, S. (1982b). Fluidity on the United States Supreme Court: A comparison of the original vote on the merits with the final vote. *Jurimetrics Journal, 22*, 287–292.

Brenner, S., & Dorff, R. H. (1992). The attitudinal model and fluidity voting on the United States Supreme Court: A theoretical perspective. *Journal of Theoretical Politics, 4*, 195–205.

Brenner, S., Hagle, T., & Spaeth, H. J. (1990). Increasing the size of minimum winning original coalitions on the Warren court. *Polity, 23*, 309–318.

Brenner, S., & Palmer, J. (1988). The time taken to write opinions as a determinant of opinion assignments. *Judicature, 81*, 179–184.

Breyer, S. (1997, January 18). C-SPAN television interview. America and the Courts.

Broder, D. (1998, April 1). Court blunder hurts presidency. *Lawrence Journal-World*, p. 6B.

Broder, D. (2003, June 29). Scalia hardly a model for appointees. *Lawrence Journal-World*, p. 6B.

Brown v. Board of Education, 347 U.S. 483 (1954).

Bugliosi, V. (1998). *No island of sanity.* New York: Ballantine.

Bugliosi, V. (2001). *The betrayal of America: How the Supreme Court undermined the Constitution and chose our president.* New York: Nation Books.

Bush v. Gore, 121 S.Ct. 525 (2000).

Caldeira, G. A. (1987). Public opinion and the Supreme Court: FDR's court-packing plan. *American Political Science Review, 81,* 1139–1154.

Caldeira, G. A., & Wright, J. R. (1988). Organized interests and agenda setting in the U.S. Supreme Court. *American Political Science Review, 82,* 1109–1128.

Caldeira, G. A., & Wright, J. R. (1990a). *Amici curiae* participation before the Supreme Court: Who participates, when, and how much? *Journal of Politics, 52,* 782–806.

Caldeira, G. A., & Wright, J. R. (1990b). The discuss list: Agenda building in the Supreme Court. *Law and Society Review, 24,* 807–836.

Caldeira, G. A., & Wright, J. R. (1994, April). *Nine little law firms? Justices, organized interest, and agenda setting on the Supreme Court.* Paper presented at the meeting of the Midwest Political Science Association, Chicago.

Callins v. Collins, 510 U.S. 1141 (1994).

Cardozo, B. N. (1921). *The nature of the judicial process.* New Haven, CT: Yale University Press.

Carelli, R. (1997, June 29). Court flexed its muscles. *Kansas City Star,* pp. A16–A17.

Carey v. Saffold, 122 S.Ct. 2134 (2002).

Carp, R. A. (2003). Joseph Tanenhaus, the "learned discipline" of public law. In N. Maveety (Ed.), *The pioneers of judicial behavior* (pp. 148–171). Ann Arbor: University of Michigan Press.

Carter, S. L. (1994). *The confirmation mess: Cleaning up the federal appointment process.* New York: Basic Books.

Cartwright, D., & Zander, A. (1960). Leadership and group performance: Introduction. In D. Cartwright & A. Zander (Eds.), *Group dynamics* (2nd ed., pp. 487–510). New York: Row-Peterson.

Charen, M. (1996, May 28). Justices act like politicians. *Lawrence Journal-World,* p. 7B.

Chase, H. W. (1972). *Federal judges: The appointing process.* Minneapolis: University of Minnesota Press.

Chemers, M. M. (1997). *An integrative theory of leadership.* Mahwah, NJ: Erlbaum.

Cheney v. U.S. District Court for the District of Columbia, 124 S.Ct. 2576 (2004).

Chicago v. Morales, 527 U.S. 41 (1999).

Choi, S., & Gulati, M. (2004). A tournament of judges? *California Law Review, 92,* 299–321.

Chong, D. (2000). *Rational lives: Norms and values in American society.* Chicago: University of Chicago Press.

Christie, R., & Geis, F. L. (1970). *Studies in Machiavellianism.* Orlando, FL: Academic Press.

City of Mobile, Alabama v. Bolden, 446 U.S. 55 (1980).

Clark, H. B. (1995). *Justice Brennan: The great conciliator.* New York: Birch Lane Press.

Clayton, C. W. (1999). The Supreme Court and political jurisprudence: New and old institutionalisms. In C. W. Clayton & H. Gillman (Eds.), *Supreme Court decision making: New institutionalist approaches* (pp. 15–41). Chicago: University of Chicago Press.

Clifford, C. (1991). *Counsel to the President.* New York: Random House.

Clinton, B. (2004). *My life.* New York: Knopf.

Clinton v. City of New York, 118 S.Ct. 2091 (1998).

Clinton v. Jones, 117 S.Ct. 1636 (1997).

Colby, W. H. (2002). *Long goodbye: The deaths of Nancy Cruzan.* Carlsbad, CA: Hay House.

Comiskey, M. (2004). *Seeking justices: The confirmation of Supreme Court nominees.* Lawrence: University Press of Kansas.

Cook, B. B. (1991). Justice Sandra Day O'Connor: Transition to a Republican court agenda. In C. M. Lamb & S. C. Halpern (Eds.), *The Burger Court: Political and judicial profiles* (pp. 238–275). Urbana: University of Illinois Press.

Cooper, P. J. (1995). *Battles on the bench: Conflict inside the Supreme Court.* Lawrence: University Press of Kansas.

Cooper v. Aaron, 358 U.S. 1 (1958).

Coyle, M. (1996, July 15). Court ducks affirmative action case. *National Law Journal,* p. A10.

Coyle, M. (1997, June 9). Line-item veto: Who'll vote how. *National Law Journal,* pp. A1, A22–A23.

Coyle, M. (1999, June 21). Whose court is it, anyway? *National Law Journal,* pp. A1, A14–A15.

Coyle, M. (2002, August 5). Tale of two justices. *National Law Journal,* pp. C1, C4.

Cray, E. (1997). *Chief Justice: A biography of Earl Warren.* New York: Simon and Schuster.

Cullinan, K. (2004, September 6). Just imagine it's the Supremes. *Legal Times,* p. 30.

Cushman, J. H., Jr. (2003, July 7). O'Connor indicates she will remain on Court. *New York Times,* p. A9.

Danelski, D. J. (1964). *A Supreme Court justice is appointed.* New York: Random House.

Danelski, D. J. (1978). Values as variables in judicial decision-making. In S. Goldman & A. Sarat (Eds.), *American court systems: Readings in judicial process and behavior* (pp. 457–466). San Francisco: Freeman.

Danelski, D. J. (2002). The influence of the chief justice in the decisional process. In W. F. Murphy, C. H. Pritchett, & L. Epstein (Eds.), *Courts, judges and politics* (5th ed., pp. 662–670). New York: McGraw-Hill.

Darden v. Wainwright, 477 U.S. 168 (1986).

Dastar v. Twentieth Century Fox, 123 S.Ct. 2041 (2003).

Davis, R. (2005). *Electing justice: Fixing the Supreme Court nominating process.* New York: Oxford University Press.

Davis, S. (1989). *Justice Rehnquist and the Constitution.* Princeton, NJ: Princeton University Press.

Dawes, R. M. (1994). *House of cards: Psychology and psychotherapy based on myth.* New York: Free Press.

Dean, J. W. (2001). *The Rehnquist choice: The untold story of the Nixon appointment that redefined the Supreme Court.* New York: Free Press.

Deck v. Missouri, 125 S.Ct. 2007 (2005).

Department of Commerce v. United States House of Representatives, 119 S.Ct. 765 (1999).

Dershowitz, A. M. (2001). *Supreme injustice: How the high court hijacked the election 2000.* New York: Oxford University Press.

DeShaney v. Winnebago County, 109 S.Ct. 998 (1989).

Deutsch, M., & Gerard, H. B. (1955). A study of normative and informational social influence upon individual judgment. *Journal of Abnormal and Social Psychology, 51,* 629–636.

Dickerson v. United States, 120 S.Ct. 2326 (2000).

Dionne, E. J., Jr. (2001). So much for states' rights. In E. J. Dionne, Jr. & W. Kristol (Eds.), *Bush v. Gore: The court cases and the commentary* (pp. 287–288). Washington, DC: Brookings Institution Press.

Dionne, E. J., Jr., & Kristol, W. (Eds.). (2001). *Bush v. Gore: The court cases and the commentary.* Washington, DC: Brookings Institution Press.

Donahue, D. (2002, January 22). Even cowgirls get to the high court. *USA Today,* pp. 1D–2D.

Dorff, R. H., & Brenner, S. (1992). Conformity voting on the United States Supreme Court. *Journal of Politics, 54,* 762–775.

Dorsen, N., & Newcomb, A. A. (Eds.). (2002). John Marshall Harlan II, associate justice of the Supreme Court, 1955–1971: Remembrances by his law clerks. *Journal of Supreme Court History, 27*(2), 138–175.

Douglas, W. O. (1961). In defense of dissent. In A. F. Westin (Ed.), *The Supreme Court: Views from inside* (pp. 51–56). New York: Norton.

Douglas, W. O. (1980). *The court years 1939–1975: The autobiography of William O. Douglas.* New York: Random House.

Dred Scott v. Sandford, 60 U.S. (19 How.) 393 (1857).

Drew, E. (1994). *On the edge: The Clinton presidency.* New York: Simon and Schuster.

Eagly, A. H., & Chaiken, S. (1998). Attitude structure and function. In D. T. Gilbert, S. T. Fiske, & G. Lindzey (Eds.), *Handbook of social psychology* (4th ed., Vol. 1, pp. 269–322). New York: Oxford University Press.

Eisenstadt v. Baird, 405 U.S. 438 (1972).

Eisenstein, J., & Jacob, H. (1977). *Felony justice: An organizational analysis of criminal courts.* Boston: Little, Brown.

Eisler, K. I. (1993). *A justice for all: William J. Brennan and the decisions that transformed America.* New York: Simon and Schuster.

Eldred v. Ashcroft, 123 S.Ct. 769 (2003).

Elk Grove Unified School District v. Newdow, 124 S.Ct. 2301 (2004).

Epstein, L., & Knight, J. (1998). *The choices justices make.* Washington, DC: Congressional Quarterly Press.

Epstein, L., & Knight, J. (2003). Walter F. Murphy: The interactive nature of judicial decision-making. In N. Maveety (Ed.), *The pioneers of judicial behavior* (pp. 197–227). Ann Arbor: University of Michigan Press.

Epstein, L. & Segal, J. A. (2005). *Advice and consent: The politics of judicial appointments.* New York: Oxford University Press.

Epstein, L., Segal, J. A., Spaeth, H. J., & Walker, T. G. (1996). *The Supreme Court compendium: Data, decisions and developments* (2nd ed.). Washington, DC: Congressional Quarterly Press.

Estelle v. Gamble, 429 U.S. 97 (1976).

Estreicher, S., & Sexton, J. (1986). *Redefining the Supreme Court's role.* New Haven, CT: Yale University Press.

Evans v. Gore, 253 U.S. 245 (1920).

Falbo, T. (1977). Multidimensional scaling of power strategies. *Journal of Personality and Social Psychology, 35,* 537–547.

Feeney, F. (1975). Conflicts involving federal law: A review of cases presented to the Supreme Court. In Hruska Commission (Ed.), *Structure and internal procedures: Recommendations for change* (pp. 93–94). Washington, DC: U.S. Government Printing Office.

Fiedler, F. E. (1964). A contingency model of leadership effectiveness. In L. Berkowitz (Ed.), *Advances in experimenal social psychology* (Vol. 1, pp. 149–190). Orlando, FL: Academic Press.

Fiedler, F. E. (1967). *A theory of leadership effectiveness.* New York: McGraw-Hill.

Fiedler, F. E. (1969). Style or circumstance: The leadership enigma. *Psychology Today, 2*(10), 38–43.

Fiedler, F. E. (1971). Validation and extension of the contingency model of leadership effectiveness: A review of empirical findings. *Psychological Bulletin, 26,* 128–148.

Fiedler, F. E., & Garcia, J. E. (1987). *New approaches to effective leadership: Cognitive resources and organizational performance.* New York: Wiley.

Fine, S. (1979). *Frank Murphy: The New Deal years.* Chicago: University of Chicago Press.

Fine, S. (1984). *Frank Murphy: The Washington years.* Ann Arbor: University of Michigan Press.

Fiss, O., & Krauthammer, C. (1982). The Rehnquist court. *New Republic, 209*(8), 14–21.

Fitzpatrick, M. A., & Winke, J. (1979). You always hurt the one you love: Strategies and tactics in interpersonal conflict. *Communication Quarterly, 27,* 1–11.

Fleishman, E. A., Harris, E. F., & Burtt, H. E. (1955). *Leadership and supervision in industry.* Columbus: Ohio State University Press.

Fortas, A. (1975). Chief Justice Warren: The enigma of leadership. *Yale Law Journal, 84,* 405–412.

Frank, J. (1949). *Courts on trial: Myth and reality in American justice.* Princeton, NJ: Princeton University Press.

Frank, J. (1963). *Law and the modern mind.* New York: Anchor Books. (Originally published in 1930).

Freedman, M. (Ed.). (1967). *Roosevelt and Frankfurter: Their correspondence, 1928–1945.* Boston: Little, Brown.

Freund, P. (1967). Charles Evans Hughes as Chief Justice. *Harvard Law Review, 81,* 4–43.

Friedelbaum, S. H. (1991). Justice William J. Brennan, Jr.: Policy-making in the judicial thicket. In C. M. Lamb & S. C. Halpern (Eds.), *The Burger Court: Political and judicial profiles* (pp. 100–128). Urbana: University of Illinois Press.

Furman v. Georgia, 408 U.S. 238 (1972).

Garnett, R. W. (2005). Hail to the Chief? Right on. *Legal Affairs, 4*(2), 34–35.

Garrett, E. (2001). Leaving the decision to Congress. In C. R. Sunstein & R. A. Epstein (Eds.), *The vote: Bush, Gore, and the Supreme Court* (pp. 38–54). Chicago: University of Chicago Press.

Garrow, D. J. (1998, April 19). Dissenting opinion. *New York Times Book Review*, pp. 26–27.

Garrow, D. J. (2005). The brains behind Blackmun. *Legal Affairs, 4*(3), 26–34.

Gaziano, T. (2002, August 5). A partisan blood sport. *National Law Journal*, p. A24.

George, T. E., & Epstein, L. (1992). On the nature of Supreme Court decision-making. *American Political Science Review, 86*, 323–337.

Gerber, S. D. (1999). *First principles: The jurisprudence of Clarence Thomas*. New York: New York University Press.

Gibb, C. A. (1969). Leadership. In G. Lindzey & E. Aronson (Eds.), *Handbook of social psychology* (2nd ed., Vol. 4, pp. 205–282). Reading, MA: Addison-Wesley.

Gibbons v. Ogden, 22 U.S. 1 (1824).

Gibson, J. L. (1983). From simplicity to complexity: The development of theory in the study of judicial behavior. *Political Behavior, 5*, 7–49.

Gideon v. Wainwright, 372 U.S. 335 (1963).

Ginsburg, R. B. (2003). From Benjamin to Breyer: Is there a Jewish seat? *Supreme Court Historical Society Quarterly, 24*(3), 1, 4–6.

Goldman, S. (1991). Federal judicial recruitment. In J. B. Gates & C. A. Johnson (Eds.), *The American courts: A critical assessment* (pp. 189–210). Washington, DC: Congressional Quarterly Press.

Goldman, S. (1997). *Picking federal judges: Lower court selection from Roosevelt to Reagan*. New Haven: Yale University Press.

Goldman, S., & Slotnick, E. (2002). Picking judges under fire. In W. Murphy, C. H. Pritchett, & L. Epstein (Eds.), *Courts, judges, and politics* (5th ed., pp. 157–159). New York: McGraw-Hill.

Goldman, S., Slotnick, E., Gryski, G., & Schiavoni, S. (2005). W. Bush's judiciary: The first term record. *Judicature, 88*(6), 244–275.

Gottlieb, S. E. (1996). Three justices in search of a character: The moral agendas of Justices O'Connor, Scalia, and Kennedy. *Rutgers Law Review, 49*, 219–283.

Granholm v. Heald, 125 S.Ct. 1885 (2005).

Gratz v. Bollinger, 123 S.Ct. 2411 (2003).

Greenfield, J. (2002). A hero to his valet: An underling spies on the Supreme Court. *Harpers, 305*(1829), 77–81.

Greenhouse, L. (1990, July 20). Supreme Court dissenters: Loners or pioneers? *New York Times*, p. B8.

Greenhouse, L. (1999, January 26). In blow to Democrats, court says census must be done by actual count. *New York Times*, pp. A1, A20.

Greenhouse, L. (2000, June 28). A turf battle's victim. *New York Times*, pp. A1, A18.

Greenhouse, L. (2001a, February 20). Election case a test and a trauma for justices. *New York Times*, pp. A1, A18–A19.

Greenhouse, L. (2001b, May 22). Court says press isn't liable for use of ill-gotten tapes. *New York Times*, p. A14.

Greenhouse, L. (2002a, July 2). Court had Rehnquist initials intricately carved on docket. *New York Times*, pp. A1, A14.

Greenhouse, L. (2002b, July 17). Pay erodes, judges flee, and relief is not at hand. *New York Times*, p. A11.

Greenhouse, L. (2002c, December 3). Justices to reconsider ruling against sex between gays. *New York Times*, p. A27.

Greenhouse, L. (2003a, January 16). Twenty-year extension of existing copyrights is upheld. *New York Times*, p. A22.

Greenhouse, L. (2003b, May 28). Justices, 6–3, rule workers can sue states over leave. *New York Times*, p. A29.

Greenhouse, L. (2003c, June 3). Court rules out using trademark law in case about old war footage. *New York Times*, p. A20.

Greenhouse, L. (2004a, March 4). Documents reveal the evolution of a justice. *New York Times*, pp. A1, A16–A17.

Greenhouse, L. (2004b, March 5). Friends for decades, but years on the court left them strangers. *New York Times*, pp. A1, A16.

Greenhouse, L. (2004c, June 2). Teenager's murder conviction is reinstated after challenge based on Miranda. *New York Times*, p. A17.

Greenhouse, L. (2004d, July 5). The year Rehnquist may have lost his court. *New York Times*, pp. A1, A12–A13.

Greenhouse, L. (2005a, January 21). Ailing Chief Justice makes good his promise. *New York Times*, p. A13.

Greenhouse, L. (2005b). *Becoming Justice Blackmun: Harry Blackmun's Supreme Court journey.* New York: Times Books.

Greenstein, F. (1982). *The hidden-hand presidency: Eisenhower as leader.* New York: Basic Books.

Gregg v. Georgia, 428 U.S. 153 (1976).

Greve, M. S. (2005, May 2). Liberals in exile. *Legal Times*, pp. 66–67.

Griffin v. California, 380 U.S. 609 (1965).

Grove, W. M., & Meehl, P. E. (1996). Comparative efficiency of informal (subjective, impressionistic) and formal (mechanical, algorithmic) prediction procedures: The clinical-statistical controversy. *Psychology, Public Policy, and Law, 2,* 297–323.

Grove, W. M., Zald, D. H., Lebow, B. S., Snitz, B. E., & Nelson, C. (2000). Clinical versus mechanical prediction: A meta-analysis. *Psychological Assessment, 12,* 19–30.

Gruenfeld, D. H. (1995). Status, ideology, and cognitive complexity in the U.S. Supreme Court: Rethinking the politics of political decision-making. *Journal of Personality and Social Psychology, 68,* 5–20.

Grutter v. Bollinger, 123 S.Ct. 2325 (2003).

Gunther, J. (1947). *Inside U.S.A.* New York: Harper.

Guttman, L. (1944). A basis for scaling qualitative data. *American Sociological Review, 9,* 139–150.

Hall, M. G., & Brace, P. (1999). State supreme courts and their environments: Avenues to general theories of judicial choice. In C. W. Clayton & H. Gillman (Eds.), *Supreme Court decision-making: New institutionalist approaches* (pp. 282–300). Chicago: University of Chicago Press.

Halpin, A. W. (1966). *Theory and research in administration.* New York: Macmillan.

Halpin, A. W., & Winer, B. J. (1952). *The leadership behavior of the airplane commander.* Columbus: Ohio State University Research Foundation.

Hammer v. Dagenhart, 247 U.S. 251 (1918).

Harlan, J. M., II. (1955). What part does oral argument play in the conduct of an appeal? *Cornell Law Quarterly, 41,* 6–11.

Harris, A. (1986, August 21). The unintended battle of Michael Hardwick. *Washington Post,* pp. C1, C4.

Harris v. Alabama, 513 U.S. 504 (1995).

Harris v. Forklift Systems, Inc., 114 S.Ct. 367 (1993).

Harris v. United States, 122 S.Ct. 2406 (2002).

Hatch, O. (2002). *Square peg: Confessions of a citizen senator.* New York: Basic Books.

Heck, E. V., & Hall, M. G. (1981). Bloc voting and the freshman justice effect revisited. *Journal of Politics, 48,* 852–860.

Hibbing, J. R., & Theiss-Morse, E. (1995). *Congress as public enemy: Public attitudes toward American institutions.* New York: Cambridge University Press.

Hiibel v. Sixth Judicial District Court of Nevada, 124 S.Ct. 2451 (2004).

Hill v. Colorado, 147 S.Ct. 597 (2000).

Hirsch, H. N. (1981). *The enigma of Felix Frankfurter.* New York: Basic Books.

H. L. v. Matheson, 451 U.S. 398 (1981).

Hoeflich, M. (1996, March 27). Judges, clerks have special tie. *Lawrence Journal-World,* p. 7B.

Holmes, O. W., Jr. (1897). The path of law. *Harvard Law Review, 10,* 457–478.

Hope v. Pelzer, 536 U.S. 730 (2002).

Hopwood v. State of Texas, 78 F.3d 932 (5th Cir. 1996).

Howard, A.E.D. (1997, June 30). Shaking up the high court. *Washington Post National Weekly Edition,* p. 33.

Howard, J. W., Jr. (1968a). *Mr. Justice Murphy: A political biography.* Princeton, NJ: Princeton University Press.

Howard, J. W., Jr. (1968b). On the fluidity of judicial choice. *American Political Science Review, 62,* 43–56.

Howard, J. W., Jr. (1992). Frank Murphy. In K. L. Hall (Ed.), *The Oxford companion to the Supreme Court of the United States* (pp. 567–568). New York: Oxford University Press.

Hudson v. McMillian, 503 U.S. 1 (1992).

Hull, A. (1997). *Strategic interaction and schema: An integration and study of judicial decision-making models.* Unpublished manuscript, Department of Political Science, University of Kansas, Lawrence, KS.

Hutchinson, D. J., & Garrow, D. J. (Eds.). (2002). *The forgotten memoir of John Knox: A year in the life of a Supreme Court clerk in FDR's Washington.* Chicago: University of Chicago Press.

Hutchinson, D. J., Strauss, D. A., & Stone, G. R. (Eds.). (2004). *The Supreme Court review, 2003.* Chicago: University of Chicago Press.

Ickes, H. L. (1953). *Secret diary* (Vol. 2). New York: Simon and Schuster.

INS v. Chadha, 462 U.S. 919 (1983).

Jackson, R. (1951, November). Advocacy before the Supreme Court: Suggestions for effective case presentations. *American Bar Association Journal, 37,* 801–804.

Jackson, R. H. (1961). The Supreme Court as a unit of government. In A. F. Westin (Ed.), *The Supreme Court from inside* (pp. 17–33). New York: Norton.

Jeffries, J. C., Jr. (1994). *Justice Lewis F. Powell, Jr.* New York: Scribner's.

Johnson, J. W. (1997). *The struggle for student rights: Tinker v. Des Moines and the 1960s.* Lawrence: University Press of Kansas.

Johnson, T. R. (2004). *Oral arguments and decision-making in the United States Supreme Court.* Albany: State University of New York Press.

Kamisar, Y. (2000, July 17). Your sort-of right to remain silent. *National Law Journal*, p. A18.

Kansas v. Colorado, 121 S.Ct. 2023 (2001).

Kaplan, D. A. (2001). *The accidental president: How 423 lawyers, 9 Supreme Court justices, and 5,953,110 (give or take a few) Floridians landed George W. Bush in the White House.* New York: HarperCollins.

Katz, D. (1960). The functional approach to the study of attitudes. *Public Opinion Quarterly, 24,* 163–204.

Katz, D. (1968). Consistency for what? The functional approach. In R. P. Abelson, E. Aronson, W. J. McGuire, T. M. Newcomb, M. J. Rosenberg, & P. H. Tannenbaum (Eds.), *Theories of cognitive consistency: A source book* (pp. 179–191). Chicago: Rand McNally.

Katz, D., & Stotland, E. (1959). A preliminary statement to a theory of attitude structure and change. In S. Koch (Ed.), *Psychology: A study of science* (Vol. 3, pp. 423–475). New York: McGraw-Hill.

Kearney, J. D., & Merrill, T. W. (2000). The influence of *amicus curiae* briefs on the Supreme Court. *University of Pennsylvania Law Review, 148,* 743–855.

Kelly v. South Carolina, 122 S.Ct. 726 (2002).

Kelman, H. C. (1958). Compliance, identification, and internalization: Three processes of opinion exchange. *Journal of Conflict Resolution, 2,* 51–60.

Kelo et al. v. City of New London, 125 S.Ct. 2655 (2005).

Kennedy, D. M. (1995). How FDR derailed the New Deal. *Atlantic Monthly, 276*(6), 87–92.

Kiesler, C. A., Collins, B. E., & Miller, N. (1969). *Attitude change: A critical analysis of theoretical approaches.* New York: Wiley.

King, W. L. (1950). *Melville Weston Fuller: Chief Justice of the United States, 1888–1910.* New York: Macmillan.

Kloppenberg, L. A. (2001). *Playing it safe: How the Supreme Court sidesteps the hard cases and slants the development of the law.* New York: New York University Press.

Kluger, R. (1976). *Simple justice: The story of Brown v. Board of Education and black America's struggle for equality.* New York: Knopf.

Kobylka, J. F. (2005, April 25). No empty robe. *Legal Times,* pp. 60–61.

Korematsu v. United States, 323 U.S. 214 (1944).

Krislov, S. (1963). The *amicus curiae* brief: From friendship to advocacy. *Yale Law Journal, 72,* 694–721.

Kritzer, H. M. (2001). The impact of *Bush v. Gore* on public perceptions and knowledge of the Supreme Court. *Judicature, 85*(1), 32–38.

Kunda, Z. (1990). The case for motivated reasoning. *Psychological Bulletin, 108,* 480–498.

Kurz, R., Crowson, C. J., & Kurian, A. (2003, April 28). What does *Moseley* mean? *Legal Times,* p. 60.

Lamb, C. M, & Halpern, S. C. (1991). The Burger court and beyond. In C. M. Lamb & S. C. Halpern (Eds.), *The Burger Court: Political and judicial profiles* (pp. 433–461). Urbana: University of Illinois Press.

Lash, J. P. (1975). *From the diaries of Felix Frankfurter.* New York: Norton.

Lassiter v. Department of Social Services, 425 U.S. 18 (1980).

Lawrence v. Texas, 123 S.Ct. 2472 (2003).

Lazarus, E. (1998). *Closed chambers.* New York: Random House.

Lee v. Weisman, 112 S.Ct. 2649 (1992).

Leuchtenburg, W. E. (1995). *The Supreme Court reborn: The constitutional revolution in the age of Roosevelt.* New York: Oxford University Press.

Lewin, K. (1951). *Field theory in social science.* New York: Harper.

Lewis, A. (1964). *Gideon's trumpet.* New York: Random House.

Lewis, N. A. (2000, December 13). Justice Thomas speaks out on a timely topic, several of them, in fact. *New York Times,* p. A14.

Lewis, N. A. (2002, September 6). Democrats reject Bush pick in battle over Court balance. *New York Times,* pp. A1, A18.

Liles v. Oregon, 425 U.S. 863 (1976).

Lubet, S. (1995, August 21). Recusal can deny cert. *National Law Journal,* pp. A19–A20.

Magrath, C. P. (1963). *Morrison Waite: The triumph of character.* New York: Macmillan.

Maltese, J. A. (1995). *The selling of Supreme Court nominees.* Baltimore: Johns Hopkins Press.

Maltzman, F., Spriggs, J. F., II & Wahlbeck, P. J. (2000). *Crafting law on the Supreme Court: The collegial game.* New York: Cambridge University Press.

Maltzman, F., & Wahlbeck, P. J. (1996a). May it please the Chief? Opinion assignments in the Rehnquist court. *American Journal of Political Science, 40,* 421–433.

Maltzman, F., & Wahlbeck, P. J. (1996b). Strategic policy considerations and voting fluidity on the Burger court. *American Political Science Review, 90,* 581–592.

Mann, J. (1983). Year-end salute. *American Lawyer, 5*(9), 94.

Marbury v. Madison, 1 Cranch 137 (U.S. 1803).

Margolick, D., Peretz, E., & Shnayerson, M. (2004, October). The path to Florida. *Vanity Fair, 46*(10), 310–322, 355–369.

Marwell, G., & Schmitt, D. R. (1967). Dimensions of compliance-gaining behavior: An empirical analysis. *Sociometry, 30,* 350–364.

Maryland v. Craig, 110 S.Ct. 3157 (1990).

Mason, A. T. (1956). *Harlan Fiske Stone: Pillar of law.* New York: Viking Press.

Mason, A. T. (1965). *William Howard Taft: Chief justice.* New York: Simon and Schuster.

Mauro, T. (1996, August 27). Thomas' role in case questioned. *USA Today,* p. 3A.

Mauro, T. (1997, June 2). Justices' private holdings can affect their public duty. *USA Today,* pp. 1A–2A.

Mauro, T. (1998, March 13–15). Justices give pivotal role to novice lawyers. *USA Today,* pp. 1A–2A.

Mauro, T. (1999a, July 6). Justice Stevens defends court ruling that let Clinton case proceed. *USA Today,* p. 4A.

Mauro, T. (1999b, October 4). Activists to ask again to meet with justices. *USA Today,* p. 8A.

Mauro, T. (2000, March 14). Burnish Supreme Court's minority-hiring image. *USA Today,* p. 19A.

Mauro, T. (2002, January 15). TV show errs, yet informs. *USA Today,* p. 13A.

Mauro, T. (2003a, March 24). Win or lose, law schools already considering changes. *Legal Times,* pp. 1, 10.

Mauro, T. (2003b, April 17). O'Connor on center stage at arguments. *Legal Times*, p. 10.

Mauro, T. (2003c, November 3). Counting the clerks. *Legal Times*, pp. 8, 10.

Mauro, T. (2003d, December 29). Recalling a battle in an ongoing war. *Legal Times*, p. 7.

Mauro, T. (2004a, March 1). Decoding high court recusals. *Legal Times*, pp. 1, 8, 10.

Mauro, T. (2004b). Glasnost at the Supreme Court. In N. Devins & D. M. Douglas (Ed)., *A year at the Supreme Court* (pp. 191–208). Durham, NC: Duke University Press.

Mauro, T. (2004c). Speak wisely. *American Lawyer, 26*(4), 81–82.

Mauro, T. (2004d). The wedding ring leader. *American Lawyer, 26*(6), 94–97.

Mauro, T. (2005a, April 25). Blackmun article triggers backlash. *Legal Times*, p. 8.

Mauro, T. (2005b, March 14). Courtside: Too many friends. *Legal Times*, pp. 12–13.

Mauro, T. (2005c). Fluent in tea leaves. *American Lawyer, 27*(5), 75–76.

Mauro, T. (2005d, April 25). Justices have ties to FAIR members. *Legal Times*, p. 12.

Maveety, N. (1996). *Sandra Day O'Connor: Strategist on the Court.* Langham, MD: Roman and Littlefield.

McAllister, S. R. (1995, April). Practice before the Supreme Court of the United States. *Journal of Kansas Bar Association*, pp. 25–43.

McConnell v. FEC, 540 U.S. 93 (2003).

McCreary County, Kentucky, v. ACLU of Kentucky, 125 S.Ct. 2722 (2005).

McGautha v. California, 402 U.S. 183 (1971).

McGuire, K. (1993). *The Supreme Court bar: Legal elites in the Washington community.* Charlottesville: University Press of Virginia.

McGuire, K. T. (1996, November). *Explaining executive success in the United States Supreme Court.* Paper presented at the conference on Scientific Study of Judicial Politics, St. Louis.

McGuire, K. T., & Palmer, B. (1995). Issue fluidity on the U.S. Supreme Court. *American Political Science Review, 89*, 691–702.

McLaughlin, G. T. (2000, November 6). Trade dress not optional. *National Law Journal*, p. A22.

Meehl, P. E. (1954). *Clinical versus statistical prediction: A theoretical analysis and review of the evidence.* Minneapolis: University of Minnesota Press.

Melone, A. P. (1990). Revisiting the freshman effect hypothesis: The first two terms of Justice Anthony Kennedy. *Judicature, 74*, 6–13.

Melton, G. B. (1989). Public policy and private prejudice: Psychology and law on gay rights. *American Psychologist, 44*, 933–940.

Mendelson, W. (1991). Justice John Marshall Harlan: *Non sub Homine . . .* In C. M. Lamb & S. C. Halpern (Eds.), *The Burger Court: Political and judicial profiles* (pp. 193–211). Urbana: University of Illinois Press.

Menez, J. F. (1984). *Decision-making in the Supreme Court of the United States: A political and behavioral view.* Lanham, MD: University Press of America.

Mennel, R. M., & Compston, C. L. (Eds.) (1996). *Holmes and Frankfurter: Their correspondence, 1912–1934.* Hanover, NH: University Press of New England.

Meyer v. United States, 364 U.S. 410 (1960).

Michael H. v. Gerald D., 491 U.S. 110 (1989).

Mickens v. Taylor, 122 S.Ct. 1237 (2002).

Miles v. Graham, 268 U.S. 501 (1925).

Miller, G. R., & Parks, M. R. (1982). Communication in dissolving relationships. In S. Duck (Ed.), *Personal relationships 4: Dissolving relationships* (pp. 127–154). Orlando, FL: Academic Press.

Miller, R. L. (2002). *Whittaker: Struggles of a Supreme Court justice.* Westport, CT: Greenwood.

Milliken v. Bradley, 418 U.S. 717 (1974).

Miranda v. Arizona, 384 U.S. 436 (1966).

Mitchell v. Helms, 147 S.Ct. 660 (2000).

Moran v. Burbine, 475 U.S. 412 (1986).

Morin, R. (1989, June 26–July 2). The case for TV in the highest court. *Washington Post National Weekly Edition*, p. 37.

Morris, R., Jr. (2003). *Fraud of the century: Rutherford B. Hayes, Samuel Tilden, and the stolen election of 1876.* New York: Simon and Schuster.

Moseley v. V Secret Catalogue, Inc. 537 U.S. 418 (2003).

Muller v. Oregon, 208 U.S. 412 (1908).

Munn v. Illinois, 94 U.S. 113 (1877).

Murdoch, J., & Price, D. (2001). *Courting justice: Gay men and lesbians v. the Supreme Court.* New York: Basic Books.

Murphy, B. A. (2003). *Wild Bill: The legend and life of William O. Douglas.* New York: Random House.

Murphy, W. F. (1964). *Elements of judicial strategy.* Chicago: University of Chicago Press.

Murphy, W. F. (1965). In his own image: Mr. Chief Justice Taft and Supreme Court appointments. In P. B. Kurland (Ed.), *The Supreme Court and the Constitution: Essays in constitutional law from the Supreme Court Review* (pp. 123–157). Chicago: University of Chicago Press.

Murphy, W. F., & Pritchett, C. H. (Eds.). (1961). *Courts, judges, and politics: An introduction to the judicial process.* New York: Random House.

Murphy, W. F., Pritchett, C. H., & Epstein, L. (Eds.). (2002). *Courts, judges, and politics: An introduction to the judicial process* (5th ed.). New York: McGraw-Hill.

Nagel, R. F. (1994). *Judicial power and American character: Censoring ourselves in an anxious age.* New York: Oxford University Press.

National Labor Relations Board v. Jones and Laughlin Steel Corp., 301 U.S. 1 (1937).

Nevada Department of Human Resources v. Hibbs, 123 S.Ct. 1972 (2003).

New York v. Quarles, 467 U.S. 649 (1984).

New York Times v. Sullivan, 376 U.S. 254 (1964).

Newman, R. K. (1994). *Hugo Black: A biography.* New York: Pantheon.

O'Brien, D. M. (1993). *Storm center: The Supreme Court in American politics* (3rd ed). New York: Norton.

O'Brien, D. M. (Ed.). (1997). *Judges on judging: Views from the bench.* Chatham, NJ: Chatham House.

O'Brien, D. M. (1999). Institutional norms and Supreme Court opinions: On reconsidering the rise of individual opinions. In C. W. Clayton & H. Gillman (Eds.), *Supreme Court decision-making: New institutionalist approaches* (pp. 91–113). Chicago: University of Chicago Press.

O'Brien, D. M. (2000). *Storm center: The Supreme Court in American politics* (5th ed.). New York: Norton.

O'Connor, K. (1983). The amicus curiae role of the U.S. solicitor general in Supreme Court litigation. *Judicature, 66,* 256–264.

O'Connor, K., & Epstein, L. (1983). Court rules and workload: A case study of rules governing *amicus curiae* participation. *Justice System Journal, 8,* 35–45.

O'Connor, S. D. (1981). Trends in the relationship between the federal and state courts from the perspective of a state court judge. *William and Mary Law Review, 22,* 801–815.

O'Connor, S. D. (2003). *The majesty of the law: Reflections of a Supreme Court justice.* New York: Random House.

O'Connor, S. D., & Day, H. A. (2002). *Lazy B: Growing up on a cattle ranch in the American Southwest.* New York: Random House.

O'Malley v. Woodrough, 207 U.S. 277 (1939).

Pear, R. (1997, June 27). Court allows Clinton the line-item veto. *New York Times,* p. A17.

Pennsylvania v. Muniz, 496 U.S. 582 (1990).

Perloff, R. M. (1993). *The dynamics of persuasion.* Mahwah, NJ: Erlbaum.

Perry, B. A. (1999a). *The priestly tribe: The Supreme Court's image in the American mind.* Westport, CT: Praeger.

Perry, B. A. (1999b). *"The Supremes": Essays on the current justices of the United States Supreme Court.* New York: Peter Lang.

Perry, H. W., Jr. (1991). *Deciding to decide: Agenda setting in the United States Supreme Court.* Cambridge, MA: Harvard University Press.

Peters, L. H., Hartke, D. D., & Pohlmann, J. T. (1985). Fiedler's contingency theory of leadership: An application of the meta-analysis procedures of Schmidt and Hunter. *Psychological Bulletin, 47,* 274–285.

Phillips, C. G. (2004). Was affirmative action saved by its friends? In N. Devins & D. M. Douglas (Eds.), *A year at the Supreme Court* (pp. 113–129). Durham, NC: Duke University Press.

Phillips, H. B. (Ed.). (1960). *Felix Frankfurter reminisces.* New York: Reynal.

Planned Parenthood of Southeastern Pennsylvania v. Casey, 112 S.Ct. 2791 (1992).

Plessy v. Ferguson, 163 U.S. 537 (1896).

Pollock v. Farmer's Loan and Trust Co., 157 U.S. 429 (1895).

Ponnuru, R. (2000, July 31). Supreme hubris. *National Review, 52*(14), 28–31.

Ponnuru, R. (2004). The Court's faux federalism. In N. Devins & D. M. Douglas (Eds.), *A year at the Supreme Court* (pp. 131–149). Durham, NC: Duke University Press.

Posner, R. A. (1996, December 15). Poetic justice. *New York Times Book Review,* pp. 16–17.

Posner, R. A. (1999). *An affair of state: The investigation, impeachment, and trial of President Clinton.* Cambridge, MA: Harvard University Press.

Posner, R. A. (2001). *Breaking the deadlock: The 2000 election, the Constitution, and the courts.* Princeton, NJ: Princeton University Press.

Presser, S. B. (1992). Samuel Chase. In K. L. Hall (Ed.), *The Oxford companion to the Supreme Court of the United States* (pp. 137–139). New York: Oxford University Press.

Prettyman, E. B. (1984). The Supreme Court's use of the hypothetical questions at oral argument. *Catholic University Law Review, 33,* 555–591.

Prewitt, K. (1999). Census 2000: Science meets politics. *Items: Social Science Research Council, 53*(1), 7.

Printz v. United States, 521 U.S. 848 (1997).

Pritchett, C. H. (1948). *The Roosevelt court: A study in politics and values, 1937–1947.* New York: Macmillan.

Provine, D. M. (1980). *Case selection in the United States Supreme Court.* Chicago: University of Chicago Press.

Purdom, T. S. (2005, July 5). Presidents, choosing justices, can wind up with surprises. *New York Times,* pp. A1, A14.

Puro, S. (1981). The United States as *amicus curiae.* In S. S. Ulmer (Ed.), *Courts, law, and judicial processes* (pp. 220–229). New York: Free Press.

Quindlen, A. (2000, November 6). The best of the Supremes. *Newsweek, 136*(19), 92.

Raines v. Byrd, 65 U.S.L.W. 4705 (1997).

Rasul v. Bush, 124 S.Ct. 2686 (2004).

Reed v. Reed, 404 U.S. 71 (1971).

Rehnquist, W. H. (1957, December 13). Who writes the decisions of the Supreme Court? *U.S. News and World Report,* pp. 74–75.

Rehnquist, W. H. (1984). Oral advocacy: A disappearing art. *Mercer Law Review, 34,* 1015–1028.

Rehnquist, W. H. (1987a). *The Supreme Court: How it was, how it is.* New York: Morrow.

Rehnquist, W. H. (1987b). The Supreme Court: Past and present. In J. H. Choper (Ed.), *The Supreme Court and its justices* (pp. 194–201). Chicago: American Bar Association.

Rehnquist, W. H. (2001). *The Supreme Court* (Rev. ed.). New York: Random House.

Rehnquist, W. H. (2004). *Centennial crisis: The disputed election of 1876.* New York: Knopf.

Reynolds v. Sims, 377 U.S. 533 (1964).

Ring v. Arizona, 122 S.Ct. 2428 (2002).

Roberts, J. G., Jr. (2005). Oral advocacy and the re-emergence of a Supreme Court bar. *Journal of Supreme Court History, 30*(1), 68–81.

Roche, J. P., & Levy, L. W. (1964). *The judiciary.* New York: Harcourt, Brace, and World.

Roe v. Wade, 410 U.S. 113 (1973).

Roesch, R., Golding, S. L., Hans, V. P., & Reppucci, N. D. (1991). Social science and the courts: The role of amicus curiae briefs. *Law and Human Behavior, 15,* 1–11.

Rohde, D. W., & Spaeth, H. J. (1976). *Supreme Court decision making.* San Francisco: Freeman.

Rohde, D. W., & Spaeth, H. J. (1989). Ideology, strategy, and Supreme Court decisions: William Rehnquist as chief justice. *Judicature, 72*(4), 247–250.

Romer v. Evans, 116 S.Ct. 1620 (1996).

Roper v. Simmons, 125 S.Ct. 1183 (2005).

Rosen, J. (2000). Pride and prejudice. *New Republic, 227*(28 & 29), 16–18.

Rosen, J. (2001, June 3). A majority of one. *New York Times Magazine,* pp. 32–37, 64, 68, 73, 76, 79.

Rosen, J. (2005a). Breyer review. *New Republic, 232*(3), 10–13.

Rosen, J. (2005b). Rehnquist the Great? *Atlantic Monthly, 295*(3), 79–90.

Rowland, C. K., & Carp, R. A. (1996). *Politics and judgment in federal district courts.* Lawrence: University Press of Kansas.

Rubin, G. C. (1998, July 13). Betraying a trust. *Washington Post National Weekly Edition*, p. 27.

Rubin, T. F., & Melone, A. P. (1988). Justice Antonin Scalia: A first-year freshman effect? *Judicature, 72*, 98–102.

Rudman, W. B. (1996). *Combat: Twelve years in the U.S. Senate*. New York: Random House.

Ruger, T., W., Kim, P. T., Martin, A. D., & Quinn, K. M. (2004). The Supreme Court Forecasting Project: Legal and political science approaches to predicting Supreme Court decision making. *Columbia Law Review, 104*, 1150–1209.

Salokar, R. M. (1992). *The Solicitor General: The politics of law*. Philadelphia: Temple University Press.

San Antonio Independent School District v. Rodriguez, 411 U.S. 1 (1973).

Savage, D. G. (2004). Anthony M. Kennedy and the road not taken. In N. Devins & D. M. Douglas (Eds.), *A year at the Supreme Court* (pp. 35–54). Durham, NC: Duke University Press.

Scalia, A. (1994). The dissenting opinion. *Journal of Supreme Court History, 19*, 33–44.

Scalia, A. (1997a). *A matter of interpretation*. Princeton, NJ: Princeton University Press.

Scalia, A. (1997b). Originalism: The lesser evil. In D. M. O'Brien (Ed.), *Judges on judging* (pp. 187–194). Chatham, NY: Chatham House.

Scheb, J. M., II & Ailshie, L. W. (1985). Justice Sandra Day O'Connor and the "freshman effect." *Judicature, 72*, 9–12.

Schechter Poultry Corporation v. United States, 295 U.S. 495 (1935).

Schenck-Hamlin, W. J., Wiseman, R. L., & Georgacarakos, G. N. (1982). A model of properties of compliance-gaining strategies. *Communication Quarterly, 30*, 92–100.

Schkade, D. A., & Sunstein, C. R. (2003, June 11). Judging by where you sit. *New York Times*, p. A29.

Schmidhauser, J. R. (1979). *Judges and justices: The federal appellate judiciary*. Boston: Little, Brown.

Schubert, G. (1965). *The judicial mind: Attitudes and ideologies of the Supreme Court justices, 1946–1963*. Evanston, IL: Northwestern University Press.

Schubert, G. (1974). *The judicial mind revisited: Psychometric analysis of Supreme Court ideology*. New York: Oxford University Press.

Schwartz, B. (1981). Felix Frankfurter and Earl Warren: A study of a deteriorating relationship. In P. B. Kurland & G. Casper (Eds.), *The Supreme Court review, 1980* (pp. 115–142). Chicago: University of Chicago Press.

Schwartz, B. (1984). *The unpublished opinions of the Warren Court*. New York: Oxford University Press.

Schwartz, B. (1987). *The unpublished opinions of the Burger Court*. New York: Oxford University Press.

Schwartz, B. (1989). Chief Justice Rehnquist, Justice Jackson, and the *Brown* case. In P. B. Kurland, G. Casper, & D. J. Hutchinson (Eds.), *The Supreme Court review, 1988* (pp. 245–267). Chicago: University of Chicago Press.

Schwartz, B. (1996a). *Decision: How the Supreme Court decides cases*. New York: Oxford University Press.

Schwartz, B. (1996b). *The unpublished opinions of the Rehnquist Court*. New York: Oxford University Press.

Schwartz, B. (1997). *A book of legal lists: The best and worst in American law.* New York: Oxford University Press.

Schwartz, B., with Lesher, S. (1983). *Inside the Warren Court.* Garden City, NY: Doubleday.

Schwartz, H. (1988). *Packing the courts: The conservative campaign to rewrite the Constitution.* New York: Scribner's.

Schwartz, H. (2004, July 19). Looking for his next job? *Legal Times*, p. 70.

Scigliano, R. (1971). *The Supreme Court and the presidency.* New York: Free Press.

Segal, J. A. (1984). Predicting Supreme Court cases probabilistically: The search and seizure cases, 1962–1981. *American Political Science Review, 78*, 891–900.

Segal, J. A. (1999). Supreme Court deference to Congress: An examination of the Marksist model. In C. M. Clayton & H. Gillman (Eds.), *Supreme Court decision-making: New institutionalist approaches* (pp. 237–253). Chicago: University of Chicago Press.

Segal, J. A., & Cover, A. D. (1989). Ideological values and the votes of the Supreme Court justices. *American Political Science Review, 83*, 557–565.

Segal, J. A., & Reedy, C. D. (1988). The Supreme Court and sex discrimination: The role of the solicitor general. *Western Political Quarterly, 41*, 553–568.

Segal, J. A., & Spaeth, H. J. (1993). *The Supreme Court and the attitudinal model.* New York: Cambridge University Press.

Segal, J., & Spaeth, H. (2002). *The Supreme Court and the attitudinal model revisited.* New York: Cambridge University Press.

Segura v. United States, 468 U.S. 796 (1984).

Selective Draft Law cases, 245 U.S. 366 (1918).

Shullman, S. L. (2004). The illusion of devil's advocacy: How the justices of the Supreme Court foreshadow their decisions during oral argument. *Journal of Appellate Practice and Process, 6*, 271–293.

Sigelman, L. (1979). Black–white differences in attitudes toward the Supreme Court: A replication in the 1970s. *Social Sciences Quarterly, 60*, 113–115.

Silvia, P. (1997). *Straw polls and fluidity on the Supreme Court.* Unpublished manuscript, Department of Psychology, University of Kansas, Lawrence, KS.

Simon, D. (2002). Freedom and constraint in adjudication: A look through the lens of cognitive psychology. *Brooklyn Law Review, 67*, 1097–1139.

Simon, D. (1998). A psychological model of judicial decision making. *Rutgers Law Journal, 30*, 1–142.

Simon, J. F. (1980). *Independent journey: The life of William O. Douglas.* New York: Harper and Row.

Simon, J. F. (1995). *The center holds: The power struggle inside the Rehnquist Court.* New York: Simon and Schuster.

Small v. United States, 125 S.Ct. 1752 (2005).

Smith, J. E. (1996). *John Marshall: Definer of a nation.* New York: Holt.

Smith, M. B., Bruner, J., & White, R. W. (1956). *Opinions and personality.* New York: Wiley.

Smolla, R. A. (1995). Introduction: Personality and process. In R. A. Smolla (Ed.), *A year in the life of the Supreme Court* (pp. 1–29). Durham, NC: Duke University Press.

Smolla, R. A. (2004). Cross burning: *Virginia v. Black.* In N. Devins & D. M. Douglas (Eds.). *A year at the Supreme Court* (pp. 153–173). Durham, NC: Duke University Press.

Solberg, R. P. (2005). Diversity and George W. Bush's judicial appointments: Serving two masters. *Judicature, 88*(6), 276–283.

Spaeth, H. J. (1972). *An introduction to Supreme Court decision making* (Rev. ed.). San Francisco: Chandler.

Spaeth, H. J. (2003, November 25). *The original Supreme Court data base.* Document 51. Available at the website of the original United States Supreme Court Judicial Data Base: PDF.

Steamer, R. J. (1986). *Chief Justice: Leadership and the Supreme Court.* Columbia: University of South Carolina Press.

Stenberg v. Carhart, 68 U.S.L.W. 4702 (2000).

Stephens v. Hopper, 58 L.Ed 2d 667 (1979).

Stern, R. L., & Gressman, E. (1962). *Supreme Court practice* (3rd ed.). Washington, DC: Bureau of National Affairs.

Stern, R. L., & Gressman, E. (1978). *Supreme Court practice* (5th ed.). Washington, DC: Bureau of National Affairs.

Stewart, D. O. (1994, October). Quiet times: The Supreme Court is reducing its workload—but why? *American Bar Association Journal, 80*(10), 40–44.

Stewart, M. L. (1998). Justice Blackmun's capital punishment jurisprudence. *Hastings Constitutional Law Quarterly, 26,* 271–305.

Stewart v. Evans, D. C. Circuit, No. 01–5036 (2002).

Stidham, R., Carp, R. A., & Songer, D. R. (2002). The voting behavior of President Clinton's appointees. In W. F. Murphy, C. H. Pritchett, & L. Epstein (Eds.), *Courts, judges, and politics* (5th ed., pp. 175–178). New York: McGraw-Hill.

Stith, K. (2005). Crime and punishment under the Constitution. In D. J. Hutchinson, D. A. Straus, & G. R. Stone (Eds.), *The Supreme Court review, 2004* (pp. 221–269). Chicago: University of Chicago Press.

Stogdill, R. M. (1950). Leadership, membership, and organization. *Psychological Bulletin, 47,* 1–14.

Strauss, D. (2004). Kerry's even keel. *Legal Affairs, 3*(5), 28–29.

Strauss, D. A. (1990). Due process, government inaction, and private wrongs. In G. Casper & D. J. Hutchinson (Eds.), *The Supreme Court review, 1989* (pp. 53–86). Chicago: University of Chicago Press.

Strube, M., & Garcia, J. (1981). A meta-analysis investigation of Fiedler's contingency model of leadership effectiveness. *Psychological Bulletin, 90* 307–321.

Sunstein, C. R. (1999). *One case at a time: Judicial minimalism on the Supreme Court.* Cambridge, MA: Harvard University Press.

Sunstein, C. R. (2004/2005). The Rehnquist revolution. *New Republic, 231*(26–28), 32–37.

Sunstein, C. R. (2005). Minimalism at war. In D. J. Hutchinson, D. A. Straus, & G. R. Stone (Eds.), *The Supreme Court review, 2004* (pp. 47–109). Chicago: University of Chicago Press.

Sunstein, C. R., & Epstein, R. A. (Eds.). (2001). *The vote: Bush, Gore, and the Supreme Court.* Chicago: University of Chicago Press.

Tanenhaus, J., Schick, M., Muraskin, M., & Rosen, D. (1978). The Supreme Court's *certiorari* jurisdiction: Cue theory. In S. Goldman & A. Sarat (Eds.), *American court systems: Readings in judicial process and behavior* (pp. 130–143). San Francisco: Freeman.

Taylor, S., Jr. (1986, July 1). High court, 5–4, says states have the right to outlaw private homosexual acts. *New York Times*, pp. A1, A19.

Taylor, S., Jr. (1988, September 23). When high court's away, clerks' work begins. *New York Times*, p. 22.

Tennard v. Dretke, 124 S.Ct. 2562 (2004).

Tennessee v. Garner, 471 U.S. 1 (1985).

Tetlock, P. E. (1983). Cognitive style and political ideology. *Journal of Personality and Social Psychology, 45*, 118–126.

Tetlock, P. E., Bernzweig, J., & Gallant, J. L. (1985). Supreme Court decision making: Cognitive style as a predictor of ideological consistency of voting. *Journal of Personality and Social Psychology, 48*, 1227–1239.

Texas v. Johnson, 491 U.S. 397 (1989).

Texas v. White, 7 Wallace 700 (1869).

Thimsen, S. (2003, May). *A psychological analysis of United States Supreme Court voting patterns.* Unpublished senior honors thesis, Department of Psychology, University of Kansas, Lawrence, KS.

Thomas, A. P. (2001). *Clarence Thomas: A biography.* San Francisco: Encounter Books.

Thomas, C. (1996, April 8). *Judging.* Speech at the University of Kansas, Lawrence, KS.

Thomas, E., & Isikoff, M. (2000, December 25). The truth behind the pillars. *Newsweek, 136/137*(26), 46.

Tinker v. Des Moines Independent Community School District, 393 U.S. 503 (1969).

Todd, A. L. (1964). *Justice on trial: The case of Louis Brandeis.* Chicago: University of Chicago Press.

Toobin, J. (2001). *Too close to call.* New York: Random House.

Tremper, C. R. (1987). Organized psychology's efforts to influence judicial policy-making. *American Psychologist, 42*, 496–501.

Tushnet, M. (1992). Thurgood Marshall and the brethren. *Georgetown Law Journal, 80*, 2109–2130.

Tushnet, M. (2005). *A court divided: The Rehnquist Court and the future of constitutional law.* New York: Norton.

Ulmer, S. S. (1970). The use of power in the Supreme Court: The opinion assignments of Earl Warren, 1953–1960. *Journal of Public Law, 19*, 49–67.

Ulmer, S. S. (1984). The Supreme Court's *certiorari* decisions: Conflict as a predictive variable. *American Political Science Review, 89*, 901–911.

Ulmer, S. S., Hintze, W., & Kirklosky, L. (1972). The decision to grant or deny *certiorari*: Further considerations of cue theory. *Law and Society Review, 6*, 637–643.

United States v. Armstrong, 517 U.S. 456 (1996).

United States v. Arvizu, 122 S.Ct. 744 (2002).

United States v. Booker, 125 S.Ct. 738 (2005).

United States v. Drayton, 122 S.Ct. 2105 (2002).

United States v. F. W. Darby Lumber Co., 312 U.S. 100 (1941).

United States v. Hatter, 203 F.3d 795 (Denied *certiorari*, 2001).

United States v. Knights, 122 S.Ct. 587 (2002).

United States v. Lopez, 115 S.Ct. 1624 (1995).

United States v. Nixon, 418 U.S. 683 (1974).

United States v. Ruiz, 122 S.Ct. 2450 (2002).

United States v. Vonn, 122 S.Ct. 1043 (2002).

Urofsky, M. I. (1981). *Louis D. Brandeis and the progressive tradition.* Boston: Little, Brown.

Urofsky, M. I. (1991). *Felix Frankfurter: Judicial restraint and individual liberties.* Boston: Twayne.

Urofsky, M. I. (1997). *Affirmative action on trial: Sex discrimination in Johnson v. Santa Clara.* Lawrence: University Press of Kansas.

USA Today. (2004, September 22). Justice Stevens defends court secrecy. *USA Today,* p. 14A.

Van Orden v. Perry, 125 S.Ct. 2854 (2005).

Vernonia School District v. Acton, 115 S.Ct. 2386 (1995).

Vinson, F. (1961). Work of the federal courts. In W. F. Murphy & C. H. Pritchett (Eds.), *Courts, judges, and politics* (pp. 54–57). New York: Random House.

Virginia v. Black, 538 U.S. 343 (2003).

Vitullo-Martin, J. (2004). Justice and Antonin Scalia: The Supreme Court's most strident Catholic. In J. L. Victor & J. Naughton (Eds.), *Annual editions: Criminal justice 04/05* (pp. 131–135). Dubuque, IA: McGraw-Hill.

Ward, A. (2003). *Deciding to leave.* Albany: State University of New York Press.

Warren, E. (1966). Mr. Justice Brennan. *Harvard Law Review, 80,* 1–22.

Warren, E. (1977). *The memoirs of Earl Warren.* New York: Doubleday.

Wasby, S. L. (1981). Oral argument in the Ninth Circuit: The view from bench and bar. *Golden Gate University Law Review, 11,* 21–79.

Wasby, S. L. (1992). *Amicus* brief. In K. L. Hall (Ed.), *The Oxford companion to the Supreme Court of the United States* (pp. 31–32). New York: Oxford University Press.

Wasby, S. L., D'Amato, A. A., & Metrailer, R. (1976). The functions of oral argument in the U.S. Supreme Court. *Quarterly Journal of Speech, 62,* 410–422.

Wasby, S. L., Peterson, S. A., Schubert, J. N., & Schubert, G. (1992). The Supreme Court's use of per curiam dispositions: The connection to oral argument. *Northern Illinois University Law Review, 13,* 1–32.

Washington Post. (2000, December 11). Closely divided public mirrors court splits. *Lawrence Journal-World,* p. 5A.

Washington University Supreme Court Forecasting Project. (2004, April 5). Available at: http://wusct.wustl.edu/.

Weaver, W., Jr. (1990). The Chief Justice. In National Press Editors (Eds.), *Eight men and a lady* (pp. 14–48). Bethesda, MD: National Press.

Webster v. Reproductive Health Services, 492 U.S. 490 (1989).

West Coast Hotel Co. v. Parrish, 300 U.S. 379 (1937).

West Virginia State Board of Education v. Barnette, 319 U.S. 624 (1943).

Westen, D., & Weinberger, J. (2004). When clinical description becomes statistical prediction. *American Psychologist, 59,* 595–613.

Whelan, J. (2005). *Jefferson's vendetta: The pursuit of Aaron Burr and the judiciary.* New York: Carroll and Graf.

White, E. (1978). *The American judicial tradition: Profiles of leading American judges.* New York: Oxford University Press.

Will, G. (1996, July 4). Expanding the boundaries of free speech. *Kansas City Star,* p. C-11.

Willing, R. (1997, August 6). Disorder on the rise in nation's courts. *USA Today*, p. 3A.

Wiseman, R. L., & Schenck-Hamlin, W. J. (1981). A multi-dimensional scaling validation of an inductively derived set of compliance-gaining strategies. *Communication Monographs, 48*, 251–270.

Witt v. Florida, 54 L.Ed 2d 294 (1977).

Wood, F. A. (1913). *The influence of monarchs.* New York: Macmillan.

Wood, S. L. (1996, August). *Bargaining and negotiation in the Burger Court.* Paper presented at the meetings of the American Political Science Association, San Francisco.

Woodward, B., & Armstrong, S. (1979). *The brethren: Inside the Supreme Court.* New York: Simon and Schuster.

Yalof, D. A. (1999). *Pursuit of justices: Presidential politics and the selection of Supreme Court nominees.* Chicago: University of Chicago Press.

Yarborough v. Alvarado, 124 S.Ct. 2140 (2004).

Yarbrough, T. E. (2000). *The Rehnquist Court and the Constitution.* New York: Oxford University Press.

Youngstown Sheet and Tube Co. et al. v. Sawyer, 343 U.S. 579 (1952).

Zelman v. Simmons-Harris, 122 S.Ct. 2460 (2002).

Index